W9-BVB-364

Fighting for MacArthur

Fighting for MACARTHUR

The Navy and Marine Corps' Desperate Defense of the Philippines

JOHN GORDON

Naval Institute Press
Annapolis, Maryland

This book has been brought to publication with the generous assistance of Marguerite and Gerry Lenfest.

Naval Institute Press
291 Wood Road
Annapolis, MD 21402

Library of Congress Cataloging-in-Publication Data

Gordon, John,
Fighting for MacArthur : the Navy and Marine Corps' desperate defense of the Philippines / John Gordon.
p. cm.
Includes bibliographical references and index.
ISBN 978-1-61251-057-6 (hbk. : alk. paper) — ISBN 978-1-61251-062-0 (ebook)
1. MacArthur, Douglas, 1880–1964. 2. World War, 1939–1945—Campaigns—Philippines. 3. United States. Marine Corps—History—World War, 1939–1945. 4. United States. Navy—History—World War, 1939–1945. 5. World War, 1939–1945—Naval operations, American. 6. World War, 1939–1945—Pacific Area. I. Title.
D767.4.G66 2011
940.54'2599—dc23

2011025475

∞ This paper meets the requirements of ANSI/NISO z39.48-1992 (Permanence of Paper).

Printed in the United States of America.

19 18 17 16 15 14 13 12 11 9 8 7 6 5 4 3 2 1

First printing

Contents

Illustrations

Photographs

Maps

Tables

Fighting for MacArthur

Introduction

The 1941–42 Philippine Campaign was clearly dominated by the Army. General Douglas MacArthur became a household name during the defense of Bataan and Corregidor. Lieutenant General Jonathan Wainwright, although captured by the Japanese when Corregidor surrendered, became a revered name in the Army and fairly well known to the public at large. Americans, at least those who knew anything at all of the campaign, were proud of the story of the defense of the Philippines, despite the fact that it is the nation's worst battlefield defeat.

As I researched the campaign I came to the conclusion that the story of the role of the Navy and Marine Corps had never received adequate attention. There were some books that told pieces of the story, the most famous being *They Were Expendable,* published in 1942. That book was a wartime telling of the story of Motor Torpedo Boat Squadron 3, the famous PT boats that fought the Japanese and evacuated MacArthur and his family from Corregidor in mid-March 1942. Like most books published during the war it contained more than a few inaccuracies, but was a stirring yarn nevertheless. A few other books and articles on the role of the Navy and the Marines were also available, some written soon after the war, others much later. However, there was no single work that told a coherent story of the Sea Services in the defense of the Philippines. Telling that story became my goal.

Because the fighting in the Philippines from December 1941 to May 1942 was primarily an Army operation I have tried to include an appropriate level of detail regarding the Army's activities due to the fact that the Army's successes and failures in the campaign had a direct effect on what happened to the sailors and Marines. Additionally, periodically describing the Army's activities puts the doings of the sea services in a proper context.

The Navy and Marines helped make the defense of the Philippines an epic story that, despite the eventual surrender of Bataan and Corregidor, was looked upon with pride by the American public at a point in the war when the Allies were suffering defeat after defeat. Sailors and Marines performed some of their most unusual missions of the entire war during this campaign. The last stand of the colorful China river gunboats, recalled so well in the classic 1960s' movie *The Sand Pebbles*, was in Manila Bay. A battalion of sailors and Marines fought as infantry against a Japanese amphibious landing on Bataan. Marines, whose primary mission during World War II was to assault defended enemy-held islands, were the main beach defense force on the island fortress of Corregidor. Sailors, who before the war were the crews of river gunboats in China, manned heavy coast artillery batteries due to a shortage of Army artillerymen. The last organized counterattack by the U.S. forces in the Philippines was by a battalion of sailors who charged with fixed bayonets into the machine-gun fire of the Japanese assault force that had landed on Corregidor.

Some Army accounts of the campaign have displayed resentment that for most of the siege the Navy and Marine Corps were receiving more and better food than the Army. This book will show that the reason the sailors and Marines had more food was because Navy leadership in the Philippines quickly grasped the seriousness of the situation in the first few days following the start of the war and took appropriate action to prepare for a long siege. The Army leaders in the Philippines, on the other hand, waited until it was far too late to stockpile Bataan. The result was wholesale starvation of the 80,000 Filipino-American Army troops on the Peninsula, one of the greatest tragedies to befall U.S. Army personnel in all of World War II.

At the highest levels of command there were problems between the services. In particular, the relationship between the Army and Navy was strained for the rest of the war due to the actions of General Douglas MacArthur. Always wanting to take credit for what went right, but avoiding any responsibility for the defeats the Americans suffered in the Philippines, MacArthur was instrumental in bringing down a four-star Navy admiral, Thomas C. Hart, the commander in chief of the U.S. Asiatic Fleet. At the lower command levels, however, there was generally good cooperation between the Army, Navy, and Marines.

The role of the Navy and Marines in the Philippine Campaign has generally been unappreciated. This is somewhat surprising considering that the Campaign accounted for by far the largest number of Navy and Marine prisoners to fall into enemy hands during World War II. Many books have been written about the defense of Wake Island during sixteen days in December 1941. Some 400 Marines were captured on Wake. In the Philippines, however, approximately 1,480 Marines were taken prisoner, as were about 2,300 officers and men of the Navy. Theirs is certainly a story worth telling.

CHAPTER 1

The Navy and Marine Corps in the Philippines

THE ASIATIC FLEET

In the fall of 1941 the Asiatic Fleet was a small, relatively well-balanced force, sufficient for its prewar mission of providing a U.S. naval presence in China and the Philippines—but woefully inadequate should there be a war with the Japanese. The senior naval officer in the Far East was Admiral Thomas C. Hart, commander in chief, U.S. Asiatic Fleet (CinCAF). Hart was one of only four four-star admirals in the Navy, along with the Chief of Naval Operations Admiral Harold K. Stark, Admiral Ernest J. King who commanded the Atlantic Fleet, and Admiral Husband E. Kimmel, the commander of the U.S. Pacific Fleet at Pearl Harbor.

Hart assumed command of the Asiatic Fleet from Admiral Harry Yarnell at Shanghai on 25 July 1939. He was then sixty-two years old, having been in the Navy since he graduated from the Naval Academy in 1897. His first command was the destroyer USS *Lawrence* from 1905–7. As he proceeded up the Navy's ranks he spent time in both submarines and surface ships, including commanding the battleship USS *Mississippi* in 1925—a prime assignment for an officer in the interwar period. He was promoted to rear admiral in 1929, clearly one of the Navy's rising stars.[1]

When Hart took command of the Asiatic Fleet his flagship was the heavy cruiser USS *Augusta*, a ship of the same class as the *Houston*, the cruiser that would be Hart's flagship when war broke out two and a half years later. Under his command were two cruisers; destroyer, minesweeper, and submarine squadrons; a few Navy seaplanes and flying boats (Patrol Wing 10 was officially formed in December 1940); the base establishment of the 16th Naval District;

Admiral Thomas C. Hart, 1939

Source: U.S. Naval Institute Photo Archive

the gunboats of the Yangtze Patrol that cruised China's rivers and coastal waters; and the Marines in the Philippines and China.

When Hart took command of the Asiatic Fleet tensions between the United States and Japan were already increasing. Known as a stickler for detail and discipline, Hart was also regarded in the Navy as highly competent and a realist. This latter characteristic would lead to much trouble with General Douglas MacArthur.

Shortly after taking command Hart visited all the elements of the Asiatic Fleet in China and the Philippines. Within a few weeks he recognized that the Asiatic Fleet had not placed sufficient emphasis on training for war against a major opponent. Firing at Chinese bandits along the banks of the Yangtze River was one thing; taking on the Imperial Japanese Navy was an entirely different matter.

This conclusion led the admiral to develop an intense training program for his small force. During 1940 and 1941 the ships of the Asiatic Fleet conducted numerous maneuvers and practiced battle drills. Hart would at times go to sea with his ships, observing training. He also scrutinized many of the details of the defense plans. For example, he personally inspected plans to mine the entrances of Manila and Subic Bays, found them inadequate, and ordered changes. His emphasis on detail and training paid off when war came. Thomas Hart was a competent, first-rate senior leader. Unfortunately, the candor that accompanied his clear, realistic judgment would cost him in the days and weeks after war started.

Admiral Hart developed a good relationship with the commander of the Army's Philippine Department, Major General George Grunert, who until July 1941 was the senior active-duty Army officer in the Islands. He was also on good terms with Philippine president Manuel Quezon.

When Hart assumed command of the Asiatic Fleet Douglas MacArthur was the military adviser to the Philippine Commonwealth government, not the commander of the U.S. Army's forces in the Philippines. MacArthur had served as the chief of staff of the Army from 1930 to 1935. From 1935 until he retired in 1937 MacArthur had been the military adviser to the Philippines; he continued to perform that role after retiring. Thomas Hart was one of the very few people who could call the General "Douglas." Unfortunately, once the General was recalled to active duty in July of 1941 their professional and personal relationship started to rapidly deteriorate.

By the time war was approaching in the fall of 1941 Hart's headquarters had moved to the third floor of the modern, air-conditioned Marsman Building near the Manila waterfront. His chief of staff was Rear Admiral William R. Purnell. Hart's senior commander afloat was Rear Admiral William A. Glassford, the commander of the Yangtze Patrol (YANGPAT) until 5 December. Glassford assumed command of Task Force 5, the Asiatic Fleet's main surface command, when YANGPAT was disestablished. The large and growing Asiatic Fleet submarine force was under Captain John Wilkes.

The 16th Naval District

The base support for the Asiatic Fleet was vested in the 16th Naval District, commanded by Rear Admiral Francis W. Rockwell whose headquarters was at the Cavite Navy Yard, southwest of Manila. Cavite was by far the largest and most important base that the Navy had west of Hawaii, but it was still a small facility with a total area of only fifty acres. Four hundred to five hundred American sailors were assigned to the Navy Yard, along with about five hundred Filipino naval reservists. Cavite had been the main naval base of the Spanish while they owned the Islands. Over eight thousand Filipino civilians were employed at the Yard; many had worked there for decades.[2] The City of Cavite occupied most

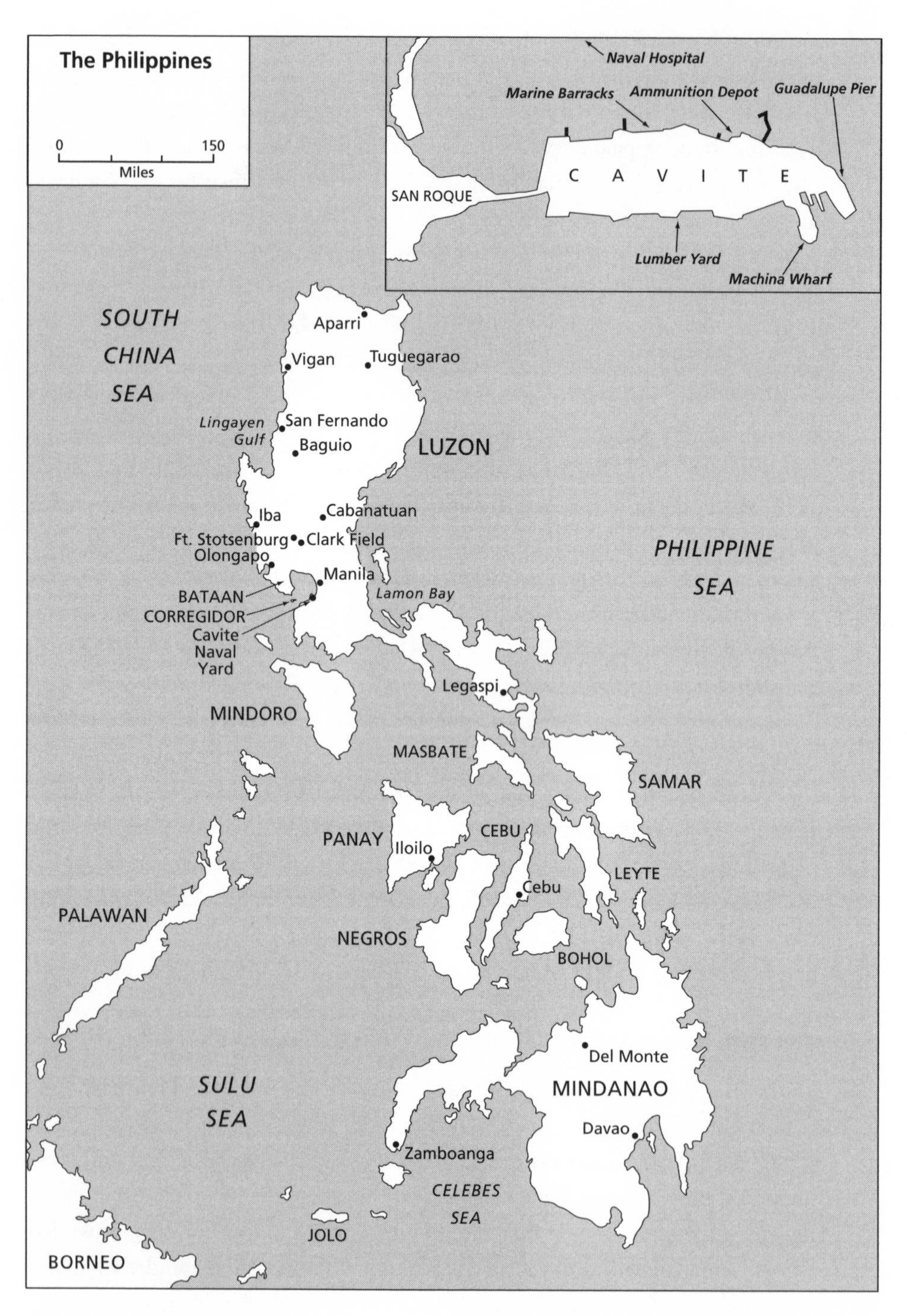

Map 1. The Philippine Islands

Rear Admiral Francis Rockwell, taken on 17 December 1941 at the Cavite Navy Yard

Source: National Archives and Records Administration

of the western end of the Cavite Peninsula, with the Navy Yard taking up the east end.

The Cavite Navy Yard had machine shops, an ammunition depot, storage warehouses, and other facilities needed to keep a naval force in operation. There was no permanent dry dock at the Cavite Navy Yard, but small ships such as gunboats and minesweepers could be pulled out of the water on the small marine railway between Machina and Central Wharves. Like most naval bases then and today Cavite was a crowded facility with wooden and light metal buildings set close to each other, although the base included the sturdy old Spanish fort that housed the commissary and the stone and masonry casemate where the ammunition depot was located.

In addition to Cavite the Navy had several other facilities in the Philippines. The Olongapo Naval Station was in Subic Bay. In the early 1900s the Navy had originally thought that this would be its primary base in the Philippine Islands. Within a few years, however, Olongapo had taken on a secondary role compared to Cavite, since the latter was set inside well-protected Manila Bay, with

An October 1941 view of the Cavite Peninsula. USS Canopus *is on the east side of Machina Wharf and MTB Squadron 3's PT boats are tied up along the pier on the northeast side of the Yard. Destroyers* Peary *and* Pillsbury *are on either side of Central Wharf. The City of Cavite occupied most of the western half of the Peninsula.*

Source: National Archives and Records Administration

Corregidor and the other harbor forts standing guard at the entrance. During the spring and summer of 1941 the Navy evacuated most of its personnel from Olongapo, including moving the floating dry dock *Dewey* to Mariveles. Moored at one of Olongopo's piers was the decommissioned 8,000-ton armored cruiser *Rochester*, originally commissioned in 1893. By the outset of war Olongapo was a minor base that could still perform some useful functions such as becoming the new home of the 4th Marines upon their arrival from China.

A small Navy Section Base was being developed at Mariveles, the town located at the southern tip of the Bataan Peninsula at the entrance to Manila Bay. For years the Navy had owned several square miles of territory on the southern end of Bataan. This area was designated as a U.S. Naval Reservation, although Filipino civilians could move easily through the area. The Navy envisioned basing some of its submarines at Mariveles Harbor, as well as small ships of the Inshore Patrol, the command that was responsible for patrolling the entrance of Manila Bay and some distance north and south along the west coast of Luzon.

The Contractors Pacific Naval Air Bases (PNAB) organization, a private consortium of firms that were constructing naval facilities around the Pacific (over one thousand PNAB employees were captured on Wake Island), was performing most of the new construction work including expanding the Navy's aviation facilities on Sangley Point and the new base at Mariveles. There were about eighty American civilian managers, technical experts, and foremen, but most of the PNAB employees (about four hundred men) were locally hired Filipinos.[3] Mr. George Colley was the senior PNAB official in the Philippines. He had direct access to admirals Hart and Rockwell.

The Army and Navy had long-standing plans to mine the entrance of Manila Bay if it appeared that war was near. During late July both services started planting mines to seal the Bay. The Navy's mines were of the contact type—once put in position the Navy mines were dangerous. The Army's weapons, which were intended to open or close the channel through the larger Navy minefield, were more sophisticated controlled mines. These weapons were put in position and electrically connected to a concrete mine casemate on Corregidor Island.[4]

Across Canacao Bay, north of the Cavite Navy Yard, was Sangley Point. Here was the Navy's main medical facility in the Far East, the Canacao Naval Hospital. A modern facility, Canacao was staffed by some 150 naval medical personnel, including twelve female nurses. Captain R. G. Davis, the senior Navy doctor in the Philippines, commanded the hospital. Sixteen other doctors and three dental officers comprised the professional staff at Canacao. There were other Navy doctors with the 4th Marines, the larger ships of the Fleet, and a small dispensary at Olongapo. Most of the hospital employees were local Filipinos. Close to the Naval Hospital were the three 600-foot-tall radio towers that the Navy erected in 1915 for long-range communications—this facility was known as Radio Cavite.

In addition to the hospital, fuel depot, and the towers of Radio Cavite, Sangley Point was a base for one of Patrol Wing 10 (PatWing 10) flying boat squadrons, VP-101, and the Wing's Utility Squadron. A large concrete ramp had been built into the south side of Sangley Point, not far from the fuel depot. PatWing 10 seaplanes used this ramp to get out of the water when in need of maintenance. In order to provide for the seaplanes large stocks of aviation fuel had been cached at various places around Sangley Point along with aircraft spare parts and ammunition. Before the start of the war the PNAB organization was working to expand the naval air base on Sangley Point.

Inside the city of Manila the Navy had several small facilities. Asiatic Fleet headquarters was in the Marsman Building that was close to the Manila waterfront

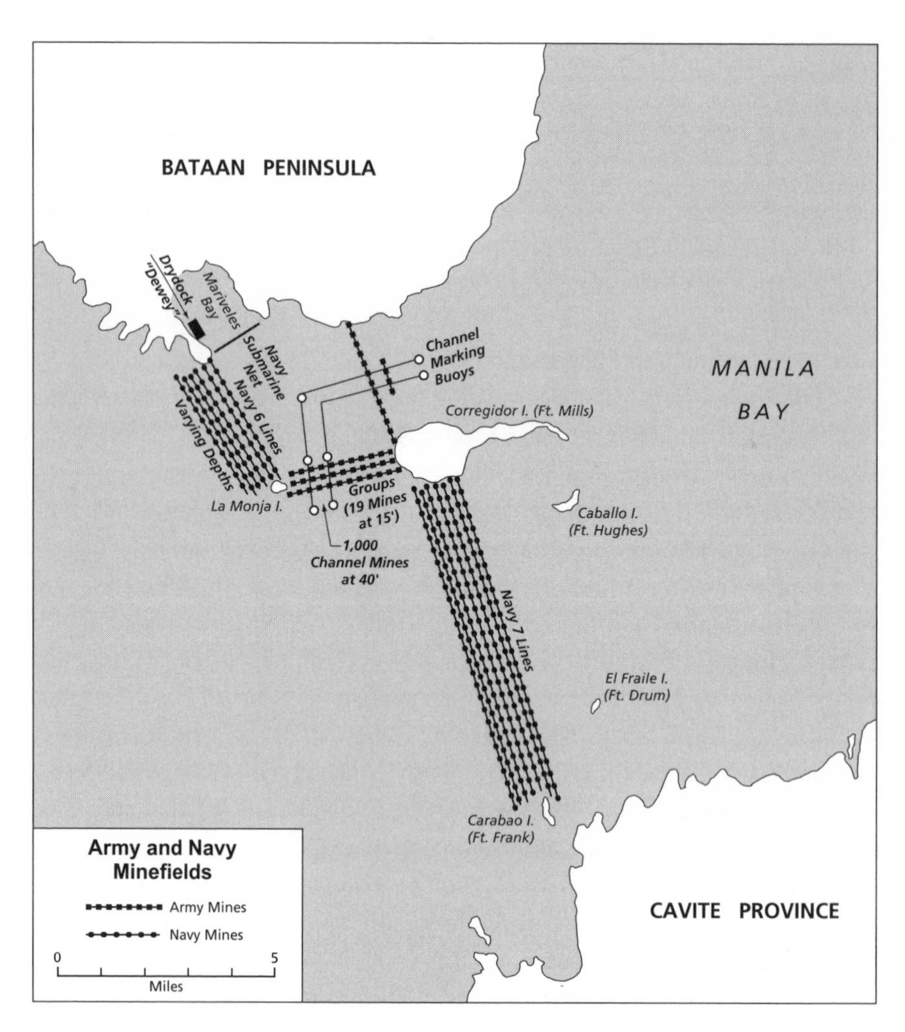

Map 2. The Army and Navy minefields at the entrance to Manila Bay

and had a good view out over the Bay from its upper floors. Additionally, the Navy had several warehouses along the Pasig River that flows from the mountains east of Manila through the city and into the Bay.[5]

The Navy had two very important facilities on Corregidor, the island fortress that was nicknamed The Rock. The first was a series of tunnels that were being dug into the south side of Malinta Hill. The Army's tunnel system, which was so vital to the defense of Corregidor, had been constructed under Malinta Hill from 1931 to 1938. The elaborate Army tunnels were large enough to hold several headquarters, portions of the treasury of the government of the Philippine

Commonwealth, and sufficient food for a 7,000-man garrison for at least six months. The main tunnel was some nine hundred feet long and thirty feet wide.

During the mid-1930s the Army had started work on an extension of Malinta Tunnel intended to exit on the southwest portion of Malinta Hill. The Army never completed this project, but the Navy decided to make use of what had already been accomplished. So in 1939 the Navy began work on its own tunnel system on the south side of Malinta Hill. There were three Navy tunnels under Malinta Hill. The largest, and nearest completion upon outbreak of war, was Tunnel Queen, roughly 250 feet in length. Concrete-lined and equipped with drainage and electric outlets, Queen was able to house several hundred personnel and considerable amounts of supplies and equipment. Before the start of war the Navy began to transfer supplies and equipment, including submarine torpedoes and spare parts, to the tunnels on Corregidor. The Navy envisioned using Mariveles Harbor as an advanced submarine base upon outbreak of war. Corregidor was so close to Mariveles that there would be little problem keeping submarine munitions there; torpedoes and other gear could be lightered out to the waiting subs when needed.[6] The second Navy facility on The Rock was its radio intercept station that will be described below.

The majority of the Asiatic Fleet's vessels were obsolescent or obsolete. For example, all thirteen destroyers were the 1,200-ton World War I "flush deck" type, armed with four 4-inch guns, a single 3-inch anti-aircraft gun, a few machine guns, and twelve torpedoes. Compared to early 1940s' Japanese destroyers the Asiatic Fleet's old "four pipers" were seriously outclassed. Hart's flagship, the heavy cruiser *Houston*, was armed with 8-inch guns, but compared to Japanese heavy cruisers was relatively lightly armed, since she lacked torpedo tubes. The light cruiser *Marblehead* was of the same era as the destroyers. The gunboats all dated from the 1920s. They were slow and intended for either coastal or river patrolling; they were not capable of standing up to a modern Japanese naval vessel of destroyer size or larger. Similarly, the six minesweepers (and the submarine rescue vessel USS *Pigeon*) were all World War I *Owl*-class vessels, although several of these had undergone significant upgrades in 1940–41, giving them a modern capability to sweep mines.[7] Appendix A provides a list of the ships and shore commands of the Asiatic Fleet at the outbreak of war.

Two of the most promising types of vessels in the Asiatic Fleet were its large number of submarines and the newly arrived Patrol Torpedo (PT) boats of Motor Torpedo Boat (MTB) Squadron 3. By December 1941 there were twenty-nine submarines in the Asiatic Fleet. This represented the largest single submarine force anywhere in the U.S. Navy. The buildup of modern fleet submarines (the Asiatic Fleet had always had a small force of World War I–era S-boats in the

1920s and 1930s) in the Philippines was a result of a late July decision to rapidly reinforce the Islands in an attempt to deter the Japanese from striking southward and as a way of putting muscle behind the U.S. embargo of oil to Japan. Together with the Army's heavy bombers based on Luzon, the Navy's submarines would provide, in theory, the means to interdict any Japanese move toward the Netherlands East Indies or Malaya. The submarines and bombers would also provide the first line of defense for the Philippines itself, attacking any approaching Japanese invasion fleet. Unfortunately, the Navy was not aware of the very poor quality of its prewar submarine torpedoes.

The other innovative addition to the defense of the Philippines was the PT boats. The Navy had started development of PTs in the late 1930s, experimenting with several different designs. In the summer of 1941 a decision was made to dispatch one of the first PT squadrons (MTB Squadron 3) to the Philippines to provide close-in defense against a possible Japanese invasion. Of the twelve PTs envisioned for Squadron 3 only six made it to the Islands before war started. The remaining Squadron 3 boats were deck cargo on board the tender USS *Ramapo* at Pearl Harbor when war began.

The Navy's decision to dispatch PTs to the Islands appealed to General MacArthur since he had for years envisioned a Philippine Navy consisting of fifty or more motor torpedo boats. Unfortunately for the fledgling Philippine Navy, funds were available for only three boats before the start of war, Q-111, -112, and -113. The Philippine Q-boats were smaller than the U.S. Navy PTs, having two rather than four torpedo tubes and fewer machine guns. Nevertheless, the Philippine Q-boats were conceptually the same as the U.S. Navy boats. Interestingly, the Philippine Q-boats were part of the Philippine Army; the officers and men of the Q-boats wore Philippine Army rank. In March of 1941 the Philippine Army placed an order for eight additional Q-boats to be built in local shipyards. None of these craft were complete by the time the Japanese attacked. The Q-boats remained under U.S. Army control even during the siege of Bataan, although their activities were coordinated with the Navy's.[8]

While apparently well suited for operations in the coastal waters of the Philippines, the PTs were an untried and unfamiliar asset when war started. Fast, and well armed with four torpedoes and four .50-caliber machine guns, the boats were capable of over 30 knots when well maintained. Squadron 3 added two additional .30-caliber Lewis machine guns (easily recognizable from their top-mounted drum magazines) on pedestals on the forecastle of each boat. PT tactics were, however, still a matter of experimentation. What operations would be like under conditions where the enemy had air superiority was not yet understood.

Another potentially valuable Navy asset were the aircraft of PatWing 10. The Navy had operated flying boats in the Philippines for many years. By 1940 there were sufficient aircraft available to form a Patrol Wing with three squadrons. Patrol Squadrons 101 and 102 each had fourteen PBY-4 Catalina flying boats. The PBY had a range of some 1,800 miles and could be armed with up to 4,000 pounds of weapons consisting of a mix of torpedoes, depth charges, and 500-pound bombs. With an endurance of sixteen to eighteen hours, the PBYs were very valuable for extended reconnaissance missions. The problem was that they were vulnerable. With a top speed of only about 180 miles per hour and self-protection limited to four machine guns, the seven to nine men on board would be hard-pressed to survive an attack by enemy fighters. The Utility Squadron added a few smaller seaplanes for errands, short-range patrols, and general duties.

Station C

The final Navy facility in the Philippines was Station C,[9] the radio intelligence unit located on Corregidor. The radio intercept station in the Philippines was always a very important part of the Navy's attempts, under way since the 1920s, to break the Japanese Imperial Navy's codes, due to the fact that it was located so close to Japan and Imperial Navy fleet operations in the Western Pacific.

In late 1938 the Army and Navy agreed to relocate Station C from the Cavite Navy Yard to Corregidor. An interservice agreement was prepared, with the Navy transferring funds to the Army to start work on a tunnel and some support buildings that would house the Asiatic Fleet radio intercept unit.

By the spring of 1939 work was under way on what was officially known as "Tunnel Afirm" at Monkey Point on Corregidor. In June of 1940 the work was nearly complete and the personnel of Station C began transferring to Corregidor. In mid-October 1940 the move was complete. Inside the tunnel were storage areas, generators, radio systems, and all the necessary equipment for processing and decoding Japanese messages. The Station's state-of-the-art equipment included IBM machines that were used to rapidly process the thousands of possible permutations of the enemy's codes.

In the months before the outbreak of war in December 1941 Station C was the most important, and successful, of the chain of intercept stations that the Navy maintained in the Pacific. Station C, along with the main OP-20-G office in Washington, had the lead in trying to break the critical Imperial Navy operational code, known to Navy Intelligence as JN-25b. Analysts in Hawaii were simultaneously tasked to attack the special code that was used exclusively by Japanese admirals (the U.S. Navy was never able to break that code).

At the outbreak of war Station C included seventy-six personnel: eight officers, forty-three radiomen, and twenty-five yeomen. All of the Station's activities were highly classified. Outside of the Station's personnel there were probably fewer than twenty Navy or Army personnel in the Philippines who were aware of Station C's mission and activities. For bookkeeping purposes Station C was given the unassuming title of "Fleet Radio Unit," under the auspices of the 16th Naval District.[10] The importance of Station C is demonstrated by the fact that one of the eight "Purple Machines" that were being used to decode Japanese diplomatic messages was located in Tunnel Afirm on Corregidor.

MARINES IN THE PHILIPPINES

The 4th Marine Regiment

The 4th Marine Regiment had been assigned to Shanghai since 1927 when it was dispatched to help protect Americans in that city as China spiraled into chaos. Other Marine Corps and Army units had periodically reinforced the regiment during the 1930s as the level of violence in China waxed and waned. During most of the period the 4th Marines were in Shanghai the regiment was organized as a two-battalion unit with a strength that varied from 1,000 to 1,200 officers and men, as well as a normal complement of sailors; most of the latter were medical personnel.

The regimental commander was Colonel Samuel L. Howard; he had taken command of the unit in May 1941. The executive officer was Lieutenant Colonel Donald Curtis, and the regimental sergeant major was Edwin D. Curry. The 1st Battalion was commanded by Lieutenant Colonel Curtis T. Beecher, and the 2nd Battalion was under command of Lieutenant Colonel H. R. Anderson.

When the 4th Marines departed from China at the end of November the regiment was considerably under strength. Admiral Hart had been withholding the regiment's replacements at Cavite for roughly a year by the time the 4th Marines arrived in the Philippines. Hart's reasoning was sound—he wanted to minimize the number of men who would be lost in China should war suddenly break out in the Pacific.

While in China the 4th Marine Regiment was organized on the Table of Organization (T/O) of a Marine Corps 1935-type separate infantry regiment. Compared to the robust midwar regiments (by 1943 a Marine infantry regiment numbered over 3,200 men, for example), the 1930s' organizations were very lean in terms of personnel and equipment. This was due, of course, to the very limited military budgets and manpower levels of the Depression era. For example, the active-duty strength of the Marine Corps was roughly 16,000 officers and men during most of the 1930s.

A 1935 Marine regiment had the following regimental-level elements: (1) Regimental Headquarters with eight officers and five enlisted men; (2) Regimental Headquarters Company that included one officer and sixty-two enlisted (plus ten Navy personnel, two of whom were doctors, one a chaplain, and seven pharmacist mates, also known as corpsmen); and (3) the Regimental Service Company with three officers, two warrant officers, and eighty enlisted men. The Service Company included the regiment's twenty-eight-member band.

A full-strength regiment had three battalions, each with a Battalion Headquarters Company that included five officers, thirty-nine enlisted, and nine Navy medical personnel (one of whom was doctor). There was also a battalion Machine Gun and Howitzer Company that had seven officers, one warrant officer (usually referred to as "Gunner," because this position was for an artilleryman), and 141 enlisted Marines. The company included three machine-gun platoons (each with four .30-caliber machine guns, for a total of twelve weapons), and a howitzer platoon armed with one M-1916 37-mm gun and one 3-inch Stokes (later 81-mm) mortar.

Each battalion also had three rifle companies, each consisting of three officers and 103 enlisted men, organized in a headquarters and three rifle platoons. The nine squad leaders, plus the platoon leaders and platoon sergeants, were supposed to be armed with a .45-caliber Thompson sub-machine gun (the "Tommy Gun," made famous during the gangster era in the 1920s). One man in each squad had a Browning Automatic Rifle (BAR). Additionally, one man per squad was issued a rifle grenade launcher that could be attached to the famous Model 1903 Springfield bolt-action rifle most of them carried.

A full-strength, three-battalion 1935-type regiment had 75 officers, 5 warrant officers, and 1,614 enlisted men for a total of 1,694 Marines. Additionally, there were 36 Navy medical personnel (5 of whom were doctors), and a chaplain. The regiment was authorized thirty-six machine guns, three 37-mm guns, and three mortars. Interestingly, the Marine rifle squads were better armed than their Army counterparts of the era because each squad was supposed to have a submachine gun and a BAR. Army squads of this period lacked Thompsons.

Unfortunately, the 4th Marines arrived in the Philippines undermanned and without its third battalion. Only 44 officers, 3 warrant officers, and 717 enlisted men took up station at Olongapo in early December 1941. In addition to the Marines, 28 Navy personnel, including 3 doctors, 2 dentists, a chaplain, and 22 enlisted men, were assigned to the regiment, bringing the total strength of the 4th Marines to 792 officers and enlisted men combined. When the regiment absorbed the 75-man Marine Barracks Olongapo on 22 December the unit's strength grew to 828 Marine Corps officers and men, plus 48 Navy personnel (20 sailors from the Olongapo Naval Station were added to the regiment when the Marine Barracks joined the 4th Marines). Despite these additions, the 4th remained well below its authorized paper strength of 1,183 officers and enlisted men combined.[11]

To compensate for the lack of Marines, Colonel Howard organized the regiment without the third rifle company in each battalion. Additionally, the rifle companies each had only two rather than the normal three platoons. This meant that by the time the regiment arrived in the Philippines it had only eight rifle platoons, as opposed to eighteen in a full-strength, two-battalion regiment. It also appears that in the Machine Gun and Howitzer Companies (D and H) the number of machine-gun platoons was reduced from three to two. Shortly after the regiment arrived in the Philippines Lieutenant Commander Thomas H. Hayes from Canacao Naval Hospital became the regiment's senior Navy medical officer.

Although undermanned, the regiment was well armed by the standards of 1941. There were not enough Thompson sub-machine guns to give every squad leader a weapon, but there were sufficient BARs to arm those squads that lacked a Thompson with two automatic rifles. Many of the platoon leaders and platoon sergeants were provided with Thompsons. The 4th Marines had considerably more than its authorized number of machine guns (the regiment had fifty-two Browning and two Lewis .30-caliber machine guns, more than double the twenty-four called for in the T/O of a two-battalion 1935 regiment).[12] Unfortunately, there were no .50-caliber heavy machine guns for anti-aircraft defense. The regiment was slightly over authorization in mortars; the 1st Battalion had two World War I–era Stokes mortars that had been modified to fire 81-mm ammunition and the 2nd Battalion one 81-mm, as opposed to the theoretical allocation of one 3-inch Stokes mortar per battalion. Additionally, the regiment had six M-1916 37-mm guns as opposed to the two that were authorized. When the regiment absorbed Marine Barracks Olongapo a few additional weapons were gained: a half dozen machine guns and three Navy 3-pounder landing guns. The regiment brought with it from China some five hundred tons of equipment and supplies, including at least ten units of fire for each weapon, two years supply of summer uniforms, and the equipment for a 100-bed hospital.[13]

1st Separate Marine Battalion

This was the second largest Marine unit in the Philippines. It was formed at the Cavite Navy Yard on 1 May 1941 when Marine Barracks Cavite was formally disbanded in order to create the new battalion. Organized into a headquarters and four line companies, A through D, there were initially 572 Marines in the 1st Separate Battalion. By 1 December of that year the unit's strength had risen to 722 officers and men, due largely to Admiral Hart's policy of withholding replacements for the 4th Marines in China. As a result, it became the largest American battalion-sized unit in the Philippines at the outbreak of the war. Under the command of Lieutenant Colonel John P. Adams, the battalion's primary mission was the anti-aircraft defense of the Cavite Navy Yard. In keeping with the Marine's tradition of every man being a rifleman, the battalion could be used as an infantry unit if need be.[14]

In order to accomplish its dual anti-aircraft/infantry mission the four lettered companies were reorganized into anti-aircraft batteries. A Company formed Battery D (located at Sangley Point, armed with a dozen .50-caliber machine guns); B Company formed Battery A (four 3-inch .50-caliber guns, also located at Sangley Point, across Canacao Bay to the north of Cavite); C Company created Batteries B and C, armed with 3-inch 50s, positioned at Carridad and Binakayan to the west and south of the Navy Yard; while D Company formed Batteries E and F, one armed with 3-inch .23-caliber weapons and the other with .50-caliber machine guns, both located inside the Navy Yard.[15] The battalion had a total of sixteen 3-inch guns; twelve long-barreled .50-caliber weapons of which four were semimobile and the rest fixed, and four short-barreled .23-caliber guns. There were also roughly twenty-four .50-caliber anti-aircraft machine guns. The 1st Separate Battalion also had a full complement of weapons in the event that it was committed in an infantry role. These included thirty-five .30-caliber water-cooled Brownings and four 37-mm guns.[16]

The Battalion Headquarters Company had recently been equipped with three still highly secret radar sets. They arrived in November and included two Army SCR-268s for short-range fire control, and one long-range SCR-270B for aircraft detection and early warning. Due to the classified nature of their mission and equipment, the 34-man radar detachment (32 Marines, one Navy corpsman, and a Filipino naval reserve cook), under the leadership of Warrant Officer John T. Brainard, was segregated from the other Marines at the Cavite Marine Barracks.

On 4 December Brainard's radar detachment moved to Nasubugu, south of Cavite, in order to provide radar coverage of air approaches south and west of Manila. Once there, the Marine radar detachment reported to the Army's Air Warning Service command. When war started the Marine radar was one of only two air warning sets ready for operations in the Philippines, the other being an Army set at Iba Field on Luzon's west coast where the Army's 3rd Pursuit Squadron was located.[17]

As the 4th Marines settled into Olongapo, the *President Harrison*, the chartered liner that helped transport the 4th Marines to the Philippines, turned around and set sail for the port of Chinwangtao where it would take on board the last sailors and Marines still in China—204 officers and men of the Embassy Guard at Peiping and the legation at Tinsing. Unfortunately, time ran out. On the day war broke out the North China Marines were preparing their equipment for departure, with the men still strung out between the port and Peiping. Overwhelming numbers of Japanese immediately surrounded them. Japanese officers gave the senior Marine present, Colonel Wiliam W. Ashurst, an opportunity to make a decision—surrender or fight. There was no question that resistance was futile, so he made the only realistic decision and surrendered his small detachments. The *President Harrison* was still near Shanghai when was broke out. Her master ran her aground after he received word of the outbreak of war.

SUMMARY

The personnel strength of the Navy in the Philippines is much harder to determine compared to the Marine Corps, where precise, name-by-name records are still available. The Navy strength can only be approximately estimated by examining the various surviving records. In some cases very accurate information is available. For example, there is an Asiatic Fleet officer's roster from early November 1941 that lists, by name and position, all the Navy and Marine Corps officers in the Philippines. According to that source, there were 750 commissioned Navy officers ashore and afloat. This total would have risen by about 80 additional officers when the submarine tender *Holland* and twelve more submarines arrived in late November and early December.

When it comes to the number of Navy enlisted men in the Asiatic Fleet the records are much less precise. The Navy accounted for its enlisted men in monthly muster rolls. These were prepared for ships, shore commands, and other organizations such as PatWing 10. In many cases the last surviving record of a shore element or ship is dated months before the start of the war. In other cases, there is no record at all for late 1941–42, especially for ships that were lost during the campaign.

It appears that in the first week of December 1941 the Asiatic Fleet included roughly 11,000 American Navy officers and men. This estimate is based on the surviving muster rolls of individual ships and shore commands, the 16th Naval District's November 1941 officer roster, and data on the planned complement of various types of ships. There were also some 650 Filipino naval reservists and 1,563 Marines in the Asiatic Fleet (not including the small Marine detachments aboard the Fleet's three cruisers). In comparison to the naval strength, there were approximately 19,150 American (non-Filipino) Army personnel in the Philippines at the outbreak of war.[18] Therefore, the Navy and Marine Corps represented approximately 40 percent of the total of about 31,800 American military personnel assigned to the Philippines when war started, keeping in mind that several of the Asiatic Fleet's combatants and auxiliaries had already moved southward to the Dutch East Indies when war started. A major difference was that the majority of the Navy sailors managed to escape from the Philippines as the ships and submarines of the Asiatic Fleet withdrew southward. Few of the Army or Marine Corps personnel in the Philippines would be so fortunate.

CHAPTER 2

The Final Days of Peace

By October it was becoming increasingly clear that U.S.-Japanese relations were deteriorating rapidly. For those few Americans who truly knew and understood Japan, General Hideki Tojo's assumption of the position of prime minister on the 18th of the month indicated a decisive political victory on the part of the country's militarists. Barring some dramatic—and very unlikely—diplomatic breakthrough, the two countries were clearly on a course toward war.

In the Philippines important command changes had taken place in July. On the 24th of that month the Roosevelt Administration froze Japanese financial assets in response to the Japanese occupying the southern portion of French Indochina (Vietnam). Two days later Douglas MacArthur was recalled to active duty with the rank of lieutenant general and placed in command of all Army air and ground forces in the Philippines. His new command was titled USAFFE (U.S. Army Forces Far East).

Since becoming the military adviser to the Philippine Commonwealth government in 1935, MacArthur was convinced the Philippines could defend itself by creating a large force of reservists who would be quickly mobilized in the event of a crisis. Although this plan was far from complete by 1941, MacArthur remained convinced the Philippines could be defended, especially now that the United States committed major reinforcements for the Islands in order to back up its embargo of Japan. Importantly, MacArthur was convinced that Japan would not attack until April 1942. He claimed that by then the Army's defensive preparations in the Philippines would be complete, including the mobilization of eleven small (8,700-man) Philippine Army divisions and the buildup of Army air power in the Islands. The Army had earmarked over 240 fighters, 52 dive bombers, and 165 B-17 and B-24 heavy bombers for delivery to the Philippines by March 1942.

CONFLICTS OVER AIRCRAFT CONTROL

As the situation worsened Admiral Hart tried to clarify several important matters with the Army, primarily regarding the control of air operations over land and water in the vicinity of the Philippines. Hart wanted the Navy to be in control of air search over water, as well as any air attacks against enemy ships. Knowing that the Navy had much better knowledge of the whereabouts of its ships and submarines than the Army would, Hart felt that the Navy should manage the over-water air operations. Conversely, he was willing to concede to the Army the tactical command of air operations over land in the Philippines (Hart suggested that either service could strike shore targets in enemy territory, e.g., Formosa). On 23 October Hart sent a memorandum to the USAFFE commander, recommending such a division of control.[1]

On 7 November Hart received MacArthur's reply. In the first paragraph the USAFFE commander stated that he found the admiral's proposal "entirely objectionable," laying out the Army's case for air operations unfettered by Navy control. As he concluded the memo MacArthur stated, "It is possible that under extraordinary conditions elements of an Army Air Force in support of a Fleet might advantageously operate under temporary Naval direction, but in this sense, the term 'Fleet' cannot be applied to the two cruisers and the division of destroyers of your command. . . . It would be manifestly illogical to assign for control of tactical command such a powerful Army air striking force to an element of such combat inferiority as your Command or that of the 16th Naval District."[2]

The tone of MacArthur's rejection of Hart's proposed division of labor was highly insulting, especially given that he was still a three-star general at this point while Hart was a full admiral. The issue soon got to the level of Army chief of staff General George C. Marshall in Washington, who in a 5 December message admonished MacArthur, reminding him that the Joint agreements between the Army and Navy provided for Army aircraft to be placed under Navy operational control to ensure unity of command against targets at sea.[3]

WAR WARNING FROM WASHINGTON

By the last week in November negotiations between the United States and Japan were in the final stage of collapse. On 20 November the Americans received a peace proposal from Japan that was deemed unacceptable. On the 24th the Chief of Naval Operations, Admiral Harold K. Stark, sent a warning to Admiral Hart stressing how serious the situation was. On 27 November, following a meeting of General Marshall and Admiral Stark with President Roosevelt, it was decided to send a formal war warning message to the senior Army and Navy commanders in the Pacific. Also included in the distribution was Mr. Francis B. Sayre, the U.S. high commissioner in the Philippines. Sayre immediately called a meeting with Hart and MacArthur to discuss the situation.

The meeting that day between the two senior military commanders and the ranking U.S. government official in the Philippines was a perfect example of MacArthur's irresponsible optimism as opposed to Hart's stark realism. Sayre recorded later that MacArthur, "paced back and forth, smoking a black cigar and assuring Admiral Hart and myself in reassuring terms that there would be no Japanese attack before the spring. Admiral Hart felt otherwise."[4]

Hart's response to the war warning message was to expedite the southward deployment of the surface elements of the Asiatic Fleet and to send a message to Admiral Glassford and Colonel Howard that they needed to get their units out of Shanghai as quickly as possible. Hart met with Admiral Rockwell, who had been commandant of the 16th Naval District for less than a month, and directed that the building of bomb shelters around Sangley Point and the Cavite Navy Yard be accelerated. Rockwell took immediate action, including ordering the dispersal of fuel drums and ammunition to a newly constructed dump on Sangley Point. Ordinary repair and refit work was stopped and priority given to getting ships already in the Yard ready to get under way.[5] The 1st Separate Marine Battalion at Cavite was placed on a war footing, with orders to have several guns in each anti-aircraft battery constantly manned.

As tensions increased in November and December, the Navy became increasingly concerned about the security of Station C. The number of guards near Tunnel Afirm was increased and Navy ships were posted off Corregidor's Monkey Point to ensure that no vessels approached from seaward. There were always a large number of fishing boats operating in Manila Bay, some of which were owned and operated by Japanese firms. On 22 November the minesweeper *Whippoorwill* was stationed in the area between Corregidor and Fort Hughes when a civilian Filipino vessel, *Remedio VIII*, approached the area near Monkey Point. When the ship ignored *Whippoorwill*'s warnings four shots were fired from one of the sweepers 3-inch guns, at which point *Remedio* hove to. A few days later the sweeper had to stop the Army Coast Artillery mine planter *General Harrison* from getting too close to Monkey Point.[6]

EVACUATION OF MARINES AND GUNBOATS FROM CHINA

In the first week of November, following many requests from the CinCAF, the Navy Department directed that the Marines and gunboats be withdrawn from China. Hart's staff decided to charter two President Liners—SS *President*

Harrison and SS *President Madison*—that normally operated in the western Pacific. These ships were directed to proceed to Shanghai where they would evacuate the largest American military contingent still in China, the 4th Marine Regiment. Once the Shanghai Marines were removed, *President Harrison* would be sent back to north China to pick up the remaining men of the Embassy and Legation guard.

Colonel Howard, commander of the 4th Marines, received orders from Admiral Hart on 10 November that the regiment would be withdrawn to the Philippines. Thus began the process of shutting down operations in Shanghai where the 4th Marines had been stationed since 1927. The plan was for the regiment to embark for the Philippines between 27 and 30 November.

Colonel Ashurst, the commander of the north China Marines, received word of the evacuation at the same time. He had far fewer personnel, barely two hundred, but was much farther north and in a very exposed position. The north China Marines were to evacuate from the port of Chinwangtao as soon as the ships carrying the 4th Marines could be turned around.

The river gunboats presented a special problem. It was now typhoon season in the South China Sea. The little river gunboats were not designed for trips in the open ocean, especially during rough weather. The commander of the Yangtze Patrol, Rear Admiral William A. Glassford, coordinated the move with the Asiatic Fleet staff. It was clear that the gunboats would be at risk during the crossing to the Philippines, so it was arranged to have them escorted by more seaworthy ships—minesweepers and the submarine rescue vessel *Pigeon*.

Oahu and *Luzon* were both at Shanghai waiting for orders to sail. *Mindanao* was at the British base of Hong Kong; she too would go to the Philippines. Two other gunboats were in Chinese waters, the little *Wake* at Shanghai and her sister ship *Tutuila*, roughly 1,400 miles up the Yangtze at the Nationalist Chinese capital of Chungking. It was decided that *Wake* would be stripped of her supplies and weapons and would remain behind as a radio watch vessel to support the U.S. Consulate in Shanghai. She would be left with a skeleton crew; the rest of her men were divided between *Luzon* and *Oahu*. *Tutuila* was far too deep in China to escape, especially with war now apparently so close. She would remain where she was at Chunking.[7]

On the morning of 27 November Colonel Howard received a message from the CinCAF directing that he expedite the regiment's preparations to depart. When that message was received the 2nd Battalion and about half of the Regimental Headquarters and Service Companies were already embarking on the liner *President Madison*. The regimental executive officer, Lieutenant Colonel Donald Curtis, was in command of the first echelon to depart, a total of about four hundred officers and men. When Admiral Hart's message to expedite the departure was received Colonel Howard met with Admiral Glassford, who was still in Shanghai, and the master of *President Harrison* to see if the rest of the regiment could load the following day despite the fact that the liner's conversion into a transport ship was still not complete. All agreed that time was clearly of the essence and the regiment needed to get out of China as soon as possible.[8]

During the rest of the day and that night the remaining men of the regiment worked feverishly to get their supplies and equipment loaded on board the ship. Colonel Howard informed the local Japanese commander that the 4th Marines was about to depart. Although the Japanese admiral was polite, he instigated a number of strikes by Chinese workers that day in an obvious attempt to hinder the regiment's departure. In a hard day of work the remaining Marines, assisted by some Chinese, managed to get the rest of the regiment's equipment, over five hundred tons, loaded into *President Harrison*.[9]

At 0900 on the morning of 28 November 1941 the remaining personnel of the 4th Marine Regiment formed up at the 1st Battalion billets and marched down the Bubbling Well Road toward the waiting liner. Thousands of Chinese, as well as some Americans and Europeans, lined the roadside cheering the Marines as they marched behind the Regimental Band. By 1400 the remaining Marines were on board the ship, which pulled away from the dock and headed downriver toward the South China Sea.

As soon as the ship was in the open sea orders were issued for a blackout during the hours of darkness. Twelve .30-caliber machine guns were broken out and mounted around the ship's upper decks. A constant radio watch was maintained. There were a considerable number of civilians on board, mostly Americans and Europeans who were trying to get out of China before war started. The first afternoon at sea Japanese military aircraft overflew the ship. Later that same day, two U.S. submarines met the ship to escort her to the Philippine port of Olongapo that would be the regiment's new home.

President Madison arrived at Olongapo early on the morning of 30 November and disembarked the first half of the regiment. *President Harrison* arrived the next day. Two lighter loads of supplies and equipment were removed from each vessel and the Marines were put ashore. The ships then proceeded to Manila where the remainder of their cargos and the civilian passengers were disembarked. The Navy contracted for civilian trucks to return the rest of the regiment's gear to Olongapo. The 4th Marines had made their escape.

Colonel Howard quickly discovered that there was not sufficient barracks space at Olongapo for the entire regiment, so about half of the unit was put into tents. Major King, the commander of Marine Barracks Olongapo, and his seventy-five men assisted the 4th Marines in establishing themselves in their new home. On 3 December Howard proceeded to Manila to report to Admiral Hart and Admiral Rockwell. Hart placed the 4th Marines under the operational command of the 16th Naval District. Meanwhile, *President Harrison* departed to pick up the 204 Marines and sailors still in north China.[10]

The same day that the second half of the 4th Marines departed the two river gunboats *Luzon* and *Oahu* sailed from Shanghai. With the larger *Luzon* in the lead, the two gunboats headed down the Whangpoo River for the open sea. Rear Admiral Glassford was on board *Luzon*, which had special accommodations for a flag officer and a small staff. It was a necessary but very dangerous journey. The Asiatic Fleet command in Manila recognized the danger and dispatched *Finch* and *Pigeon* to meet the two gunboats and assist them if the weather got too rough.

On 1 December the two gunboats rendezvoused with *Pigeon* and *Finch*. The four ships were sailing together when at 1045 they spotted a Japanese warship traveling on an opposite course. Not long after a Japanese seaplane circled them. By 1300 they were passing through a formation of Japanese ships that included several warships and four transports that were seen to be loaded with troops, headed north. As the American vessels turned southward, one of the Japanese transports hoisted an international flag that when translated read: "Enemy escaping on course 180 degrees."[11]

The next day the weather became very bad. The two gunboats were tossed and shaken violently in the storms that were sweeping through the South China Sea. The 2nd and 3rd of December were appalling. *Oahu* rolled an incredible 56 degrees to starboard and 50 degrees to port, but managed to right herself. With only about three feet of freeboard above the surface of the sea (in calm weather) the two gunboats were taking tons of water over their bows and sterns. Both ships had extra crew on board from *Wake*, and all hands were needed to repair damage and keep the machinery in operation. The worst day was 4 December. By then nobody on board either ship had slept for forty-eight hours, and there had been no hot food for several days. Even the two larger escorting ships were taking a beating. *Finch* had her anchors swept away and *Pigeon*'s rudder was damaged.[12]

Finally, on 5 December the weather changed to beautiful clear sky and calm seas. The two gunboats put on their best speed and headed for Manila, which they reached that day. Also on that day the U.S. Navy's Yangtze Patrol officially came to an end. It had been a colorful period in U.S. Navy history.[13]

On 2 December Lieutenant Commander Alan McCracken, the skipper of the river gunboat USS *Mindanao*, received word to proceed to Manila. The ship was still at Hong Kong when the orders arrived. The tug *Ranger*, owned by the Luzon Stevedore Company, was also at Hong Kong; she was placed at the disposal of the gunboat. Preparations to make the dangerous voyage across the South China Sea were made, including loading extra supplies and equipment on board the gunboat and the tug. Eight hundred rounds of 3-inch ammunition that *Mindanao* had stored in a British magazine were loaded on board the tug. The two ships split 250,000 rounds of .30-caliber machine-gun ammunition.

On the morning of 4 December *Mindanao* bid farewell to Hong Kong for the last time—she had been the Yangtze Patrol's south China gunboat for over a decade. *Ranger* was not yet ready to go; she was directed to follow as soon as possible. As soon as the gunboat left the shelter of Hong Kong harbor she encountered heavy seas and high winds. Not long after leaving the port a Japanese cruiser approached and looked the gunboat over but did not linger. The *Mindanao* was soon being tossing violently in the gale. McCracken was forced to take an easterly course—generally toward Formosa.

For three days the little gunboat beat her way through the storm. At one point she rolled 49 degrees before righting herself. Finally, on 7 December, the weather allowed the ship to turn toward the Philippines. On that day an American PBY was sighted. By this point the deckhouse had started to work loose from the constant pounding from the sea. Due to the heavy use of the engines the fuel supply was starting to get low but McCracken determined she could make Luzon. There was no sign of *Ranger* despite multiple attempts to reach her on the radio (the tug made it to Manila). *Mindanao* pressed on toward the Philippines.[14]

THE SHIPS MOVE SOUTH

Hart took Washington's war warning message very seriously. On 24 November, upon receipt of Admiral Stark's message, the destroyer tender USS *Blackhawk* along with the destroyers *Whipple*, *Alden*, *John D. Edwards*, and *Edsall* departed Manila en route to the Dutch port of Balikpapan on the southeast coast of Borneo. The light cruiser *Marblehead* and destroyers *Paul Jones*, *Stewart*, *Barker*, and *Bulmer* left for Tarakan, an important oil port north of Balikpapan.

The heavy cruiser *Houston*, the Asiatic Fleet flagship and the largest surface combatant in the fleet, rushed preparations to depart from Cavite. The ship was being fitted with four 1.1-inch, four-barreled, automatic anti-aircraft guns. The Yard personnel rushed the job and on the morning of 1 December the big cruiser departed for the port of Iloilo on the southern coast of the island of Panay in the central Philippines.

The last convoy to reach Manila arrived on 4 December. The five merchant ships in the convoy, which carried little military cargo, were escorted by the light cruiser USS *Boise*. Hart was able to retain *Boise* to bolster his fleet although she was part of the Pacific Fleet at Pearl Harbor. After fueling at Sangley Point she was dispatched to Cebu in the central Philippines. With fifteen 6-inch guns *Boise* was a much more powerful ship than the older *Marblehead*, which had long been part of the Asiatic Fleet.

While the surface ships were dispersing southward PatWing 10 stepped up its air patrols west of the Philippines. The arrangement that had finally been worked out with the Army in November was for the better-armed Army B-17s to conduct reconnaissance out to sea near Formosa while the more vulnerable PBYs would patrol the area near the Indochina coast. During the first week in December PBYs scouting the area around Camranh Bay discovered over twenty merchant ships in the harbor. These spottings confirmed the work of Station C, which through traffic analysis had detected the buildup of Japanese shipping in Formosa and Indochina as early as mid-November.

ADMIRAL PHILLIPS' VISIT

Just as the Americans were trying to rapidly increase their forces in the Far East in an attempt to deter the Japanese, so too were the British rushing what forces they could to Asia. By far the most important of the eleventh-hour British reinforcements were the battleship HMS *Prince of Wales* and the battle cruiser *Repulse*.

British prime minister Winston Churchill was personally involved in the decision to dispatch the two ships to Singapore—a move that was resisted by much of the uniformed British naval leadership in London. The battle cruiser was already in the Indian Ocean when the decision was made, but *Prince of Wales* had to be dispatched from England. The commanding officer of the British force, which was intended to be the centerpiece of London's attempt to deter the Japanese, was Vice Admiral Sir Tom Phillips. While his ships were still en route, Phillips flew ahead to Singapore, arriving on 1 December to be briefed on the overall situation. Within a day of Phillips' arrival British intelligence (which was already sharing much information with their American counterparts, including Station C on Corregidor) was warning that the Japanese were massing shipping in Camranh Bay and a dozen submarines had been spotted headed south into the South China Sea. Realizing that war might be imminent, Phillips decided to fly to Manila to confer with MacArthur and, especially, Hart. He departed in a British flying boat on the night of 4 December for secret meetings with the Americans the next day.[15]

The formal meeting that included MacArthur and his chief of staff, Brigadier General Richard K. Sutherland, took place at noon on 6 December. MacArthur made a speech where he described the growing power of his ground forces, stressing that all would be ready to meet Japanese aggression—by April 1942. The USAFFE commander told the British admiral that, "Admiral Hart and I operate in the closest cooperation. We are the oldest and dearest friends." Hart's staff officers who were present could barely restrain their incredulity, given the increasingly insulting, condescending attitude of the USAFFE commander toward their admiral.[16] Once MacArthur and Sutherland departed, Hart and Phillips continued their discussions about the relationship of American and British naval forces in East Asia.

Phillips wanted Hart to commit Asiatic Fleet destroyers to supporting his capital ships. Given the tremendous strain of the battle against German U-boats in the Atlantic very few of the Royal Navy's destroyers could be spared for the Far East; Phillips had only half a dozen available. Knowing that the Asiatic Fleet had already dispatched some of its destroyers to the Indies along with their tenders, the British admiral wanted a commitment that in the event of a Japanese attack the American vessels would operate in direct conjunction with his heavy ships. Although very impressed with Phillips, Hart was not at liberty to make such an open-ended commitment given that the United States was not yet at war.

While they were discussing the destroyer issue on the afternoon of the 6th word was received that a large Japanese convoy had been spotted moving southward from Indochina into the Gulf of Siam. That brought the meeting to a halt. Both admirals agreed that they would continue to coordinate their actions as much as possible. Phillips soon departed for Singapore on an American PBY (his British aircrew was somewhere in Manila and could not be found on short notice). It appeared that war could soon break out, although the senior American and British leaders still did not know exactly when or where.[17]

ROOSEVELT'S GAMBLE

On 1 December Hart received a top-secret communication from Admiral Stark in Washington. Under direct orders from the president, Hart had two days to

> charter three small vessels to form a "defensive information patrol." Minimum requirements to establish identity as a United States man of war are command by a naval officer and to mount a small gun and one machine gun would suffice. Filipino crews may be employed with minimum number of naval ratings to accomplish purpose which is to observe and report Japanese movements in West China Sea and Gulf of Siam. One vessel to be stationed between Hainan and Hue one vessel off the Indochina coast between Camranh Bay and Cape St. Jaques and one vessel off Pointe de Camau. Use of *Isabel* authorized by president as one of these three but not other naval vessels. Report measures taken to carry out president's views.

> At same time inform me as to what reconnaissance measures are being regularly performed at sea by both army and navy whether by air surface vessels or submarines and your opinion as to the effectiveness of these latter measures.[18]

Hart thought the orders were risky since PatWing 10 was already conducting extensive aerial reconnaissance off the Indochina coast. Clearly, the ships assigned to the mission would be at great risk. Nevertheless, the orders originated with the president himself and had to be obeyed. One of the three vessels was already available in Manila Bay—the patrol yacht USS *Isabel.* In keeping with the strict secrecy associated with the message, Hart had a personal one-on-one meeting with the ship's commanding officer, Lieutenant John W. Payne, on the morning of 3 December. Hart carefully went over the instructions with the young officer and told him that only the ship's executive officer (XO) could be told of the mission, and he only once the ship was out to sea. Meanwhile, efforts were made to quickly arm, crew, and commission the other two vessels, per Roosevelt's instructions. These were the recently acquired schooners *Lanikai* (which was placed under the command of Lieutenant Kemp Tolley, the former XO of the gunboat *Wake*), and *Molly Moore*. Neither schooner managed to get to sea before war started, but *Isabel* did.[19]

On the evening of 3 December *Isabel* cleared Manila Bay and headed toward the Indochina coast. By the evening of the 5th she was less than twenty-five miles from the shore. Earlier that day the little ship, which was prominently displaying an American flag, was overflown by Japanese single-engine aircraft, but not attacked.

Shortly after dusk orders from the CinCAF were received directing the ship to return to Manila at once. Throughout the 6th the ship plowed through stormy weather, once being observed by a Japanese twin-engine bomber. The patrol yacht was literally within sight of Corregidor in the early morning hours of 8 December when a radio warning was received that war had broken out.

There can be little doubt what this mission was all about. Station C and the patrolling PBYs of the Asiatic Fleet had detected the buildup of Japanese shipping in southern China and Indochina in late November. The Japanese were clearly on the verge of a major move southward. But when and where would it take place? If the Japanese only attacked Thailand it was unlikely that the U.S., the British, or Dutch could respond. More seriously, if the Japanese only went after the British in Malaya and Singapore would Roosevelt be able to convince his still strongly isolationist nation to go to war if the United States or the Philippines was not attacked directly?

Roosevelt and his inner circle in Washington clearly understood that the situation in the Far East was deteriorating fast—that is why Admiral Stark and General Marshall sent the 27 November "war warning" messages to their senior commanders in the Pacific. What was not known was the specific timing and intent of the Japanese. It is virtually certain that the purpose of sending *Isabel* into the likely path of a southward-bound convoy was to maximize the chance that the vessels—all officially U.S. men-of-war—would be attacked by the Japanese. Roosevelt and his closest advisers almost certainly realized that it would be politically very difficult to convince a still-wary Congress to authorize American entry into the war if only Thailand or Malaya were invaded.

Admiral Hart was glad that he was authorized to recall the slow and poorly armed *Isabel*, which would not have stood a chance had the Japanese attacked her. For the rest of his life he remained convinced that the purpose of sending the ship into the South China Sea was to maximize the chances of an incident that would ensure the United States would be involved in a Pacific War.[20]

THE ASIATIC FLEET ON THE EVE OF WAR

As the first week in December came to an end the Asiatic Fleet had taken important steps to prepare for war. All three cruisers had moved southward to the central Philippines or Borneo, as had nine of the thirteen destroyers. Most of the fleet's twenty-nine submarines were in Manila Bay; many had already received orders about their war patrol stations. The fleet's gunboats, with the exception of *Mindanao*, stood ready in the bay as well, while the fleet's minesweepers and most of the tenders took up station nearby. The small seaplane tender *Heron* was southwest of Manila at the island of Palawan while the larger *Preston* was at Mindanao in the extreme southern Philippines. Finally, the six PT boats of MTB Squadron 3 were at the Cavite Navy Yard. Of PatWing 10's twenty-eight PBY flying boats, all but three were in the Manila Bay area or Olongapo; the final three aircraft were with *Preston*.

At Olongapo the 4th Marines were settling into their new home; meanwhile, the 1st Separate Battalion was at a high state of readiness in and around the Cavite Navy Yard. It was hoped that within a few days two hundred more Marines would arrive from north China; they were to be immediately added to the 4th Marines. The 1st Separate Battalion's radar unit was operating southwest of Manila, tied in with the Army's Air Warning Service headquarters.

The Asiatic Fleet had clearly heeded the war warnings it received during the past two weeks. For the most part the Fleet was ready for war. They did not have long to wait.

CHAPTER 3

War Begins

It was 0257 on the morning of 8 December when the radio message: "Air raid Pearl Harbor, this is no drill" was received by the Asiatic Fleet radio watch. Within minutes the senior duty officer, Lieutenant Colonel William T. Clement, USMC, notified Admiral Hart at his residence at the Manila Hotel. The Asiatic Fleet commander quickly penned out the following message to be transmitted to all ships and shore commands: "Priority. Japan started hostilities, govern yourselves accordingly."[1] The United States was in World War II.

At Olongapo the 4th Marines received Admiral Hart's "govern yourselves accordingly" message at 0350. A follow-on message that arrived before the sun came up warned all ships and the 16th Naval District to be prepared for enemy air attacks at dawn. Before the sun rose Marines were establishing defensive positions around Olongapo; thirty-six light machine guns were emplaced for air defense. With the limited number of men at his disposal Colonel Howard was restricted in what he could do to defend the Olongapo area. Patrols were sent into the nearby hills and contact established with the Army's coast artillery garrison on Grande Island (Fort Wint) at the entrance of Subic Bay. The Regimental Band dug foxholes along the beaches near the town of Olongapo. Lastly, in accordance with a recent decision to have the 4th Marines take over the defense of southern Bataan, the 1st Battalion (less Company D) was embarked in the large Navy tug *Vega* and dispatched to Mariveles early that morning.

Colonel Howard had already been in touch with the Philippine Army's 31st Division that was mobilizing north of Olongapo. It was important for the 4th Marines to be aware of what was going on to their north and east because the only viable road exit from Olongapo ran through the easy-to-block Zig Zag Pass. Therefore, during the morning of the 8th Howard dispatched 1st Lieutenant Lewis H. Pickup to serve as the regiment's liaison officer with the 31st.[2]

The Marines of the 1st Separate Battalion at Cavite had maintained partial manning of all anti-aircraft batteries since late October. Now the guns were fully manned and all positions readied for possible air attack. The battalion had been on such a high state of alert since the "war warning" message on 27 November that relatively little additional work needed to be done on the first day of hostilities.

As ground forces made their final, hasty preparations to defend the area, radar and aerial elements sprung to action. Southwest of Manila, Warrant Officer Brainard's radar detachment had been in position since 4 December. Linked in with the Far Eastern Air Force's air warning center, the Marine radar scanned the area west and south of Manila for aerial intruders. Meanwhile, the two PBY squadrons, VP-101 at Sangley Point and VP-102 at Olongapo, readied their aircraft for reconnaissance and strike missions. A number of the flying boats were armed with four 500-pound bombs and all were loaded with machine-gun ammunition. Crews were to stand by to take off on short notice in order to be prepared to launch attacks against targets of opportunity. By 0600 the first armed reconnaissance missions of the war took off to scan the ocean west of Luzon.

Patrol Wing 10 had a well-rehearsed plan for the outbreak of hostilities. Seven planes of VP-102 based at Olongapo conducted the initial scouting missions. Meanwhile, seven aircraft from VP-101 were held in readiness near Sangley Point as an attack group. Five additional aircraft at Sangley Point formed a second scouting element, while four planes were dispatched to Laguna de Bay, the large lake south of Manila, to be ready as a backup attack force—some ammunition and fuel had already been cached near the lake to facilitate operations. The three flying boats with the seaplane tender USS *William D. Preston* in the Gulf of Davao and two planes in hangars at Sangley Point completed PatWing 10's total of twenty-eight flying boats. By mid-morning the Asiatic Fleet's air element was at its war stations and ready for operations.[3]

In the week immediately before the war started, and continuing for the next two days following the start of hostilities, Allied and neutral merchant shipping was accumulating in Manila Bay. Before dawn the 16th Naval District's Radio Cavite broadcast a message to all U.S. merchant ships in the area to proceed to the nearest friendly port. Realizing that Manila was farther from the Japanese than Hong Kong, most merchant ships in the South China Sea decided to head for the Philippines. By the morning of the 10th some 200,000 tons of ocean-going merchant shipping, roughly forty vessels of various sizes, were lying at anchor near Manila and Mariveles.[4]

One of the first hostile actions taken by the Japanese was to attack the seaplane tender *Preston* that was anchored in Malang Bay at the southern end of Mindanao, the second largest island in the Philippines. *Preston* was a converted World War I "flush deck" destroyer. With some of her boilers removed to accommodate parts and fuel for her aircraft, the ship was now limited to a speed of about 25 knots, compared to her original 34.

Preston received Admiral Hart's message alerting the Asiatic Fleet to the outbreak of war. Before dawn one of her three PBYs took off on patrol, the other two flying boats remaining at anchor near the ship. Just after 0700 she was attacked by a group of six Japanese Navy A5M *Claude* fixed-landing-gear fighters from the Imperial Navy's light aircraft carrier *Ryujo* operating east of Mindanao. It was the first Japanese attack on the Philippines and the first action of the U.S. Navy in the Far East. Despite anti-aircraft fire from the *Preston*, the Japanese fighters left both moored PBYs in flames. On board one of the aircraft Ensign Robert Tills was killed and an enlisted radioman wounded; they were the first American casualties in the Philippines.

Preston got under way as quickly as possible, but was soon attacked by seven B5N *Kate* bombers from the Japanese carrier. Fortunately, their bombs missed as she gained speed, firing back with her limited anti-aircraft armament. As the ship stood out toward the entrance of Davao Gulf her one airborne PBY radioed a warning that three unidentified warships were some fifteen miles away, heading in the ship's direction. Assuming that the ships were Japanese destroyers (which they were), the seaplane tender poured on all possible speed to clear the area.[5] At 0730 an entry was made in the 16th Naval District war diary noting that the *Preston* was under attack. The Army's USAFFE Headquarters was notified a few minutes later.

HAMMERING THE AIRFIELDS

A key element of the Japanese plan for the seizure of the Philippines was to rapidly gain air superiority. During the months before the start of the war Japanese agents had tried to determine the size of MacArthur's Air Force. By early December they estimated that there were about 300 American aircraft in the Philippines, which proved to be a pretty good guess. There were actually 270 planes of all types in the Far Eastern Air Force inventory. The Philippine Army Air Corps had about 60 additional aircraft, mostly biplane trainers of no combat value.[6]

Due to the distance from the airfields on Formosa to the most important targets—the Army's Clark Field in central Luzon and the Manila Bay area—it would be the Japanese Navy that would lead the effort to break the back of U.S. airpower in the Philippines. Japanese Army bombers could only reach the middle of Luzon from their bases on Formosa; short-ranged Japanese Army fighters needed bases on Luzon in order to operate. On the other hand, the Imperial Navy's twin-engine medium bombers, the G4M (soon to be code-named Betty by the Allies) and the older G3M (shortly to be nicknamed Nell) could easily reach targets in the Manila area. Importantly, the Imperial Navy's superb A6M2 Zero fighter had sufficient range to escort the bombers. That was a remarkable performance for a 1941 fighter plane—from the bases on Formosa to the Manila area was roughly five hundred miles, one way.

For the critical first strikes on 8 December the Japanese committed fifty-four G4M bombers and fifty-three A6M Zeros against Iba Field on the west coast of Luzon. The strike force intended to hit Clark, the main U.S. bomber base in the Philippines, consisted of twenty-five Nells and twenty-seven Bettys, accompanied by thirty-six Zeros. A small number of Japanese Army bombers would attack targets that were within their range farther north on Luzon.[7]

There remains to this day considerable controversy about the actions of General MacArthur, Brigadier General Sutherland, and Major General Louis H. Brereton, the Far Eastern Air Force (FEAF) commander, on the morning of 8 December. Evidence suggests that well before dawn General Brereton attempted to see MacArthur, wanting authorization to launch an attack on Formosa using the B-17s that were based at Clark Field. For whatever reason, General Sutherland prevented Brereton from seeing MacArthur for several hours. Permission to conduct an armed reconnaissance of Formosa was not given to the Air Force until very late in the morning, too late for the Army bombers to depart before the big Japanese air raid arrived.[8]

The Army expected enemy air activity over Luzon to start at first light, but instead there were only minor attacks by Japanese Army bombers against Baguio and Tuguegarao around 0830. Army fighters were in the air early, but by mid-morning they had to start rotating in to land for fuel, having failed to intercept any of the Japanese aircraft. The strange lack of large-scale enemy air activity during the morning hours was because the Japanese Navy's air bases on Formosa were badly fogged in when the sun rose; takeoff was delayed by several hours. By the time they finally got into the air the Japanese expected to arrive over Luzon with the element of surprise lost and with large numbers of American fighters waiting for them.

False alarms during the morning resulted in the B-17s at Clark being scrambled to avoid being caught on the ground. They landed before lunch to start fueling and arming for a possible strike against Formosa late that afternoon. Unfortunately, FEAF's fighter controllers were very inexperienced. Despite having radar plots of approaching enemy aircraft transmitted to them from the Army's radar set at Iba Field, they made numerous errors in allocating and scrambling fighters that morning. The Army's fighter controllers were, without question, alerted by the radar at Iba Field about the approach of two large Japanese air formations. They delayed too long in ordering fighter units on the ground and in the air to respond. The Iba radar sent the first reports of the approach of the enemy aircraft at 1120, over an hour before the bombing of the airfields. There was also considerable confusion between the Army's fighter and bomber commands. It appears that word of the approach of enemy aircraft was not passed to the 19th Bombardment Group Headquarters at Clark Field.

The air strikes on Clark and Iba Fields started at approximately 1230. Very few Army fighters were in the air in the vicinity of either base. Additionally, the Army's 200th Coast Artillery Regiment (Anti-Aircraft) at Clark was incapable of disrupting the enemy raid. Of the several air bases the Army had on Luzon Clark was the only one with a significant anti-aircraft capability. However, neither the Imperial Navy Betty and Nell bombers that attacked first from roughly 22,000 feet nor the Japanese Navy Zero fighters that went in next at low altitude to strafe the field suffered significant losses from the air defenses at Clark. Iba Field was nearly totally defenseless, with only a few machine guns for base protection.[9]

All the factors listed above ensured the virtual destruction of Iba Field and very serious damage to Clark. At Iba the very heavy bombing that smashed the little base destroyed the only operational radar that the Army had on Luzon. At Clark, the Japanese naval bombers struck first, dropping their bombs mostly on the buildings of the base. Almost half the Army's B-17s in the Philippines were caught on the ground. Incredibly, few of the parked B-17s were hit during the first part of the raid. When the bombers departed, however, many of the escorting Zero fighters descended to low altitude to strafe. It was at that point that most of the B-17s were destroyed (nineteen B-17s were Clark-based; sixteen additional heavy bombers were at Del Monte Field on Mindanao when war started).

A few air battles did take place. Some of the fighters of the 3rd Pursuit Squadron at Iba were airborne when the raid arrived. They tried, without much success, to engage the enemy. Similarly, a handful of the P-40s of the 20th Pursuit Squadron based at Clark managed to get airborne and challenge the raiders. They too achieved little. Toward the end of the raid at Clark the P-35As of the 34th Pursuit Squadron from Del Carmen Field arrived in a belated attempt to come to the rescue of the beleaguered base.

Over nine hours after receiving word of the Pearl Harbor attack, the Army Air Force in the Philippines had been caught largely on the ground. Inexperience, bad luck, poor training, miscommunication, and some undeniable incompetence resulted in the Army's Far Eastern Air Force suffering a disastrous defeat. By the time the Japanese Navy planes departed, forty-nine American aircraft had been destroyed on the ground at Clark and Iba, including twelve of nineteen B-17s.[10] In addition, nine P-40 fighters were either shot down or crashed when they ran out of fuel. More aircraft, including fighters and bombers, were damaged in the attack. Only fifty-eight of the Army's ninety-two P-40 fighters remained operational at the end of the first day of battle. Of the Army's five pursuit squadrons, two (the 3rd and 20th) had been eliminated. Seventy-seven Army Air Force officers and men had been killed, and about 150 more wounded. No Japanese bombers had been lost over Luzon; one Betty crash-landed upon return to base in Formosa. A total of seven Zero fighters failed to return to their bases on Formosa.[11]

A DISASTER WITH DEVASTATING CONSEQUENCES

Although the exact sequence of events during the morning of 8 December will never be known (historians have tried unsuccessfully for years to reconcile the statements of MacArthur, Sutherland, Brereton, and other key Army Air Force personnel), there is no question that the senior Army leaders in the Philippines were completely responsible for the disaster. Indecision at the highest levels resulted in hours of delay that cost the defenders of the Philippines dearly. It was the B-17s that were supposed to provide the first line of defense against the Japanese, interdicting enemy shipping far out to sea and attacking Japanese bases. On the first day of war nearly half of the heavy bombers in the Philippines had been destroyed or damaged and the Army Air Force's main base heavily bombed. Nearly 40 percent of the Army's modern fighters had been damaged or lost. It was a deadly blow.

MacArthur clearly should have shouldered much of the blame for this disaster. Indeed, in some militaries he, his chief of staff, and his air commander would all have been relieved, or worse. Fortunately for MacArthur, the thousands of miles between the Philippines and the most senior U.S. political-military decision makers in Washington shielded him from direct scrutiny and blame. There was no denying, however, that the defense of the Philippines was off to a terrible start. As events went from bad to worse in the next few days MacArthur started looking for scapegoats to whom he could deflect blame and criticism. In his mind the U.S. Navy made an ideal target.

INITIAL NAVAL ACTIONS

By the evening of the first day of war the Navy leadership in the Philippines was aware that it had been a very bad day at Clark Field, although they did not know the details yet. Hart's main concern was the safety of his ships and getting them to locations that would do the most good for the defense of the Islands, as well as the longer-term mission of helping the Dutch and British defend Malaya and the Indies to the south.

During the remainder of the day the Navy and Marine elements in the Philippines continued to get ready for combat. As already noted, a major portion of the 4th Marines moved from Olongapo to Mariveles. The Naval Hospital at Canacao started transferring one-third of its supplies to Mariveles and another third to Manila. Admiral Rockwell and Captain Davis, Canacao's commanding officer, were concerned that the hospital was very vulnerable to attack, sitting as it was midway between the Cavite Navy Yard and the other facilities on Sangley Point, all of which were legitimate military targets. During the day several reports were received from Guam that the island was under air attack.

MTB Squadron 3 was dispersed among several locations in Manila Bay. At the end of the first day three of the PT boats were positioned at Mariveles with full loads of torpedoes, and three other boats were in the Manila-Cavite area available for whatever duties either the CinCAF or Com16 required.

On Sangley Point were stored thousands of drums of aviation fuel and gasoline. Late on the first evening of war the dispersal of the gas started, with five thousand drums of aviation fuel going to Mariveles and the remaining stores of gas broken up into smaller caches along the Peninsula. Given the magnitude of the task it would take a couple of days' work to accomplish the move.

Most of the Asiatic Fleet's twenty-nine submarines were in Manila Bay on the day war started. Their tenders were all there, too. Hart ordered that eight of the subs get under way to seek out Japanese shipping around Formosa and Indochina. Eight other boats would take up positions off the north, west, and east coasts of Luzon to guard against an invasion. That would leave about a third of the available submarines in reserve in Manila to surge out as events demanded or to relieve the first wave of subs that would soon be headed toward their designated stations. Two submarines were already on patrol. *S-36* was off Lingayen Gulf, long suspected to be the main landing point of a would-be invader. *S-39* was patrolling to the southeast of Luzon. Three submarines, *Seadragon*, *Shark*, and *Sealion* were at the Navy Yard being refitted; it would be several days before they could go to sea. Before dawn on the first day of war the commander of the Asiatic Fleet sent the following message: "Submarines and aircraft will wage unrestricted warfare."[12] Great things were expected from the submarines, recently issued the new, secret Mark VI magnetic detonator for their torpedoes. This new device was intended to explode the "fish" under the keel of an enemy ship, with the goal of breaking the target's back. Unfortunately, it would soon be apparent that the performance of the subs was to be the bleakest part of the Asiatic Fleet's efforts to defend the Philippines.

CHAPTER 4

The Bombing of the Cavite Navy Yard

The war in the Pacific was only three days old, but Wednesday 10 December was a decisive day for the defense of the Philippines. The Japanese set out to destroy MacArthur's already crippled Air Force. Simultaneously, the first Japanese landings on Luzon took place at Vigan and Aparri in the north. For the U.S. Navy this day would bring the worst damage inflicted on one of its shore installations by an enemy since the British burned the Washington Navy Yard in 1814.

The Japanese were unable to make major air attacks on the Philippines on 9 December due to bad weather. The U.S. Army used the absence of enemy air raids that day to reposition its remaining fighter assets. Two of the Army's five pursuit squadrons had been destroyed on the 8th, as had over a third of its heavy bombers and a number of support aircraft. Despite tremendous losses on the first day of the war, the Army remained determined to resist the Japanese onslaught. Army Air Force leadership in the Philippines ordered the remaining B-17s moved from Del Monte Field on Mindanao to Luzon in preparation for strikes against Formosa. Its three remaining fighter squadrons, the 17th and 21st Pursuit armed with the modern P-40E and the 34th Pursuit with the much less capable P-35A, were readied to intercept the expected Japanese air attacks. Each of the Army fighter units had about eighteen aircraft. A provisional detachment of fifteen P-40s was also created to defend Manila. The Americans were aided by the Philippine Army Air Corps' only fighter unit, the 6th Pursuit Squadron, which was armed with a dozen fixed-landing-gear P-26A "Peashooter" fighters, an early-1930s machine. Although brave, the Filipino pilots were at a hopeless disadvantage against the Imperial Navy Zeros.[1]

American airpower was limited in other ways. Due to the destruction of the early warning radar that was at Iba Field there was little warning of approaching

Japanese air units coming from the north. The Marine air warning radar detachment at Nasugbu remained in place and continued to monitor the air situation west and southwest of Manila Bay. Had it been repositioned on 9 December to search north of Luzon it might possibly have been able to provide better warning of the massive Japanese air attack that would occur the next day.

Supplementing the limited radar capability, aerial reconnaissance flights were conducted by PBYs from Olongapo. Early on the morning of the 9th one aircraft discovered a suspicious ship less than one hundred miles off the northwest coast of Luzon. When the flying boat went in for a close look it was sprayed by machine-gun fire from the vessel, which the American crew assumed to be Japanese. When the patrol plane's report was received at Olangapo, PatWing 10 dispatched three more PBYs, each armed with four 500-pound bombs. After a short flight, the PBYs arrived over the target and dropped their weapons. Fortunately for the crew of the Norwegian ship SS *Ulysses*, the Navy planes missed their vessel. Illustrating the nerves and uncertainty that engulfed the Americans, another PatWing 10 flying boat was accidentally fired on by friendly troops as it approached Subic Bay to land. The aircraft made a successful water landing, but was badly shot up; one of the enlisted crewmen died.

The Navy used the lull on 9 December to prepare for the inevitable renewal of Japanese attacks. Captain Wilkes, who had been preparing to return to the United States when the war started, was restored to command of the Asiatic Fleet's submarines. During the day the first wave of boats moved to their war patrol stations. Admiral Hart met with Admiral Rockwell and Captain Frank Wagner, the commanding officer of PatWing 10. Hart, obviously fearing air attack, directed that the Patrol Wing's fuel supplies be dispersed, a process that had actually started on the evening of the 8th.

Fears of an attack were indeed high. Beyond taking the necessary defensive steps to prepare for the next round of attacks, female civilian employees were directed not to report to work until further notice, and a partial evacuation of civilians from the towns of Cavite and San Rogue was ordered. On the ninth the 185 patients at the Navy's Canacao Hospital were transferred across the Bay by ferry to the Army's Sternberg Hospital in Manila. Captain Davis coordinated the move with his Army medical counterparts. Canacao's naval medical staff remained in place in order to be ready to accept a new, war-generated, patient load certain to arrive soon.

On the 9th Admiral Hart received word that the little river gunboat *Wake* had been captured by the Japanese in Shanghai harbor the day before. The small caretaker crew had not been able to scuttle the ship before the Japanese boarded her. *Wake* was the only U.S. warship captured by the enemy in World War II while crewmen were still on board. Additionally, the CinCAF was informed of the surrender of the 204 Marines and sailors in north China.

10 DECEMBER, DAY OF DISASTER

The Japanese intended to make a major effort in the air on 10 December. They planned to strike several targets, mostly in the Manila Bay area, and provide support for their amphibious assaults in northern Luzon. Again, it was to be the air units of the Imperial Navy that would take the lead against the Americans; until bases were established on Luzon the Japanese Army's shorter ranged fighters and bombers could not reach targets in the Clark Field–Manila Bay area.

Seventeen Zero fighters from the elite Tainan Kokutai were allocated to provide cover for the landings in north Luzon. The Japanese Army's Ki-27 Nate fighters based on Formosa had enough range to allow them to help protect the landings. The main effort, however, was the attack directed against airfields and other targets in the Manila Bay area. Several formations were assembled for those missions. The first consisted of twenty-seven Betty bombers of the Takao Kokutai intended for Nichols Field near Manila.[2] Twenty-seven additional Bettys from the same unit were earmarked to strike Del Carmen Field near Clark Air Base. Finally, twenty-seven Nell bombers of the 1st Kokutai under command of Lieutenant Commander Takeo Ozaki were dispatched to attack the Cavite Navy Yard. Escorting the bombers were fifty-six Zeros of the Tainan and 3rd Kokutais. Japanese Army bombers were allocated to strike battered Iba Field, a target that was within their range from Formosa. Including reconnaissance planes that accompanied the strike forces, roughly two hundred Japanese Army and Navy aircraft set off toward the Philippines.[3]

From the Americans' point of view the best part of 10 December were the early actions. Just after dawn a Navy PBY piloted by Lieutenant Clarence Keller, one of three flying boats that took off from Manila Bay, spotted ships some 250 miles off the west coast of Luzon that the crew mistook for the British capital ships HMS *Prince of Wales* and *Repulse*. PatWing 10 headquarters was not convinced and ordered that the PBY firmly establish the identity of the ships. Dutifully, the Catalina swung back to find the ships again. When the ships were relocated a hail of anti-aircraft fire convinced Keller that the vessels were indeed *not* British.

Within minutes of Keller's 0800 report that the ships were hostile Captain Wagner ordered five bomb-loaded PBYs to launch from their temporary base at Laguna de Bay. Just after noon the five Catalinas, led by Lieutenant Commander J. V. Peterson, dropped a total of twenty 500-pound bombs at the Japanese ships. The bombs missed just astern of the Japanese heavy cruiser *Ashigara,* whose return fire hit one of the Navy flying boats. Although postwar Japanese records do not mention damage to the ship, Peterson and his crew clearly observed the cruiser slow down and move in a circle as the other vessels sped away. It may be that the bombs impacting so close to the stern caused temporary steering damage. All five PBYs returned to base. Captain Wagner next ordered four flying boats at Sangley Point to be loaded with torpedoes for a follow-up strike. The Americans were, however, soon overwhelmed by the day's events; the mission never took place.[4]

Even before the PBY attack Army aircraft had launched strikes against the Japanese landings at Vigan and Aparri. The Japanese landings had started before dawn. Roughly 5,900 troops went ashore at Aparri, and another 4,400 at Vigan.[5] The purpose of these small initial landings was to gain airfields on Luzon and to provide flank protection for the main landings at Lingayen Gulf, slated for 22 December. There was virtually no opposition ashore at either landing site.

When confirmation of the landings was received at Far Eastern Air Force Headquarters groups of Army fighters and bombers were dispatched to attack. At 0600 the first B-17s took off from Clark for Aparri (these were the bombers that had flown up from Mindanao the day before). Several of the bombers attacked the Japanese ships from altitudes above 12,000 feet, but with little effect. Some of the B-17s had been forced to take off from Clark before being fully armed due to an air raid alert. As the bombers departed they thought they had inflicted considerable damage (including the supposed sinking of the Japanese battleship *Haruna* by Captain Colin Kelly, USA), but in reality a Japanese minesweeper, *W-19*, had been forced to beach and another was slightly damaged. The ship that Kelly's crew had just missed was probably the Japanese light cruiser *Natori*, which reported slight damage. A destroyer and a cargo ship were also hit, the *Takao Maru* being driven ashore.[6]

At Vigan five B-17s started the aerial attack, followed by P-40s and P-35s that went in at low altitude to machine-gun the Japanese landing force and the barges plying between the beach and the ships offshore. The low-level fighter attacks were more effective compared to the bombers' effort, but at higher cost. The brave commander of the P-35s of the 34th Pursuit Squadron was killed as he repeatedly strafed the Japanese minesweeper *W-10* that finally exploded as he passed directly over the ship. The Army bombers also inflicted slight damage on the light cruiser *Naka* and a greater amount on the transport *Oigawa Maru*; the cargo ship was run aground. Despite the efforts of the Army pilots, the Japanese were firmly ashore in north Luzon, with minimal losses. Now, as the Army aircraft returned to their bases to refuel and rearm, the big Japanese aerial striking force from Formosa appeared.

The situation started to become serious just before 1230 when Zeros of the Tainan Kokutai arrived over Del Carmen Field at low altitude and discovered the fifteen P-35s of the 34th Pursuit Squadron, recently returned from the attack on the Vigan landing site, lined up on the ground. In a few minutes of strafing ten of the American fighters were destroyed and the others damaged, thus effectively eliminating one of the three remaining American Army fighter units. Unfortunately for the U.S. Navy, twenty-seven Bettys of the Takao Kokutai had been forced to abort their bombing mission against Del Carmen due to cloud cover. The Bettys pressed on toward their secondary targets in the Manila Bay area where they would soon make their presence felt.

News of the attack on Del Carmen sent the P-40s of the 17th and 21st Pursuit Squadrons skyward from Clark where they had been refueling after the morning attacks at Vigan and Aparri. Some of the Army fighters headed for Del Carmen while the rest went south toward Manila. While they were en route, Japanese bombers appeared over Manila Bay.

The first group of Bettys of the Takao Kokutai arrived over the Bay at roughly 1240. Their targets were Nichols and Nielson airfields and merchant shipping in the Bay. When the Japanese arrived over Manila a group of eight P-40s had just taken off to relieve seven other Army fighters from the standing patrol that was being maintained over the Manila area. When the Army fighter pilots spotted the approaching Japanese formation they maneuvered to intercept, although half of them had only enough fuel left for ten minutes of fighting. Thus began a series of swirling dogfights that raged from Manila to Subic Bay as American and Japanese fighters tangled. The P-40s racing south from Clark also entered the fray. While the dogfights were under way four P-26s arrived. One of the Filipino pilots attempted to ram a Zero with his much slower fighter. The Filipino squadron commander, Captain Jesus Villamor, engaged a Japanese bomber and left it smoking. Incredibly, all four P-26s made it back to their base, Zablan Field, outside Manila.[7]

The air battle was a one-sided contest. There is no question that at this stage of the war the majority of the fighter pilots of the Imperial Navy were much better than their U.S. Army counterparts. Many of the Zero pilots were veterans of fighting over China, and on average had hundreds more flying hours than the majority of the young U.S. Army flyers in the Philippines. Of at least equal importance, the tactics of the Army pursuit squadrons at this stage of the war were simply not appropriate for fighting nimble, highly maneuverable Japanese fighters. The American pilots had been indoctrinated to dogfight in their prewar training. Unfortunately, they did not realize that their heavy P-40s were far less maneuverable than the Japanese fighters that could turn tighter and thus quickly get behind the surprised Americans. The results were devastating. Of roughly thirty-five Army P-40s that engaged the Japanese in the Manila Bay area on 10 December, twenty were lost, either shot down (at least one due to friendly fire) or crashed as their fuel ran out. Three Japanese Zeros were shot down and four others ditched on their way home due to battle damage. Critically, the Army fighters had not been able to interfere at all with the Japanese bomber formations that converged over the Manila area.[8]

BOMBING OF THE NAVY YARD

It had been a busy morning at 16th Naval District Headquarters in the Navy Yard. At 0745 that morning the river gunboat *Mindanao* arrived from Hong Kong, reporting that she had ten prisoners on board. They were the crew of the Japanese fishing vessel *No. 3 South Advance Maru* that the gunboat had intercepted in the South China Sea while en route to Manila; the prisoners were turned over to the 16th Naval District.[9] The gunboat was ordered to proceed to Sangley Point to refuel and take on water; she was then to report to the

A mid-1930s view of the Cavite Navy Yard, showing the crowded conditions of the base. The 600-foot radio towers of the 16th Naval District are in the distance on Sangley Point. The Canacao Naval Hospital is in the wooded area between the radio towers and the beach of Sangley Point.

Source: U.S. Navy

commander of the Inshore Patrol for duty. The 16th Naval District staff was planning to equip all three river gunboats with minesweeping gear and depth charges. The refitting of the three ships was to be performed by the Yard's maintenance and repair staff.

At 1115 the destroyer USS *John D. Ford* moored at the Sangley Point fuel dock, refilling her oil bunkers. The 16th Naval District staff, as a normal security precaution, was destroying war plans documents. Per Admiral Hart's instructions of the day before, hundreds of fuel drums in the Sangley Point area were being dispersed. The detail moving the fuel was under Lieutenant (junior grade) Malcolm Champlin, Admiral Rockwell's flag lieutenant. Champlin and his detail had worked most of the night, and the job was nearly done. At the waterfront of the Yard there was much activity, with ships and submarines that were under repair hastening their preparations to get under way. Not all would make it.

Entering Manila Bay that morning were two old, small British destroyers that had just made a high-speed dash from Hong Kong, HMS *Thanet* and *Scout*. The two British ships were to be provisioned and fueled at Manila before they departed for Singapore.

There were a number of vessels at the Cavite Navy Yard piers that morning. Moored along the west side of Machina Wharf was a nest of vessels. Closest to the pier was the submarine *Seadragon*. Next to her was another *Sargo*-class sub, *Sealion*. On *Sealion*'s outboard side was the *Owl*-class minesweeper *Bittern*, followed by another minesweeper, *Quail*, and, finally, the submarine rescue vessel *Pigeon*, herself a converted *Owl*-class vessel. *Quail*, *Bittern*, and *Pigeon* were all in the Yard to complete various repairs and refit work. *Quail*'s crew had worked furiously over the past three days to get their ship ready to go back to sea. On the 8th and 9th personnel of the Yard had worked closely with *Quail*'s crew to finish reassembling the engines and completing other repairs. Yard personnel, most of them skilled Filipino civilians, had worked around the clock on behalf of several of the ships, pushing as hard as they could to provide needed parts and other services. On the morning of the 10th *Quail* was nearly ready; her engines were being tested, but there was little ammunition on board and the ship needed to refuel.

Pigeon had just entered the Yard for some quick repair work, particularly on her steering gear, storm damaged a few days earlier when she was escorting *Oahu* and *Luzon* from Shanghai. Her crew had also toiled hard to complete work as quickly as possible, but on the morning the Japanese bombers arrived the little ship's steering gear was still being reassembled. Due to the extensive amount of topside equipment required for the submarine rescue mission, *Pigeon* was armed only with machine guns. *Bittern* was even less ready than the two ships outboard of her. On the morning of the 10th her engines were still partly disassembled and much other work was needed to get the sweeper ready for sea. Although her crew was working as fast as possible to get their ship out of the Yard, it was estimated that several more days' effort would be needed before *Bittern* could get under way.

Otus, which had just arrived at Cavite that morning from Mariveles in order to complete conversion from a merchant vessel to a destroyer tender, was moored at the end of Machina Wharf. At 5,700 tons, she was by far the largest ship at the Yard that morning.

Anchored a few hundred yards south of *Otus*, where the water started to become very shallow, was the river gunboat *Luzon*. Also a few hundred yards from the base was the patrol yacht *Isabel* that was being armed with depth charges, now that her "reconnaissance" mission off the coast of Indochina was over. During the morning a floating crane, which brought with it the depth charge racks, was towed out to the yacht. After positioning the barge alongside *Isabel* the little yard tug *Santa Rita* backed off and anchored about thirty yards astern.

Two old "flush deckers," *Peary* and *Pillsbury*, were moored on either side of Central Wharf that morning. The two destroyers had suffered damage in a collision in October and were completing repairs. Of the two, *Pillsbury* was closer to being ready to return to action, but neither destroyer was operational that morning. *Pillsbury* had been fueled and had steam up in her number one boiler room to provide power for ship operations. However, the ship's communications system was not fully operational and her main engines, although refitted, had not been tested. The ship's machine guns and 3-inch anti-aircraft gun were ready, but her torpedoes and 4-inch main battery were not. Many of her crew were in the Yard, assembling equipment and supplies so the ship could get under way within the next few days.

Peary was in a less ready state. She was receiving power from the Yard and her engines were being reassembled. The ship's bow was still under repair; she was incapable of independent movement. For self-defense the old destroyer only had .50- and .30-caliber machine guns.[10] Neither her 4-inch main battery nor the 3-inch .23-caliber anti-aircraft gun on the stern were operational that morning.

Two submarines, *Seadragon* and *Sealion*, were moored side-by-side along Machina Wharf, with minesweepers and the rescue vessel outboard of them. Both submarines were undergoing overhaul and not ready to put to sea. Realizing the vulnerability of being immobile in the Yard, every ship captain of the vessels moored at Cavite was working hard to complete repairs or overhaul and get his ship or submarine back out to sea. *Sealion* was not capable of moving that morning; her engines were still partly disassembled. *Seadragon* was planning on leaving Cavite in three or four more days, and was being repainted that morning; paint cans were stacked on her deck.

The 16th Naval District staff had been monitoring the various Navy reports generated that morning, and, to the extent they could, Army reports of enemy air activity. The first air raid warning of the day for the Navy Yard had actually sounded at 0120. A second alarm went off about an hour and a half later. In the second case it was suspected Japanese planes flying over Manila Bay.

At 1230 Admiral Rockwell's staff received an ominous report of approximately fifty enemy bombers near San Fernando, flying southward toward Manila. That prompted the air raid sirens to be sounded again at 1235. Simultaneously, a (incorrect) report was received from the Olongapo Naval Station that it was under air attack. Minutes earlier the destroyer *Ford* completed fueling at Sangley Point and quickly headed out into Manila Bay to gain maneuvering room.

At 1245 a formation of Japanese bombers was spotted over the Bay, heading east toward Manila. Within minutes the Army's Nichols Field was under attack. Parachutes were observed over the Manila area at the same time (these were U.S. Army fighter pilots bailing out of their stricken P-40s). Fifteen minutes later a formation estimated at thirty bombers was seen heading for the Navy Yard from the direction of the city.

The 1st Kokutai's Nell bombers crossed Manila Bay from the north as they approached their target. Most of the twenty-six Nells (one bomber had aborted en route) were armed with twelve 60-kilogram (132-pound) general-purpose bombs, although a few 250-kilogram (550-pound) weapons may have been on board some of the aircraft. It was approximately 1300 as they approached Sangley Point.

Marine 2nd lieutenant William F. Hogaboom was the officer in charge of Battery A, 1st Separate Marine Battalion. Hogaboom's battery had four fixed, Navy-type 3-inch, .50-caliber anti-aircraft guns on Sangley Point. Alerted when the air raid alarm was sounded at the Navy Yard just after 1240, Hogaboom's men were at their guns when aircraft were seen approaching from the direction of Manila where Nichols Field was already under attack and dogfights were taking place over the city. Thinking that the second of two approaching aircraft was Japanese, Battery A opened fire and shot the aircraft down into the Bay between the Navy Yard and Sangley Point. Unfortunately, the 1st Separate Battalion's first kill was an Army P-40 piloted by Lieutenant Jim Philips. Philips was attempting to engage Zeros that were attacking Navy float planes that were trying to take off from the Sangley Point area when the Marine fire struck his aircraft. He managed to ditch the fighter in the water between Cavite and Sangley Point. Sailors from the Navy Yard went out in a banca to rescue him.

Nearby, four of PatWing 10's PBYs, each heavily laden with a torpedo and two 500-pound bombs, were racing to get airborne and, hopefully, to safety as the sky filled with Japanese aircraft. One flying boat, piloted by Ensign McConnell, was riddled by fire from *Zeros* and barely managed to reach Laguna de Bay where it made a forced landing. A second PBY had just taken off under command of Lieutenant Harmon T. Utter when it was jumped by several Japanese fighters. Fighting hard with its bow and waist guns, the flying boat's gunners were sure they had downed one of the Zeros in a daring head-on duel. Chief Boatswain Earl D. Payne, the PBY's bow gunner, was credited with the kill, the first enemy aircraft shot down in air-to-air combat by the U.S. Navy in World War II. Damaged, the PBY made a hard landing on Manila Bay, at which point the remaining enemy fighters raced off for other targets. Four of PatWing 10's smaller float planes (three J2F "Ducks" and one OS2U "Kingfisher") also made desperate escapes from Sangley Point, with enemy fighters chasing them part of the way. By now the Japanese bombers were over the Navy Yard.[11]

According to the 16th Naval District report and the observations of several survivors, on its first pass over the Yard the 1st Kokuai did not drop bombs. At 1302 the formation of bombers was directly over Sangley Point. As the Japanese planes approached, the Marine Corps anti-aircraft batteries in and around the Navy Yard opened fire.

At Sangley Point Battery A's height finder section estimated that the enemy bombers were flying at over 24,000 feet. Nevertheless, Battery A tried its best to thwart the enemy's attack. The shell bursts were, however, below the enemy formation, which swung around for another pass without dropping its bombs.[12]

This formation, clearly the 1st Kokutai, circled back over the Bay lining up for a second pass over the Yard. This time Lieutenant Commander Ozaki meant business. As the Japanese bombers approached from the east, Battery E inside the Yard opened fire with its 3-inch .23-caliber weapons mounted atop the Ammunition Depot. With a maximum vertical range of about 18,000 feet, the old weapons had no chance of reaching the high-flying Japanese. The Nells, who actually attacked by nine-plane squadrons, dropped their first bombs just before 1314. Many bombs from the first attack struck the water in Canacao Bay between Sangley Point and Cavite, not surprising considering that the Cavite Peninsula presented a rather narrow target. Nevertheless, enough bombs from the first pass hit the Navy Yard to start the process of destruction. Although the Nells did not carry large weapons, the 60-kilogram bombs that struck the base did massive damage.

Among the first buildings to be hit was the power plant, which was knocked out. Inside the burning plant Lieutenant J. A. Steward, USN, a Civil Engineering

Corps officer, remained at his post, despite being wounded. After realizing he could not contain the blaze, Steward shut down some key machinery in order to minimize the chance of an explosion, and then helped evacuate wounded men from the plant. He was recommended for the Navy Cross for his actions. The loss of power was a major blow, since it cut off pressure to the fire mains.

Like most Navy bases then and now, Cavite was a densely packed establishment with wooden and light metal buildings located very close to each other. Early in the raid fires broke out and started to spread. The Nells also rained bombs down on the mostly immobile ships moored along the piers. Exploding bombs also killed or wounded firefighters. As more bombs fell the fires grew in intensity and started to spread throughout the Yard. One of the first buildings hit was the base dispensary; six Navy corpsmen were killed and a doctor wounded. Admiral Rockwell's headquarters building, the Commandancia, was not hit directly by bombs but was destroyed by fire later in the raid.

The patrol yacht *Isabel* was straddled by bombs that burst all around her. As the little ship started to cut the lines to the floating barge so she could get under way, the tug *Santa Rita* took a direct hit and immediately sank. As the yacht pulled away from the Yard her crew watched the devastation of the base.

When the first wave of bombers appeared over the Yard *Quail*'s skipper, Lieutenant Commander John Morrill, ordered his two 3-inch guns mounted forward of the bridge to open fire. The noise was incredible. Glancing over to the bridge of *Pigeon*, tied up next to *Quail*, Morrill could see her commanding officer, Lieutenant Commander Dick Hawes. Through a series of arm signals (the noise of gunfire and exploding bombs was far too great for a shout to be heard), the two skippers came to an understanding that they would go out as one, while their ships were still lashed together. *Pigeon* needed the help since her steering was still not fully operable. *Quail*'s engines had been slowly turning over that morning, but were not yet certified for operations by the Yard foreman. None of that mattered—*Quail* and *Pigeon* were going out, tied together.

As soon as the lines to *Bittern*, on *Quail*'s inboard side, were cut Morrill rang up "full speed astern." Firing as they went, the two ships pulled away from Machina Wharf as bombs exploded in the water and on the pier. Maneuvering around the bulk of *Otus* at the end of the wharf was a trick, but Morrill managed it. A collision with the China river gunboat *Luzon*, herself maneuvering to get out of the area, was barely averted by using both *Quail* and *Pigeon*'s engines. Still lashed together, the two ships headed out into Canacao Bay with *Quail* firing at any enemy plane that appeared to be in range.

Once in the Bay the lines that held the two ships together were cut. By that point *Pigeon* had managed to rig temporary rudder control with lines and tackles.

Although now relatively safe, both ships' commanders elected to head back into the Navy Yard to help rescue other ships. As they prepared to do so the mine-sweeper *Whippoorwill* returned from a mission in the outer Bay and announced its intention to go to the aide of other ships and to try to fight fires in the Yard. *Quail* and *Pigeon* followed her back into the hail of bombs and fire. Meanwhile, the destroyers and submarines were taking a beating.[13]

Lying immobile alongside Central Wharf the destroyer *Peary* was near-missed by several bombs early in the raid. Not until the third wave of bombers released their weapons was the destroyer finally hit. One bomb burst on the foremast, above the unarmored bridge. The entire forward part of the ship was showered with fragments and the mast crashed down. The bomb also had a pronounced incendiary effect. Burning fragments set *Peary*'s bridge afire. Structures and supplies on the pier and *Pillsbury* on the other side of Central Wharf were also set on fire by hot fragments from the hit on *Peary*. The ship's commanding officer, Lieutenant Commander H. H. Keith, who was on the bridge, was seriously wounded in both legs and the XO, Lieutenant A. E. Gates, was hit and died later. All the men on the gun director platform above the bridge were killed. The ship's injured quartermaster managed to implement the wounded skipper's command to signal "any ship" to tow them away from the pier. About that time power was lost as bombs cut the connections from the ship to the Central Wharf (it is likely that the destruction of the base power plant also played a role).

As men from nearby sister ship *Pillsbury* on the other side of the pier began to play hoses on the stricken *Peary*, help appeared in the form of the mine-sweeper *Whippoorwill*, commanded by Lieutenant Commander C. A. Ferriter. *Whippoorwill* had been in Manila Bay when the bombing started. Her commander elected to proceed into the Yard to provide assistance, knowing that there were several vessels that were immobile. This was certainly a brave move, given the severity of the ongoing air attack. As "*Whip*" approached with her bow to *Peary*'s stern in order to fasten a line to pull the burning destroyer to safety, torpedoes in sheds on the end of Central Wharf began to burn and then explode. Fragments flew in all directions as men of the three ships tried desperately to free *Peary*. Bombs continued to fall as the effort was made to attach a line; during the second attempt the line was cut by bomb fragments.

The situation was becoming desperate, with torpedoes along the wharf exploding, as a final attempt was made to free the destroyer. Lieutenant Commander Ferriter placed his ship's bow directly against *Peary*'s stern and men on board the destroyer, working with some of the minesweeper's crew on the forecastle, attached a line and slipped *Peary*'s moorings with the dock. This time it worked, and the little minesweeper pulled the burning destroyer away from the increasingly dangerous Central Wharf. *Peary* would survive, for now, but she had been grievously hurt, with 23 dead or missing and 19 wounded out of a ship's company of roughly 130 officers and men. Unfortunately, more than half of the ship's casualties were wounded men (and uninjured sailors sent along to assist the wounded) who left the ship to obtain medical care just as the ship was pulled free of the wharf. The ongoing bombing or fires in the Navy Yard killed these men as they sought medical help.

Although *Pillsbury* did not suffer a direct hit, the nearby burst on *Peary*'s mast showered the ship with fragments. Dead and wounded lay all over *Pillsbury*'s upper decks. Although the ship's just-overhauled engines were untested the senior officer on board, the executive officer Lieutenant R. W. Germany, ordered the destroyer to get under way because staying alongside Central Wharf was clearly too dangerous. Backing away from the pier, *Pillsbury* slowly made her way from the Yard into more open water in the Bay. She had suffered two dead, sixteen wounded, and twelve men missing. As was the case with *Peary*, most of the missing men were almost certainly killed in the Yard, having been ashore during the bombing.

The two submarines, *Sealion* and *Seadragon*, also took a pounding, one that the former never recovered from. When the first stick of bombs fell into the Yard one struck Machina Wharf, destroying a mess hall. Both submarines shot back with their .50-caliber machine guns, but the enemy aircraft were far too high.

As the bombers swung around for a second pass the two submarine commanding officers, Lieutenant Commander Richard Voge and Lieutenant Commander William Ferrall, ordered their men below. It did little good. Two bombs scored direct hits on *Sealion*, one on the conning tower and the other on the aft engine-room hatch. Four sailors in the engine room were killed. Fragments from this bomb penetrated the conning tower of the nearby *Seadragon* and killed Ensign S. J. Hunter.

More bombs fell, stoking the fires. On the opposite side of Machina Wharf a lighter full of nearly fifty torpedoes intended for the two submarines was hit and capsized, spilling the weapons into the harbor. Fires spread along Machina Wharf as *Sealion*'s crew abandoned ship; their submarine was sinking by the stern. On board *Seadragon* the topside paint cans were now on fire. More ominously, tied to the submarine was the immobile minesweeper *Bittern* that had been struck by bomb fragments and was now ablaze. Some of the sweeper's crew escaped to the submarine and reported that their ship's magazines might blow up. At that point Lieutenant Commander Ferrall ordered his crew ashore. The crews of both subs moved through the blazing Yard and assembled on the base's baseball diamond.

Seadragon's crew had not been ashore long when Ferrall decided to try to get back on board his ship. Leading his men through the fires, they reached Machina Wharf just as the *Pigeon* was returning, looking to help any ship that could be taken out. Dick Hawes had his deck detail pass a line to *Seadragon*. Moored just behind the sub were two lighters, one filled with gasoline. Two men from *Pigeon* got in a small boat and pulled the lighters to a safer distance. Once the line to *Seadragon* was secured, the submarine rescue vessel lived up to her intended role and pulled the damaged sub out to safety.

It was an amazing escape. As the sub was being towed into the channel just south of the Yard's three piers a big fuel tank on the wharf exploded, sending a wall of flame in a horizontal direction that came so close to the ship and sub that both vessels' hulls were scorched. *Pigeon* helped the sub reach open waters; from there *Seadragon* made for the sub tender *Canopus*, lying camouflaged alongside the Manila City waterfront. For *Sealion*, however, there was no escape. Half sunk by the stern, she was the first U.S. submarine lost in action in World War II.[14]

While *Pigeon* was helping the submarine, *Quail* had also returned. Seeing the burning *Bittern*, Lieutenant Commander Morrill decided to try to help her out of the Yard. With torpedoes blowing up on Machina Wharf, *Quail* struggled to get her stricken sister ship to safety. Some of *Bittern*'s crew continued to fight fires, while others aided *Quail*'s deck crew. A line was run between the two sweepers. A motor launch from *Otus* came along and lent a hand. Finally, with much effort, the badly damaged sweeper was pulled clear and taken out into the Bay. She survived, but never was an active ship again. Her damage was bad, and the bombing and fires destroyed much of the ship's machinery that was still in the shops of the Yard. After getting *Bittern* to temporary safety Morrill returned once more and towed out a barge of torpedoes that was moored on the east side of Machina Wharf, close to where the barge loaded with torpedoes intended for the two submarines had rolled over into the Bay.[15]

Otus was very lucky. She had moored at the end of Machina Wharf at 1000 that morning, having spent the night at Mariveles Harbor. The crew was told that they would spend the day loading equipment and machinery. When ready, the ship would depart for another port to the south in order to complete conversion into a tender. The plan was that the ship would be under way by 12 December. By 1100 lighters and barges were alongside, and equipment was being loaded into the ship. The men working topside transferring gear from the lighters heard the air raid sirens wail and saw the bombers approaching the Yard. As the crew raced to make preparations to get under way, bombs from the 1st Kokutai's first salvo fell into the water about one hundred yards off the starboard beam.

The next stick of bombs hit the water about one hundred feet to starboard, and the shock opened up some seams in the hull, letting water in. Both generators were knocked out. The next bombs landed in the water seventy-five feet to port, peppering the ship with fragments. This was the same salvo that hit *Sealion* and *Seadragon*.

As soon as one of the generators was placed back in operation *Otus* started to get under way. She nearly fouled *Quail* and *Pigeon* as those two ships went out together. The ship seemed like she would get clear when a near-miss from a bomb ruptured the hull, starting flooding. Immediate damage control work prevented a serious situation. Slowly gathering speed, *Otus* headed out into the Bay where she could get some maneuvering room.[16] A number of the ship's officers and men were ashore during the air raid, mostly gathering supplies and equipment. Some of them never made it back on board, including her gunnery/torpedo officer—Lieutenant (junior grade) Trose Emmett Donaldson—who nevertheless won the Navy Cross for his actions during the bombing of the Navy Yard. Donaldson would later die while in command of a former Army tug the day Bataan fell in April. *Otus* had no men killed, but two officers (including the CO, Commander Joel Newsom) and six men were wounded.[17]

Many of the Marine anti-aircraft gun crews had narrow escapes. Battery E manned the old 3-inch guns atop the Ammunition Depot. Through no fault of their own, the Marines' firing was futile; the Japanese bombers were well above their maximum altitude. Battery F, manning .50-caliber machine guns, was spread throughout the Yard, including firing positions on the main piers. One of these young Marines, Private First Class Thomas Wetherington, was killed in the bombing. He was the first Marine to die in the defense of the Philippines.

As the fires intensified, some of the Marines of Battery F found themselves trapped on Guadalupe Pier; they could not move northward off the pier into the main part of the Yard due to the intensity of the flames. Captain Ted Pulos, USMC, the Battery F commander, was there with his men. Seeing no other way out, Pulos had his men quickly build rafts from materials on the pier in order to escape. The Marines brought their ammunition and machine guns with them.[18]

The Japanese Navy bombers apparently made four runs over the Yard. Probably due to the narrow nature of the target, the bombing was actually done in nine-plane groups. A formation of twenty-seven aircraft would have been too broad—too many bombs would have fallen into the water north and south of the Yard. As mentioned earlier, on their first run no bombs were dropped. It is virtually certain that the initial attacking unit was the twenty-six G3M Nells of the 1st Kokutai. At some point, possibly the last bombing run, the Takao Kokutai's twenty-seven G4M Bettys appeared. The Takao Kokutai was the unit that had been forced to abandon its primary target, Del Carmen Field. The Takao bombers first attacked shipping in Manila Bay, but managed to disable only one merchant vessel, the American freighter SS *Sagoland*, with part of their bomb load. They then turned toward the Navy Yard and disposed of their remaining bombs. According to Japanese records, losses among the eighty Nells and Bettys that struck the Manila Bay area that day were light. One Betty force-landed at the just-captured airfield at Vigan, another ditched in the sea near Formosa. Two Nells of the 1st Kokutai also ditched near their home base.[19]

At least one of the Japanese bomber formations departed by flying out via the North Channel between the island fortress of Corregidor and the southern tip of Bataan. When the Japanese aircraft came within range Corregidor's anti-aircraft guns engaged them. The 60th Coast Artillery fired several hundred 3-inch rounds and claimed to have shot down one enemy aircraft. In nearby Mariveles Harbor the river gunboat *Oahu* lay at anchor. She opened fire on the same Japanese formation as it headed northwestward. After shooting eleven 3-inch rounds she ceased fire—the enemy bombers were flying too high.[20]

If all the Japanese aircraft carried the standard load of twelve 60-kilogram bombs, and assuming that the Takeo Kokutai aircraft had dropped half of their ordnance on shipping in the Bay, a total of roughly 450 bombs fell into the area of the Navy Yard, a fair number of which landed in the water. It was more than enough. The raid was over by approximately 1500. By then the Cavite Navy Yard was ablaze from end to end.

FIGHTING THE FIRES

Admiral Rockwell and his staff were personally involved in rescue operations and the effort to save as much equipment as possible. Within the first thirty minutes of the raid Rockwell could see that the fires were raging out of control. His main concern was the Naval Ammunition Depot. There was some seven hundred tons of explosives (an amount comparable to what had exploded in the forward magazine of the battleship *Arizona* at Pearl Harbor two days earlier) in the old Spanish stone and masonry casemate located along the Yard's north shore. Fires raged all around the Ammunition Depot. Amazingly, no bomb had directly hit the structure itself, or if one did it did not penetrate. The solid construction of the old Spanish casemate helped, as did the small size of the bombs that the Japanese had used. Nevertheless, the threat of a massive explosion was real enough. Rockwell decided to let the crews fight the fires for a while in an attempt to save what they could. By this time about a third of the City of Cavite was also on fire. While the fire fighting was under way wounded were being

The wrecked Cavite Navy Yard after the raid

Source: National Archives and Records Administration

evacuated. It was at this point that the PT boats of MTB Squadron 3 came in from the Bay to help.

When the air raid started the PTs had gotten under way and moved out into the Bay where they could maneuver at high speed. While in the Bay they were attacked by some of the bombers from the Takao Kokutai that were going after merchant shipping near the Manila waterfront. The highly maneuverable PT boats avoided every attack by the Japanese, and in the process claimed to have shot down three of the enemy.[21] When the air raid ended, the PTs returned to the Yard and helped evacuate wounded directly across Canacao Bay to the Naval Hospital. The PT boat base, including most of the squadron's spare parts, was destroyed in the bombing and fires.

Within the Navy Yard the situation was dire. With the power to the water mains gone, there were only the base's two fire trucks. The City of Cavite, itself ablaze, could spare nothing to help. Later two additional fire trucks capable of pumping water directly from the Bay arrived from Manila. Once the Japanese bombers had departed many of the Marine gun crews from outlying batteries were brought into the Yard to help fight the fires.

Lieutenant (junior grade) Champlin, Admiral Rockwell's flag lieutenant, had been at his quarters outside the Yard following the all-night job of dispersing fuel drums. When the raid began he quickly raced back to the base. As he entered the gate he passed trucks and cars leaving with wounded men, heading toward the Naval Hospital. When he found his admiral, Rockwell was hatless, his shirt covered with blood from carrying wounded men.

Champlin was with Admiral Rockwell, conferring with most of the senior officers in the Yard, when Lieutenant R. T. Whitney, the assistant captain of the Yard, limped up stating that a warehouse that contained hundreds of gas masks was threatened by the fires. Champlin led a group of sailors in an attempt to get the masks out, along with other valuable gear. When the dangerous job was done Champlin thanked his men. At that point he discovered that most of them had been released from the brig when the bombing started. Several asked the lieutenant if he would testify on their behalf at their court-martials, which he said he would, of course, do.

Many wounded were loaded into small craft for transport across Canacao Bay to the Navy Hospital. One fifty-foot motor launch was packed with wounded and sent across Manila Bay to the Army's Sternberg Hospital in the city. An Army nurse remembered a Navy officer who, despite his mortal wounds, remained upbeat to the end, insisting that the medical staff treat others before him. At Canacao it was the first mass casualty event the vast majority of the staff had ever experienced. Many of the wounded were terribly burned. The nurses and corpsmen performed triage on the arriving patients, noting that some could not be saved. The hospital staff worked through the rest of the day, that night, and into the next tending to the wounded.

Back at the Yard the effort to control the fires went on all afternoon and into the early evening. The manpower the Marine gun crews provided was of great assistance. Lieutenant Colonel Adam's men set up a field kitchen inside the Yard to feed the personnel who were fighting the fires. Priority was give to preventing the flames from reaching the Ammunition Depot and trying to save unburned areas. Through heroic efforts of all hands the fires were being brought under control by roughly 1800. At that time a careful inspection was made of the Yard and it was discovered that the fires were out. Details were posted at key locations to ensure that sparks did not reignite the blaze. Exhausted sailors, Marines, and civilian firefighters took their first break in hours. A huge amount of damage had been done to the base, but it at least looked like the worst was over.

Shortly after 1800 a group of officers were taking a break, sitting on some barrels, drinking coffee and eating sandwiches when a Marine came running up—a very large fire had restarted in the lumberyard. Before a fire truck could be brought up the lumberyard was a roaring inferno, and the blaze was spreading to nearby buildings. All the men who were not completely exhausted were assembled and the effort began anew to control the fires, but it was hopeless.

By 2100 it appeared that the fire would reach the Ammunition Depot. At that point Admiral Rockwell, who had been leading the effort all afternoon, ordered the Yard abandoned. All sailors and Marines moved out of the base and assembled in the yard of the Dalahiean School at the town of San Roque. A Marine armed guard was posted at the entrance to the base with instructions that no one, military or civilian, was to be allowed in until further notice. Admiral Rockwell directed Lieutenant Champlin to proceed by car to Manila and personally report to Admiral Hart that the Cavite Navy Yard was totally destroyed, but that the 16th Naval District would continue to support the ships of the Asiatic Fleet as best it could from its remaining facilities.[22]

Admiral Hart had watched the attack from atop the Marsman Building in Manila. It did not take long for him to reach several important conclusions. First, the Navy Yard was destroyed. Although confirmation from Admiral Rockwell was several hours away, there was no doubt in the minds of Hart and his staff that it was a devastatingly effective attack. Second, the Army had lost control of the air over Luzon. Air defense of the Philippines was the Army's responsibility and it had failed completely, despite the bravery of the individual fighter pilots who tried to intercept the Japanese. The second point led directly to the third. The Navy had to abandon Manila Bay; it was clearly untenable as a major base. Hart directed that a number of the large ships, including *Holland*, *Otus*, the gunboat *Isabel*, and the destroyers *Ford* and *Pope* sail that evening and proceed southward toward the Dutch East Indies, per the prewar plans. Another, slower, group of ships was also formed with the seagoing gunboats *Tulsa* and *Ashville* along with the minesweepers *Whippoorwill* and *Lark*. Those ships would depart shortly after the first group.

Yet more bad news arrived that day. Hart received word that Japanese aircraft had sunk the two British capital ships, the battleship *Prince of Wales* and the battle cruiser *Repulse*, off the coast of Malaya that afternoon. British vice admiral Thomas Phillips, who Hart had met just five days earlier, was dead along with over eight hundred British sailors from the two big ships. It was terrible news for the Allied cause in Asia, coming but two days after the Pearl Harbor debacle. Guam also fell that day.

A FINAL ASSESSMENT

The Japanese bombing of the Cavite Navy Yard was the most devastating attack on a U.S. naval installation since the British burned the Washington Navy Yard in 1814. The Pearl Harbor raid two days before had focused on the ships of the Pacific Fleet—little damage had been inflicted on the Navy's shore facilities in Hawaii. That was not the case with Cavite.

The destruction of the base was due to four reasons. First, the primary blame must lie with the inability of the Army to defend the air space over Luzon. With its fighter force on Luzon reduced by nearly 40 percent on the first day of war, the remaining Army fighters, manned mostly by inexperienced pilots employing inappropriate tactics, were incapable of seriously interfering with the massive Japanese air raid of 10 December. It was the Army's responsibility to defeat aerial attacks, and the Far Eastern Air Force manifestly failed in its task. Second, the Marine anti-aircraft weapons were inadequate for the job. The Japanese bombed from above 24,000 feet, at least at the start of the raid.[23] The 1st Separate Battalion's 3-inch shells used the old model powder-train fuze, which had a maximum ceiling of roughly 25,000 feet.[24] That figure, however, applied to aircraft flying within a relatively short horizontal distance of the firing unit. The farther this distance to the aircraft, the lower the effective altitude that the shells could reach. Second Lieutenant Willard Holdredge's Battery B at Binacayan south of the base was too far away from the flight path of the Japanese bombers, which approached the Yard from due east. Lieutenant Hogaboom's Battery A at Sangley Point north of the Yard was better positioned, but even that battery was not well sited to engage Japanese bombers approaching at over 24,000 feet from the east. Battery E, located atop the Ammunition Depot inside the Yard, was armed with the older 3-inch .23-caliber gun that only had an 18,000-foot reach. So, the anti-aircraft guns had no chance of seriously disrupting the Japanese attack. Third, Cavite was a crowded base, very vulnerable to blast damage and, especially, fire. Once the fires started to rage, the base was in serious trouble. Finally, the Imperial Navy's air units were at peak efficiency at this point of the war, with highly trained aircrew. Just as the Zeros decimated the Army P-40s that tried to intercept their formations, the Imperial Navy bombers put in an excellent performance against Cavite.

Two American journalists, Carl Mydans of *Life* magazine and Mel Jacoby of *Time*, watched the attack from the Manila waterfront. They were amazed at the accuracy of the Japanese bombing. Mydans had covered the Russo-Finnish War the year before. He remarked to his colleague that he had never seen such an accurate air attack.[25]

What was the final cost of the devastating air raid on the Cavite Navy Yard? The issue of personnel losses is the hardest part of the Cavite story. Compared to the detailed, name-by-name accounting of casualties in the Pearl Harbor attack the records concerning the Cavite attack are woefully inadequate. Over the years there have been various statements on the number of casualties, American and Filipino. Numbers such as "over 500 dead" and "500 dead and wounded" have been reported. The unfortunate reality is that it is impossible to determine precisely how many Americans and Filipinos lost their lives or were wounded in the Yard, although data on ships' casualties are more detailed.

Rockwell's report and some other sources mention that when Navy personnel reentered the Yard on 13 December 122 badly decomposed bodies were buried in a common grave; a trench dug by a bulldozer in the yard of the Commandancia, Rockwell's destroyed headquarters building. A Marine source mentions 250 dead being buried, but makes no distinction between American military personnel and Filipino civilians.[26] Another source says that 167 bodies were disposed of inside the Yard after the fires burned themselves out, with 285 wounded treated at Canacao Naval Hospital within the first twelve hours of the raid.[27] Most of the bodies were so badly burned that identification was impossible.

It should be noted that Admiral Rockwell and Commander R. G. Deewall, the captain of the Yard, showed great foresight when on the first day of the war they minimized the number of civilians working on the base. Realizing that some of the Filipino workers were absolutely vital to the machine shops and other activities (they were desperately needed, for example, to finish the work on submarine and other ships' repairs and refits) and could not be spared, they nevertheless decided to reduce the workforce on the base to a minimum. Additionally, on 8 and 9 December they worked with the mayor of Cavite to start evacuating the civilian population. This certainly helped reduce casualties, considering that on a normal day there could be over eight thousand civilian workers in the Yard. Had the full workforce been on the base when the Japanese bombers arrived the number of dead could have been horrendous. Additionally, the personnel shelters that both Hart and Rockwell had insisted on preparing before the start of the war saved many lives. Admiral Rockwell is correct when he stated, "in this connection it may be pointed out that the surprisingly low number of casualties was due to the fact that the great majority took shelter in accordance with previous instructions and drills."[28]

The U.S. Navy's official list of casualties in World War II offers important insights on how many Navy personnel were probably killed during the bombing of the Cavite Navy Yard. The Navy's casualty data shows that for December 1941 in the "Asiatic" area of operations (which at that time was only the Philippines and the Dutch East Indies) the service suffered 10 officers and 97 enlisted dead. If correct, those figures include the data on all the Navy organizations that suffered casualties in the month of December. For example, PatWing 10 suffered roughly 30 killed ashore or in its aircraft during December. When the seaplane tender *Preston* was attacked at Davao on the first day of the war 1 man died. The destroyer *Peary* and the minesweeper *Heron* each had 2 men killed by air attack as they withdrew from the Philippines at the end of the month. When the submarine tender *Canopus* was bombed in Mariveles Harbor on 29 December 6 men died. When all those losses are subtracted from the December total of 107 officers and men killed, and assuming the official Navy data is correct, it means that about 65–70 Navy personnel died during the bombing of the Cavite Navy Yard. Of those, 5 were on board the submarines *Sealion* and *Seadragon* and approximately 37 were from the destroyers *Peary* and *Pillsbury*. The latter figure includes the 26 men *Peary* and *Pillsbury* listed as missing, and probably killed ashore; the remains of these men were quite likely interred during the mass burials that took place in the days following the raid. Apparently only 1 Marine died during the bombing. It therefore appears that roughly 25–30 Navy officers and men of the 16th Naval District shore establishment were killed, a remarkably low number and a tribute to the precautions of placing bomb shelters around the base before the start of the war. Of the remainder buried by the salvage parties on 13 December, whether some of the 122 men mentioned by Rockwell or the 250 in some Marine accounts, most were almost certainly Filipino naval reservists and civilians who were employees of the Navy.[29]

Finally, it must be noted that the number of Filipino civilians killed in the City of Cavite exceeded those lost in the Yard. As an earlier photo showed (see page 8), the city shared the claw-like promontory with the Navy Yard. From the vantage point of a Japanese bombardier over four miles up it would have been virtually impossible to differentiate the Navy Yard from the civilian areas, assuming that the enemy was even inclined to try to spare the city. Enough bombs fell into the city to start major fires, and when combined with the blast damage from exploding bombs it is certain that numerous civilians perished. Just how many died will always remain unknown, but it was probably several hundred. Some accounts mention piles of bodies heaped in parts of the city. One report stated that some one hundred civilians were killed when a bomb burst in the crowded plaza of the City of Cavite. According to another story, a Navy chief lost his entire family in the city; his Filipino wife and eight children all killed by Japanese bombs. As was the case with the Navy Yard itself, the death toll would have been far higher had not the evacuations of civilians been started in the two days before 10 December.[30]

There is no question regarding the material losses. The Yard was burned out and almost totally destroyed. Amazingly, the Ammunition Depot did not explode, although the fear of such a blast is what prompted Admiral Rockwell to order the evacuation of personnel around 2100 that evening. Although the Navy was able to salvage some equipment after the fires burned out, almost all the shops and major warehouses were destroyed. Importantly, there was a major loss of torpedoes, although there is some controversy. Several sources have stated that the Asiatic Fleet submarines were effectively crippled due to the loss of 230 torpedoes that day. Admiral Hart, in a postwar letter to the Army team writing the service's official history of the 1941–42 Philippine Campaign, stated that most of the torpedoes that were lost were destroyer weapons, and that the majority of the submarine torpedoes (which were quickly shown to be highly unreliable) had been shipped to Corregidor before the start of the war. This is supported by a 9 December entry in the 16th Naval District war diary that shows roughly two hundred torpedoes at Corregidor, aboard *Canopus*, or stored at other locations outside the Navy Yard.[31]

Of the ships at the Yard the Asiatic Fleet was perhaps luckier than one would expect, given the overall accuracy of the attack. The submarine *Sealion* was lost. Sunk by the stern, it would have taken many weeks to refloat and repair her, time that was not available. When the ruins of the Navy Yard were finally abandoned during the withdrawal to Bataan depth charges were set inside the stricken submarine's hull to damage it so badly that the Japanese could not possible repair her; American troops saw the wreck in 1945 when they returned to Cavite. A few days after the attack, however, the submarine rescue ship *Pigeon*, herself in need of a more powerful armament, used one of her cranes to partly lift the sub's hull in order to remove the 3-inch deck gun. *Pigeon* took the gun to *Canopus*, moored at the Manila Bay waterfront, where the tender's machinists and armaments men properly mounted the weapon on board the vessel.

The minesweeper *Bittern* was another loss. Although not sunk, she had been badly damaged by bomb fragments and fire. Parts of her disassembled engines were destroyed in the Yard's workshops and could not be replaced. Initially towed to near Fort Hughes at the entrance of the Bay, she was later moved to Mariveles Harbor on Bataan where she remained, used as a hulk. Some of her crew went to other minesweepers; *Quail* got several, for example. *Pigeon* gained a second 3-inch gun by removing one from *Bittern*. Unlucky *Bittern* was scuttled the night Bataan fell in April.[32]

Seadragon was temporarily patched together by *Canopus* and *Pigeon* and sailed south a few days later. She continued to participate in the defense of the Philippines and survived the war. Damaged *Otus* cleared Manila Bay the next day, heading southward toward the Indies.

Peary was in bad shape. The bomb that hit her foremast had destroyed the gun director equipment atop the bridge; the mast itself came down. The bomb blast had torn off the overhead of the bridge, and the torpedo directors were damaged. Some steam lines were cut up and the four funnels were all riddled by fragments. The ship's searchlight was also destroyed. A very effective bomb burst, indeed. Only temporary repairs could be made prior to the ship's departure for the Indies and Australia in late December.

Out on Corregidor the sailors at Station C were proud of themselves. That morning they had produced the first significant decrypt of the JN-25b code. It was a huge step, and the first time that any location in the OP-20-G network had had such a success. Some of the men were outside the Monkey Point tunnel when they saw one of the Japanese bomber formations pass by Corregidor en route to Manila. Not long afterward they could see the huge column of smoke rising from the Cavite Navy Yard. The mood was no longer so cheerful.[33]

Waiting for the Main Attack

With the destruction of Cavite the Navy leadership in the Philippines realized that the situation was rapidly deteriorating. On the 10th Admiral Hart ordered most of the larger Navy ships still in Manila Bay to move south to the Indies. With the Japanese so obviously in control of the air over Luzon there was no other option.

Despite the fires raging in Cavite, on the night of 10 December a few ships moved in close to the burning Yard to see if there was an opportunity to salvage something of value. *Quail* had done well that day, helping to get *Pigeon* out of the Yard and then saving the badly damaged *Bittern*. However, the minesweeper was very short of ammunition. Lieutenant Commander Morrill brought *Quail* close to the north shore of the Yard where the Ammunition Depot was located. Several of her crew went ashore, led by Gunner Donald Taylor. Although fires were blazing everywhere, the Ammo Depot itself did not appear to be threatened. Realizing that this might be a unique opportunity, Taylor and his detail broke into the depot and began to move 3-inch shells to their ship waiting at the nearby Mine Wharf. It took several hours of work, but *Quail* was filled with 3-inch rounds, far more than she normally carried. Indeed, so much ammunition was brought on board that some had to be placed on the crew's wire bunks, with the mattresses then put back in place on top of the shells.[1] Until the gunners needed the ammo, some of *Quail*'s men would sleep on top of 3-inch projectiles.

The tug *Napa* also got in on the act and put men ashore to see what could be retrieved. Despite the nearby fires, her detail brought on board several hundred 3-inch shells from the Ammunition Depot. That was more ammunition than she could store for her own 3-inch gun, so the tug donated 120 shells to the gunboat *Mindanao*.[2]

The following day, the 11th, Admiral Rockwell and his chief of staff Captain Ray reentered the Navy Yard where fires were still burning. Much of the City of Cavite was also still on fire. The admiral decided that no further attempt would be made to reenter the area until the fires had burned themselves out. Most of the survivors from the Yard were concentrated on Sangley Point, which had only suffered a few stray bombs during the attack the previous day. A bivouac was established and the men started to disperse supplies around the area. The remaining population of the City of Cavite and the towns of San Roque and Caridad were evacuated farther inland. Admiral Hart insisted that the large diesel fuel tanks on Sangley Point be emptied and the fuel dispersed. Bringing barges over from Manila and pumping the fuel into them accomplished this. The work continued over several days. Some of these barges were sent to Mariveles where their cargos would prove vital during the siege of Bataan and Corregidor.

There were a large number of merchant vessels sheltering in Manila Bay. On 11 December Hart held a meeting with the masters of the roughly forty oceangoing merchant ships, plus the captains of a number of smaller interisland vessels. The larger ships were from many Allied and neutral nations. Hart advised the ships' captains that if they remained in the Manila Bay area it was only a matter of time before they would be sunk, so they should depart for the south as quickly as possible. He told them that the Navy could not provide close escort, but its actions would help cover their movement southward. Simultaneously, he advised the masters of the interisland ships that were in the Bay that they would probably be relatively safe in the central and southern Philippines—at least for now. The captains of all the merchant ships needed little convincing; on the previous day they had seen firsthand the effectiveness of Japanese airpower. That evening the ships started to depart from Manila Bay under cover of darkness. Within a few days most of the larger ships were gone, some 200,000 tons of oceangoing merchant shipping had been saved, although in the coming days a number of small interisland ships would be sunk in the Bay.

PREPARATIONS FOR THE LONG HAUL

The events of the 10th clearly showed that the Japanese could attack any target on Luzon with impunity, with the possible exception of the very heavily defended fortified islands at the entrance of Manila Bay. Therefore, Admiral Hart wanted to start moving the Navy's remaining supplies and equipment to the tunnels on Corregidor and the new Section Base at Mariveles. This was a critical decision, and one very different from the Army's perspective at that time.

On 13 December Navy and Marine personnel reentered the burned-out Cavite Navy Yard to bury the dead and to try to salvage what they could. In addition to *Quail* and *Napa*, other ships had also put small parties ashore in an attempt to salvage what had survived the fires. After the dead were buried the details in the Navy Yard began to sort through the burned-out and wrecked buildings. Stacks of torpedoes, damaged by fires and fragments, sat useless on the piers. Most of the workshops and supply sheds had been destroyed by fire, but occasionally something of value was found. For example, *Pigeon* managed to salvage fourteen usable torpedoes and brought them to the tender *Canopus*, which was still tied up and camouflaged along the Manila waterfront.

Canopus, built in 1919 and commissioned into the Navy in 1922, was one of the Navy's most important ships in the Manila Bay area. At 5,975 tons she was much larger than the gunboats and minesweepers of the Inshore Patrol; she would be the largest Navy ship in Manila Bay during the Bataan campaign. Although slow and rather unimpressive in appearance, she was a much-loved ship that had long served with the Asiatic Fleet. To her crew she was known either as "The Old Lady" or "Mamasan." She was to be truly a jack-of-all-trades during the siege of Bataan.

Some other important equipment had also survived. When the heavy cruiser *Houston* departed for the southern Philippines on 1 December she left behind a spare 1.1-inch automatic anti-aircraft gun mount. The Yard had mounted four of these four-barreled, rapid-fire systems on the cruiser. The spare mount had remained on a dock, and had somehow survived the bombing. In the next few days several of the smaller ships such as *Pigeon* and *Quail* considered "borrowing" it, but realized it was too large for them. The weapon, and 25,000 rounds of ammunition, was moved on a Navy barge to Corregidor and later turned over to the Army.

The sturdy old Spanish casemate that housed the Ammunition Depot contained not only hundreds of tons of ammunition of various types, there were also a large collection of Navy guns, although most of them were obsolete. When it was discovered that the guns and their ammunition had survived the bombing Hart decided to offer them to the Army. Lieutenant Colonel Clement informed USAFFE Headquarters that the Navy would provide these weapons to the Army, along with all the available ammunition. With the Philippine Army desperately short of all types of equipment this offer was eagerly accepted. On 18 December the Army took possession of the Navy weapons and ammunition at Cavite. The transfer included six 4-inch guns (the type mounted on the "flush deck" destroyers), along with over 6,000 rounds of ammunition; eleven 3-inch .50-caliber guns with 1,200 rounds; twelve 6-pounder landing guns with 2,000 rounds; twenty-eight 3-pounder landing guns with 2,400 rounds; and nine 1-pounders with 4,500 rounds.[3] Most of the weapons were sent to Bataan where they were used as beach defense guns along the east and west coasts.

On 13 December Hart and key members of his staff met in the Marsman Building. The CinCAF ordered that the movement of Navy supplies to Corregidor and Mariveles be expedited and that actions to conserve resources be taken. As part of Hart's desire to husband supplies, Navy personnel were put on two meals a day, effective 16 December.[4] Interestingly, this action to reduce rations was taken nearly a month before the Army was forced to make a similar decision on Bataan in early January (Colonel Howard had already placed the 4th Marines on two meals a day several days before the CinCAF's order took effect). Mr. Colley's PNAB contractors were directed to speed up the work on several tunnels around Mariveles that the Navy wanted to use as supply and personnel shelters. The five tunnels already under construction or planned at Mariveles totaled some three thousand linear feet, a considerable amount of storage space. Colley's men were also directed to start work on earth and sandbag personnel shelters at Mariveles; sailors and some of PNAB's personnel did the same at Sangley Point. Importantly, Admiral Hart also directed that the movement of Navy supplies to Bataan and Corregidor be accelerated.

Hart's decisions to expedite the movement of supplies to Bataan and Corregidor meant that the Navy began transferring critical supplies, including food, over ten days before the Army started to do so.[5] At this point in World War II, supply, including provision of food, was the responsibility of each service; the Navy supplied its personnel (and usually the Marines), while the Army took care of its own. Even within the Army, the Air Force elements maintained their own supply system.

Along the Pasig River in Manila were several warehouses leased by the Navy. Some were stocked with spare parts and other supplies, but others held food, including both dry goods and cold storage. One warehouse was managed by Lieutenant (junior grade) Kenneth Wheeler, a Naval Reserve Supply Corps officer who had a business degree from the University of California, Berkeley. On 14 December Wheeler received orders to start shipping a portion of his food stocks to Mariveles and the Navy tunnels on Corregidor. Food such as meat that required refrigeration was placed in the Army's large cold storage plant on Corregidor. For the next ten days Wheeler dispatched several trucks daily to Bataan and during the same period a number of barges were loaded with food at his warehouse on the Pasig and towed across Manila Bay to The Rock where their cargos were transferred into Tunnel Queen or the Army cold storage plant.[6]

By 17 December the Navy had already accumulated a significant amount of food at Bataan and Corregidor. That day the 16th Naval District estimated that it had food for 3,000 men for 90 days at Mariveles, plus enough for another 250 personnel for 180 days in the tunnels on Corregidor. Additional rations for 4,500 men for 90 days were still at Sangley Point and in Manila. The effort to move the remaining food to Bataan continued each day using trucks and barges.[7] It is important to note that at this point USAFFE had not yet ordered the withdrawal to the Bataan Peninsula.

The Navy ships remaining in the Bay also stocked up on supplies. The fuel depot at Sangley Point was still in operation, so during cover of darkness the gunboats, minesweepers, and the destroyers *Peary* and *Pillsbury* (both of which were still in Manila Bay) docked at the fueling pier and filled their bunkers. The ships also helped themselves to ammunition from the Depot in the Navy Yard, and sought additional weapons, including machine guns obtained from PatWing 10's supply and maintenance sheds on Sangley Point. Most ships stocked up on as much food as they could make room for, so great was the uncertainty about what the future held.

The Army was taking a very different approach. Despite the virtual destruction of his air force and the lack of opposition to the initial Japanese landings on north Luzon, where an enemy regiment was steadily expanding its lodgment, MacArthur clung to his original plan of defending the beaches rather than planning to fall back on Bataan and Corregidor per the original Plan Orange and the more recent (May 1941) Rainbow 5 plan. This meant that whereas the Navy started to move supplies and food to Mariveles and Corregidor soon after the disasters on 10 December, the Army quartermasters continued to move supplies *away* from Manila and Bataan in the direction of the still-mobilizing Philippine Army divisions that were now taking up beach defense positions along Lingayen Gulf and at locations south of Manila.

MORE ENEMY ATTACKS

The Far Eastern Air Force was now very weak. By the end of the day on 10 December only twenty-two of the original ninety-two P-40 fighters were still operational, roughly the equivalent of one squadron. A few obsolescent P-35As were also available. The Army made a decision to limit its remaining fighters to reconnaissance missions; attempts to intercept enemy air raids were ended. With the Japanese now clearly in control of the air over Luzon, there was no way that the remaining B-17s could operate from Clark or any other Army air base in the northern part of the Islands; the remaining bombers were pulled back to Mindanao, and soon sent all the way to Australia. With the seizure of the airfields at Vigan and Aparri the Japanese Army began to redeploy fighters to northern Luzon. By the end of the day on the 11th nearly forty short-ranged Ki-27 fighters were operating from the two bases.

On 12 December the next enemy landings took place, this time at the port of Legaspi on Luzon's southeastern tip. Similar to the landings at Aparri and Vigan in northern Luzon, the purpose of this move was to gain airfields ashore and to provide flank protection for the main landings south of Manila, now less than two weeks off. There was no opposition ashore at Legaspi when the 2,500 men of the Japanese Army's Kimura Detachment and the 575 Imperial Navy sailors of the Kure 1st Special Naval Landing Force came ashore.[8]

There was still some aerial opposition to the Japanese, but not nearly enough to seriously interfere with the enemy's plans. The brave Filipino pilots of the 6th Pursuit Squadron clashed with Japanese bombers and fighters over central Luzon, their commander Captain Villamor shooting down a Nell bomber of the unit that had battered Cavite two days earlier. However, shortly after this victory several Zeros jumped the old P-26s and three were shot down, with others damaged. A few individual P-40s apparently attempted interceptions of Japanese formations, but it was clear that the enemy had won command of the air over Luzon. It was on this day that PatWing 10 suffered its first major loss of the war.[9]

In the early morning hours on the 12th the Army coast artillery unit at Fort Wint at the entrance of Subic Bay received word from Filipino coast watchers that two Japanese "battleships" were offshore at San Antonio, northwest of Olongapo. The Army passed the information to the 4th Marines' command post, which immediately sent it on to Lieutenant Commander Clayton Marcy, the senior officer of VP-102 then at Olongapo. Taking the report seriously, VP-102 immediately armed the seven PBYs that were at the base for a predawn takeoff. At 0500 the seven flying boats took off and headed north.

The search was futile. For four hours the planes scoured the sea, searching 150 miles north and south and up to 70 miles west of San Antonio for any enemy shipping, but found nothing. The report, like so many made by untrained, excitable soldiers and civilians in the early days of the war, was false. By 0900 the planes were landing back at Olongapo. The crews immediately started to refuel the aircraft while their officers checked with VP-102 operations to see if any other targets had been identified.

The Japanese made a number of air attacks around Luzon that day, hitting Clark and Iba Fields—again—as well as Manila. They also conducted several fighter sweeps, looking for targets of opportunity. Lieutenant Masuzo Seto led nine Zeros of the Tainan Kokutai to Olongapo where the Japanese knew there was a U.S. base. Up to this point the Subic Bay area had not been hit. That was about to change.

Shortly after 1000 a group of enemy planes at roughly six thousand feet were spotted flying near the Naval Station. The alarm was sounded. When nothing happened, the "all clear" was given at 1020. Five minutes later disaster struck. The Japanese fighters swung into Subic Bay from the south, flying close to Fort Wint. The Army's anti-aircraft guns opened fire on the Zeros, and claimed one shot down into the Bay. Whether any of the Japanese fighters were shot down or not, what appeared to the Marines on the ground as seven enemy planes swept in low and proceeded to shoot up the PBYs moored on the water near the Naval Station. The Marines' heaviest weapons were .30-caliber machine guns, which were inadequate to the task—their effective range against aircraft was very limited and they lacked hitting power. Colonel Howard later reported that .30-caliber tracer rounds were seen bouncing off the enemy planes, which sounds unusual since the Zero was completely unarmored. Several PBY crewmen on board the moored aircraft fought back with their .50-caliber machine guns, but it did no good. In the crow's nest in the mast of the old, decommissioned armored cruiser *Rochester* a couple of Marines on lookout duty fired at the Japanese planes with a BAR.

By the time the Japanese fighters departed all seven of the PBYs were on fire or sinking. Eleven VP-102 crewmen were dead and another four wounded, mostly men who were on board their moored aircraft when the enemy arrived. To add insult to injury, three more Zeros (that the Marines reported as "Messerschmitts") came by to strafe the base at 1225 as they were on their way back to Formosa. By this point a total of ten of PatWing 10's twenty-eight PBYs had been destroyed in combat or by accident. The Asiatic Fleet staff realized that it was time to get the rest out of the northern Philippines, lest the entire force be destroyed.[10]

On the 12th the Naval Hospital at Sangley Point was evacuated. Some Navy officers regarded it as nearly a miracle that the hospital was not hit during the raid on the Navy Yard two days earlier. In fact, only a few bombs had struck Sangley Point during the attack on the Yard. It was clear, however, that the hospital was far too exposed, and with military targets along Sangley Point including the Navy fuel depot and the seaplane base, it was only a question of time before the Japanese bombers would return. During the day most of the hospital staff and patients moved initially to the Philippine Union College just outside the capital where a makeshift hospital was established. Many of the casualties from the bombing of the Navy Yard were already at the Army's Sternberg Hospital in Manila. An aid station manned by a few doctors and corpsmen remained behind on Sangley Point to continue to serve the sailors working to salvage what they could from the wreckage of the Navy Yard and the 1st Separate Marine Battalion that was still manning anti-aircraft guns.

More air attacks followed the next day, 13 December. The enemy was still mostly concentrating on airfields, which were by now home to very few remaining American and Filipino planes. Twenty-six Imperial Navy G4M Betty bombers of the Takao Kokutai headed toward Olongapo, escorted by Zeros. That morning Colonel Howard inspected the Marine defensive positions and directed that a better job of camouflaging needed to be done of the machine-gun emplacements. Coincidentally, just after Colonel Howard completed his inspection a message was received from the 16th Naval District stating that even shallow trenches had provided good protection during the bombing of the Cavite Navy Yard three days earlier.[11]

At 1120 the air raid sirens sounded at Olongapo as twenty-six enemy planes were spotted, heading north, probably the Takao Kokutai. At first it appeared that the planes would pass the base by, but at 1155 the aircraft reappeared and dropped bombs after having already attacked Army airfields. Several bombs hit the town of Olongapo, starting fires. Because most of the regiment had by this point moved into the hills east of Olongapo there were few Marine casualties; one man was seriously wounded when he was blown through a bamboo fence by the concussion of a bomb blast. Unfortunately, about a dozen civilians in the town were killed and another forty or more wounded. The Navy doctors and corpsmen of the 4th Marines tended to the civilian casualties as well as the wounded Marines.[12]

That day Colonel Howard and Lieutenant Colonel Anderson conducted a reconnaissance of the Bagac Bay–Moron area on the west coast of Bataan. Colonel Howard was concerned that if the Japanese landed at Bagac Bay they could cut the 4th Marines in two, with part of the regiment at Olongapo and the rest at Mariveles. He noted that the Army had few troops in the area guarding this potentially vulnerable point, although two 155-mm guns manned by Philippine Scouts (PS) had been dispatched to the area from Corregidor.[13]

By the 13th most of PatWing 10's remaining PBYs were at Laguna de Bay, camouflaged along the shores of the lake. Ten of the twenty-eight flying boats had already been destroyed and several others were damaged and out of commission. That night Admiral Hart directed Captain Wagner to redeploy PatWing 10 to the Indies. The planes started flying out on the 14th. Captain Wagner, several pilots, and most of his staff departed on board the sea plane tender *Childs*, like the *Preston* a converted "flush decker." Most of the Wing's aircrews escaped the Philippines, but the majority of the ground crews and some of the pilots were destined to fight ashore on Bataan and Corregidor.

On the 14th, on Admiral Hart's order, two Vichy French merchant ships, *Marchal Joffre* and *Si-Kiang* were seized in Manila Harbor. The first of the two ships was a nice prize. A new, large, fast cargo ship, she was clearly of value. A small Navy "prize crew" was put on board. Those crewmen who were willing to side with the Free French cause were allowed to remain on the ship; they would help the Americans get her out of the Philippines. When she departed for the Indies she had aboard fourteen officers and sixty-two enlisted men from PatWing 10. Later she was renamed *Rochambeau* and spent the rest of the war in U.S. service.

The older ship, *Si-Kiang*, was of considerable value due to her cargo. She had been en route to Indochina with a cargo of thousands of gallons of gasoline and 2,500 tons of flour. The ship was moved to Mariveles Harbor where Marines from the 1st Battalion, 4th Marines, already located at Mariveles, were put on board to guard the vessel. Within a few days her cargo of gasoline had been removed. For some reason there was less urgency about off-loading the flour, a delay that was to prove tragic.

At a meeting on the 15th between the Asiatic Fleet staff and representatives from USAFFE the Army proposed to use the 4th Marines in a rather unusual way. In addition to continuing to mobilize the Philippine Army, the Philippine Constabulary was being formed into regimental-sized units. The Constabulary was the Islands' militarized national police that had been in existence since the early years of the American presence in the Philippines. USAFFE wanted to break the 4th Marines into two regiments, and merge each half with a regiment of Constabulary troops, thus forming a brigade-sized unit. It was suggested that Colonel Howard would become the brigade commander.

The next day Lieutenant Colonel Clement responded for the Asiatic Fleet, tentatively agreeing with the proposal. Shortly thereafter Admiral Hart changed his mind, stating that the 4th Marines needed more opportunity to continue their training as a unit following their many years in Shanghai where field training was very limited. In addition, there was still a need to protect the naval facilities in the Philippines, technically the Marines' primary mission. General Sutherland was told that Admiral Hart preferred that the 4th Marines be used as a unit, and when the time came they would be released to the control of the Army for tactical employment.

THE SS *CORREGIDOR* TRAGEDY

One of the greatest maritime tragedies of the twentieth century occurred at the entrance of Manila Bay on the night of 17 December when the interisland steamer SS *Corregidor* struck a mine as it was leaving Manila en route to the southern Philippines. The ship was packed with Filipino civilians, most of whom were attempting to reach the hoped-for safety of the southern islands or trying to get back to their homes in the southern islands before it was too late. Five members of the Philippine Legislature were on board, all from districts in the south. Apparently some 150 Philippine Army soldiers were also on the ship, heading for units in the southern islands. Interestingly, there were only seven Americans on board, two of whom were Army officers en route to the Visayan-Mindanao Force.

Compania Maritima, the ship's owners, did not know how many people were on board when it departed. All that can be said is that there were somewhere between 1,200 and 1,500 people on board when the ship pulled away from its dock in Manila at 2000 on the 16th. Apparently the Navy was not informed of the ship's intention to depart Manila Bay that night. No word of *Corregidor*'s intent to leave the Bay was passed to the Seaward Defense Command on Corregidor, where the Army's electrical mines were controlled. The gunboat *Mindanao* spotted *Corregidor* as she headed toward the entrance of the Bay. Since the ship had not been officially cleared to depart, the gunboat tried to force her to stop, but to no avail.[14]

The ship's master, Apolinar Calvo, was an experienced captain who had already made trips through the tightly controlled entrance to the minefields that ran between Bataan and the Cavite shore; the minefields had been in place since late July. Interestingly, *Corregidor* was the fastest ship among the small fleet of interisland steamers that worked among the Philippine Islands. The ship had a colorful history. In an earlier life she had been HMS *Engadine*, a Royal Navy seaplane carrier. At the Battle of Jutland in 1916 she had launched the only fixed-wing aircraft to participate in that great clash of battleships.

At 0100 in the morning of the 17th the ship was close to the island fortress of Corregidor. Army observers on The Rock spotted her approaching the North Channel and preparing to turn into the lane through the minefield. There was confusion at the Army's Seaward Defense Command headquarters on Corregidor. Some duty officers recommended that the Army's electrically controlled mines be switched to the "safe" setting (essentially, temporarily disarmed). According to several accounts, Colonel Paul Bunker, the Seaward Defense Commander who controlled not only Corregidor's big guns but also the Army's mines, ordered that the mines remain active, having not received any word of the ship being cleared to leave the Bay.

As the ship moved through the lane in the direction of the tiny island of La Monja there was a huge explosion on the starboard side toward the stern.

Corregidor immediately took on a list and quickly started to sink. The ship was badly overcrowded, which certainly resulted in many people being trapped belowdecks by the surge up the passageways. According to some survivors, the ship sank so quickly that there was virtually no time for a large scale panic to start. Almost before they could realize what had happened, the survivors were struggling in the water. They soon saw searchlights from nearby Corregidor Island playing across the water, illuminating the scene of the sinking.

At nearby Sisiman Cove on Bataan the men of MTB Squadron 3 were in the process of setting up their new home. Most of the PT boats' spare parts, including precious engines, had been lost when the Navy Yard was bombed out. Sisiman Cove was an excellent location from which to patrol the entrances to Manila and Subic Bays, even though the amenities left much to be desired. There was a dock and a few huts that the men could use, and the small base at Mariveles was not too far away, either by foot or boat.

When the men heard the explosion PT-32, -34, and -35 got under way to see what was happening. Soon they were at the entrance to the minefield, surrounded by wreckage and struggling survivors. Ladders were put over the sides of the little vessels and the crews worked frantically to bring on board as many people as they could find. Eventually the three PT boats picked up 296 survivors. The 32 Boat alone was crammed with 196 people.[15] Some of the survivors were temporarily put on board the recently seized Vichy ship, *Si-Kiang*. At dawn many of the badly injured were transported across the Bay to hospitals in Manila.[16]

No one will ever know how many died on board the ill-fated *Corregidor* because there is no accurate count of the number of people on the ship. It appears that 900–1,200 men, women, and children went down with the vessel. Two of the Philippine legislators were lost, as was the ship's captain. Also on board were Army supplies, most importantly the majority of the field artillery weapons allocated to the Visayan-Mindanao Force. It was a real blow to the Army forces in the southern islands. Fourteen naval 3-inch guns along with their ammunition were lost. These were weapons that the Navy had turned over to the Army several months before the start of the war, above and beyond the naval guns given to the Army after Cavite was bombed. Additionally, a few old 2.95-inch mountain howitzers also went down with the ship. The loss meant that between them the three Philippine Army divisions in the southern islands had to fight the war with a total of eight ancient 2.95-inch weapons as their entire artillery strength.[17] In addition to the guns and ammunition, Army medical supplies and other equipment intended for the Visayan-Mindanao Force went down with the ship.

The tragic sinking of *Corregidor* was never properly investigated. There was a war on and events were moving too fast. Apparently some Army officers unofficially told a reporter from a Manila newspaper that the mines were set to the safe position immediately *after* the explosion. Since no investigation was conducted and the ship's master was lost, it will never be possible to determine who was to blame for the sinking. It appears that the owners of *Corregidor* had not informed the Navy's Inshore Patrol of the ship's intent to leave Manila Bay that night. It also appears that the Navy changed procedure that day, placing lighted buoys near the channel through the Army mines rather than posting a gunboat near the channel as had been done for several nights previously. The Army, not knowing of *Corregidor*'s plan to depart, left its mines on the "armed" setting. Therefore, it appears that a combination of mistakes by the ship's owners, captain, and the U.S. military resulted in the tragedy.[18]

INCREASED ENEMY PRESSURE

Sangley Point was finally bombed in a systematic manner on 19 December. The Japanese encountered heavy anti-aircraft fire from the 1st Separate Battalion, but pressed home their attack, which began at approximately 1330. Most of the aviation fuel drums that remained (much had already been evacuated to Bataan and Corregidor) were burned as a result of the bombing. One of the 600-foot radio towers collapsed and the power plant for the radio station was destroyed by a direct hit. Fortunately, the drums of diesel fuel and gasoline had already been removed across the Bay. Surprisingly, the now-vacant Naval Hospital grounds, very close to the radio towers, were not touched. The hospital staff and patients had already been transferred to Manila. Five Marines from the 1st Separate Battalion were killed on Sangley Point during this air raid and others were wounded.[19] The gunboat *Oahu* was near Sangley Point when the air attack began. She fired nineteen 3-inch anti-aircraft rounds as she maneuvered to avoid the Japanese bombers.[20]

On the 20th Admiral Rockwell met with Hart in the Marsman Building. It was determined that the immediate area of Manila was no longer tenable for operations and the move to the outer part of the Bay needed to be completed. It was hoped that the strength of Corregidor's anti-aircraft defenses and the shelter afforded by the tunnels would provide better protection from enemy air attacks.

Hart directed Rockwell to move the 16th Naval District Headquarters to Tunnel Queen on Corregidor as quickly as possible. It was also decided that the 1st Separate Marine Battalion would move from Sangley Point to the Mariveles area. The Marines were to take with them as much of their equipment and supplies as possible. Rockwell said that he would leave a detachment on Sangley

Point under the control of Captain J. H. Dessez who would continue to salvage as much as possible for shipment to Corregidor and Mariveles and also be prepared to destroy whatever facilities and equipment remained if a final move to Bataan and the fortified islands was ordered.

The next day, 21 December, Rockwell and his immediate staff departed for Corregidor aboard the minesweeper *Tanager*. When the admiral arrived on The Rock he met with Major General George Moore, USA, the harbor defense commander. Rockwell and Moore discussed better integrating the activities of the Inshore Patrol with the Army. By this time the Inshore Patrol was under the command of recently promoted Captain Kenneth Hoeffel who was on board the gunboat *Mindanao*. While the minesweepers continued to conduct daily sweeps of the ship channels through the minefields, the gunboats patrolled to the east of Corregidor. The ships still in the Bay continued to refuel at the still-usable Sangley Point fuel dock when they were not needed to conduct a specific mission.

On the 21st Lieutenant Colonel Adams was ordered to begin transferring his men and equipment to Mariveles. This was accomplished over the next several days. Four 3-inch anti-aircraft guns, all the battalion's machine guns, and most of the men had moved by the 23rd. Lieutenant Hogaboom's Battery A departed for Mariveles on the 22nd, leaving behind its four fixed 3-inch anti-aircraft guns. These were later destroyed in place by Captain Dessez's detail. As the 1st Separate Battalion moved into the Mariveles area the unit went into bivouac outside the town, linking up with the 1st Battalion, 4th Marines that was already in the area. When four mobile 3-inch guns arrived via barge from the Sangley Point area they were set up near Mariveles to provide anti-aircraft protection for the Navy Section Base. The .50-caliber machine guns were also set up to drive off low-level attacks. Nineteen Marines from the battalion who had been wounded during the bombing of the Cavite Navy Yard and Sangley Point remained in Manila under the care of Navy medical personnel.[21]

Thus by the end of the second week of war the Navy and Marines were clearly concentrating in southern Bataan and on Corregidor, including moving most of their remaining supplies there. The regimental headquarters and 2nd Battalion of the 4th Marines remained near Olongapo, awaiting orders. PatWing 10 was already moving out of the Philippines. In Manila Bay were still a collection of vessels, including *Canopus*, two destroyers, the gunboats, minesweepers, PT boats, and various small craft. Submarines were still entering and leaving Manila Bay. During daylight they remained submerged, sitting on the bottom. When darkness fell, a sub would be quickly serviced by the *Canopus* before departing again. Although very few naval personnel knew it at the time, by this point MacArthur had turned on the Navy in a very major way.

BLAMING THE NAVY

By 12 December it was clear that the situation in the Philippines was extremely serious. Although it was only the fifth day of the war, the Army's Far Eastern Air Force had been reduced to a handful of fighters and bombers whose bases were under constant attack. The FEAF had no ability to challenge the Japanese in the air; enemy bombers were attacking the Philippine capital every day. The Philippine Army was very much unprepared for war; it needed months of additional training and far more equipment to have a chance of successfully defending the beaches against the best army in Asia. Besides, the enemy was already ashore in north and south Luzon, was establishing air bases, and expanding his lodgment. The Navy's only major base in the Far East, the Cavite Navy Yard, had been destroyed. In addition, most of the surface ships of the Asiatic Fleet had departed from Manila Bay, heading toward the Indies. With the enemy in command of the air, those ships were not coming back any time soon. Given the number of warships the Japanese had around the Philippines at this point, the entire surface element of the Asiatic Fleet could not have stopped them, even if the enemy had not had air superiority. The situation was grim, and getting worse.

During this period MacArthur was sending a stream of messages to General Marshall that can only be described as delusional. For example, on 10 December, three days after the Pearl Harbor debacle, MacArthur radioed to Marshall the following:

> The mass of enemy air and naval strength committed in the theater from Singapore to the Philippines and eastward establishes his weakness in Japan proper and definite information available here shows that entry of Russia is enemy's greatest fear. Most favorable opportunity now exists and immediate attack on Japan from north would not only inflict heavy punishment but would at once relieve pressure from objectives of Jap drive to southward. Information being secured establishes that heavy air attack on Jap objectives would not only pull in much of present widely dispersed air strength but could destroy much of their exposed oil supply. A golden opportunity exists for a master stroke while enemy is engaged in overextended air effort.[22]

How the United States was going to conduct this "master stroke" when it was not yet clear whether the Japanese were going to invade the Hawaiian Islands was unexplained by the USAFFE commander. Marshall apparently took this and other messages from MacArthur in stride. What these messages should have done was show the Army chief of staff that his Far Eastern Commander was out of touch with reality.

On the same day as MacArthur's message to Marshall, Admiral Purnell sent a far more realistic appreciation of the situation to General Brereton, the FEAF commander. It read:

> Navy's estimate of the situation as of today; with the initiative in the hands of the enemy, consideration of his early successes, and the preponderance of forces available to him is the contemplation of a long war, facing the loss of, and ultimate recapture of the Philippines. Navy decision is to employ the forces available, primarily air and submarines, to inflict maximum losses on the enemy as he makes his commitments. The air force is scouting for enemy forces on which attacks can be delivered by air or submarines, or both. An air attack is now being delivered on enemy force reported this morning. Eight submarines are on offensive missions, thirteen are on offensive-defensive missions in Philippine waters, and eight are repairing or overhauling in Manila Bay area, in preparation as reliefs on the offensive missions; of the number, four are available to respond to an urgent call to local action. Surface forces available are capable of rendering defensive action only.[23]

Written on the day the Cavite Navy Yard was destroyed, and two days after the Army's Far Eastern Air Force was caught on the ground, this was a realistic appraisal of the situation, including the likely loss of the Philippines. Although the memo was sent to the FEAF commander a copy was soon in MacArthur's hands. The General did not like the message. His attacks on the Navy were about to start.

When the war started a convoy of several merchant ships was southwest of Hawaii, with Manila as its destination. Since the heavy cruiser USS *Pensacola* was the escort ship the convoy was generally referred to by her name. On board the merchant ships were the fifty-two A-24 dive bombers of an Army light bombardment group whose personnel were already in the Philippines, eighteen P-40 fighters, thousands of tons of supplies and ammunition, and several battalions of Army National Guard field artillery. All together, about 4,500 Army troops were in the *Pensacola* convoy. MacArthur, of course, wanted the convoy to reach the Philippines as quickly as possible.

In the aftermath of the attack on Pearl Harbor the initial impulse in Washington was to reroute the convoy back to Hawaii. With the enemy's intentions unclear, the whereabouts of his aircraft carriers following the strike on the Pacific Fleet unknown, and with Hawaii possibly threatened by invasion, the safe bet was to pull the convoy back rather than let it proceed to the Philippines. Due to pleas from MacArthur and a genuine desire to try to help the Philippine garrison, the Army leadership in Washington reversed its decision and insisted that the convoy proceed westward. On 12 December the *Pensacola* convoy was redirected to Brisbane, Australia. The cruiser, the submarine tender *Niagra*, and the seven transports and cargo ships entered that harbor on 22 December, the same day as the main Japanese landings on Luzon.[24]

While the convoy was en route to Australia a series of increasingly terse exchanges took place between Admiral Hart and the CNO, Admiral Stark, on one side, and MacArthur and General Marshall on the other. When MacArthur was informed by the Army chief of staff that the *Pensacola* convoy was heading for Australia, the former insisted that it be escorted onward to the Philippines by the Asiatic Fleet. MacArthur met with the CinCAF on 13 December to discuss getting the convoy through. Hart, in all things far more the realist than MacArthur, knew that the enemy already had sufficient air and naval strength in and around the Philippines to conduct a blockade of the Islands. Hart understood that any attempt to bring such a large convoy northward to Manila was impossible given the Japanese control of the air, and he told MacArthur so.

Later on the 13th MacArthur sent a radio message to Marshall complaining that Hart was insisting that by the time the *Pensacola* convoy could proceed northward the Japanese would have put a blockade into effect and that the Islands were ultimately doomed. Hart was, of course, absolutely correct. That was not, however, what MacArthur wanted to hear. In his message to Marshall the USAFFE commander stated that the defense of the Philippines was so vital that: "Every resource of the Democratic Allies in sea, air, and land should be converged here immediately and overwhelmingly. The Philippine theater of operations is the locus of victory or defeat and I urge a strategic review of the entire situation least a fatal mistake be made. . . . It justifies the diversion here of the entire output of air and other resources."[25] MacArthur suggested that the Dutch and Australian navies should participate in escorting convoys northward to the Philippines.

On the 14th MacArthur sent another radiogram to Marshall stating that his immediate need was ten pursuit squadrons (he had five at the start of the war) of some two hundred fighters, plus fifty dive bombers. He said that *if* the planes could be ferried from Australia by 1 January they could easily be dispersed and would start immediate operations against the enemy. He also suggested that the Army planes could be ferried by Navy aircraft carriers to within range of the Philippines.[26]

These messages are significant, for they demonstrate that MacArthur was desperate (which is understandable), but also out of touch with reality. These were not some idle statements not meant to be taken seriously; rather, they were official messages from a very senior Army field commander to the chief of staff of the Army at a critically important point in the war.

Over the next few days more messages went from MacArthur to General Marshall, urging reinforcements be dashed to the Philippines and complaining that the Navy was not supporting him. On the 19th MacArthur sent a memo to Admiral Hart, saying that General Marshall had informed him that President Roosevelt had "generally concurred" with messages that USAFFE had sent to the Army chief of staff, thus implying that MacArthur's goal of reorienting American grand strategy around the Philippines was now official U.S. policy, which was clearly not the case. MacArthur insisted that Hart make arrangements for the escort of *Pensacola* and subsequent convoys to the Philippines, possibly with the assistance of the Dutch and British navies.[27] An increasingly concerned General Marshall was taking MacArthur's messages to the secretary of the Army, Mr. Henry L. Stimson who at least partially echoed the USAFFE commander's claims that the Navy was "defeatist."

Hart could clearly see what was going on. As MacArthur became increasingly shrill in his demands that the small Asiatic Fleet push convoys northward to the beleaguered Philippines, Hart was in communication with Admiral Stark in Washington. On 13 December, following his meeting with MacArthur, Hart sent a message to the CNO advising him of the real situation in the Philippines, including the fact that the Japanese were rapidly gaining control of the air and sea around the Islands. On the 17th the Chief of Naval Operations sent the following message to the CinCAF:

> CNO recognizes that you cannot guarantee safe transport to Philippines of shipborne Army supporting units, but suggests effort when appropriate to pass through such support as may be practicable. Cooperate with Army in the aircraft transport when practicable of items the Army particularly needs. Army sending out several Pan American Clippers [large commercial flying boats] via Africa to assist. When in your judgment you can from elsewhere more effectively direct the operations of your fleet CNO approves your departure from Manila and the prior transfer southward of advance base personnel and material. Assure MacArthur you will continue your full support of the defense of the Philippines and upon your departure place all remaining naval and Marine personnel under MacArthur's command and make available to him naval munitions, stores, and equipment. SECNAV authorizes you to commandeer such shipping in the Philippines as you require for your operations.[28]

On the 20th Hart sent a memo to MacArthur, following a meeting with General Sutherland. In it Hart stated that he was examining ways to get the convoy through to the Philippines. He stated that the Navy understood the importance of the convoy's contents to the Army, and if possible a way would be found to escort it to the Philippines, but no decision could yet be made as to whether an onward voyage from Australia would be possible or when. In the same memo, Hart also reminded MacArthur of the 4th Marine Regiment, stating that it would be a valuable addition to the Army forces in the Islands and that the time was drawing near when they needed to make a formal agreement regarding how the Marines would be employed.[29]

On the 23rd Hart received a message from the Navy staff in Washington telling him, "Army in Manila and here are bringing heavy pressure for greater naval activity in Philippine waters. As my information on this subject is meager, desire you submit by dispatch as soon as possible as may be convenient a full account of naval operations in support of Army."[30] By this point the fate of the Philippines was already sealed. On the day before Hart received the message from OPNAV (Navy Operations staff, located in Washington, D.C.) that the main body of the Japanese 14th Army had stormed ashore at Lingayen Gulf, about one hundred miles north of Manila.

The Retreat to Bataan and Corregidor

THE MAIN JAPANESE LANDINGS

The largest Japanese convoy of the entire Pacific War arrived in Lingayen Gulf in the early morning hours of 22 December. On board the eighty transports was the majority of the 48th Division (the most powerful unit in the 14th Army), an infantry regiment from the 16th Division, two tank regiments totaling about ninety light and medium tanks, several independent artillery regiments and battalions, plus engineer, anti-aircraft, and logistics units. A total of roughly 43,000 men were about to come ashore. Also on board the ships was Lieutenant General Masaharu Homma, the commander of the 14th Army.[1]

The landings started before dawn on the 22nd, with infantry from the 48th and 16th Divisions going ashore along the northeast beaches of Lingayen Gulf. There was very little resistance at the landing sites. A Philippine Scout 155-mm artillery battery near the beaches opened fire on the transports, but did not hit any. Wasting no time, the Japanese infantry started expanding their lodgment while tanks and artillery came ashore to add their weight to the attack. Almost immediately the poorly trained and badly equipped Filipino troops of the 11th and 71st Divisions that were in the landing area started to fall back in disorder, abandoning much of their equipment and ammunition. MacArthur's cherished plan to defend the landing beaches with the Philippine Army had collapsed.

During the next two days the Japanese established a firm beachhead and continued to advance inland, sweeping southward down the shore of Lingayen Gulf. A few Army P-40s and P-35s attempted strafing runs against enemy ships and ground troops. Four B-17s from Mindanao also attacked, but hit nothing. By this time the Japanese Army had numerous fighters and light bombers based on the airfields in northern Luzon. These aircraft bombed and strafed the Filipino troops and drove off most of the U.S. Army aircraft that tried to enter the area.

Had it not been for the valiant efforts of the Philippine Scouts of the elite 26th Cavalry Regiment the campaign on Luzon would have ended very quickly. The 26th Cavalry was in reserve behind the beaches when the Japanese landed. A battalion-sized unit, it only had about six hundred men available at that time and no anti-tank weapon heavier than .50-caliber machine guns firing armor-piercing ammunition. Although partly motorized, the regiment was primarily a horse-mounted formation. It was the last U.S. Army horse cavalry unit ever to engage in combat.*

Fighting desperate delaying actions over the next few days, the Scout cavalrymen covered the retreat of the disorganized Philippine Army units. At times the 26th Cavalry fought entire regiments of Japanese infantry reinforced with tanks. As one would imagine, the Scouts suffered heavy casualties, but they bought precious time for their poorly trained fellow Filipinos to retreat behind the Agno River south of the Lingayen beaches where they could start to reform. The other key units that covered the retreat of the Philippine Army divisions were two American National Guard tank battalions that had arrived in the Philippines during the summer and fall. Although the cavalry and tanks had prevented a rapid collapse, it was now very clear that the enemy was firmly ashore in great strength.[2]

More bad news arrived on 24 December when seven thousand Japanese troops of the 16th Division landed at Lamon Bay southeast of Manila. The enemy was now set up for dual drives to converge on Manila from the north and south. MacArthur's scheme of defeating the enemy at the beaches had been a complete and utter failure.

FAILURE OF THE SUBMARINES

In the prewar plans to defend the Philippines it had long been recognized that Lingayen Gulf would probably be the site of the main Japanese landings on Luzon. When the 27 November war warning message was received the old *S-36* had been dispatched to patrol the area north of Lingayen. Once war started more submarines were posted off western and northern Luzon.

---

*The Philippine Scouts were an element of the regular U.S. Army. Formed in the early 1900s and always considered an elite organization, the Scouts were Filipino enlisted men serving under mostly American officers; a few Scout officers were Filipinos.

The first two weeks of the war had been frustrating for the Asiatic Fleet submarine force. Some of its boats had been positioned close to the Philippines to help guard against major enemy landings, while others had been sent farther to interdict Japanese shipping off the coast of Indochina and Formosa. Results had been disappointing, to say the least.

One of the first attacks was by *Seawolf*. On 10 December she was routed to North Luzon to attack the Japanese landings. She fired a total of eight torpedoes at Japanese ships near Aparri, but scored no hits. *Pickerel* fired five torpedoes at a gunboat off the coast of Indochina on 14 December, but all of them missed or failed to detonate. *Sargo* attacked several ships off the same coast on 14 and 24 December, but no hits were scored. By the time *Sargo* headed back to Manila she had fired thirteen torpedoes in six separate attacks, but not one scored.

Pike attacked a cargo ship near Hong Kong on 17 December. She fired one torpedo, but missed. On 21 December *Sturgeon*, operating off the coast of Formosa, made a surface torpedo against an enemy cargo ship. Four torpedoes had been fired, but all missed or failed to explode. By this time the commanding officers of the subs were becoming very suspicious that something was seriously wrong with their torpedoes.[3]

A few successes were achieved. *Swordfish* was dispatched to patrol the vicinity of Hainan Island, south of Hong Kong. She torpedoed the Japanese Army transport *Kashii Maru* on 14 December. Two days later she scored against the merchant ship *Atsutasan Maru*. On 23 December *Seal* sank *Soryu Maru* off Vigan.

SUBS AT LINGAYEN GULF

In the early morning hours of 20 December the Navy sent a warning to USAFFE Headquarters that a large convoy had been located moving south from Formosa toward Lingayen Gulf. Shortly after 1700 the next day, 21 December, the submarine *Stingray* spotted several columns of smoke approaching from the north. The sub radioed a sighting report, but did not attack. By the time *Stingray* tried to attack the large Japanese convoy was inside the Gulf where the water was very shallow, often less than one hundred feet, hardly a good environment for submarines to operate. *Stingray* had not fired a single torpedo.

Captain Wilkes, the commander of Asiatic Fleet submarines, directed more of his boats toward Lingayen. Six additional subs—*S-38*, *S-40*, *Salmon*, *Permit*, *Porpoise*, and *Saury*—were all ordered to attack the convoy; all were already within a day's sailing of the Gulf. Wilkes directed the sub captains to take the risk of entering the shallow waters of Lingayen in order to attack enemy shipping.

In the predawn hours of 22 December the *S-38* slipped into the Gulf. Shortly after sunrise Lieutenant Commander W. G. Chapple fired his four bow tubes at enemy transports at a range of about one thousand yards. All of the torpedoes either missed or—as was so common in the first year of the war—failed to detonate. An enemy destroyer hunted the S-boat, but did not locate her. Frustrated, Chapple took his sub even farther into Lingayen Gulf, reloading his torpedo tubes as he slowly and quietly advanced. From his periscope Chapple could see dozens of enemy ships either moving or already anchored as they started to land their troops.

Closing to within about five hundred yards of an enemy transport, Chapple set the next spread of torpedoes for a mere nine-foot depth. Less than a minute after firing the old submarine was rocked by the explosions of several of its torpedoes detonating against the 5,400-ton *Hayo Maru*. It was to be the only kill by U.S. submarines against the huge enemy convoy that was depositing the 14th Army ashore on Luzon.

S-38 was immediately counterattacked by two Japanese destroyers that dropped a lot of depth charges, but none very close. As she attempted to escape, the old sub went aground in about eighty feet of water. It took several hours to dislodge the boat. Finally *S-38* reached deeper water and surfaced that evening to reload torpedoes and recharge batteries. The next day Chapple attempted another strike, but was attacked by a Japanese aircraft that spotted the submerged submarine in the shallow water. The enemy aircraft barely missed *S-38* with its depth charge or bomb. On the evening of the 23rd the sub was forced to head back to Manila following an internal explosion.

The other subs had even less luck. Once the convoy entered Lingayen Gulf the Japanese established a screen of destroyers in an attempt to seal the entrance. Because the water was so shallow, it was very dangerous for the American submarines to operate inside the Gulf—the Japanese plane spotting the submerged *S-38* provided plenty of evidence of that. On the 22nd and 23rd, *Saury*, *Salmon*, and *S-40* all attempted to penetrate the enemy screen at the entrance to the Gulf, even taking shots at the Japanese destroyers. All the torpedoes either missed or malfunctioned. Violent counterattacks by enemy destroyers forced the submarines to remain submerged and generally in the outer reaches of the Gulf. A fair number of torpedoes were launched, mostly at destroyers, but none hit other than *S-38*'s early score. By Christmas Day it was clear that the submarines had failed to seriously interfere with the landing of the 14th Army.[4]

What had gone wrong? The submarines represented the greatest potential of the Asiatic Fleet, like the B-17s had for the Army Air Force in the Philippines. Several factors contributed to the poor performance of the submarines off Lingayen Gulf. First, not enough boats were positioned to block the entrance, although several were within a day's sailing of Lingayen. Admiral Hart and

Captain Wilkes can be criticized for that error. Knowing the importance of Lingayen as a likely landing spot, more submarines should have been north of the Gulf to intercept an approaching convoy. Second, *Stingray* did not act aggressively and was slow in getting the word to Captain Wilkes that the main enemy convoy had been spotted headed into Lingayen Gulf. When *Stingray* returned to Manila Wilkes relieved her commanding officer, Lieutenant Commander Raymond Lamb. Third, the water of Lingayen Gulf was very shallow. Once the Japanese convoy was inside the Gulf attacks by submarines were very difficult and risky. Finally, the performance of the American torpedoes was very bad. It was only the third week of the war and it was already becoming apparent that there was something very wrong with U.S. submarine torpedoes. Several boats on patrol off the coast of Indochina had already experienced trouble with their weapons. Frustrated commanding officers were already trying to vary the depth settings before firing, thinking that the problem was torpedoes running too deep, passing under enemy ships. They did not know that the new Mark VI magnetic exploders were faulty and the traditional contact detonators were also unreliable. It would be well over a year before the Pacific Fleet submarine force had consistently reliable torpedoes.

The fact remains that the Asiatic Fleet submarine force failed to seriously threaten the largest Japanese convoy of the entire Pacific War. Given the poor quality of the torpedoes, it is possible that even if more boats had succeeded in intercepting the Japanese before they entered Lingayen Gulf the overall results would have been no better. Even so, the Army, which was now fighting a desperate battle against the rapidly advancing 14th Army, was upset that the submarines had failed to seriously interfere with the enemy landing. Clearly, the Army had a right to feel that way. It was the worst performance of U.S. Navy submarines in the Pacific War.

REVERTING TO WAR PLAN ORANGE—"WPO-3 IS IN EFFECT"

By the afternoon of 23 December the Japanese were firmly ashore and preparing to advance into the great valley that runs southward toward Manila. It was quite clear to the USAFFE leadership that if the poorly prepared Philippine Army formations that made up the overwhelming majority of the North Luzon Force attempted to stand and fight in the Lingayen area the Japanese would overwhelm them and bring the campaign to a swift end. A major change in plans was needed—right away. On the evening of the 23rd the commander of the North Luzon Force, Major General Jonathan M. Wainwright, was informed by USAFFE Headquarters that "WPO-3 is in effect"—the retreat to Bataan was on. The following morning, as the Japanese landed at Lamon Bay southeast of Manila, Major General George M. Parker, the South Luzon Force commander, was also informed of the decision to withdraw.

The Army forces on Luzon, now closely engaged by the Japanese, were reverting to the decades-old original plan to retreat to Bataan and the fortified islands of Manila Bay. The North Luzon Force was expected to delay the enemy north of Manila until about 1 January in order to buy time for the South Luzon Force to march north, pass through Manila, and turn into Bataan. Also, and critically, the Army's quartermasters would have to rush as many supplies as they could into the Peninsula and to Corregidor. They would have about a week to move food, ammunition, and medical supplies for the Filipino-American Army forces now moving toward Bataan. According to the original War Plan Orange Bataan was supposed to be stocked with supplies for a six-month siege. However, due to MacArthur's plan to fight at the beaches the Army had not moved anything toward Bataan up to this point in the campaign. Given the amount of time that was now available, the Army quartermasters had an impossible task on their hands.

On 22 December MacArthur reported to General Marshall that the enemy had made his main landing, estimating that the Japanese were putting ashore 80,000–100,000 men at Lingayen Gulf. Actually the Japanese force at Lingayen was about half that size. Including the troops that had also landed at Vigan, Aparri, Legaspi, and Lamon Bay, there were at most 65,000 Japanese ashore on Luzon by this point, including Army Air Force personnel. In the same message MacArthur told Marshall that he had on Luzon about 40,000 men in "units partly equipped." This number was clearly far below the true size of the Philippine Army and U.S. Army forces on Luzon. Relatively few American and Philippine Army casualties had been suffered by this point in the campaign—a few hundred at most prior to the Lingayen landings.

Several hundred Air Force personnel had moved southward to Del Monte Field on Mindanao. Additionally, a couple hundred air and ground crewmen had flown to Australia in the remaining B-17s. And while none of the Philippine Army divisions on Luzon had reached their planned strength of 8,700 men, most were probably well over 7,500 by this point in their mobilization. A number of non-divisional Philippine Army organizations had also been formed, including engineers as well as coast artillery and field artillery units of battalion and regimental size. Therefore, there were probably close to 100,000 American and Filipino Army troops on Luzon at the start of the retreat, including roughly 6,000 who were already on the fortified islands. About 80,000 managed to reach Bataan. The rest, about 14,000, either became casualties or deserted during the withdrawal.[5]

The Navy first learned of the Army's intent to revert back to War Plan Orange on the evening of 22 December. The 16th Naval District intelligence officer, Lieutenant Commander M. C. Cheek, maintained close contact with the Army's Philippine Department G-2. In the evening of the 22nd Cheek was told by his counterpart in the Philippine Department staff that the Army was on the verge of starting to pull back to Bataan. When he tried to confirm that with Colonel Charles Willoughby, the USAFFE G-2, he was told that the Army had no plans to withdraw. Cheek informed Admiral Hart's office of what he had discovered and was surprised that the Army had told no one on the CinCAF's staff that a retreat was being considered.[6]

Late on the following day Admiral Hart was told that the Army was probably going to order a withdrawal. On the morning of Christmas Eve official word was received that the Army was pulling back to Bataan. The Navy was told that USAFFE Headquarters and key officials of the Philippine government, including President Quezon, would move to Corregidor that day. Importantly, the Army also announced that it was going to declare Manila an Open City the next day—Christmas—in an attempt to spare the Philippine capital further destruction. This meant that all military forces had to withdraw from the city; it would not be defended once the Open City edict went into effect. Although the Asiatic Fleet staff realized that a move to Bataan and Corregidor was probably inevitable, the very short notice that they were given surprised them. Now final preparations had to be rushed. There was, however, some confusion as to exactly when Manila would become an Open City. The Navy was under the impression that the city had to be evacuated by the end of Christmas Day. In fact, it was not until the 26th that the edict went into effect.

Hart met with his staff on the afternoon of the 24th to finalize plans to get the remaining Navy and Marine personnel and equipment to Bataan and Corregidor. It was unclear how long the Army could delay the enemy north and south of Manila. All the Navy knew for certain was that the capital was about to be declared an Open City. To the Navy's great advantage, many of its supplies, including food, had already been transported to the area where the siege would take place.

During the staff meeting it was decided that the Asiatic Fleet submarines would continue to operate from the Manila Bay area for as long as possible. In order to support the subs, the old tender *Canopus* would remain in the Bay. The little ships of the Inshore Patrol would also stay in order to support the Army on Bataan. Hart decided that it was time to move his headquarters south to the Dutch East Indies in order to better control the main body of the surface ships of the Asiatic Fleet, most of which were already operating in the south. The plan was to send the staff out by PBY on two consecutive nights.

Admiral Rockwell was at the meeting. Hart informed Rockwell that he would now take command of all remaining Navy and Marine Corps units in the

Philippines, although it was clear that it was now time to transfer most of the Marines to Army tactical control. Rockwell told Hart that he fully concurred with the CinCAF's decision to move to the Indies; only from there could he control the main surface elements of the Asiatic Fleet.

Colonel Howard was en route to Manila when Hart's staff meeting took place. He arrived as the port of Manila, close to the Marsman Building, was under air attack. Hart told the colonel that the time had come to transfer tactical control of the Marines over to the Army. The admiral said that Colonel Howard would gain control of the 1st Separate Marine Battalion, which was still moving from Sangley Point to Mariveles. There would be a need to retain a few Marines of the 1st Separate Battalion for anti-aircraft duties around Mariveles, but the majority of the unit would join the 4th Marines as the regiment's new 3rd Battalion. Hart then directed Colonel Howard to report to USAFFE Headquarters for detailed instructions from the Army.

Howard, accompanied by Lieutenant Colonel Clement, went to a now very hectic USAFFE Headquarters at Fort Santiago in downtown Manila. The two Marines first reported to General MacArthur. The USAFFE commander was very pleasant to the two senior Marines. He told them that his chief of staff would provide them with detailed instructions on how the 4th Marines would be employed.

When Colonel Howard met Sutherland he suggested that the 4th Marines could be used to provide beach defense for the area around Bagac Bay on Bataan's west coast. Howard had already personally reconnoitered that area after his 1st Battalion moved to Mariveles. If the enemy landed at Bagac it could jeopardize the Army's move into the Peninsula. Sutherland had different plans. He told Colonel Howard that the 4th Marines would become the primary beach defense unit on Corregidor. Although this was not the field role that Howard sought, it was nevertheless a very important assignment. The Army had no infantry unit on Corregidor and with the campaign entering a very critical stage there was clearly a pressing need to ensure the protection of the ultimate U.S. bastion in the Philippines. Before returning to Olongapo Colonel Howard stopped to see Admiral Hart to inform him of the Army's plans for the regiment. The CinCAF told Howard that he was not going to release the 1st Battalion of Howard's unit to the Army just yet, because it was still needed to protect the Naval Base at Mariveles. Other than that, Howard was to comply with the Army's orders.[7]

Before departing for Olongapo Colonel Howard ran into Admiral Rockwell. It was then that Howard learned that the 16th Naval District was moving to The Rock. Howard told the admiral of his instructions to place the regiment, less the 1st Battalion, under Army control. Rockwell then ordered Howard to destroy the Olongapo Naval Station at once.

Some have suggested that the "relegation" of the 4th Marines to Corregidor reflected the Army's bias (in particular, MacArthur's) against the Corps by thus keeping the Marines off the front lines on Bataan. There may have been some element of truth to that—MacArthur clearly did not particularly care for the Marine Corps, and occasionally would openly say so. It should be pointed out, however, that days earlier Lieutenant Colonel Clement, at a USAFFE staff meeting where he was representing the Asiatic Fleet and the 16th Naval District, had pointed out to General Sutherland that the 4th Marines had not had a chance to operate in the field as a regiment for years due to the limited training areas available in Shanghai.[8] That clearly influenced the Army's thinking about the regiment. As mentioned above, the beach defense assignment at Corregidor was, without question, a vitally important mission since Corregidor had no infantry element and it was there that USAFFE Headquarters and the Philippine government was moving.

GOODBYE OLONGAPO

When Howard returned to Olongapo late that day he issued instructions for the destruction of the Naval Station. A detachment to perform the mission was formed under control of Major Francis "Joe" Williams. Williams was ordered to destroy anything of value to the Japanese before pulling out for Bataan. Meanwhile, the remainder of the regiment, Headquarters and Service Companies and the 2nd Battalion, loaded supplies on board the limited number of trucks that were available and prepared to depart for Mariveles. By this time the regiment was better armed with anti-aircraft weapons. The Marines had salvaged nineteen .50-caliber machine guns from the PBYs that had been burned or sunk in the Japanese strafing attack of 12 December.

There was concern that if the Japanese advanced rapidly southward from the Lingayen area the escape route from Olongapo along the only road that led to the east might be cut. The rapidly changing situation in the North Luzon Force area was a real concern to Colonel Howard. He therefore dispatched radio-equipped motorcycle patrols into the area northeast of Olongapo to provide him with information about the progress of the Japanese as they advanced southward.

The Regimental R-4, Major Ridgely, supervised the loading of supplies and equipment. The movement started at 2000 hours on the night of the 24th and continued over the next two days. Lieutenant Colonel Curtis, the regimental XO, departed with the first group to head south. The 4th Marines requested ten trucks from the Army to help them make the move to southern Bataan, but none could be spared. The 16th Naval District, however, was able to send trucks with Navy drivers to help the regiment upload its supplies. Fortunately, the distance from Olongapo to Mariveles was not very great, thus permitting most of the trucks to make a couple of roundtrips each day, even as the roads became increasingly clogged with Army troops and vehicles retreating into Bataan.

On Christmas Day the garrison on nearby Fort Wint started to evacuate from Grande Island. Having only a limited amount of motor vehicles (which was normal for a coast artillery unit), the Army needed help moving their equipment and ammunition into Bataan. There were over five hundred American and Philippine Army troops on Fort Wint. The most important assets that could be evacuated were two 155-mm guns and four 3-inch anti-aircraft guns, plus their ammunition. The 4th Marines provided some of its limited quantity of vehicles for the Army troops to move these guns and other supplies. As they left Grande Island the Army personnel rendered inoperable the fixed coast artillery weapons that could not be moved. The Japanese were to get Fort Wint without a fight. The only real hindrance the Japanese encountered when they took control of Subic Bay was the Navy mines that were left in place when the area was evacuated. The Japanese had to sweep the mines before they could make use of the harbor.[9]

Once the majority of the regiment had departed on the evening of 26 December Major Williams and his men burned or blew up most of the facilities of the Olongapo Naval Station. The old armored cruiser *Rochester* was towed out into Subic Bay in an attempt the block the entrance. After the charges were set in the ship the scuttling party departed expecting the explosion would sink the old cruiser in the ship channel, thus blocking it. However, the mooring lines separated and *Rochester* drifted into deeper water by the time the explosion blew part of the ship's bottom out; she sank in about eighty feet of water. At least she would be of no possible use to the enemy.

Most of the buildings of the base were destroyed. One of the last to go was the Naval Station power plant. It went up in a spectacular explosion that sent flames several hundred feet into the air. Since the Marine Barracks was located so close to the town of Olongapo Williams decided to leave it untouched. Shortly after the regiment pulled out for Mariveles the residents of Olongapo set fire to some of the buildings in the town. The fire spread to the abandoned Marine Barracks, consuming it in the blaze. Major Williams and his men were heading south to Mariveles before midnight.[10]

During the 24th the various Navy elements in the Manila area were informed of the order to fall back to Bataan and Corregidor. Lieutenant (junior grade) Wheeler received word that Manila was to be declared an Open City the next day. Using sailors and civilian labor, several commandeered trucks were loaded with food and dispatched to Bataan. On Christmas Day Wheeler, his senior chief, and several enlisted men departed for the Peninsula. Prior to leaving he received permission to throw the warehouse open so the local population could take what they wanted from the remaining stocks, most of which was cold storage food items that were difficult to transport and store on Bataan. Better the Filipinos get the goods rather than the Japanese.[11]

At the ruined Cavite Navy Yard and nearby Sangley Point sailors loaded the few remaining supplies, mostly fuel drums, on board minesweepers and barges for movement to Bataan. The PNAB contractors on Sangley Point were directed to either evacuate their heavy equipment to Mariveles or destroy it. The Japanese made heavy air attacks on the port area of Manila that day. Several small inter-island steamers were hit and sunk or set on fire.

On the morning of the 24th *Canopus*, still camouflaged at the Manila waterfront, received orders to load supplies and proceed to Mariveles Harbor. By this time the Old Lady had increased her own anti-aircraft armament by mounting weapons salvaged from Cavite. She now had sixteen machine guns, including ten .50-caliber weapons. During the day her crew moved supplies on board while simultaneously servicing the submarines *Shark* and *S-39*. When the two subs departed, the tender completed her preparations to get under way. She backed away from Pier 4 at 2300 hours on Christmas Eve and anchored during the early morning hours in the North Channel between Corregidor and Bataan. The next day Mamasan moved into Mariveles Harbor and began to set up shop for the siege. As *Canopus* pulled away from the Manila waterfront the gunboat *Mindanao* was entering the harbor. The next day Lieutenant Commander McCracken topped off his ship's fuel tanks at Pier 7 before heading back out to Corregidor.[12]

THE DEPATURE OF ADMIRAL HART

Christmas Day, 1941. The situation in the Philippines was becoming increasingly chaotic. It was time for Admiral Hart to depart for the Indies to take command of the surface elements of the Asiatic Fleet that were operating in the south. The remaining Navy and Marine elements in the Manila Bay area would revert to the command of Admiral Rockwell.

The fastest way for Hart to get to Java was by Navy PBY flying boat. Early that morning a PBY had flown Major General Brereton, USA, and nineteen other passengers from Laguna de Bay to Java. The much-overloaded flying boat had just managed to take off from the lake. Now preparations were being made to get the CinCAF out by the same means. There were few PatWing 10 aircraft left in the Philippines, and every day the enemy was tightening his control of the sky over Luzon as increasing numbers of Japanese Army fighters and bombers moved into airfields in the Philippines.

Two PBYs were moored near the shore of Laguna de Bay waiting for final instructions to pick up Admiral Hart and his immediate staff when suddenly two enemy twin-engined bombers swept in at low altitude and machine-gunned the moored Navy planes. They made several passes, and although clearly hit by return fire from PBY crewmen who fought back using the guns on board their aircraft, the Japanese destroyed one of the flying boats and left the other riddled with holes. The only other PBY still on Luzon was an unserviceable aircraft in a hangar on Sangley Point. It was clear that Admiral Hart was not going to get out via aircraft.[13]

The only option at this point was to go by submarine. Still in Manila Bay was the submarine *Shark*. At 0200 on 26 December Admiral Thomas Hart and fifteen members of his staff boarded the sub for the voyage to Soerabaya, Java. It was not until the evening of New Year's Day that *Shark* arrived at the Dutch naval base. During that time Hart was largely out of contact with his own command and Washington. When he arrived and reestablished communications it became apparent that relations with the Army had continued to deteriorate.

When Hart arrived in Java, waiting for him was a 29 December message from Admiral Stark. In it the CNO highlighted extracts from a 26 December message from MacArthur to General Marshall, complaining of a lack of naval support in the Philippines. Admiral Stark explained to the CinCAF that he realized MacArthur's messages were based on "impression," but that MacArthur's complaints were so persistent that the Navy needed to undertake some "calculated risks" to try to help the Army.[14] Hart had not seen these messages while on board *Shark*. On 2 January Hart felt compelled to send the following message to the OPNAV staff in Washington:

> Having sensed since about 10 December that this fleet might be charged with the loss of the Philippines I have kept record straight to prove otherwise. I really think that my preceding dispatches with your general knowledge of the situation should be sufficient to combat erroneous impressions. A defeat in the Philippines will be primarily incident to total loss of control of the air which followed close upon first Japanese attack made nine hours after that on Pearl Harbor. It is axiomatic that fleets must have basing facilities for their operations and our base had had no fighter protection whatsoever which as made effective by radar system I have repeatedly pointed out as the first essential. In consequence of enemy's complete freedom in the air even our submarines have now been forced out of Manila Bay. Incidentally I fear that they held there too long. Withdrawal of surface ships was according to your plan and please recall

> that on 27 October I proposed to fight the campaign from Manila Bay with this entire fleet. Your rejection of that proposal was correct and we should receive your full defense against criticism in following the plan. After making due allowance for the fact that results with submarines come slowly I confess disappointment with their effect as thus far known but as yet I am unable to judge whether this is due to their inefficiency or to the excellence of enemy antisubmarine measures. As regards taking greater risks I have followed your message which mentioned the sacrifice of British major units and I feel that I should not expend my surface forces except on chances of large results. At present those chances are slim due to coverage of enemy surface by air and to our own lack of any air protection. . . . I will project my own operations as far northward as possible. I was personally reluctant to leave Manila largely because I expected unfounded criticism of the step. I am now making estimate of situation as seen from here and will confer with allies at Batavia on 4 January.[15]

At this point Admiral Hart's role in the defense of the Philippines essentially ended. From the time he arrived in Java he was completely consumed with the desperate Allied attempt to stem the Japanese power drive into the Indies. Despite the formation of the American-British-Dutch-Australian (ABDA) command in an attempt to coordinate the multinational effort to hold Singapore, Sumatra, and Java, the Japanese quickly overwhelmed the Allies.

By 15 February Singapore fell, and on 8 March the Dutch surrendered on Java, so rapid and powerful was the enemy offensive to seize the key objectives south of the Philippines—the areas that the Japanese had really gone to war for. The Japanese isolated the Philippines much faster than anyone could have imagined before the start of the war. MacArthur's claims that the Islands could have been reinforced if only the Navy would put its mind to it were just so much nonsense, yet another one of his delusions.

From early January until the fall of Java Japanese strength moving south into the Indies was overwhelming. There was never any chance that the Asiatic Fleet, even had it received assistance from the British, Dutch, and Australians, would be able to fight its way northward to the Philippines. Indeed, the Allies were barely able to slow the Japanese advance into the Indies and were, of course, unable to stop it.

On 12 February Dutch admiral Helfrich replaced Admiral Hart as the commander of Allied naval forces in the Indies. On the 16th of that month Hart left Java for the United States. Publicly the reason given was ill health and his age (Hart was sixty-four, already beyond the normal retirement age). Senior Navy officers in the Asiatic Fleet and in Washington who knew better realized what had really happened. Highly competent, always a realist, and never concerned about personal publicity, Hart's reputation had been seriously damaged by MacArthur's attacks—and the Navy knew it. As more and more information about what was *really* going on in the Philippines gradually got out, the Navy developed its own impressions of Douglas MacArthur.[16]

RETREAT TO BATAAN

The Army started falling back to Bataan on 24 December when the WPO-3 order was issued. A number of delaying positions from Lingayen Gulf back to Bataan were manned for a day or so each as the Japanese advanced southward. The roughly 20,000 men of the South Luzon Force had to quickly pass through Manila and then turn westward toward Bataan while the 38,000-man North Luzon Force tried to delay the enemy long enough for their companions to make their escape. Meanwhile, thousands of Army Air Force, anti-aircraft, and logistics personnel evacuated their air bases and headed toward Bataan.

The most important units during the withdrawal were the 26th Cavalry Regiment (PS) and the 192nd and 194th Tank Battalions of the Army National Guard. Were it not for the actions of the Scout cavalrymen and the American tanks the Japanese would have overrun the retreating Philippine Army divisions and defeated MacArthur before the end of December. Time and again, the Scout cavalrymen and the tanks covered the retreat of the Philippine Army units as they withdrew toward Bataan. By the end of the first week of January the surviving American and Filipino units were in the Peninsula.

A JAPANESE VICTORY?

As the Americans and Filipinos fell back into the Bataan Peninsula the Japanese thought they were on the verge of victory. Air superiority had been won with unexpected ease in the first three days of the war. The initial landings had gone very well. The U.S. Navy had been forced to withdraw most of its ships well south of Manila Bay. Attacks by American submarines had been little more than a nuisance. The Japanese Army had routed the Americans and Filipinos from the beaches of Lingayen Gulf and Lamon Bay where the main landings were made. Although there had been some stiff opposition from the American tanks and the Scout cavalry, for the most part the Japanese had swept all before them. By the first day of 1942 the 14th Army stood poised north and south of Manila ready for a victorious entry into the capital. Imperial General Headquarters in Tokyo had allocated fifty-five days for the Philippine operation. By the end of December the war was only twenty-four days old and it appeared that with the exception of eliminating the Americans on Corregidor and the other fortified islands—which would clearly require a siege operation—the campaign was virtually over.

Or was it? The 14th Army staff had noted the retreat of Filipino-American forces into Bataan; such a move had not been entirely unexpected. The general feeling in Homma's staff was that there were only 25,000 to 30,000 American and Filipino troops on Bataan, and they must have low morale considering the pounding they had taken during the ten days since the landings at Lingayen Gulf.

On 2 January the Japanese entered Manila. That same day Lieutenant General Homma was informed that Imperial General Headquarters had decided to move up by about a month the planned invasion of Java, which together with Malaya and Sumatra was one of the key objectives that Japan went to war for. Since operations in the Philippines were obviously going so well, Imperial General Headquarters decided that the 14th Army's best formation, the 48th Division, would be withdrawn from the Philippines to give it time to prepare for the accelerated offensive into the Indies. Along with the 48th Division would go most of the Imperial Army and Navy air units that had proved so vital to the rapid success achieved thus far. Despite Homma's protests, the decision stood. Tokyo recognized that the early withdrawal of the best air and ground units from the Philippines might cause operations to slow down a bit, but in their opinion the situation in the Islands was now so favorable that what remained would essentially be mopping up operations.[17]

This turn of events is critical in order to understand what subsequently took place on Bataan. By the end of December the Japanese thought that the campaign was nearly over, with the notable exception of siege operations that would be needed to take the fortified islands at the entrance to Manila Bay. Prior to assaulting Corregidor they expected to meet no more than 30,000 demoralized troops on Bataan, which they thought they would eliminate in a couple of weeks of fighting. Little did the Japanese know that by the beginning of January there were some 80,000 Americans and Filipinos on Bataan alone, with about 10,000 more on Corregidor and the other harbor forts. Although exhausted from the retreat, the Filipino and American troops on Bataan were digging in and preparing their defenses as the Japanese made their victory parade into Manila. The Japanese were to face a far tougher battle than they expected.

CHAPTER 7

Settling in for the Siege

During the last week of December the 14th Army pursued the Filipino-American troops as they retreated toward the Bataan Peninsula. Some pitched battles were fought as the troops fell back, but strangely the Japanese made little use of their air forces to interdict the movement of the Americans and Filipinos as they retreated. Instead, the enemy's air units continued to attack Manila (despite it having been declared an Open City on 26 December), interisland merchant ships still in the Bay, the already-battered American air bases, and the fortified islands at the entrance of Manila Bay.

Meanwhile, considerable numbers of American and Philippine Army troops were already in the Peninsula, taking stock of the supplies that had been accumulated during the hectic week of retreat, and preparing their defenses for the inevitable enemy attack. By this time the Navy and Marine Corps had concentrated their personnel on Bataan and Corregidor.

ONGOING OPERATIONS

While the retreat to Bataan was under way the Navy continued to perform missions to support the Philippine garrison. Now that the Filipino-American forces were concentrating around the entrance of Manila Bay it was the Navy's responsibility to help secure the area. By the start of the last week in December most of the Navy's larger ships had departed for the south, but there were still a few in the Manila Bay area.

The destroyers *Peary* and *Pillsbury* were still in the Bay when WPO-3 was put into effect. Without question the most powerful surface ships the Navy still had in the northern Philippines, they were also the most attractive targets for enemy air attack. Between 17 and 25 December the two destroyers participated in night patrols off the entrance of Manila Bay, including some distance to the north and south. At times one or more of MTB Squadron 3's PT boats accompanied the destroyers. On the night of the 21st *Pillsbury* made a run down part of the eastern side of the island of Mindoro, southwest of Luzon. On the night of the 23rd *Peary* made the same run, accompanied by several PT boats.[1]

With the enemy in control of the air, daylight patrols much beyond the range of Corregidor's anti-aircraft guns was a risky proposition. Both ships were still recovering from the damage that they had suffered during the bombing of the Navy Yard two weeks earlier. *Peary* still lacked a mast and her torpedo and 4-inch gunnery control were both still affected by the damage to their directors. With the Navy Yard bombed out, repairs were now a difficult proposition. The machine shops on the tender *Canopus* were the Navy's best repair facilities left in the Bay, but she was fully occupied in servicing the submarines that were still operating from Manila.

On 24 December as the Navy and Marines received word of the evacuation of Manila, the Japanese made their first air attack on the Mariveles area. There was very little in the way of anti-aircraft fire since the 1st Separate Battalion was still moving some of its guns from Sangley Point, the Army's anti-aircraft units on Luzon were still en route to Bataan, and Corregidor was too far away to be of much hindrance to the Japanese. Bombs hit the former Vichy French cargo ship *Si-Kiang*; she took on a list and started to burn. The minesweeper *Finch* came close alongside and played her fire hoses on the burning ship, but she could not be saved. By this time most of the ship's cargo of gasoline had been off-loaded onto Bataan—and would be of considerable use during the siege. Unfortunately, indeed tragically, for the men on Bataan the ship's 2,500 tons of flour was lost. *Si-Kiang* burned four more days before she sank. There was a squad of Marines on board guarding the ship when she was attacked; men from A Company of the 1st Battalion, 4th Marines. Two Marines were killed, Private First Class George Moore and Private First Class Grady Poole. Three more Marines were wounded, one seriously. Also on the 24th the skippers of the two destroyers still in the Bay went to the Marsman Building, requesting that they be allowed to make a break for the Indies. Their request was denied.[2]

On the 26th Japanese aircraft went after the two destroyers. *Peary* and *Pillsbury* were both just east of The Rock when the enemy aircraft arrived. Fortunately, both had steam up and could quickly get under way and start to maneuver. However, their commanding officers were ashore on Corregidor meeting with Admiral Rockwell. With their XOs at the con, both ships headed for the open water in the middle of the Bay farther to the east of Corregidor. The two ships made radical high-speed maneuvers as they fired their 3-inch anti-aircraft weapons and machine guns at the attackers. It was here that the speed and maneuverability of a destroyer proved to be a great advantage. Waiting until the enemy planes had dropped their loads, the ships' helms were then put hard over to avoid the falling bombs. Five separate attacks were made on *Peary* and one on *Pillsbury*.

Ashore on Corregidor men from all the services held their breath as they watched the Japanese aircraft make attack after attack, with geysers of water rising close to the ships when the enemy made a near miss. Apparently no Japanese aircraft were lost, but neither did the bombers score a hit on the nimble destroyers. The worst that happened were some near misses that peppered the ships' hulls with fragments. There were no casualties.

That evening the two destroyer captains discussed their situation with Admiral Rockwell. It was clear that if they stayed in Manila Bay it was only a matter of time before the Japanese damaged or sank them. They either had to make their escape—soon—or should be regarded as good as lost. Rockwell agreed; both destroyers were ordered to make their run to the south that night under cover of darkness. Both ships took some passengers on board before they sailed. With their departure the largest surface combatants the Navy still had in the northern Philippines were the river gunboats and minesweepers of the Inshore Patrol.[3]

The three Philippine Army Q-boats established a new base at Lamao on Bataan's east coast. Two Coast and Geodeytic Survey ships, *Research* and *Fathomer*, accompanied the Q-boats to their new home. The *Fathomer* carried supplies and equipment for the Filipino boats. The *Research* was grounded off the mouth of the Diginin River on Bataan's east coast and became a berth for the crews of the Q-boats. Several Q-boats that were under construction at local shipyards were destroyed when Manila was evacuated. The Philippine Army Off Shore Patrol (OSP) therefore consisted of the Q-111 "Luzon," the Q-112 "Abra," and the Q-113 "Agusan," under the command of Captain Alberto Navarete, Philippine Army. Each boat had a crew of 8–10 officers and men, and all were armed with two 18-inch torpedoes, two .50-caliber machine guns, and four depth charges. The OSP had 42 officers and 173 men, more than enough to provide two crews for each Q-boat, plus maintenance personnel.[4] Later in January the OSP squadron took over a few small motor vessels that were armed with machine guns and used to patrol in the Bay.[5]

Due to their smaller size and more limited armament it seemed appropriate that the Q-boats patrol inside the Bay, while the larger American PTs took responsibility for the area north and south of the entrance to the Bay, including off the west coast of Bataan. A strange command system was developed for the Q-boats, since they were still under Army control. The OSP was attached to the

A Philippine Army Q-boat passing the U.S. submarine S-41 *in Manila Bay*
Source: MacArthur Memorial, Norfolk, Va.

Army's II Philippine Corps, the unit responsible for operations on the eastern half of Bataan. The activities of the Q-boats were to be coordinated with the Navy, who would also help maintain the Philippine Army boats.

Already the lack of spare parts was starting to affect PT operations. When the Cavite Navy Yard was bombed Squadron 3 lost most of its spare parts. Upon arrival of the squadron in the Philippines in September Lieutenant John D. Bulkeley had ordered that nine of the spare engines be stored in private garages in Manila in an attempt to disperse some of the most critical equipment. Three of these had not been retrieved in time when the Japanese entered the capital and were lost. Of the remaining six that had been moved across the Bay by barge, two were destroyed on Corregidor. With each boat mounting three 1,200 horsepower Packard engines, a total of four spares to share among the six boats of the squadron was not much. The squadron was going to have to rely a lot on the ability of *Canopus* and *Pigeon* to perform maintenance and repairs. Fortunately, the dry dock *Dewey* was also available in case the boats needed to get out of the water for repairs or servicing.[6]

THE MOVE TO CORREGIDOR

When the last elements of the 4th Marines reached Mariveles they bivouacked west of the town in an area known as Camp Carefree. By the evening of Christmas Day most of the Marines in the Philippines were located there. Tents were pitched, foxholes dug, and supplies inventoried as the men waited orders for the next move. Batteries A and C of the 1st Separate Battalion worked to emplace their 3-inch guns and .50-caliber machine guns to protect the area around the Naval Section Base. Although Colonel Howard now had command of the 1st Separate Battalion, it was technically not yet the 3rd Battalion, 4th Marines. That administrative change took place on 1 January.

On the morning of the 26th orders were issued to start transferring the regiment to Corregidor. That evening, 14 officers and 397 men from the 1st Separate Battalion were ferried to The Rock on minesweepers. Landing at Corregidor's North Dock, the men were moved on the island's trolley system to their temporary home, Middleside Barracks, an early 1900s' structure originally built to house part of the island's Army coast artillery garrison.

The next night more of the regiment followed, the remainder of the 1st Separate Battalion (less the two batteries that would stay at Mariveles for air defense), most of the 2nd Battalion, and part of the Regimental Headquarters and Service Companies. During the night of the 28th almost all of the remainder of the regiment completed the crossing, mostly the 1st Battalion and the rest of the Headquarters and Service units. A few men from Service Company remained at Mariveles to complete the transfer of the rest of the regiment's supplies and equipment to Corregidor.

When the 4th Marines arrived they were well supplied by the standards of the Philippine Campaign. In addition to six months rations, the regiment had a two-year supply of summer khaki uniforms, a complete 100-bed hospital, and a minimum of ten units of fire for all weapons. By this time the 4th Marines was considerably overstrength in mortars, machine guns, and 37-mm guns compared to what was called for in its 1935 T/O. The regiment's tents would soon be turned over to the Army; they would be used by the field hospitals on Bataan. The rest of the medical equipment not needed for the battalion aid stations was handed over to the Army's hospital in Malinta Tunnel.[7]

When the main body of the 4th Marines moved to Corregidor some Marines remained on Bataan. This included Batteries A and C from the 1st Separate Battalion that manned 3-inch and .50-caliber machine guns around Mariveles, the Marine radar detachment that was now located on Bataan's east coast, and a detachment to guard MacArthur's forward command post on Bataan, about five miles up the west coast from Mariveles. Altogether, about 230 Marines remained on Bataan.

CORREGIDOR—AMERICA'S GIBRALTAR IN THE FAR EAST

The Marines had heard many rumors about the famed fortress of Corregidor, although few, if any, had ever been on it before. The Rock was about four miles long from east to west. Officially, the 1,735 acres of Corregidor Island was Fort Mills. For twenty years before World War II Corregidor was considered very good duty by Army personnel.

Shaped like a huge tadpole, the island was divided into four distinct areas. Farthest to the west was the head of the island, known as Topside. Most of the fixed concrete gun emplacements were located there. The island's parade ground was surrounded by officers' quarters, the Post Headquarters, and the so-called "Mile Long Barracks," long home to the U.S. Army Coast Artillery Regiments that garrisoned the fortress. At its highest elevation Topside was 628 feet above sea level. Steep cliffs rose from the sea along much of its perimeter.

Next came Middleside. It was the somewhat lower ground to the east of Topside. The island's power and cold storage plants were there, along with the large concrete barracks that the Marines were occupying. The southern part of this portion of the island ended in what was known as Government Ravine, where vaults to store the Philippine government's gold and silver reserves were located. The eastern portion of Middleside sloped down to the next part of the island, Bottomside. The old Spanish fort was located at just about the point the two areas merged.

Bottomside was the lowest portion of the island. A narrow strip of land with three concrete piers (including the large North Dock where the Marines had landed) on its north side and another pier, the Mine Wharf, on the south side, Bottomside was also the home to most of the Filipino civilians who lived on Corregidor. Barrio San Jose occupied most of Bottomside; its population made their living as employees of the U.S. Army.

Immediately to the east of Bottomside, and totally dominating it, was Malinta Hill. Rapidly rising to a height of nearly four hundred feet, Malinta Hill was the site of the famous tunnel system that the Army had built during the 1930s. Skirting the letter of the law of the Washington and London Naval Treaties that prohibited improvement to fortifications in the Western Pacific, Malinta Tunnel was build under the auspices of a storage system, which it clearly was. However, the tunnel system was also intended to house the Army headquarters in the Philippines in the event of war, a hospital system, and provide protection for a large part of Corregidor's garrison. Importantly, there was sufficient space to store huge amounts of supplies. The main tunnel running from east to west was some nine hundred feet long and thirty feet wide. It had twenty-four side, or lateral, tunnels, each about two hundred feet in length. To the north of the main shaft was the hospital complex, and to the south an extensive storage system. A long narrow passageway connected the southern part of the storage area to the

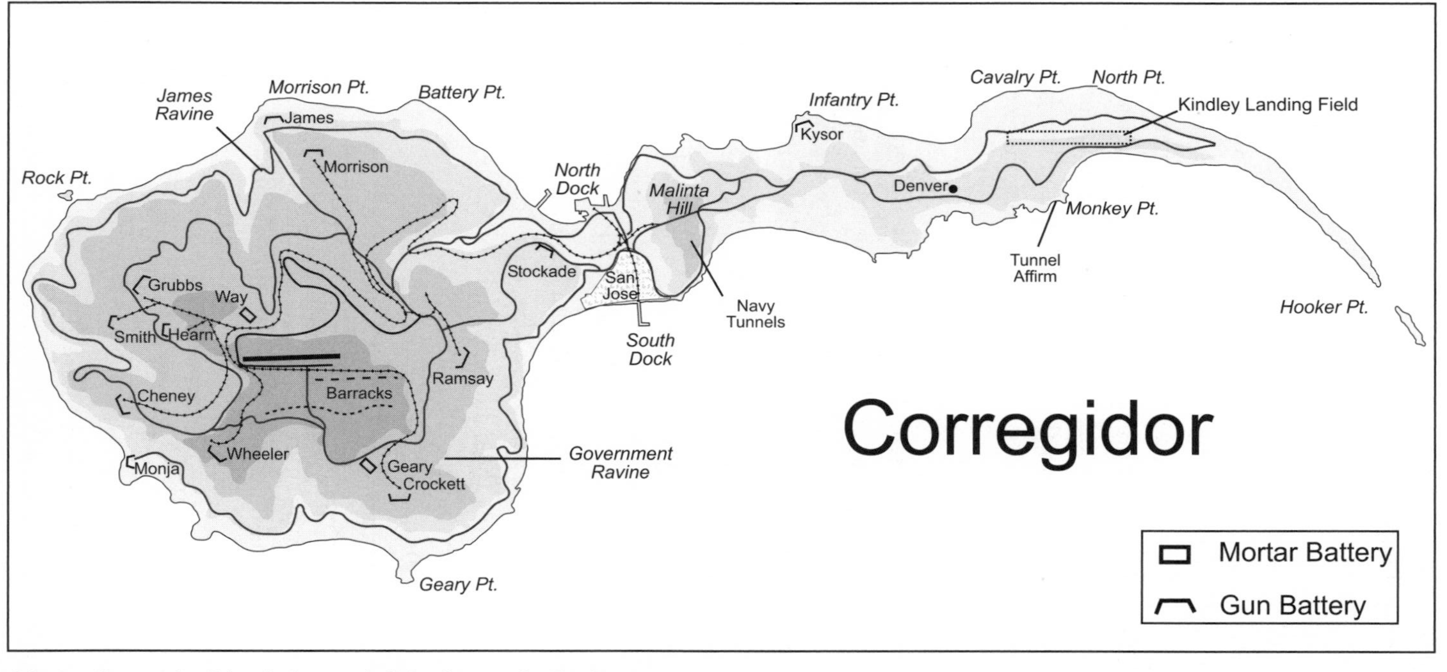

Map 3. Corregidor Island, America's Gibraltar in the Far East

Navy's Tunnel Queen on the southwest side of Malinta Hill. It was an extensive tunnel system, and of vital importance to the garrison.

Beyond the east entrance to Malinta Tunnel was the Tail, the easternmost portion of The Rock. Long and narrow, the Tail extended nearly four thousand yards from the tunnel to Hooker Point, the extreme eastern tip of the island. As one proceeds farther to the east the Tail narrows to only one to two hundred yards width. Much of the north and south shore of the Tail is sheer cliffs twenty to fifty feet straight up from very narrow beaches, although there are a few points where the hillsides of the Tail slope more gently down to the water's edge. There were few gun prewar batteries in this area of the island, but Corregidor's small airstrip, Kindley Field, occupied the flattest portion of the Tail. Just south of Kindley Field on Monkey Point was Tunnel Afirm, the Asiatic Fleet's secret radio intercept facility.[8]

Running from Kindley Field through Malinta Tunnel and all the way to Topside was the electric trolley system. Built long before World War II, the trolley served the needs of the island's military and civilian communities with numerous stops, including at all the major fixed gun batteries. Most of the Marines had ridden the trolley from North Dock to Middleside Barracks when they arrived on the island. Corregidor's seacoast armament will be described in detail later.[9]

When the Marines arrived on the island there were already about seven thousand Army troops there, the vast majority of whom were the prewar garrison. On 24 December USAFFE Headquarters had moved from Manila to the island. Long before that Corregidor had been home to the Headquarters of the Harbor Defenses of Manila and Subic Bays, under command of Major General George F. Moore, USA. The main Army units on Corregidor were the all-American 59th and 60th and the Philippine Scout 91st and 92nd Coast Artillery Regiments. The 59th manned most of the fixed heavy guns and mortars while the 60th was the primary anti-aircraft unit. The two Scout regiments mostly manned the mobile 155-mm guns and smaller fixed coast artillery weapons, the beach defense light artillery, and controlled the Army's mines. Elements of all these Army regiments also manned the other three, much smaller, forts at the entrance to Manila Bay.

About a mile south of Corregidor was Caballo Island—Fort Hughes. While the eastern portion of this small island was just above sea level, the center and western portions rose high above the ocean, mostly flanked by steep cliffs. Two single-gun 14-inch batteries were the heaviest weapons on Fort Hughes. Additionally, in the center of the island was Battery Craighill with four 12-inch mortars. Smaller 6-inch, 155-mm, and 3-inch batteries completed the armament of this fort. A 350-foot-long tunnel ran beside the mortar battery and also housed the island's headquarters during wartime. Two batteries from the 59th Coast Artillery were the pre-war garrison of Fort Hughes, nowhere near enough personnel to man the weapons and defend the beaches. This lack of Army manpower resulted in a considerable Navy and Marine Corps presence gradually being built up on Caballo Island.

About five miles farther to the south was tiny El Fraile Island. In the decade before World War I this island of less than one acre had been turned into an amazing concrete fortress, Fort Drum. Looking very much like a warship, Fort Drum was manned by E Battery of the 59th Coast Artillery Regiment. The two heavily armored 14-inch gun turrets of the so-called "concrete battleship" were to prove the most effective of all the weapons in the harbor defenses during the siege.

Finally there was Fort Frank on Carabao Island. Sitting a mere five hundred yards from the Cavite shoreline, this fort was recognized as being exposed to enemy attack. However, an underground tunnel system connected most of the gun batteries, which included two single-gun 14-inch emplacements, an eight-weapon 12-inch mortar battery, four 155-mm guns, and a battery of 3-inch anti-aircraft weapons. Because most of the island's shoreline was steep cliffs, it was thought that taking Fort Frank would be a tough proposition. Following the evacuation of Fort Wint at the entrance of Subic Bay Fort Frank's garrison was reinforced so that by the end of December it consisted of two batteries of Philippine Scouts and some Philippine Army coast artillery personnel.

Fort Drum, the U.S. Army's concrete battleship at the entrance to Manila Bay

Source: MacArthur Memorial, Norfolk, Va.

A summary of the seacoast armament of Corregidor and the other forts is shown in the table below. For comparison purposes Fort Wint at the entrance to Subic Bay is also included. DG refers to disappearing guns, LRG are long-range guns, and Ped is a pedestal-mounted weapon. All the weapons listed in the table were fixed except the 155-mm guns, most of which were on mounts that allowed the gun to be removed. The weapons listed below represent a total of thirty-one fixed batteries, not including the semimobile 155s. Anti-aircraft weapons and light beach defense artillery are not listed in the table (the 3-inch guns included in the table were rapid-fire coast defense weapons).

TABLE 7.1
Seacoast Armament of the Harbor Defenses of Manila and Subic Bays

	Turrett	14" DG	12" LRG	12" DG	12" Mortar	10" DG	155-mm gun	6" DG or Ped	3" gun
Mills			2	6	12	2	19	5	10
Hughes		2			4		2	2	2
Drum	4							4	1
Frank		2			8		4		
Wint						2	2	4	4

Source: Ancheta, *The Wainwright Papers*, vol. II, 54–57.

On Corregidor were twenty 3-inch anti-aircraft guns and about forty .50-caliber machine guns of the 60th Coast Artillery Regiment. The 60th also had one 3-inch battery on southern Bataan to interlock with the island's fire. There were also four 3-inch guns on Forts Frank and Hughes, plus two on the top deck of Fort Drum. At the start of the war one battery of the 60th Coast Artillery was armed with the more modern mechanical time fuze for its 3-inch shells, thus allowing it to reach altitudes of about 30,000 feet. This was the only anti-aircraft battery in the entire Philippines with this capability when war started.

Although the coast artillery troops always had a secondary mission to fight as beach defense troops the Army had never dedicated an infantry unit to defend Corregidor's beaches. This is why the assignment of the 4th Marines to that role was an important mission. As the siege progressed the number of personnel assigned to the 4th Marines steadily grew.

FIRST BOMBING OF THE ROCK

At 0800 on the morning of the 29th Colonel Howard met with Major General Moore, Corregidor's commander. Moore appointed Howard as commanding officer of the beach defense of Corregidor, taking the place of Lieutenant Commander D. Asmus, an Army coast artillery officer. With Howard now the beach defense commander, Asmus took over as the officer in charge of the beach defense artillery, mostly 75-mm weapons manned by Philippine Scout coast artillerymen. Following the meeting with General Moore, Howard made a tour of Corregidor with Moore's intelligence officer, Colonel Samuel McCullough.

Colonel Howard returned from his reconnaissance of the island around 1100. Defense sectors for each battalion were being mapped out by the regimental staff and the men were settling in to their new surroundings when the island's air raid sirens sounded. It was 1140 and the first Japanese air attack to strike Corregidor was about to begin.

Thinking that they would have no real problem mopping up resistance on Bataan, the Japanese were already looking ahead to the siege of Corregidor. For the first three weeks of the war few enemy aircraft had ventured close to the fortified islands. On those few occasions that the islands' anti-aircraft guns had fired it was on formations of enemy planes going to or returning from bombing raids on other targets in the Manila area. On 10 December, for example, The Rock's

Colonel Howard (center), with Major General Moore, USA, (right), the harbor defense commander, and Lieutenant Colonel Anderson, the commander of the 2nd Battalion, 4th Marines

Source: USMC Historical Division, Quantico, Va.

anti-aircraft gunners had fired over three hundred rounds at a Japanese bomber formation departing from raids on Manila. There had been many air raid alerts in the past three weeks but no enemy bombs had fallen on Corregidor, nor Forts Hughes, Drum, or Frank. That was all about to change.

It was a rare joint Imperial Army-Navy air attack, and a big one. Eighteen Japanese Army Ki-21 Sally and twenty-two Ki-48 Lily medium bombers were joined by forty-one Imperial Navy Bettys and thirty-six Nells. The Army also committed eighteen Ki-30 light bombers in a dive-bombing role. 29 December was to be the first of several days of raids intended to reduce the fortified islands—particularly Corregidor. A few Ki-27 Nate fighters were also hovering in the area, not really expecting any resistance from the few remaining P-40s and P-35s of the FEAF. They were correct; none of the twenty-one American fighters now based on Bataan attempted to interfere with the raid.

Although they encountered no aerial opposition, the Japanese bomber formations were met with fierce anti-aircraft fire. Possibly due to the general ineffectiveness of American anti-aircraft defenses on Luzon up to this point, the initial wave of Japanese Army bombers approached Corregidor at about 18,000–20,000 feet. That put them well within range of the twenty 3-inch anti-aircraft guns on The Rock. The four anti-aircraft guns at nearby Fort Hughes were also close enough to engage many of the enemy bombers that concentrated on Corregidor, as was the battery located on southern Bataan. When the light bombers went into their dives they were met with intense fire from the island's .50-caliber machine guns, much of it coming from specially built wooden and metal towers that placed the weapons above Corregidor's foliage.[10]

The Marines at Middleside Barracks heard the air raid sirens. The scream of the sirens was followed by the sharp crack of the Army 3-inch anti-aircraft guns. Next came the bombs, lots of bombs. The entire area of Middleside and Topside erupted in a hurricane of explosions. Almost the entire regiment took cover on the bottom floor of the building. As one Marine put it, "There we were,—the whole regiment flat on our bellies on the lower deck of Middleside Barracks!"[11] The movement of the men into the barracks without question saved many lives.

When the Army constructed most of its big barracks buildings on Corregidor in the early 1900s they were designed so that the bottom floor of the structure had a thick ceiling of reinforced concrete intended to resist bombs and shellfire. Several bombs hit the top floors of the structure, but the thick roof of the ground floor stopped the blast effect. Windows and doors were blown out and nearby light structures destroyed or badly damaged, but Middleside Barracks weathered the bombing well. Only one bomb penetrated all the way to the bottom floor before it exploded. Despite the intense bombing, only one Marine was killed that day, Corporal V. W. Murphy.

Not all of the Marines had moved to Corregidor by the time the first raid took place on 29 December. In addition to Batteries A and C that were still at Mariveles to provide air defense, there were a small number of men from the Regimental Service Company still loading supplies for movement to Corregidor. Several Marines were on one of the hills above Camp Carefree to the west of Mariveles when the raid started. For the next two hours they watched in amazement as the Japanese bombers made run after run over the island in the face of intense anti-aircraft fire from the defenders. As the last wave of enemy planes approached the Marines noticed that some Japanese aircraft were attacking the Mariveles Harbor area. Suddenly they saw many bombs exploding on the hillsides and in the water around *Canopus*. Next they saw smoke erupt from the ship. The Old Lady had been hit.

Canopus had arrived at Mariveles on Christmas morning. She tied up in Caracol Cove, a tiny inlet on the eastern side of the harbor. Just south of the ship was a little hill that had been the home of Station C in the mid-1930s. Commander Sackett immediately started setting up shop in the area. It was expected that *Canopus* would continue to service submarines as long as possible. Few could have guessed at the time that as the siege progressed *Canopus* would become the most important repair facility on Bataan. Nowhere else were there machine shops, mechanics, and electricians of the quality that the Old Lady brought to Bataan.

Attempts were made to camouflage the ship with nets, but the nearby terrain did not really lend itself to hiding such a large ship. Her deck was painted green in an attempt to help her blend in with the nearby hills. Branches and foliage were attached to the stack and masts. However, the efforts at concealment certainly did not fool the Japanese who arrived over Mariveles around 1345. The ship was at Battle Stations, with her 3-inch anti-aircraft guns and machine guns manned and ready. Some of the crew were ashore when the enemy attacked. A few of the men manned machine guns atop the little hill just south of where the ship was moored. From their hilltop they had a perfect view of the bombing of Corregidor. These men and the crew still on the ship saw one of the last groups of Japanese planes veer off to attack *Canopus*.

The nine planes dropped thirty-six bombs. Only one hit, but it nearly destroyed the ship. The bomb, which may have been a 250-kilogram (550-pound) delayed fuze weapon, struck aft near the centerline of the ship. It penetrated several decks and burst atop the propeller shaft casing, underneath the aft magazine. The blast buckled several of the decks in the area around the explosion. Six sailors in the engine room and the aft casualty dressing station were killed or later died of wounds and another six were injured by the blast, fragments, or due to scalding from smashed steam pipes. Immediately a fire started almost directly beneath the magazine that was loaded with 3-inch and 5-inch ammunition.

The crew turned to fighting the fires. Commander Sackett ordered the after magazine flooded, but damage to bulkheads and decks allowed water to escape and resulted in the flooding progressing slowly. The boilers were secured until the breaks in the steam lines could be dealt with. As the men fought the blaze, small explosions could be heard as some of the shells that had been flung from the magazine burst after coming into contact with the fire. There was clearly a real danger that the ship would blow up.

At this point Gunner's Mate 1st Class Zygmond Budzja crawled into the magazine with a fire hose to put the main blaze out at the source. Were it not for this courageous act the ship might have been lost. By 1715 the last of the fires were out. The crew then set to work controlling and repairing the rest of the damage. A considerable amount of the ammunition in the after magazine was rendered useless due to the fires and flooding, but the ship was saved. That evening one of her motor launches was the scene of a burial at sea in the middle of Mariveles Harbor for the sailors killed in the bombing.

Despite her damage, the Old Lady continued to service submarines that entered Mariveles Harbor after the sun went down. *S-36*, *S-39*, *Permit*, *Sturgeon*, and *Stingray* loaded supplies and some Asiatic Fleet submarine personnel before they departed for either safer waters in the south or for patrols around the Philippines.[12] *Canopus* was still in the fight.

Canopus was not the only Navy ship to have a narrow escape that day. For the past week *Mindanao* had been a busy ship. She had led a number of merchant ships through the minefield channel and patrolled the area along the south shore of Manila Bay where the Japanese approaching from southern Luzon might appear at any time.

On the morning of the 29th the gunboat was swinging on her anchor, just off Corregidor's Tail in South Harbor. When the Japanese bombers approached from the east she opened fire with her 3-inch guns, followed by her machine guns as the enemy light bombers went into their dives. As the bombers dropped their loads on Kindley Field a number of bombs went into the water, very close to *Mindanao*.

Ashore on a ridgeline not far from the ship was the Army's Battery D, 60th Coast Artillery (Battery "Denver"). The Army gunners also opened fire on the first wave of enemy planes, their fire being directed by the unit's strong and respected 1st Sergeant Dewey Brady who supervised the firing of the four 3-inch guns from atop a large concrete water tank that overlooked the sandbagged gun pits. Suddenly bombs burst in the gun position, driving the personnel to the bottom of the pits. Denver Battery temporarily ceased firing; a few gunners had been wounded.

Some of the Army personnel looked down from their hilltop and saw little *Mindanao* disappear behind multiple geysers as Japanese bombs straddled the ship. Rocking back and forth from the wash created by the near misses, the gunboat continued to fire at the enemy aircraft. That was enough for the Army gunners—if the Navy could continue to shoot, so could they.

Mindanao was straddled four times within twenty minutes; several bombs landed less than one hundred yards from the ship. One bomb struck a cliff on Corregidor. Since the ship was only about sixty yards offshore, she was pelted with fragments. Four men, including one of the gunboat's Chinese cooks who had elected to sail with the ship from Hong Kong, were wounded. Fortunately the damage from the bomb fragments was slight. Having expended thirty 3-inch shells and about three thousand machine-gun rounds, *Mindanao* got under way around 1530 to gain some maneuvering room in the Bay, just in case the enemy bombers returned.[13]

Mindanao was not the only gunboat anchored near Corregidor during the first bombing attack. Also in South Harbor was *Oahu*. When the Japanese aircraft were spotted approaching from the east her commanding officer, Lieutenant Commander D. E. Smith, ordered the crew to Battle Stations. As the first Japanese Army bombers approached, *Oahu* opened fire with both her 3-inch guns; the enemy aircraft were well within range. Before the raid was over she had expended ninety-eight rounds from her main battery, plus a large quantity of machine-gun ammunition. Her topside crew watched as the nearby *Mindanao* disappeared behind the geysers from the bombs that barely missed her. Like *Mindanao*, *Oahu* got under way as soon as she could to get some maneuvering room to the east of The Rock.[14]

WEEK OF AIR RAIDS

It is not clear from Japanese records how many aircraft they lost during the first air attack on Corregidor. The 60th Coast Artillery, Corregidor's anti-aircraft regiment, claimed nine medium and four light bombers shot down, with others seen departing the area smoking. It was almost always the case in World War II that estimates of enemy aircraft shot down by air defenses were too high, often by considerable margins. There is, however, no question that the Japanese met fierce anti-aircraft fire over Corregidor during their first big raid. The 60th Coast Artillery's batteries fired about 1,200 rounds of 3-inch ammunition that day. It was the .50-caliber machine guns ashore and afloat that brought down the Ki-30 light bombers.[15]

Considering that about eighty tons of bombs had been dropped during the first raid on 29 December, casualties were surprisingly light. Twenty people, military and civilian, were killed (including one Marine) and about eighty wounded. The island had, however, been thoroughly laced with bombs, especially the western portion. Light buildings were blasted or burned. Exposed supply dumps were destroyed. On the Tail of the island two observations planes at Kindley Field were wrecked. The island's little trolley system was also knocked out. There were so many breaks in the rail lines that no attempt was made to repair the damage. Interestingly, that meant that the ride of the 1st Battalion from the North Dock to Middleside Barracks on the night of 28 December was the last major use of the system. Importantly, none of Corregidor's seacoast or anti-aircraft weapons had been knocked out.

Corregidor's fire had been so effective that the enemy bombers did not return until 2 January. When they did come back for raids from 2–6 January most of the bombing was done from much higher altitudes. With the exception of 2 January when a formation of enemy aircraft slipped through heavy cloud cover for a sudden attack at 5,000 feet, the rest of the raids on the clearer subsequent days were from 24,000 to 28,000 feet. Several more enemy aircraft were shot down on those days, although at times only the single 3-inch battery equipped with the superior mechanical fuzes could engage the high flying bombers. An important effect of the heavy anti-aircraft fire that drove the Japanese to higher altitudes was that the enemy's bombing accuracy suffered badly. On the 3–6 January raids many bombs fell into the North Channel and South Harbor. In the latter case, many of the Navy's ships were already using South Harbor between Corregidor and Fort Hughes as an anchorage. Although none were hit, there were enough geysers of water thrown up to keep the ships' crews nervous. Many got under way and moved into the middle of Manila Bay while the raids were in progress. On several of the days that the Japanese bombed Corregidor from 2–6 January a few enemy aircraft broke off from the main group and struck Mariveles.

THE MARINES' BEACH DEFENSE

As soon as the first raid ended in midafternoon on the 29th Colonel Howard started to disperse the 4th Marines around the island. No one knew when the enemy would return, and although Middleside Barracks had stood up well to the first attack, keeping the regiment concentrated there was clearly the last thing Howard wanted to do.

The 1st Battalion was dispatched to the East Sector, basically from Malinta Hill eastward to Hooker Point at the far tip of the island. The 3rd Battalion (less some important detachments) was posted in the center portion of The Rock to defend the area from Bottomside westward to about James Ravine. On 4 January the 3rd Battalion assumed control of four Army 3-inch Stokes mortars that were located in a fixed emplacement not far from the Middleside Barracks.[16] The 2nd Battalion was to defend the western portion of Corregidor. In each case the battalions would be responsible for the north and south sides of the island. Regimental Headquarters was initially established in the Middleside area.

Starting on the 30th detachments from the 1st Separate Battalion were formed for duty at various locations. Two platoons were sent to Fort Hughes. One (one officer and twenty-eight men) had four .50-caliber machine guns for low-altitude anti-aircraft defense. The other platoon consisted of a lieutenant and forty-six men with four .30-caliber machine guns for beach defense. Ten more men and four more .30-caliber weapons supplemented this initial group on 3 January. A platoon of one officer and thirty-five men with six .50-caliber machine guns was attached to the 60th Coast Artillery to help bolster Corregidor's defense against low-altitude attack. Finally, a group of fifteen Marines with two .50-caliber machine guns went to Fort Drum.[17]

Most of these detachments were formed from the regiment's 3rd Battalion, which the 1st Separate Battalion had officially become on 1 January. By 5 January the 4th Marines regimental command post had moved into Tunnel Queen under Malinta Hill. The Marines were already starting to dig in and get The Rock ready for an eventual enemy amphibious assault.

Another group of Marines had also managed to reach Bataan before the enemy closed the gate. Warrant Officer Brainard's radar detachment had remained near Nasugbu southwest of Manila, monitoring the air situation and making constant reports to the Army's Air Warning Service. By 12 December, however, there were so few Army fighters left that even considerable warning of an approaching enemy air formation could not result in interception. Finally, on Christmas Eve, the new commander of the Army Air Forces remaining behind on Luzon, Colonel Harold H. George, instructed Brainard to move his men and their radar to Bataan. Brainard commandeered several Filipino trucks to move his unit and its precious radar. Finally, they managed to reach Bataan on Christmas Day after driving through Manila the day before. Initially setting up at Orani in the northern part of the Peninsula, it was soon clear that this position was far too exposed. The radar was moved southward to near the shoreline at Limay, about halfway down the east side of Bataan. By 28 December the radar was in place and Brainard reported his location to Colonel George and the headquarters of the 4th Marines.[18]

MANILA ABANDONED

On the last day of 1941 the submarine rescue vessel *Pigeon* headed toward Sangley Point for a final visit before the Japanese arrived. On board was Lieutenant Champlin and a detail of twenty-five armed sailors. Their mission was to complete the destruction of any remaining Navy supplies at Sangley Point. All concerned knew that this was a dangerous mission, since no one was sure just how close the Japanese were at this point.

When the men landed they checked the area for anything of possible value to the enemy. A moored lighter was found loaded with mines and aerial depth charges. *Pigeon* towed the lighter about four miles offshore and sank it by ramming—gunfire was too dangerous with its load of weapons.

While *Pigeon* was returning to the Point, Champlin's detail destroyed the PatWing 10 aircraft repair shop, including the unserviceable PBY that was still inside. A call was put through to Pan American Airways asking them to complete destruction of the Pan Am flying boat base on Sangley Point. Forty-five drums of aviation fuel were destroyed. Unfortunately, one man of the detail, Yeoman 3rd Class Kenneth Grisham, died when a tractor he was driving overturned, killing him. When Champlin and his detail reboarded *Pigeon* to return to Corregidor Admiral Rockwell thought that all naval personnel had cleared the Manila area. Unfortunately, it was not so.[19]

The following morning, New Year's Day, a telephone call came into Tunnel Queen from Manila. It was Lieutenant Pollock from PatWing 10. He reported that he was with a group of about twenty-five Army and Navy personnel who needed evacuation and that they had several truckloads of supplies that would be useful if they could be saved. Pollock asked that a boat be sent to pick them up from the waterfront at the Army-Navy Club after the sun had set. Due to the uncertain situation, as well as the possibility of the Japanese taking reprisals if a military boat arrived in Manila, now an Open City, Admiral Rockwell decided against sending a boat, instead telling the men to make their way to Mariveles as best they could. By this point, the Japanese were poised just to the north and south of Manila, ready to enter the city the next day.

On New Years' Day Lieutenant Pollock and Chief Radioman Burton Fuller searched for a way out of Manila. Finally, they managed to commandeer a small Filipino tug and a barge that they could use to carry the equipment they had accumulated. Departing from the Manila waterfront just before midnight, the tug and barge, heavily loaded with Americans and Filipinos, plus considerable equipment and ammunition, slowly moved across Manila Bay. They reached the safety of Corregidor around 0230 on 2 January. Along with the personnel that had been rescued, a large quantity of 3-inch anti-aircraft ammunition and fifty-five precious machine guns had been brought out on the barge. Pollock and the others were very lucky to make it. As they were crossing Manila Bay Japanese troops started to enter Manila. The day before the last group of four Navy trucks that had tried to escape from Manila by driving northward ran into a group of enemy tanks. Only one driver survived.[20] Pollock's group was the last Navy personnel to escape from Manila before the Japanese entered the city on 2 January.

CANOPUS HIT AGAIN

In the days following the attack on 29 December the crew of *Canopus* repaired most of the damage to the ship and simultaneously moved a considerable portion of her stores ashore into the tunnels in the Mariveles area. The PNAB contractors continued to work on the tunnels to extend them while the sailors did what they could to make them more livable. Offices were set up, telephone

USS Canopus

Source: U.S. Naval Institute Photo Archive

lines rigged from the ship into the tunnels, bunks were set up for much of the crew, and a galley established. Most of the ship's remaining machine guns were also moved ashore into the nearby hills where they could get good fields of fire.

On the morning of 5 January there were less than thirty crewmen on board, mostly manning the three 3-inch anti-aircraft guns. Commander Sackett and Lieutenant Otter, the ship's gunnery officer, were both present. Suddenly, at 0745 four Zeros from the Tainan Kokutai roared in at low altitude. Moored in the water not far from *Dewey* were the remaining seaplanes of PatWing 10's Utility Squadron. Despite some machine-gun fire from the Old Lady and Marine .50-caliber guns in the hills near the dry dock, the Japanese managed to destroy all the aircraft—two Curtis Seagulls, two Kingfishers, and a Grumman Duck. The latter partly sank in shallow water just off the beach. As the Japanese fighters pulled up and headed east they spotted two P-40s that had just taken off from the Army's Bataan Field, one of the airstrips in the southern part of the Peninsula.

Around 1245 enemy air attacks started on Corregidor. Simultaneously, a small number of enemy bombers attacked Mariveles. *Canopus* and the Marine 3-inch anti-aircraft battery outside the town both opened fire, but did not hit any of the Japanese raiders. More enemy aircraft were seen attacking Corregidor in groups of six to nine, staying at high altitudes in an attempt to avoid The Rock's anti-aircraft fire.

At 1315 a formation of seven enemy twin-engine bombers approached from the north and dropped their loads at *Canopus*. As on the 29th, only one bomb struck, hitting the side of the tall smoke stack. Apparently the bomb had an instantaneous fuze, for it burst upon striking the thin plating of the stack and showered the upper works with fragments. The exposed gun crews took the brunt of the effect. Men were struck down all over the topside area. Although the bridge was damaged, Commander Sackett and the other men there were not hurt. Lieutenant Otter continued in action despite multiple wounds in his back. He and fifteen members of the gun crews were injured. Bomb fragments damaged two of the 3-inch anti-aircraft guns. The ship's side had also been liberally sprinkled with fragments, creating holes that were later patched using wooden plugs.[21]

That night the process of off-loading the tender was accelerated. It was now quite clear that the Japanese knew exactly where the ship was, despite the best attempts to conceal her. A new type of camouflage was needed. During the night, while part of the crew moved supplies and equipment ashore, others set to work with paint and conducted controlled flooding to give the ship a list. In her holds fore and aft smoke pots were positioned for use when the sun came up. Cargo booms were left askew and her decks strewn with rubbish.

The next day, 6 January, the regular early morning Japanese photo-reconnaissance aircraft appeared overhead, circling the Mariveles area. What it saw was an apparently derelict hulk, listing, and with smoke coming from the hull. Although Japanese aircraft appeared overhead later in the day, they did not attack. Nor was the ship bothered during the next three months. The clever deception worked, convincing the enemy that the ship had been wrecked and abandoned. And so she seemed during daylight hours.

At night *Canopus* returned to life. Many of her crew would come on board to operate machinery and equipment that could not be removed to the tunnels. The Old Lady was about to enter her new role of providing maintenance support not only for the Navy and Marines at Bataan, but also for the Army. The ship's personnel repaired many an Army vehicle, including tanks, in the months to come. *Canopus* was also to provide a considerable number of her crew to fight as infantrymen ashore, not once, but twice before the campaign ended, as we will see.

NAVAL FORCES AT THE START OF THE SIEGE

There are still precise, name-by-name muster rolls available for the Marines in the Manila Bay area. The data on the Navy is far less precise, but still useful. On 14 January there were about 2,400 American Navy officers and enlisted men on Bataan, Corregidor, and on board the ships in the Bay, including the Navy medical personnel attached to the 4th Marines. There were also roughly 600 Filipino naval reservists. On the same day 1,562 Marine Corps officers and men were on the 4th Marines' rolls (including 4 men still listed as being in Shanghai and 22 wounded men who had been captured in Manila with the majority of the Navy's medical personnel). Therefore, whereas there were some 87,000 U.S. and Philippine Army military personnel on Bataan and the fortified islands in early January, the Sea Services had about 4,600 officers and men in the Manila Bay area.[22] The Navy totals do not include about 80 American and some 400 Filipino PNAB civilian contractor personnel around Mariveles. The Army had over 6,000 civilian employees on Corregidor and Bataan at the start of the siege. Of the Filipino naval reservists, 105 were serving with the 4th Marines as mess attendants.

On 6 January Battery A at Mariveles was directed to provide personnel to guard the advance USAFFE command post on Bataan. MacArthur's advanced command post (CP) was located approximately five miles up the west coast road from Mariveles. This duty was maintained until the 14th when the battery's personnel returned to Mariveles to help create the newly formed Naval Battalion that we will soon learn about. The following day the regiment dispatched a new guard detachment to the forward CP: two first lieutenants, Mann and

Dobervich, and forty-seven enlisted Marines. This detachment would remain with the Army command post until the end of the Bataan campaign.[23]

There were a surprising number of Navy ships in Manila Bay, although most were fairly small. In mid-January the Navy had the following vessels in the Bay organized as the Inshore Patrol under the command of Captain Hoeffel. The "Bataan Navy" now consisted of:

- Inshore Patrol:
  - Gunboats—*Mindanao*, *Oahu*, and *Luzon*
  - Minesweepers—*Quail*, *Finch*, and *Tanager*
  - 16th Naval District tugs—*Genesee*, *Vega*, and *Napa*
  - Civilian tugs under Navy control—*Tranajador* and *Ranger*
  - Converted yachts—*Maryanne*, *Perry*, and *Fisheries II*
- Submarine forces:
  - Tender—*Canopus*
  - Rescue vessel—*Pigeon*
- Motor Torpedo Squadron 3:
  - PT boats—31, 32, 34, 35, 41
- Elements of PatWing 10:
  - Approximately 13 officers and 140 enlisted men; no aircraft
  - Various yard craft, barges, and motor launches, plus the floating dry dock *Dewey* moored at the western side of Mariveles Harbor

Later the Navy took control of several other small vessels, including the former British oceangoing tug *Henry Keswick* that the Army had taken over.

The three little converted yachts made an interesting story. All were taken from civilian owners in the Manila area. Being diesel powered, they were economical to use and there was a fairly large amount of diesel available in both Navy and Army stocks on Bataan and in the tunnels on Corregidor. Given small crews of eighteen to twenty-two men each under the command of an ensign or lieutenant (junior grade), the little ships were armed with a number of .50- and .30-caliber machine guns. Later in the campaign they were allowed to fly commissioning pennants, which made the crews feel like their ships were really part of the Navy. Although not fast (9–15 knots), they were very useful for patrolling, often accompanying the PT boats on nighttime ventures outside Manila Bay. No pictures survive of these vessels, but according to one account *Maryanne* looked very much like the presidential yachts of the 1920s and 1930s.

The Army also had a number of vessels in the Bay at the start of the siege. It was normal for an Army harbor defense command to have a number of small vessels assigned to it. The most important of these were Army mine planters. These were the little ships, roughly the size of large tugboats, that were used to emplace, service, and if need be remove Army mines. Indeed, the Army's first use of the rank Warrant Officer was for the masters of these coast artillery vessels. The largest mine planter in Manila Bay was the 172-foot *General Harrison*. In addition, there was a smaller auxiliary mine planter, the *Neptune*. The Army also had the 138-foot *General Miley* and the 150-foot *General Hyde*. These were small cargo and transport ships that had been used in peacetime to move men and supplies from Manila to the fortified islands. Additionally, the Army had a number of diesel- or gasoline-powered motor launches for administrative runs between the fortified islands and over to Bataan.[24]

Not included in the Navy personnel totals were those who were still in Manila when the city was evacuated. When the Navy and Marines pulled out of Manila and the Sangley Point area most of the medical personnel and their patients remained behind. Many of the roughly 150 Navy and Marine Corps patients were men who had been badly wounded during the bombing of the Cavite Navy Yard. Some of them had been so badly wounded that they could not be moved far. Captain Davis and twenty-six other doctors and dentists, about one hundred Navy corpsmen, and eleven nurses stayed with their patients. On 3 January, the day after Manila fell, Japanese troops took over the Saint Scholastica campus where the temporary Navy hospital was located. Only one Navy nurse, Ann Bernatitus, had escaped to Bataan along with Navy doctor lieutenant commander Carey M. Smith, a surgeon with whom she frequently performed operations.[25]

The Navy medical personnel and their patients remained at Saint Scholastica school until early March when the doctors, corpsmen, and the patients were shipped to Bilibid Prison in Manila. The Japanese, who had no women in their military at that time, were at first not quite sure what to do with the female nurses. When the men were sent to Bilibid the women were shipped to Santo Thomas University where several thousand American, British, Australian and other Allied civilians were being interned. They were still there when American forces liberated Manila in early 1945.

THE STATUS OF SUPPLY

By the middle of the first week in January all of the Army's troops had withdrawn into Bataan. It had been a near-run thing. On several occasions the Japanese had threatened to cut off the retreat of major portions of the Filipino-American force, but they had never been able to close the noose. There was a short lull as the enemy reorganized, withdrawing the 48th Division and substituting for it the much-inferior 65th Brigade. The lull gave the defending troops a bit of a rest and provided time to start preparing defenses along the Abucay-Moron Line in northern Bataan. It also gave the Army a chance to take stock of its supply situation. The results of the inventory were shocking.

Brigadier General Charles Drake was the USAFFE supply officer. Prior to the retreat to Bataan, as the situation deteriorated in the Philippines, he had suggested that some of the Army's supplies be moved to the Peninsula as a hedge against the possibility that a siege would eventually take place. This request was denied by MacArthur who insisted on maintaining the policy of defeating the enemy at the beaches. The effect of that decision was tragic for the garrison.[26]

When WPO-3 went into effect on 24 December the Army quartermasters did their best to stockpile Bataan with supplies for the retreating Army. Corregidor was easy. The Malinta Tunnel complex already held food for a garrison of 7,000 men for six months. In one day of shipments by barge across Manila Bay the quartermasters brought that up to a level of 180 days' food for 10,000 men. Bataan was a much harder task.

Drake had estimated that it would take fourteen days to move sufficient supplies to Bataan to sustain 43,000 men for six months—the numbers specified in Plan Orange before MacArthur implemented his "hold the beaches" scheme. In actuality the quartermasters had eight days (24–31 December) to move supplies for 80,000 personnel on Bataan. Some supplies had been stored at small Army bases on Bataan before the war (in particular, the Army had a large cache of gasoline at Limay, which was vital during the siege), but nothing like what was needed to sustain an Army of the size that was now on the Peninsula. With no rail line leading into the Peninsula and the roads increasingly clogged with retreating units, barges moving from Manila to Bataan's few small docks became the best means to get a lot of tonnage to the Peninsula. For eight days the Army quartertmasters made a Herculean effort, but it was not nearly enough.[27]

During the first week of January when the quartermasters took stock of the situation they discovered that there was about twenty to forty days of food on Bataan, depending on the specific item. When MacArthur was given that grim news he placed all Army personnel on half rations, effective 5 January. Additionally, a desperate attempt to forage was started. The quartermasters began to strip Bataan for food, particularly rice, the key staple of the Filipino diet. Calls were sent out to the Army forces in the southern Philippines to assemble food and ship it to Manila Bay on small interisland steamers, an order much more easily issued than executed, as we will see. This dismal supply situation was the effect of delaying so long the decision to start stockpiling Bataan in anticipation for a siege. The time had been available from 12–22 December, the period between the first enemy landings and the main assault at Lingayen Gulf. Now the Army was in a desperate situation, particularly in terms of food. Due to Drake's efforts there appeared to be an adequate supply of ammunition on the Peninsula, as long as some economical measures were taken.

Meanwhile, the Navy and Marine Corps had been serving two meals a day since mid-December. Although a reduced amount, the Navy-Marine messes were still serving significantly more than a half ration. The critical difference in the supply situation between the Army and Navy was that the latter had started moving food to Mariveles and Corregidor as early as 14 December following the destruction of Cavite. Additionally, when the Marines arrived on Corregidor they brought with them sufficient food for two thousand men for six months at full rations. Many of the little ships in Manila Bay had used the last days before the move to Bataan to stock up on food from sources in Manila. The net effect was that the Navy and Marines were far better prepared to endure a long siege than the Army on Bataan. Corregidor appeared to be well stocked in terms of food since so much had long been stored in Malinta Tunnel. Not knowing how long the siege would last, the Navy and Marines maintained their two meals per day policy. Although not as much as the normal prewar ration, it was a relatively well-balanced one. To be sure, as the weeks went by the sailors and Marines would be tightening their belts—literally—but they did not face anything compared to the privation that was to soon beset the Army troops on Bataan. For this the sailors and Marines could thank their senior leaders whose realistic assessment of the situation in early December resulted in proper actions being taken to stockpile supplies.

The biggest supply shortfall that the Navy had was fuel oil for its ships in the Bay. Most of the ships had managed to get one final top off at the Sangley Point fuel depot before that facility was destroyed. Lieutenant Commander Morrill brought *Quail* to the Sangley Point fuel depot late on Christmas Day to top off her tanks in what he believed was the last time any Navy ship was able to get fuel from that source before the depot was finally destroyed.[28] It was clear, however, that without additional fuel the ability of the ships of the Inshore Patrol to operate would gradually decline. One of the consequences of the dash to get out of Manila in the short amount of time the Navy was given (basically two days, 24–25 December) was that there was little time to try to find more fuel barges or commandeer ships to act as floating fuel tanks. Had this been done the Inshore Patrol would have been able to patrol more aggressively in the later stages of the siege, or possibly escape to the southern islands.

As the Army troops on Bataan got ready for the Japanese to renew their attack there was a need to expand the number and capacity of the airfields on the Peninsula. Although there were not many planes available, there was hope that more could be ferried in from the southern islands, assuming that additional aircraft could be brought into the Philippines. During January one of the important activities of the PNAB contractor personnel was to help the Army engineers build new airfields, both near Mariveles and at Cabcaben on Bataan's southeastern coast. The PNAB contractors were professional engineers, well equipped with heavy construction gear. Working alongside the Army's 803rd Engineer Battalion (Aviation), the PNAB contractors helped ready Cabcaben Field and made significant progress on Mariveles Field just to the northwest of that town.[29]

SQUADRON 3's FIRST ACTIONS AND LOSSES

As the siege got under way the Navy continued to conduct patrols inside and outside Manila Bay. It was only a matter of time before the enemy would extend his activity along the Cavite shoreline in the direction of the harbor forts. Minesweepers and gunboats could take care of the area inside the Bay, working with the Philippine Army Q-boats that focused their activities on the east coast of Bataan. Outside the Bay, Japanese destroyers and other ships could already be seen moving north and south well past the range of Corregidor's guns. It was clear that the Japanese intended to start using Subic Bay as a supply point as soon as they could clear the entrance of mines.

The Navy craft best suited for patrolling outside the entrance to the Bay were the fast PT boats of Squadron 3. Prior to the departure of *Peary* and *Pillsbury* on the 26th the PTs had accompanied the destroyers on patrols as far south as the island of Mindoro. Now they were on their own, with the possible exception of armed yachts like *Perry* and *Maryanne* that sometimes departed with them to scout north and south of the entrance to the Bay. Due to the enemy's control of the air, these patrols had to be done at night.

Even before the destroyers departed, the PTs suffered their first casualty. On Christmas Eve the 33 Boat was patrolling south of Manila with *Pillsbury* when she went hard aground on a coral reef. On Christmas Day the 31 and 35 Boats tried hard to pull their sister off the reef, but it was to no avail. The next day the stricken boat was stripped of all useful gear and burned to prevent the Japanese from taking her. The squadron was down to five boats and the campaign was less than three weeks old.

The new home of the PT boats was Sisiman Cove on the southern tip of Bataan. It was from that location that three boats had dashed to help the survivors of the ill-fated SS *Corregidor* when she sank on 17 December. Soon problems were encountered with fuel that contained a waxy substance that clogged engines. As already mentioned, Squadron 3 was starting the Bataan campaign very short of spare parts due to the losses suffered at Cavite.

On 18 January Lieutenant Bulkeley was ordered to dispatch two boats to Subic Bay to attack several Japanese transports reported by the Army. PT-34 with Bulkeley in command was accompanied by the 31 Boat, commanded by Lieutenant E. G. DeLong. They cleared the minefield around midnight and headed north toward Subic.

As they approached their target area the two boats separated, with the 31 Boat proceeding slowly up the Bataan coast, while PT-34 came in from the west. The plan was to rejoin near the entrance of Binanga Bay on Bataan's west coast near the entrance to Subic Bay. It was there that they expected to find the Japanese ships, hopefully lying at anchor and unprepared for a sudden attack.

Just after midnight the 34 Boat slowly moved toward its objective, trying to remain undetected. Suddenly, a weapon from onshore near Binanga Bay fired on the PT boat. When the 34 flashed a challenge more enemy weapons opened fire from ashore and on Grande Island. Before departing, and without spotting the 31 Boat, Bulkeley spotted a freighter and fired two torpedoes. One stuck in the tube, causing a very dangerous situation. The other ran toward the target. Although the crew saw an explosion, apparently no Japanese vessel was hit. With enemy firing increasing from several directions, it was time for the PT boat to clear the area fast and head south for the safety of Corregidor. It took four hours of work before the defective torpedo could be ejected from its tube into the sea. Meanwhile, there was no sign of the 31 Boat.

It was several days before the Navy learned what had happened to PT-31. As she slowly proceeded northward up Bataan's west coast toward Subic Bay, engine trouble had started, apparently due to the waxy gasoline. With power lost, the boat drifted onto a reef. Shortly thereafter she was spotted by the Japanese at Ilinin Point who started shelling the boat. Lieutenant DeLong tried hard for three hours to get the boat off the reef, but it was beyond hope. He ordered abandon ship. He remained behind to destroy the boat by throwing hand grenades into the gasoline supply. Then he took to the water to join the twelve members of his crew. When he reached the shore he linked up with nine of the crew. His XO and two other men were missing and never found.

Due to a battle that was developing around the coastal village of Moron, the sailors had to use extreme care when trying to get back to friendly lines. On the 20th they finally encountered Filipino troops of the 91st Division who were engaged with the Japanese advancing down Bataan's west coast. By that evening they were back in Mariveles. With the loss of the 31 Boat MTB Squadron 3 was down to four boats.[30]

While the two PTs were engaged at Subic Bay, the 41 Boat had been sent to reconnoiter the south shore of Manila Bay near the town of Ternate. Japanese troops had occupied the ruins of the Cavite Navy Yard and Sangley Point on 3 January, the day after the fall of Manila. Troops of the 33rd Infantry Regiment next began to slowly advance westward along the south shore of the Bay with the goal of establishing observation points and artillery positions from which to engage the fortified islands.

On the evening of the 18 January Ensign Cox's 41 Boat, with the 16th Naval District intelligence officer, Lieutenant Commander M. C. Cheek, and an Army coast artillery observer on board, ran along the coast close to shore looking for signs of the enemy. Filipinos had reported enemy tunneling activities in the area and had claimed they had seen some Japanese cannons.

When they were between Ternate and Naic the 41 Boat spotted a small party of Japanese troops on the beach and opened fire with her .50-caliber machine guns. Apparently having no way of responding to the fire from the fast-moving PT boat the enemy troops scattered for cover in the trees. The PT boat's firing was too high and the enemy escaped. Nevertheless, this patrol confirmed that the Japanese were moving into the Cavite shoreline not far from Forts Drum and Frank.[31]

Although a Japanese move westward along the Cavite shoreline was a potentially serious matter, it was by no means the main point of concern. By 20 January the tide of battle on Bataan had clearly shifted in favor of the Japanese.

Longoskawayan Point

While the first battles of Bataan raged along the Abucay Line the Navy continued to consolidate its position on the extreme southern tip of the Peninsula. The Mariveles Navy Section Base, still incomplete, was the focal point of the Navy's presence on Bataan. The officer in charge of the little base, and the senior Navy officer on Bataan at that time, was Captain Dessez.

In its prewar planning the Army had recognized the need to defend Bataan's east and west coasts against the possibility of an enemy amphibious landing. The problem was that the best troops were needed along the main line from Moron to Abucay. Therefore, all that was available to defend the beaches along Bataan's vulnerable west coast were a mix of Philippine Constabulary, now-planeless Army Air Force squadrons, and some Philippine Army units that had been badly battered during the retreat to Bataan (such as the remnants of the 71st Division). There were no prepared defenses along the beaches as this motley collection of units took up their assigned positions in the first and second weeks of January.

THE NAVAL BATTALION

Following consultation with the Army it was agreed that the Navy would assume the responsibility for the defense of the extreme southern part of Bataan. Therefore, on 9 January 1942 Admiral Rockwell formally directed Captain Dessez to form a naval battalion. The three missions of the new unit were: (1) security of the Mariveles area, (2) defense of naval activities in the Mariveles area, and (3) support of the Army, particularly along the west coast of Bataan. Dessez was directed to employ personnel from PatWing 10, *Canopus*, Marines in the Mariveles area, and general detail personnel manning the Section Base (many of whom were survivors of the bombed-out Cavite Navy Yard). The admiral suggested that Commander Francis J. Bridget, PatWing 10's senior remaining officer in the Philippines, become the battalion commander—a suggestion Dessez accepted. Finally, Rockwell reminded Dessez that the Navy's mission was to support the Army in the Manila Bay area.[1]

Commander Bridget began forming the Naval Battalion right away. Although there were some 1,500 Navy and Marine Corps personnel in the Mariveles area, including the crew of *Canopus*, few could be dedicated full-time to the battalion. Bridget was able to assemble a total of 602 sailors and Marines for the unit, although we will see that far fewer than that would actually be committed at any one time against the Japanese.[2] The battalion executive officer was Lieutenant Commander Goodall, who was also the XO of *Canopus*.

In terms of being equipped and trained for land combat the Marines were, of course, the best prepared. Unfortunately, there were only about 150 Marines in the Mariveles area. The primary mission of Batteries A and C was to man four 3-inch anti-aircraft guns and nine .50-caliber anti-aircraft machine guns. Battery A, the machine-gun unit, was under the command of recently promoted 1st Lieutenant Hogaboom. Its .50-caliber weapons were located near the Quarantine Station close to the point where the dry dock *Dewey* was moored. Battery C's 3-inch guns were in an abandoned rice paddy between the Section Base and the town of Mariveles. First Lieutenant Holdredge was in command. A month earlier Hogaboom and Holdredge had both tried to defend the Cavite Navy base during the devastating Japanese bombing raid. Now they were preparing to defend the airspace over southern Bataan. The two young Marine officers had known each other since Annapolis—they were both graduates of the Class of 1939. Both Marine batteries were augmented with sailors, since neither had sufficient Marines to man all their weapons. Battery A received one officer and sixty-five sailors, while another officer and forty men went to Battery C.[3]

Bridget incorporated the few Marines who were available into the Naval Battalion, deliberately spreading them throughout his five companies (Battery A, Battery C, Asiatic Aircraft, General Detail, and Naval Ammunition Depot) to mentor and train the sailors who formed the majority of the personnel. While the Marines had been trained in infantry tactics and were appropriately armed with small arms and machine guns, the sailors were much more of a mixed bag when it came to ground combat.

During the period prior to World War II it was not uncommon for the Navy to form landing parties from a ship's company for action ashore. At times landing parties were composed of sailors and Marines, while in some cases when no Marines were available armed sailors would be the only force to go ashore, led by Navy officers. This type of experience was fairly common for Navy ships assigned to the Caribbean region and, especially, the Asiatic Fleet. Some sailors on ships assigned to the Asiatic and Caribbean stations received a modicum of training in the use of small arms and rudimentary infantry tactics. Indeed, compared to today the typical sailor of the pre–World War II period would have received noticeably more training in ground combat. Some of the petty officers and chiefs had, however, not fired a rifle in years, while others would have had more recent experience due to their service in China. It is important to remember that while some sailors, especially some of the "old hands" of the Asiatic Fleet, had basic knowledge of the use of small arms, they were by no means trained infantrymen. That is why Bridget sensibly spread the few Marines that he had throughout the battalion so the sailors could learn from them.

Commander Sackett, *Canopus*' commanding officer, who provided some 130 members of his crew for either full- or part-time duty in the naval battalion, noted that:

> Equipment was a serious problem. The Marines were, of course, ready for field duty. But the others were sailors, and the Navy doesn't provide much equipment for land operations at best, to say nothing of the fact that several of these groups had been separated from their normal supplies by unforeseen circumstances. However, rifles and ammunition of some sort were finally begged, borrowed or stolen for most of the men. Their white uniforms were dyed in coffee grounds to what was supposed to be khaki color, but which turned out to be "a sickly mustard yellow." Only about one canteen could be found for every three men, but the great American tin can was pressed into service to make up the deficiency.[4]

Steel helmets were also in short supply. Sackett went on to note: "Training was the next essential. Perhaps two-thirds of the sailors knew which end of the rifle should be presented to the enemy, and had even practiced on a target range, but field training was practically a closed book to them. The experienced Marines were spread thinly throughout each company in the hope that through precept and example, their qualities would be assimilated by the rest."[5]

Training began immediately after the battalion was formed, although as noted above most of the unit's personnel were doing double-duty and therefore were not available for full-time training in infantry tactics and weapons. Nevertheless, marksmanship training and unit marches were conducted in the area around Mariveles. The Marines held classes on infantry tactics and oversaw the efforts at target practice. It has been estimated that on average the sailors in the Naval Battalion received the equivalent to about two to three days of training in ground combat before the Japanese landed. As the Naval Battalion prepared, as best it could, during mid-January, events were taking a turn for the worse along the front line to the north.

THE COLLAPSE OF THE ABUCAY LINE

The first battle of Bataan started on 9 January 1942 when the heavily reinforced Japanese 65th Brigade attacked down the east coast road toward the Filipino-American forces manning the line just north of the town of Abucay.[6] Following several days of heavy fighting the initial Japanese attack was stopped due to fierce resistance, which included hand-to-hand fighting, by the elite 57th Infantry (Philippine Scouts). Realizing that he could not break through along the main road that paralleled the Bay, Japanese lieutenant general Akira Nara, the 65th Brigade commander, shifted one of his infantry regiments inland to outflank the II Philippine Corps' positions.

During the fighting along the Abucay Line a few Marines showed up to participate. Warrant Officer Brainard, in charge of "Radio Bataan," the new title for the Marine Corps radar detachment, was discovering that he had to scrounge for supplies. Positioned in a mango grove near the Manila Bay waterfront between the towns of Orion and Limay, the Marine radar detachment observed air activity over Manila Bay, providing information on enemy aircraft to the Army's Bataan Field Flying Detachment as well as the Army anti-aircraft units on Bataan and Corregidor. The problem was that logistically his outfit was somewhat of an orphan. With the Naval Base at Mariveles a good distance away, his original parent unit, the 1st Separate Battalion, having been absorbed into the 4th Marines as its 3rd Battalion, and the Army unsure about supplying Marines, Brainard found himself sending groups of his Marines around Bataan to bring in supplies—however they could. Brainard was rather liberal, if that is the right word, in allowing his men to visit Army units, including letting them participate in combat.

On 15 January five Marines from Radio Bataan were in the area of the Philippine Scout 57th Infantry. This was the period when the Scouts were engaged in heavy combat against the Japanese 65th Brigade along the east coast road. That night the Marines joined Captain Arthur Wermuth, USA, on a raid into Japanese lines. The Japanese had established themselves in a sugar cane field to the Scouts' front and had to be dislodged. Captain Wermuth received permission from the Regimental Commander of the 57th to form a provisional "anti-sniper platoon" composed of three expert Scout marksmen from each company in the 57th—and the five Marines from Radio Bataan who had arrived at the front, with Brainard's permission, looking to get into the fight.

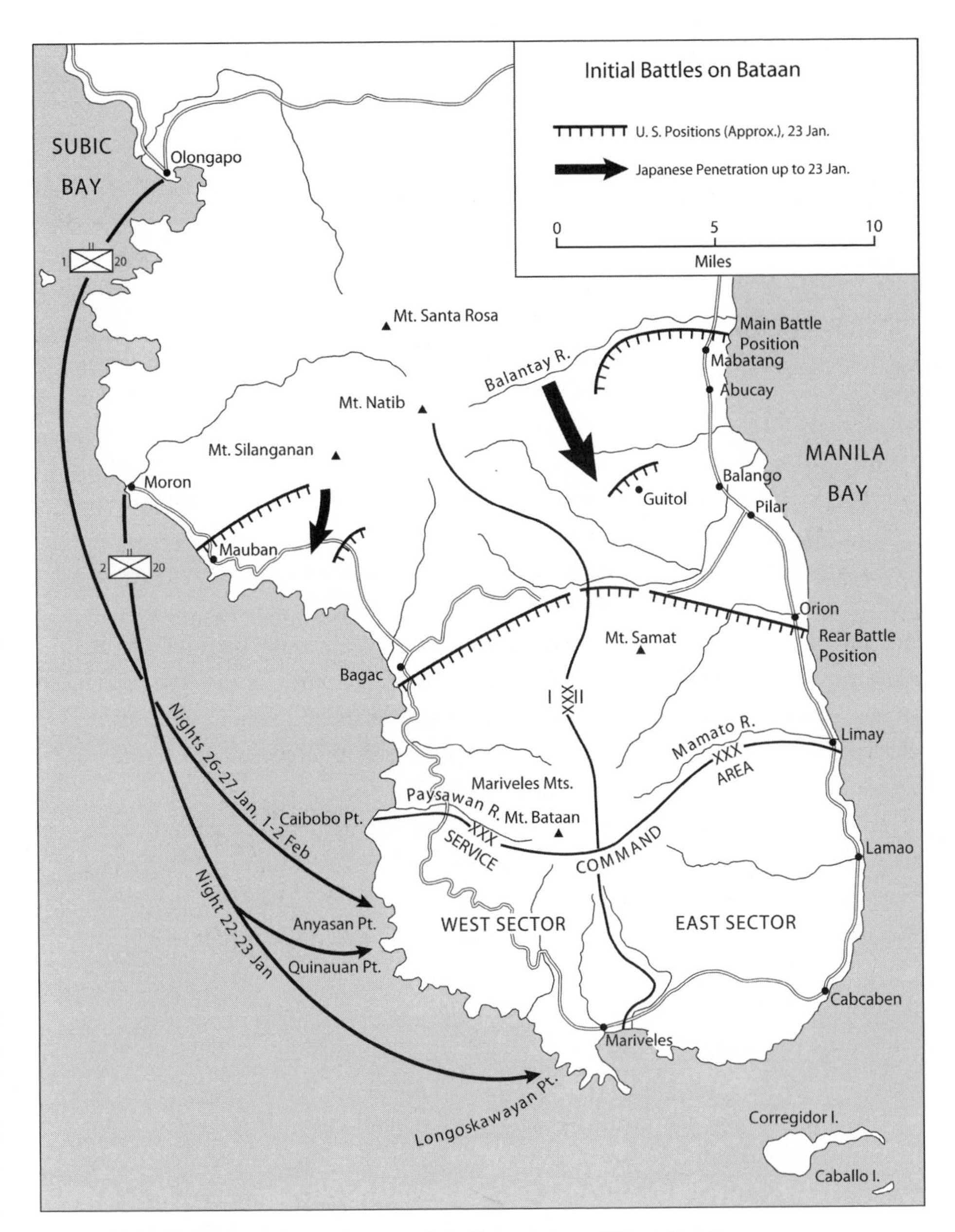

Map 4. The initial battles on Bataan, and the Japanese amphibious landings

On the night of 15–16 January Wermuth led the raid into enemy lines. They brought with them some small phosphorous bombs provided by the Bataan Field Flying Detachment. About thirty Scouts, and the five Marines, formed the patrol. The raid succeeded in setting fire to a building the Japanese were using, but the enemy then attacked the patrol. Private First Class Robert Brown, USMC, was hit and died the following morning after the patrol had returned to American lines. Two other Marines, Sergeant Charles Eskstein and Private Richard Watson, were wounded.[7]

When Headquarters 4th Marines learned of these casualties 1st Lieutenant Lester A. Schade was sent to Bataan to take over command of the radar detachment from Brainard, whose men had already earned the title of "rogues of Bataan." Brainard stayed with the detachment due to his technical expertise. Meanwhile, the situation on Bataan was taking an ominous turn for the worse.

Starting on 14 January the Japanese heavily attacked the poorly trained and ill-equipped Philippine Army 51st Division that was positioned on the jungled eastern slopes of Mount Natib on the left flank of II Philippine Corps. The inexperienced Filipino troops broke on 16 January, allowing the Japanese to advance through the jungle toward Manila Bay, threatening to envelop the II Corps. At that point General MacArthur authorized the commitment of the all-American 31st and Philippine Scout 45th Infantry Regiments to counterattack in an attempt to seal the breach in the line.

By 22 January it was apparent that the counterattack had failed. That night, following a visit to Bataan by General Sutherland who was sent by MacArthur to assess the situation, a decision was made to fall back to the Reserve Battle Position in the valley that runs east–west across the middle of the Bataan Peninsula. The decision came none too soon, because on the west side of the peninsula a further disaster was in the making.

Due to the lack of a road from Olongapo southward along Bataan's west coast it took the Japanese until 15 January to reach the advanced positions of I Philippine Corps located at Moron. Major General Naoki Kimura, the commander of the 16th Division infantry group, led the force advancing down Bataan's west coast; it was less than half a division in strength, about five thousand men. For the next few days relatively minor fighting took place between Moron and Mauban. It appeared to the American Corps commander, Major General Wainwright, that he was holding the Japanese advance. Unfortunately, the enemy then employed an outflanking maneuver over the jungle-covered western slopes of Mt. Natib, very similar to the move that had outflanked II Corps on the other side of the mountain. In midmorning of 21 January the majority of the 3rd Battalion, 20th Infantry Regiment reached the west coast road, in the rear of the I Corps troops located to the north at Mauban. Despite counterattacks that included the understrength Philippine Scout 26th Cavalry and some American tanks—attacks personally led by General Wainwright—the enemy roadblock could not be eliminated. Some five thousands troops trapped to the north of the block were forced to abandon their vehicles and artillery pieces and withdraw southward via the beach.[8]

By the night of 22–23 January the American position on Bataan was perilous. I and II Philippine Corps had both been outflanked and were now forced to withdraw to the Reserve Battle Position, with the Japanese hot on their heels. As the exhausted troops of II Corps pulled back along Bataan's east coast, Japanese aircraft attacked throughout the daylight hours. Fortunately, the move to the next position was only about ten miles and the number of aircraft available to the enemy was small—less than fifty fighters and light bombers.[9] The roughly sixty remaining light tanks of the National Guard 192nd and 194th Tank Battalions proved vital, covering the withdrawal of the infantry and artillery units as they had done during the long retreat toward Bataan in December. For several critical days the Army command on Bataan would have no reserves; every infantry, artillery, and tank unit was committed to establishing the new line across the Peninsula. It was during this hazardous withdrawal to the new, and final, defense line on Bataan that the enemy made his first attempt to outflank the defenders by conducting amphibious assaults along the Peninsula's west coast.

THE JAPANESE LANDINGS

Even before the Americans started their withdrawal to the Reserve Battle Position, the Japanese were considering amphibious landings along the west coast. By 22 January, with the battle against I Corps going well, the time appeared right for the attempt. The relatively small number of landing craft available in Subic Bay and the fact that there were only five battalions of Japanese infantry in western Bataan limited the size of the force that could conduct the landings. Nevertheless, General Kimura had high hopes for a landing at Caibobo Point, south of Bagac. Kimura believed that this move would prevent the Americans, who by 22 January were showing signs of withdrawing southward, from consolidating a new line. Kimura directed that Lieutenant Colonel Nariyoshi Tsunehiro's 2nd Battalion, 20th Infantry Regiment embark on barges at Moron for a landing set for the early hours of 23 January. The landing force was reinforced with some elements of the 33rd Infantry's regimental gun company. With less than a day to prepare for the operation, the leaders of the Japanese battalion examined the poor maps available to them and got ready to depart.

If the 2nd Battalion had been at full strength it would have numbered some 1,100 officers and men in a battalion headquarters and supply train, four rifle companies, a machine-gun company, and a battalion gun platoon with two short-barreled 70-mm infantry guns. In terms of automatic weapons a Japanese infantry battalion was better armed than a similar American unit of that phase of the war, and far better equipped than a Philippine Army infantry battalion. With twelve tripod-mounted Nambu 6.5-mm heavy machine guns in the machine-gun company and a total of thirty-six light 6.5-mm machine guns in the rifle companies the defensive firepower of a Japanese battalion was formidable. In addition, each of the twelve rifle platoons in the battalion had three 50-mm grenade dischargers, later to be known to American troops in the Pacific as "knee mortars" due to the erroneous assumption that the curved base plate of the weapon was intended to be fired from the thigh of a kneeling infantryman. The "knee mortars," which had no direct counterpart in the U.S. military, were capable of throwing a grenade-sized projectile 175–650 yards, depending on the model of the grenade launcher.[10] Had the 2nd Battalion's parent unit, the 20th Infantry, been at full strength the entire regiment would have numbered roughly 3,800 personnel.

Although strong compared to American and Filipino infantry battalions on Bataan, the 2nd Battalion, 20th Infantry was not up to full strength. Indeed, the entire regiment numbered only 2,880 men when it landed on Luzon in December, roughly 1,000 men below its theoretical full complement. It appears that including attached units from the 33rd Infantry, also a unit of the 16th Division, the 2nd Battalion departed on its mission on the night of 22–23 January with a strength of between 950 and 1,000 men. It was transported in landing barges manned by elements of the 10th Independent Engineer Regiment. The Japanese Army barges were Daihatsu Model A, which was 50 feet long, could do about 10 knots, and carry up to 100 troops.[11]

Departing from Moron around 2300 on 22 January, the 2nd Battalion expected a three-hour voyage to Caibobo Point. Initially the bright moon helped navigation. Unfortunately, the tides along Bataan's west coast proved stronger than expected and in the darkness the coves, inlets, and promontories tended to blur and merge into each other; as the battalion proceeded southward it lost track of where it was. The moon set around 0100, considerably reducing visibility. Poor quality maps did not help the situation. Much worse was soon to follow.

As Tsunehiro's force proceeded southward some two to three miles offshore, it came under fire from Filipino and American troops manning shore defenses along Bagac Bay, a good potential landing site and long a point of concern for the American command on Bataan. Searchlights along the shore illuminated some of the barges. A torrent of—inaccurate—automatic weapons' fire forced the barges farther off shore and started the process of scattering them. The now-disrupted formation continued its movement south.[12]

Engine trouble plagued some of the boats. One, carrying Captain Hidaka of the 33rd Infantry, broke down and fell behind the main body of the formation. Another boat full of infantry came along and towed Hidaka's barge. Several other barges formed up with Hidaka's group. By now this cluster of barges was separated from the main force that included the battalion commander.[13] Hidaka was the commander of the Rapid Fire Gun Company of the 33rd Infantry Regiment.

Patrolling along Bataan's west coast was PT-34 commanded by Lieutenant Robert Kelly, with Ensign Barron Chandler as the XO. PT-34 had left Sisiman Cove several hours earlier for the standard night patrol along Bataan's west coast. Also on board was MTB Squadron 3's commanding officer, Lieutenant Bulkeley. Still very concerned about the fate of PT-31 and its crew—missing from the raid on Subic Bay the night before—Bulkeley and the crew of the 34 Boat peered into the darkness. Some distance behind them was the converted patrol yacht *Fisheries II*. It had become normal for a single PT boat to go to sea on night patrol accompanied by either *Fisheries II* or *Maryanne*. Given the increasingly frequent problems with the PT boats' engines, it was somewhat comforting to have one of the converted patrol yachts along for the ride; if worse came to worst they would be available to tow a broken down PT back to port. This night's patrol took the PT boat almost to Subic Bay. When nothing was found, they turned south toward home base.

At roughly 0440, about two miles off Canas Point, the 34 Boat spotted a small craft showing a dim light off in the darkness. Increasing speed, Kelly closed in on the intruder that started to blink the light in his direction, obviously as a recognition signal. When the PT boat approached to within fifty yards Lieutenant Bulkeley hailed the still-unknown small vessel. Suddenly a hail of small arms fire erupted from what was now seen as a Japanese landing barge, headed south and full of troops. Rifle fire penetrated the thin plywood sides of the PT's cockpit and went through one of Ensign Chandler's ankles and then lodged in the other.

Despite the enemy firing first, the 34 Boat quickly overpowered its opponent. Four .50-caliber machine guns, two .30-caliber Lewis guns mounted on pedestals on the bow, and crewmen firing BARs and rifles at the enemy soon shredded the barge, probably killing most of the enemy soldiers on board. The enemy barge sank after some fifteen minutes of firing. Not stopping to look for any survivors, the 34 Boat conducted a search of the immediate area. Friendly fire from shore forced the PT boat to move farther out to sea to seek the protection of the offshore darkness. Finding nothing else, and with the ensign in considerable pain from his wounds, Bulkeley directed the 34 to head home.

As she headed south the PT boat spotted another enemy barge some three miles offshore, headed north, just after 0600. Although the enemy craft increased speed, it could not hope to avoid the much faster torpedo boat, which opened fire with its .50-caliber machine guns at roughly four hundred yards range. Soon the barge was on fire. Coming close aboard at 0725, Bulkeley pitched two grenades into the enemy craft and then boarded the sinking vessel. It was noted that the Army-supplied grenades that Bulkeley threw into the landing barge failed to explode, not the first—or last—time that old Army ammunition proved unreliable. Only three Japanese were on board, one dead and two wounded, including a noncommissioned officer. The two were taken on board the 34 Boat, along with various documents. The barge literally sank underneath Bulkeley as he struggled to save the two Japanese. As they proceeded south, the Navy men were not aware that this northward-bound barge had already deposited its passengers ashore on Bataan.[14]

Although the Americans did not know it at the time, PT-34 had seriously disrupted the southward movement of the 2nd Battalion. Already confused when the American torpedo boat encountered the first barge off Canas Point, the firing threw the Japanese barge formation into disarray. It is likely that around fifty men were lost in the first, still-loaded, barge that the 34 Boat sank. The majority of the Japanese unit, Lieutenant Colonel Tsunehiro and about six hundred men, came ashore at Quinauan Point, some four miles south of their intended landing point at Caibobo. Fortunately for the American command on Bataan, the Japanese force, which easily drove off the men of the now-planeless 34th Pursuit Squadron who were manning outposts on the point, was utterly bewildered and lost. Also fortunate for the Americans was the fact that Tsunehiro's force was about as far from the vital west coast road as it could have been.

The remainder of the 2nd Battalion, 7 officers and 294 men carried in six landing barges, came ashore much farther south on little Longoskawayan Point, less than a mile and a half from Mariveles. Once they deposited their troops, the barges headed north toward Subic Bay. It is likely that one of these returning barges was PT-34's second victim.

The Japanese who landed at Longoskawayan Point were a small but cohesive force. The 301 men were from various units of the 2nd Battalion, 20th Infantry and attached elements of the 33rd Infantry. Included in the Japanese force was the battalion gun platoon of two 70-mm infantry howitzers. It is virtually certain that Captain Hidaka was the senior officer present. Before his barge pulled away from Longoskawayan Point Hidaka gave its skipper a note: "Captain Hidaka, commanding 5th Company, Battalion Gun, and Field Hospital Units, is trying to gain ground by advancing. Cannot make contact with the main force. Request Headquarters make contact."[15] Hidaka surveyed the area around him, noting the 11–22-meter-high cliffs. He ordered some of the men to scale them to expand their bridgehead and to get an idea of where they were.

Hidaka dispatched part of the 5th Company, his main infantry unit, under Lieutenant Ikugawa to the right and another portion of the company under Warrant Officer Nakashima to the left, hoping that the main body of the 2nd Battalion was nearby. Alas, the rest of the battalion was nowhere to be found. Little did Hidaka realize that Lieutenant Colonel Tsunehiro and the rest of the force were over five miles away to the northwest on Quinauan Point. With dawn approaching, the Japanese found a trail leading up the cliffs and started to dismantle their field guns in order to get them to the top.

At 0830, with most of the force now atop Longoskawayan Point, Hidaka dispatched a lieutenant and three men on a reconnaissance to find out where they were and to locate the main road that they knew paralleled the west coast of Bataan. Meanwhile, elements of the 5th Company moved into nearby Lapiay Point to the northwest. A few men from the company began to ascend the nearest high ground, 617-foot-high Mt. Pucot. Soon they made contact with Americans atop the small mountain. The battle of Longoskawayan Point was under way.

BATTLE IS JOINED

There was an American observation post atop Mt. Pucot, which provided an excellent view of all of southern Bataan and for many miles out to sea. The men manning the outpost on the morning of 23 January were a couple of Marines and four Army personnel from the 60th Coast Artillery, the anti-aircraft regiment on Corregidor. At about 0830 Private First Class Robert McKechnie, USMC, was fired on from nearby bushes. Jumping to the ground from his observation post in a tree, he immediately called the Naval Battalion command post using the field phone that was located atop the hill, telling Commander Bridget: "Longoswkayayan, Lapiay, and Naiklec Points are crawling with Japs, sir. We're getting the hell out of here, right now!"[16] McKechnie and his companions then ran all the way to the Battery A's position, arriving just as Lieutenant Hogaboom hung up the phone with Bridget, who had already called Lieutenant Holdredge at Battery C. McKechnie briefed Hogaboom on what they had seen atop the hill.

At about the time that first contact was made with the enemy atop Mt. Pucot, PT-34 arrived in Mariveles Harbor. At 0830 the 34 Boat pulled alongside *Canopus* where Ensign Chandler was put ashore and the two prisoners were handed over. The documents that Bulkeley had found on board the second barge were also turned in.

Within minutes of being told of the presence of the enemy by Commander Bridget both Holdredge and Hogaboom were assembling platoons to head into the hills to the west to make contact with the enemy. At this point the situation was very unclear; nobody had any idea how many enemy troops were nearby. Hogaboom soon had two platoons of sailors ready to move out. There were a few Marines with each group. Lieutenant (junior grade) Les A. Pew, USN, who had started the war as a PBY pilot in VP-102, led one platoon, while Hogaboom elected to lead the other platoon himself. That left sufficient men behind to man the .50-caliber anti-aircraft machine guns that were still Battery A's responsibility. Altogether, Hogaboom and Pew had about sixty men, most of them sailors.

At about the same time Lieutenant Holdredge assembled three platoons from Battery C. He led one; another was under command of Ensign George T. Trudell who had been a pilot in PatWing 10's Utility Squadron. Like Hogaboom, Holdredge left men behind to continue to man the battery's 3-inch anti-aircraft guns. A third platoon, composed mostly of Marines under 1st Lieutenant Carter Simpson, was directed to check out Naiklec Point, to the south of Longoskawayan. There were about seventy sailors and Marines in the three Battery A platoons.

Unfortunately, these five platoons were now largely on their own. Lacking field radios or even telephone wire, once they set off into the jungle to the west of Mariveles they would be largely out of contact with each other, much less their parent batteries or battalion headquarters. By midmorning Holdredge had set out for the area east of Longoskawayan Point with his own platoon, while sending Ensign Trudell toward Mt. Pucot. Not knowing of Holdredge's plans, Hogaboom also dispatched Pew's platoon directly toward Mt. Pucot. He initially took his own platoon toward Mt. Mauankis. The Naval Battalion personnel carried no machine guns during the initial move toward the Japanese, but they did have a number of BARs to supplement the '03 Springfields that most of the men carried. A number of the men also had hand grenades. So, roughly 130 Marines and sailors, many of the latter wearing their "sickly mustard-colored" uniforms, headed into the jungle to make contact with the dreaded Japanese.

One effect of Commander Bridget issuing instructions separately to Holdredge and Hogaboom by phone, and not meeting with them together before

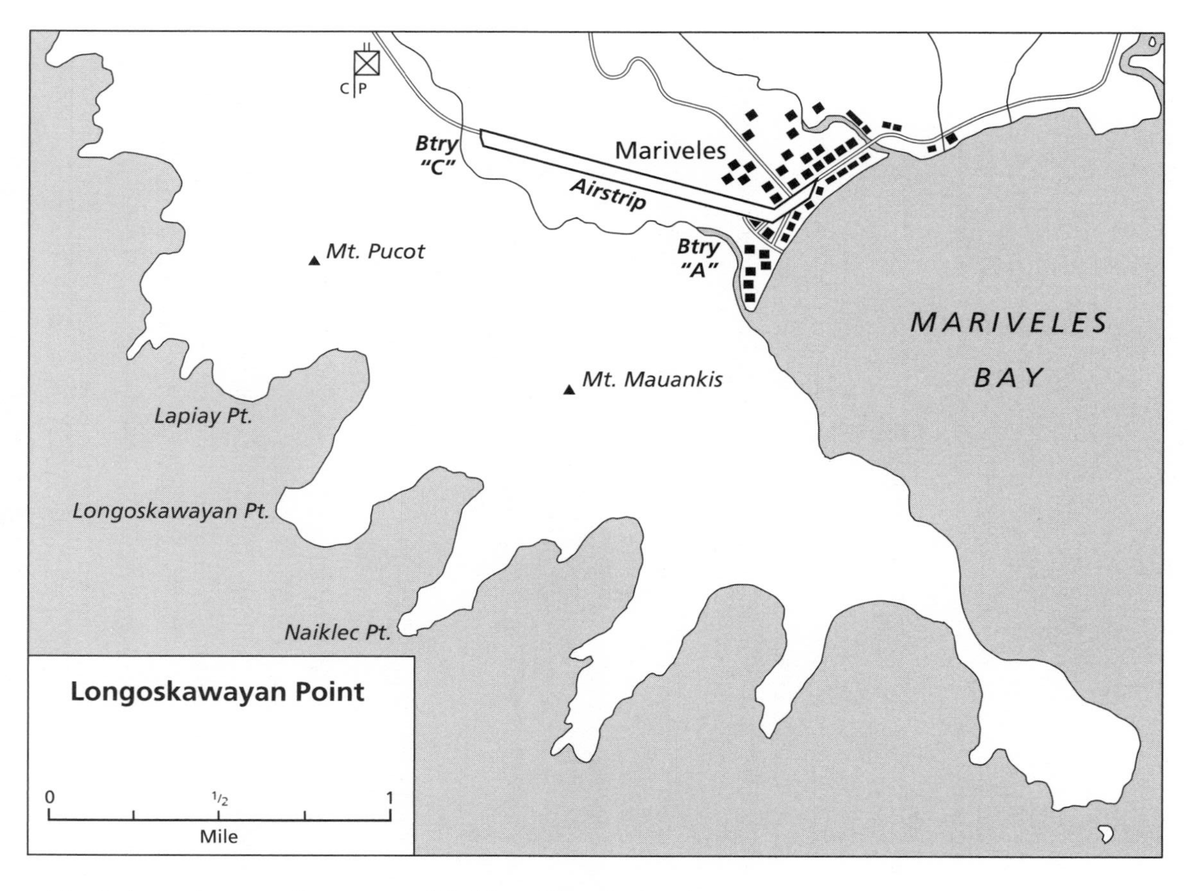

Map 5. Longoskawayan Point, scene of the Naval Battalion's action

they departed for the hills, was that the actions of the two Marines officers were largely uncoordinated. Indeed, as they moved toward the Japanese, Hogaboom and Holdredge were initially unaware of each other's actions or even presence.

As the five initial platoons moved out Bridget was already taking action to reinforce them. Word was sent to *Canopus* that the Japanese had landed nearby, with instructions directing the ship to be prepared to provide support to the coming action. Bridget directed Platoon Sergeant Robert Clement to quickly form a platoon of thirty-six sailors and follow Hogaboom and Holdredge. Clement asked for, and received, the assistance of another Marine sergeant. He also managed to round up a small number of junior enlisted Marines to go along. One can only imagine the feelings of the two Marine NCOs as they headed toward the enemy alongside their eager, but untrained, Navy comrades. As they were preparing to depart one sailor holding a rifle asked, "Hey Sarge, how do you get the bullets in this thing?"[17]

Hogaboom's first move was to Mt. Mauankis, only about half a mile west of Battery A's location. Discovering that no Japanese were there, he dropped off one squad under Corporal Fred Paulson, with instructions to hold the hill. This was a sound move, considering the fact that the 580-foot hill overlooked Mariveles Harbor. Hogaboom then led the remainder of his platoon toward Mt. Pucot to the northwest, searching for any Japanese along the small ridge that ran between Pucot and Mauankis. The going was slow due to the thick foliage. Nothing was found as they gradually moved along the jungle-covered ridge.

The first Americans to return to Mt. Pucot shortly after noon were Ensign Trudell's platoon. They initially found no enemy atop the hill, and started to sweep down the southern slope when they were fired upon by a small group of Japanese, no doubt a patrol from the 5th Company. Trudell was leading the men down a jungle trail when suddenly a group of Japanese appeared at very short range, heading directly for them. The Japanese fired first; Trudell was hit, including a round that bounced off his helmet and knocked him unconscious for a few minutes. A Marine was also wounded. At that point the remainder of the platoon—composed overwhelmingly of sailors—started to blaze away into the jungle to their front, pouring fire toward the now unseen enemy. The sailors did not realize that there were also Japanese behind them.[18]

When the firing broke out Lieutenant Pew's platoon was approaching the summit of Mt. Pucot from the east. Advancing toward the sound of battle, Pew's men were fired on as they reached the top of the hill, by the Japanese who were behind Ensign Trudell's force. Within a few minutes, the sailors drove the small party of enemy into the jungle.

Hogaboom was nearing the hill from the southeast after passing by the entrance of Longoskawayan Point. When Hogaboom heard the firing he moved in to engage the Japanese. Within a few minutes his group encountered Ensign Trudell's platoon, still firing into the jungle. The Marine lieutenant conferred with the wounded Trudell, who reported that he thought the Japanese had withdrawn. Trudell needed to be evacuated quickly; he was paralyzed on one side of his body. A quick sweep of the area around the southwest slopes of Mt. Pucot showed that the Japanese had indeed pulled back—at least for now.[19]

Hogaboom next proceeded to the top of Mt. Pucot and reported to Commander Bridget by way of the phone that had been abandoned earlier in the morning when the Japanese first appeared. Bridget directed him to hold his position there. Shortly thereafter Lieutenant Simpson's platoon arrived, also drawn to the sound of firing. Simpson's group had earlier reconnoitered Naiklec Point, where they found no trace of the enemy.

By this time it was late afternoon, and four of the American platoons were concentrated around the top and southern slopes of Mt. Pucot, still very uncertain as to the enemy's location and strength. Pew took some of his men down the slopes of Mt. Pucot in an attempt to locate the enemy. There were some brief encounters, but after a few shots were fired the Japanese melted away into the jungle. While the fight on Mt. Pucot was under way, Platoon Sergeant Clement and his men arrived in the area. Having moved over the ridge between Pucot and Mauankis, Clement pushed on toward the beach—the farthest westward movement by any element of the Naval Battalion that day. When they reached the beach Clement and his men spotted two Japanese, who immediately ran. Nearby were a large number of stacked rifles and bags of fresh water hanging on poles. Directing each of his men to take one of the Japanese rifles, the platoon started to move back inland. It is likely that the beach Clement had reached was the head of the little bay between Longoskawayan and Lapiay Points.

As Clement's men moved eastward up the trail from the beach they were ambushed by a group of Japanese in the jungle. Clement was among the first hit. The sound of firing attracted Lieutenant Pew's men who were sweeping down the southern slopes of Mt. Pucot. When Pew's force joined the firefight the enemy broke off the engagement and fell back into Lapiay Point. During the fighting Marine private first class Quentin Sitton was killed, the first Naval Battalion death in the battle.[20]

While the first four platoons congregated on Mt. Pucot, Lieutenant Holdredge, after sweeping the area near the base of Longoskawayan Point, positioned his men along the ridge between Pucot and Mauankis. Following orders from Commander Bridget, other men were also positioned along this ridge before darkness set in. A light machine-gun squad arrived from Mariveles; it joined Holdredge's men on the ridge between the two hills.

As darkness approached the first, confusing, day of action came to an end. Few Japanese had been encountered. This led Hogaboom to report to Commander Bridget that roughly a platoon of Japanese were in the area. The inexpert, uncoordinated action by the leading elements of the Naval Battalion had been effective. By taking prompt action, the sailors and Marines had established a rough cordon around the enemy on Longoskawayan and Lapiay Points. Critically, they had retained control of the high ground—Mounts Pucot and Mauankis—that dominated the coast, as well as Mariveles.

While the fighting was under way, Bridget was assembling more men, with the intention of reinforcing the units already in contact with the enemy. Brigadier General Clyde Selleck, USA, commanding the forces manning the beach defenses along Bataan's west coast, promised Bridget reinforcements. During the fighting on the 23rd, he dispatched the sixty-man American 301st Chemical Company and a 2.95-inch pack howitzer from the Philippine Army 71st Division to bolster the Naval Battalion. That evening the 2.95-inch pack howitzer,[21] under the command of 3rd Lieutenant A. A. Perez, Philippine Army, arrived. The weapon was emplaced on the ridge between the two hills. Perez and his eight-man crew were eager to give it their best, despite the fact that they had never fired their old gun before. An additional request for reinforcements went to the 4th Marines on Corregidor. Bridget's plan was for the Naval Battalion to attack toward the sea early the next morning.[22]

If the first day of action was confusing to the Americans, it also was for the Japanese. Around 0900 Captain Hidaka on Longoskawayan Point dispatched a lieutenant and three other men to press inland to scout the situation. By midmorning Hidaka was aware that he had lost contact with most of the 5th Company that he had sent toward Lapiay Point and Mt. Pucot. He retained most of his men near the western tip of Longoskawayan Point, where the two 70-mm infantry guns were set up.

About noon one of the privates from the morning patrol returned, reporting that the main road was about four kilometers to the east. Around 1700, as the sound of firing from the east grew louder (obviously the little battle taking place on the slopes of Mt. Pucot), Captain Hidaka ordered the infantry guns dismantled and moved about 550 yards inland from the tip of the little peninsula. When warned that the Americans were close by, he ordered the infantry guns to return to near the cliffs and set up again. As darkness approached he established a line around the middle of the peninsula and sent out another patrol, still not knowing where the 5th Company was.[23]

24 JANUARY, THE SECOND DAY

During the night the Army personnel of the 301st Chemical Company, led by Lieutenant Colonel L. E. Roemer, arrived and were put in position northwest of Pucot, tying in with the now-planeless 3rd Pursuit Squadron manning beach positions northwest of the Naval Battalion's area of operations. This move effectively prevented enemy infiltration northward along the beach.

Shortly after dawn the men along the slopes of Mt. Pucot began to move out toward the coast. Lieutenant Hogaboom's group headed initially for Latain Point. En route a couple of Japanese were encountered, but they ran off. Finding no enemy at Latain, Hogaboom turned toward Lapiay Point. At the base of Lapiay, Hogaboom's leading group of men encountered the Japanese. Without firing, they dashed back to report what they had seen.

Hogaboom established a base of fire near the entrance to Lapiay and began to advance into the Point, intent on clearing it. As he and his men advanced they were met with close range machine-gun fire, which drove them to cover. They attempted to knock out the enemy machine gun with hand grenades. Corporal Raymond Collins threw about half a dozen grenades at the enemy while under intense fire; he was later awarded the Silver Star for his actions. The thick vegetation held up the movement of the men and interfered with throwing grenades.

Two lieutenants, Pew and Simpson, brought their men into action when they heard the sound of firing taking place near the entrance to Lapiay Point. They fed their men into the line and the intensity of the fight grew. From Latain Point about two dozen rifle grenades were fired at the enemy holding the entrance to Lapiay. Japanese machine-gun fire held up all attempts to advance. The firefight continued into the afternoon.

Captain Hidaka was overjoyed when just after dawn he was informed that the 5th Company had been found on Lapiay Point. Shortly thereafter he dispatched a patrol that ran into an American attack. By 1000 heavy firing could be heard from the 5th Company area. Hidaka formed up most of his men, leaving the wounded under the care of the medical unit that was set up near the southwest tip of Longoskawayan Point. The medical officer, 1st Lieutenant Kamiyama, promised, "I shall take care of the patients and will share their fate with them. I will put all my men under your command." Already the Japanese were running very short of water, which made their dry rations of bread, cereal, and crackers difficult to eat.

Collecting most of the men on Longoskawayan, Hidaka advanced toward the base of the point in order to support the 5th Company. As they approached the base of the little peninsula at 1330 they encountered the Americans (probably men from Holdredge's platoon that had been holding the ridge south of Mt. Pucot). As the Americans attacked from the south side of the point, Hidaka directed machine-gun fire against them at a range of fifty yards. Three Japanese were killed, but the Americans were driven back. When the Japanese troops followed cautiously behind them, abandoned rifles and blood-stained ammunition belts were found.

By 1600 the Americans at the base of Longoskawayan had been driven back, but the 5th Company was under intense pressure. Hidaka then directed fire from the two 70-mm battalion guns against the Americans on the southern slopes of Pucot. More machine-gun fire was also directed into the area in support of the hard-pressed 5th Company. By dark things were settling down. Hidaka's men were desperately short of water. The only source they could find was a spring flowing into the Bay between Lapiay and Longoskawayan Points. The 5th Company still held this area, providing an opportunity to bring water from the stream for the thirsty men, some of whom had lost the ability to talk.[24]

Lieutenant Hogaboom had felt the exploding shells of the Japanese 70-mm battalion guns. This fire, and the increasingly intense machine-gunning from the enemy, forced the advance to a halt. The severity of the day's action had convinced him and Holdredge that a sizable enemy force was present. The two Marine officers now estimated that about two hundred enemy troops were in the area. That was roughly the same number that the Naval Battalion had committed to action thus far. The situation was reported to Commander Bridget. It was now apparent that a much larger force would be needed to drive the enemy into the sea; Holdredge and Hogaboom estimated a full infantry battalion.

25 JANUARY, THE THIRD DAY

Early that morning 2nd Lieutenant Richard Fulmer, USA, of the 59th Coast Artillery, the all-American heavy gun regiment on the fortified islands, reported from his observation post atop Mt. Pucot the locations of the Japanese on the points. Realizing at once that the enemy was within range of the big 12-inch mortars of Battery Geary on Corregidor, the Seaward Defense Command on Corregidor requested permission from Major General King, the artillery commander on Bataan, to engage the targets. At 1000 word came back from King's command post: "Do nothing at present." Disappointed, the coast artillerymen on Corregidor waited. At 1400 Battery Geary fired four practice rounds into the sea to ensure all was in readiness should they be called upon to fire in anger against the enemy.[25]

At 1000 that morning 2nd Lieutenant Michael Peschek, USMC, and two platoons from the 2nd Battalion, 4th Marines departed for Bataan from

Corregidor's North Dock. Peschek had about forty Marines and two Navy corpsmen in a small machine-gun platoon and a two-gun 81-mm mortar platoon. The 81-mm mortars had 260 rounds of ammunition available. As soon as the Marines arrived at the dock at Mariveles they moved out into the hills to support the Naval Battalion. Peschek positioned the two mortars in a saddle of ground northwest of Mt. Pucot. Once the weapons were in position, Peschek joined Lieutenant Hogaboom atop Mt. Pucot to direct the mortar fire. As soon as the mortars reported ready around 1430 a bombardment of Lapiay and Longoskawayan Points began.

With Hogaboom directing the fire, the Marine mortars worked over both points. Accuracy of the fire was described as excellent. During the shooting a group of twenty to thirty Japanese on Longoskawayan Point were seen to run between two clumps of trees to avoid the mortar fire. With a correction of "right 100" the 81s were ordered to fire for effect. No Japanese were seen to emerge from the trees after the barrage ended. Hogaboom noted that there did not seem to be any duds among the mortar ammunition—all the rounds exploded as intended.

In midafternoon the Marine and Navy platoons started to move forward toward the coast, descending from the slopes of Mounts Pucot and Mauankis and the ridge that connected them. Hogaboom's platoon headed toward Lapiay Point and soon discovered that the enemy had abandoned it. He returned to Mt. Pucot to await events. While Hogaboom's group had it easy, the other platoons had a much harder time.

Lieutenant Holdredge was in overall command of several platoons that moved forward toward Longoskawayan Point. The Japanese were ready for them. Early that morning Captain Hidaka had ordered the 5th Company to evacuate Lapiay Point and rejoin the main group on Longoskawayan. Together with 1st Lieutenant Yokochi, the leader of the 5th Company, Hidaka planned to advance that night toward the coast road that he now knew was less than two miles to the east. Hidaka also intended to attack Mariveles.[26]

These Japanese moves took place in the relative peace of the morning, before the Marine 81-mm mortar barrage began. By evacuating Lapiay Point early in the morning, Hidaka negated the effects of the Marine mortar bombardment of that area, although from Hogaboom's observations there must have been Japanese casualties during the bombardment of Longoskawayan. By the time the sailors and Marines started to attack in the afternoon the enemy had concentrated his strength on Longoskawayan in preparation for his own attack that night. Holdredge ran straight into the enemy's main strength.

For the first few hundred yards of their advance the sailors and Marines encountered little resistance. As they approached the midpoint of Longoskawayan

Point they were met with heavy fire. Holdredge, in the lead of a group of fifteen men, reached a clearing in the jungle. A Japanese machine gun on the other side of the clearing opened fire, hitting the lieutenant and a dozen others. Private First Class Warren Carver was killed in the exchange.

Holdredge turned over command to Ensign Lowell Williamson, USN, a PBY pilot from PatWing 10. Williamson continued to push southward for another hundred yards or so, employing decent fire and maneuver tactics by leapfrogging groups of his men forward as others provided covering fire. Suddenly the leading group of sailors and Marines came under intense fire at close range. This forced them to fall back again to the clearing where Holdredge and the others had been hit. The Japanese now had this area well covered. As some of the men attempted to dash across the clearing they were cut down by enemy fire. Others crawled to the other side of the clearing. Meanwhile, some of the men who had been with Holdredge tried to provide covering fire as their comrades attempted to pull back.

Darkness was falling as the men reached the ridge between the two hills—their starting point. Casualties were heavy. Twenty-nine sailors and Marines had been hit. In addition to PFC Carver, four crewmen from *Canopus* had been killed: S1c Robert Barrow and S2c Harold Kelly, Mark Koep, and Jacob Mathis. Eleven of the wounded, including Lieutenant Holdredge, were Marines, along with thirteen sailors. Fortunately, the Japanese made no attempt to pursue the men as they fell back toward the ridge, in an orderly manner, taking their wounded with them.

It is not known how many Japanese were killed or wounded that day. What is certain is that 25 January is the last entry in Captain Hidaka's diary. The final entry refers to events in the late morning, before the day's heavy fighting began. It is possible that Captain Hidaka was killed or badly wounded that day, or it may be that he was too exhausted and busy to continue making diary entries, although that seems unlikely since he had made a journal entry nearly every day since mid-November.

The first few days of fighting against the Naval Battalion had been a strange experience for the Japanese. Not realizing that they were fighting mostly sailors, the Japanese were baffled as to the American's uniforms and fighting technique. On the body of another dead Japanese soldier was a diary that included a telling entry. The Americans were "a new type of suicide squad, dressed in brightly colored uniforms. Whenever these apparitions reached an open space, they would attempt to draw Japanese fire by sitting down, talking loudly, and lighting cigarettes."[27] Obviously this was some fiendish Yankee trap. On the body of yet another Japanese soldier was a diary that referred to the Americans as being utterly fearless.

It was at this point that Commander Bridget requested fire support from the heavy guns on Corregidor.

26 JANUARY, THE FOURTH DAY

It was about 2000 on the evening of the 25th when word was received on Corregidor to commence a bombardment of Longoskawayan Point. Colonel Paul Bunker, the Seaward Defense Commander of the fortified islands, was on the phone with Commander Bridget at 2230, determining when they could begin the shoot. It was not until an hour later that Bridget was sure that the last of his men were at a safe distance and gave permission to open fire. Army Coast Artillery's Lieutenant Fulmer, atop Mt. Pucot, directed the firing.

Battery Geary fired its first round just after midnight. It was the first combat firing by heavy-caliber American coast artillery since the Civil War. The 700-pound high explosive projectiles were tipped with instantaneous fuzes in order to burst on contact. With over 100 pounds of high explosive filler, the land attack version of the big mortar shells were formidable weapons, ideal for bombardment of troop-type targets ashore. The range from Battery Geary to the target was over 14,000 yards; Geary's maximum range was just over 15,000. The weapons were firing with Zone 10, the highest powder charge allowed.

After the fourth round Lieutenant Fulmer reported that the shooting had started such large fires on Longoskawayan Point that he could no longer see the target area. A total of nine rounds were fired, but the last two-gun salvo drifted to the right, up the slope of Mt. Pucot. A frantic call from Commander Bridget brought the firing to a halt. Battery Geary had two mortars loaded, ready to fire. Corregidor requested permission to shoot, but Bridget refused. According to Lieutenant Hogaboom, who was on Mt. Pucot observing the firing with Fulmer, the first four shells landed on the shoreline of the Point, but the rest fell wide.[28]

After the sun came up Hogaboom led a patrol to recover the bodies of four of the men killed the day before. That was accomplished without incident. The rest of the day was spent conducting patrols. There was only minor contact with the Japanese, who were now clearly concentrated on Longoskawayan Point. During the day Commander Bridget sent additional men forward to replace casualties and to prepare for a major attack the next morning.

As word of the action spread around the Mariveles area, sailors in small groups or as individuals obtained weapons and headed up into the hills, seeking action. Most of these men unofficially attached themselves to the platoons that were already in contact. After dark additional reinforcements arrived in the form of F Battery of the Philippine Scout 88th Field Artillery Battalion. The battery's four 75-mm guns were set up behind Mt. Pucot. The tired men settled down to get as much rest as they could, knowing that they would make a big attack the next morning.

While the fighting was going on Lieutenant Colonel Clement had come over from Corregidor to observe the battle and provide advice to Commander Bridget. Clement also worked closely with the Army command on Bataan and Corregidor, helping to coordinate the Naval Battalion's needs and actions with the Army.

27 JANUARY, THE FIFTH DAY

At 0700 all the artillery that was available, the two 81-mm mortars, the 2.95-inch mountain howitzer, the four 75s of the 88th Field Artillery, and four of Battery Geary's 12-inch mortars, opened fire on Longoskawayan Point. Within a few minutes Lieutenant Fulmer was reporting back to Corregidor that the Point was being smothered with fire. He wondered how anything could survive such a pounding. Twenty-four of the big 12-inch shells were fired. This time a mixture of high explosive and armor piercing shells were used, the latter intended to penetrate the caves that some of the Japanese were reported hiding in near the waterline. Many of the mortar shells impacted on Longoskawayan Point, while others landed in the water. Later, when several Japanese prisoners were taken, one of them stated that, "We were terrified. We could not know where the big shells or bombs were coming from, they seemed to be falling from the sky. Before I was wounded, my head was going round and round, and I did not know what to do. Some of my companions jumped off the cliff to escape the terrible fire."[29] While the artillery firing was under way, the men of the Naval Battalion moved into position to launch their attack.

For about an hour the shelling continued at various levels of intensity. There were some constraints, however. Lieutenant Perez's 2.95-inch gun had a very limited amount of ammunition available. The Marine 81-mm mortars had received an additional sixty rounds from Corregidor, but still did not have enough ammunition to thoroughly saturate the entire Point with fire.

There were about two hundred men available for the actual attack on the morning of the 27th. Of these, sixty to seventy were Marines, the rest sailors. At a prearranged time the 81-mm mortars shifted their firing deeper into Longoskawayan and the Naval Battalion began its attack. It was now mid-morning.

Just as the men started to advance, the Scout 75-mm battery started to spray rounds all over the Point. It took about a quarter of an hour to check their fire. Once that was done, the advance resumed. It quickly became apparent that many of the enemy had survived the shelling—resistance was heavy.

When it became obvious that the advance was slowing, Hogaboom personally went forward to the center of the line. Quickly conferring with some Marine NCOs, he directed them to get the advance moving. The attack started again, but slowly.

Soon an intense firefight developed near the center of the Point, with the sailors and Marines engaging dug-in enemy machine guns that were well camouflaged. Marine Lewis machine guns were brought forward and attempts were made to outflank the enemy, but there was little room to maneuver in the thick jungle. The enemy started to get the better of the firefight, pinning the men to the ground. Hogaboom had to order his group to fall back.

Returning to the forward command post, he reported the situation to Commander Bridget, who was located near the Mariveles airfield. Hogaboom stated that the advance could not continue in the face of such heavy resistance. The battalion commander ordered the men to dig in and hold where they were—even that was not possible.

Although Hogaboom's group in the center had halted its advance, other groups of men had not received the word to stop. One platoon on the south side continued to press forward toward the tip of the Point, encountering heavy resistance as it advanced. This created a gap between the halted units and those still advancing. The Japanese either slipped men into the gap, or enemy soldiers who had been bypassed in the fighting started to fire upon the advancing platoon from the flanks and rear. What few men still in reserve were sent to eliminate this threat.

The next thing to occur was a Japanese counterattack. Preceded by what the Americans described as "mortar" fire (probably from the 70-mm guns), the Japanese tried to outflank the exposed left flank platoon that had advanced farthest along the south side of the Point, exploiting the gap that had been created. They also shelled Hogaboom's forward command post, having obviously spotted it. However, prompt action by the two Marine 81-mm mortars and Lieutenant Perez's old 2.95-inch gun saved the situation. Lieutenant Peschek's mortars knocked out or silenced the enemy mortar fire before the Japanese could fire their third round at the CP. Next, the Marine mortars and the mountain gun hit the enemy counterattack, giving the exposed platoon a chance to fall back. At that point permission was requested from Commander Bridget to withdraw to the ridge. Permission was soon received, and the men moved back to the east to take up defensive positions. During this critical phase of the fight Lieutenant Perez used the last nine rounds that were available for his old howitzer.

Three more men from *Canopus* were killed on the 27th: Chief Gunner's Mate Joseph Granes, Seaman Second Class Earnest Hubal, and Seaman Second Class William Meyers. The exhausted men moved back into position along the ridge they had occupied since the first day of the battle. No one was sure what would happen next. Around midnight the men on lookout for the Japanese were surprised to hear Filipino voices coming from behind them: "OK Joe, I take over now." The Philippine Scouts of the 2nd Battalion, 57th Infantry had arrived.

28 JANUARY, THE SIXTH DAY

By the 27th the new front line across Bataan's "waist" had stabilized sufficiently that the American command could free some troops for action at both Longoskawayan and Quinauan Points. The best troops available were the 45th and 57th Infantry Regiments (Philippine Scouts). Both Scout infantry regiments had been heavily engaged during the fight at the Abucay Line.

At 1600 27 January Lieutenant Colonel Hal Granberry, USA, the commander of the 2nd Battalion, 57th Infantry, received orders to move his unit to Mariveles to relieve the Naval Battalion and complete the destruction of the Japanese landing force at Longoskawayan Point. Granberry had only joined the 57th Infantry on 18 January, while the fight for the Abucay Line was still under way. The 2nd Battalion had 13 officers and 460 men, fairly strong for an infantry battalion at that point in the Bataan campaign. The unit had suffered a few casualties during the Abucay battle, but morale was high, as was always the case in the elite, highly professional Philippine Scout units. This was a very well-trained, experienced infantry unit—just what was needed to finish the Japanese off.

Compared to the Naval Battalion, the Scouts were much better armed. The battalion had three rifle companies and a heavy weapons company. The weapons company had four 81-mm mortars and twelve .30-caliber water-cooled machine guns. The rifle companies each had a weapons platoon with three air-cooled .30-caliber machine guns and four 60-mm mortars (although there was no ammunition available for the 60-mm weapons). The three rifle platoons in each company had three squads each, with one BAR per squad. At the regimental level the 57th had an Anti-Tank Company with nine 37-mm guns. These weapons proved to be very useful for providing direct fire against enemy defenses.[30] For this battle the 2nd Platoon of the Regimental Anti-Tank Company was attached to the 2nd Battalion. By 1800 the first elements of the 2nd Battalion were arriving in the rear of the Naval Battalion, starting preparations to move into the hills to take over from the sailors and Marines.

By midmorning on the 28th the Scouts had assumed control of the line facing the Japanese. The Navy and Marine officers on the scene briefed the newly arrived Army personnel on their experiences of the past five days. Lieutenant Hogaboom was thoroughly impressed with the professionalism and esprit of the Scouts. During the day, the 2nd Battalion deployed G and E Companies along the ridge between Pucot and Mauankis, which they intended to use as their jump-off point for their attack the following day. An outpost line was deployed closer to the Japanese, and a cordon of Scouts was deployed from Naiklec Point inland, to prevent the enemy from infiltrating south. During the 28th the Scouts reconnoitered the area, including sweeping the area in their rear to ensure that none of the enemy had managed to get behind the troops as they prepared to attack.

There was fighting on the 28th as the Scouts swept through the ground around the ridge and the low ground between it and the base of Longoskawayan Point. The Japanese had infiltrated the area and resisted the arrival of the Scouts. Some sharp little engagements took place. In one case Scout sergeant Gervacio Cinco, leader of one of the weapons platoons, was killed in hand-to-hand fighting with a Japanese armed with a sword.[31] In another, Corporal Legaspi (PS) continued to man his machine gun and drove off a group of Japanese who were attacking. Legaspi later died of his wounds. By midafternoon the Scouts had driven the enemy back entirely inside Longoskawayan Point. During the course of the day three Scouts had been killed and nine wounded. An unknown number of Japanese had died. Excellent fire support from Battery F, 88th Field Artillery (PS) and the Marine mortars had helped make the battle a rather one-sided fight.[32]

Granberry's planned his main attack for the morning of the 29th following a heavy artillery bombardment that would "prep" Longoskawayan Point. E Company would be on the left, attacking down the southern side of the Point. G Company would attack on the right, beside E, with the mission of clearing the northern half of the point. Both companies were to advance all the way to the tip of the Point. In reserve was F Company. H Company, the battalion heavy weapons unit, was positioned to use its mortars and machine guns to support the advance of the riflemen. One platoon of machine guns was sent to Lapiay Point to fire across the bay directly onto Longoskawayan. The M-1916 37-mm guns of the Regimental Anti-Tank platoon would follow the advancing infantrymen, ready to be committed against dug-in enemy positions. The Scouts knew what they were doing.[33]

At 1730 Commander Bridget's command post relayed to Corregidor a message from Lieutenant Colonel Granberry, "I would like 12-inch mortar fire on the southwest tip of Longoskawayan Point from 7:00 to 7:30 in the morning, fire not to go inland more than 100 or 180 yards. We believe we have located the caves in which the Japs seek cover."[34]

While the Scouts prepared for the attack on the morning of the 29th the men of the Naval Battalion assumed a supporting role. Lieutenant Hogaboom requested that he be allowed to remain in the area to observe the Army attack, but instead was directed to take his men back to the area of the Quarantine Station for rest and to form a reserve for the Scouts, should they require it. During the course of the 28th most of the Navy and Marine Corps personnel of the Naval Battalion redeployed back to the area of Mariveles. Lieutenant Peschek's machine-gun and mortar platoons remained in position to support the Army attack. Lieutenant Perez's 2.95-inch gun detachment, now out of ammunition, left its position on the ridge, receiving Commander Bridget's hearty thanks as they departed.

29 JANUARY, THE SEVENTH DAY

At 0630 on the morning of the 29th the forward elements of E and G Companies pulled back several hundred yards to the base of the ridge between the two hills. This cleared the way for the artillery bombardment. The Japanese detected the departure and sent some men to follow the Scouts through the jungle. At 0700 the 12-inch mortars of Battery Geary opened fire, hurling sixteen big shells at nearly maximum range. At 0720 the four 75s of F Battery added their fire to the bombardment. At 0725 the Army and Marine mortars joined in. Finally, the battalion machine guns started to sweep the area in front of the infantry at 0730.

Battery Geary's firing was not effective. At 0925 the following message was passed to USAFFE Headquarters by Lieutenant Commander Goodall, the XO of the Naval Battalion. The message originated from Lieutenant Colonel Granberry: "Mortar fire from Corregidor was entirely ineffective. We have had to attack to regain terrain we gave up this morning in preparation for this fire. We are now about back to where we were before the firing started. Don't know yet the effect of fire from the gun boat."[35] Unfortunately, all sixteen of the 12-inch mortar shells had landed in the sea. The fire from the "gun boat" that Granberry mentioned was proving to be much more effective.

On the evening of 28 January Lieutenant Commander Morrill, the commander of the minesweeper *Quail*, was called to Corregidor. Arriving late that night, Morrill was briefed by Captain Hoeffel, the commander of the Inshore Patrol, for a special mission. Commander Bridget had requested that naval gunfire from the sea be provided to support the attack of the 2nd Battalion, 57th Infantry that would take place the following morning. *Quail* was selected for the mission because she was the only Navy ship in the Manila Bay area with armored shields to protect the gun crews on the upper deck. *Quail* mounted two 3-inch, .50-caliber dual-purpose guns on a platform just forward of the bridge, as well as a dozen .50-caliber machine guns. Admiral Rockwell and Captain Hoeffel were concerned about sending *Quail* for the mission, since she was one of only two minesweepers in the Bay equipped to sweep magnetic mines. The gun shield issue is what decided the matter.

At 0435 on the morning of the 29th Commander Bridget, Major Pugh, USA, and an Army captain boarded the ship at Mariveles. By 0520 *Quail* had cleared the channel through the minefield near little La Monja Island. It was very dark, which made navigation up the coast difficult. *Quail* was on a heading of 320 degrees, slowly moving northwestward toward Longoskawayan Point.

Just before 0600 *Quail* came under machine-gun fire and was then illuminated by American searchlights. A quick—and profane—radio call from Commander Bridget caused the lights to go out. By 0645 the ship had reached a point about eight thousand yards southwest of the Point. Morrill turned the ship toward its objective, proceeding forward at Slow Ahead speed.

At 0659 Army artillery from the units ashore started to hit the Japanese. Bridget provided spotting for that firing from *Quail*'s bridge. A minute later Corregidor's mortars joined in. Morrill and Bridget saw the first salvo from the big guns fall in the water, close to the Point. Bridget also sent corrections for that fire, but the 12-inch shells continued to miss.

At 0723 *Quail* commenced firing at the western tip of the Point at a range of 2,200 yards. Since Chief Gunner's Mate Taylor was hospitalized ashore, Morrill acted as gunnery officer, leaving two chiefs on the bridge to con the ship. The XO, Lieutenant (junior grade) J. E. Lee, was positioned at the aft control station. While one of the 3-inch and the .50-caliber machine guns were trained skyward in case of air attack, the other 3-inch weapon engaged targets ashore.

Within a few minutes Morrill spotted four men hiding behind bushes on the south side of the point. It seemed they had a small mortar (possibly one of the little "knee mortars"). The first round burst right among them, at which point both 3-inch guns engaged the spot, firing four two-gun salvos. The next target was a group of men in a cave near the waterline. Three rounds took out that group.

Quail was steadily closing the range. By 0745 it was down to roughly 1,300 yards as the ship engaged its next target, more men hiding in bushes along the beach. Bridget and Pugh requested that the ship search out every cave and clump of bushes along the shoreline. Two-gun salvos were fired into every possible hiding place along the shoreline that could be identified.

Around 0800 Navy headquarters in Corregidor became aware that an enemy warship was approaching the area of the fighting. A warning was sent to *Quail.*

It soon became clear that Admiral Rockwell and Captain Hoeffel were concerned for the ship, to the point that they wanted the bombardment mission curtailed. Bridget told Morrill to keep shooting, which the latter was more than willing to do.

At 0835 enemy aircraft were spotted in the distance. Morrill redirected one of his 3-inch guns to track the planes, leaving him with the second gun to continue shelling the beach. Ten minutes later a message from ashore arrived, requesting the ship to engage targets along the top of the cliffs. A number of rounds were firing against suspected enemy locations just below the edge of the cliffs. By 0850 another message from shore came in to cease fire against those targets, friendly troops were too close.

At 0854 another report was received that an enemy "cruiser" had been spotted offshore, headed in the direction of Longoskawayan Point. Army coast artillery observers high on Corregidor saw what appeared to be a three-funneled Japanese light cruiser about 40,000 yards to the northwest, heading toward the Point. By that time *Quail* had fired ninety-five rounds of 3-inch "common" (Navy terminology for a high explosive shell, with a limited armor piercing capability). The ship had sustained no damage or casualties. The only Japanese fire that had been directed its way was one mortar round and some machine-gun fire. None of this fell closer than five hundred yards from the ship. At 0855 the little ship set course for Mariveles, following stern orders from the Inshore Patrol Headquarters.[36]

The combined effects of *Quail*'s direct fire and the indirect shooting of the Army guns and Marine Corps mortars had greatly assisted the advance of the Scouts. Nevertheless, despite the heavy fire, the Japanese were resisting. As the Scouts reoccupied the area they had evacuated prior to the bombardment Army captain Arthur Wermuth, who had become famous during the fighting at Abucay, was hit and evacuated.

By midmorning the Scouts were making good progress toward the end of the point. Due to the close nature of the jungle terrain some hand-to-hand fighting took place. One Scout sergeant fought a Japanese armed with a sword. The Scout lost his hand but continued to fight until he was killed by an enemy bayonet. The commander of G Company was in hand-to-hand fighting with a Japanese who was about to stab him with a bayonet. A young Scout, only recently recruited, dashed forward and saved his commander by killing the Japanese with a point blank shot with his .45-caliber pistol.[37]

By 1430 the Scouts had reached the tip of the Point. Organized enemy resistance was over. As the Scouts closed in on the remaining Japanese, some threw themselves over the cliffs onto the rocks below rather than surrender. About twenty-five of them tried to escape in Filipino bancas across the little bay to

Naiklec Point to the southeast. All were killed by Scout machine-gun fire from the top of the cliffs.[38]

By late afternoon on the 29th the Battle of Longoskawayan was effectively over. American casualties during the seven days of fighting were, according to Commander Bridget, eleven naval personnel killed (including two Marines) and twenty-six injured. He listed eleven Army personnel as killed and another twenty-seven wounded.[39] It may be, however, that the casualties in the 2nd Battalion, 57th Infantry (PS) were a bit higher. According to Olson, who was the Regimental S-1 (personnel officer), there may have been thirty-nine to forty wounded in the battalion.[40]

Most of the enemy who had landed in the early morning of 23 January were dead. Some were, however, still hiding in the caves and underbrush around the point. They would have to be ferreted out.

When *Quail* arrived in Mariveles Harbor following its successful bombardment mission, word was received from Navy headquarters in Tunnel Queen that Commander Bridget and Lieutenant Commander Morrill were to report, immediately. Knowing that they had "pushed it" by staying on station as long as they had with a superior enemy warship apparently descending upon them, the two were expecting a dressing-down by Captain Hoeffel, if not Admiral Rockwell himself. When they arrived at the Navy tunnel the atmosphere was much better than they expected. It seems that while the pair were en route to the Navy headquarters Major General Wainwright, the I Corps commander on western Bataan, had called Admiral Rockwell full of complements and praise for *Quail*'s actions. All was forgiven.

MOPPING UP—30 JANUARY TO 1 FEBRUARY

Before the end of the day on the 29th groups of Scouts, aided by men from the Naval Battalion, started to comb the area for any remaining Japanese. This could be dangerous work. During the Abucay fighting the Filipinos and Americans started to understand that they were fighting an opponent who almost always preferred death to surrender and who fought ruthlessly. Already the troops on Bataan had learned to cautiously approach what appeared to be dead or wounded Japanese, lest the enemy have a concealed weapon waiting, usually a grenade, for a final attempt to kill Americans or Filipinos. It was during the mopping-up operations on the 30th that a new Navy capability was brought into action, the so-called "Mickey Mouse Battleships."

All during the past week of fighting *Canopus* had been of great assistance to the Naval Battalion. Over one hundred of her crew were part- or full-time members of the unit; seven of her men were among the eleven naval personnel killed in the fighting. Lieutenant Commander Goodall, the ship's XO, was doing double-duty as the exec of the Naval Battalion. While the fighting was under way *Canopus* had provided equipment, replacement personnel, food, and ammunition to the forward platoons fighting in the jungle. Several days into the battle, work had started to convert three of the ship's forty-foot motor launches into mini-gunboats.

Canopus had the best machine shops anywhere on the Bataan. The ship's machinists placed armor plate around the bow, stern, and engines of the launches. M-1916 37-mm guns were obtained from the Army and one was mounted in the bow of each vessel. Also near the bow were two .50-caliber machine guns, one on each beam. Toward the stern there were two .30-caliber machine guns. The boats were large enough to take gun crews and about a squad of men on board. Work on the first boat was finished on the morning of 30 January. It was immediately put to use. Lieutenant Commander Goodall and a scratch crew from *Canopus* manned the boat. Departing from Mariveles Harbor, they made two roundtrips on the first day, shooting up Japanese hiding places in the bushes and caves along the shoreline of Longoskawayan Point. During their first day of operations two Japanese prisoners were taken and six were confirmed killed.

Few of the enemy were left alive by this point. During that day the Scouts and Naval Battalion personnel found thirty dead Japanese in one cave and twenty in a second. Perhaps they had committed suicide, or they might have been killed by *Quail*'s firing the day before. Lieutenant Hogaboom accompanied a patrol of Scouts who flushed out and killed half dozen of the enemy at Lapiay Point, obviously a small group who were attempting to escape northward along the beach.

On the 31st a second "battleship" was put into use and joined the first vessel in searching the coastline. Four more Japanese were killed. A final effort on the 1st of February yielded a few more enemy, but that was the end of the fight.

As mentioned earlier 22 American Army, Navy, and Marine Corps personnel had died during the week of major fighting, with somewhere between 50–70 wounded. According to most accounts, including statements from captured Japanese, 301 enemy troops had landed at Longoskawayan Point on the morning of 23 January. Six prisoners had been taken, not including the two that Bulkeley had seized from the sinking landing barge. Therefore, about 295 had been killed. Captain Hidaka was certainly among them, although there is no way to know at what point during the fighting he died. No officer prisoners were taken.

THE IMPORTANCE OF THE BATTLE

The fighting at Longoskawayan Point is certainly a very unusual chapter in the history of the Navy and Marine Corps. The Naval Battalion, formed on

9 January and committed to battle exactly two weeks later, was very much an ad hoc organization created due to the increasingly desperate situation that the Americans on Bataan found themselves in.

The actions of the hastily organized, ill-equipped Naval Battalion were very important to the defense of Bataan. The Japanese landings at Quinauan and Longoskawayan Points took place in the middle of the withdrawal from the Abucay-Moron Line. For several critical days there were no Army reserves available to commit against the landing near the southernmost tip of Bataan. The Naval Battalion was the only nearby unit. Commander Bridget lost no time in committing his force against the enemy, thus preventing the Japanese from moving out of their little lodgment area of Lapiay and Longoskawayan Points. The prompt action of the Naval Battalion contained the enemy landing.

The Japanese force at Longoskawayan was certainly small, and therefore limited in its overall combat potential. Nevertheless, had a couple of hundred Japanese suddenly blocked the west coast road or fought their way into Mariveles it would have been a major crisis for the American command, especially since the difficult withdrawal from the Abucay position was under way. In that regard, great credit must go to the sailors and Marines of the Naval Battalion.

The sailors were much better in defense than attack—a common characteristic of rather poorly trained troops. When they encountered the Japanese the sailors tended to stubbornly stand their ground and blaze away into the jungle. They showed little concern for, indeed awareness of, the need for flank protection. Groups of Japanese infiltrated around and behind them, but rarely did it seem to concern the sailors much. Perhaps they did not know any better. Again, one can imagine the thoughts of the Marines who led and fought alongside the eager, but untrained, sailors. According to one source the sailors' morale was kept high because many of them took turns during the nights, after a hard day of fighting, to go back to *Canopus* for a short break, where the ship's ice-cream machine was operating at maximum capacity on their behalf.[41]

The presence of the Marines was absolutely vital. Representing only about a third of the men committed from 23 through 27 January, the Marines provided the critical leadership and example for the inexperienced sailors. Three Marine lieutenants—Holdredge, Hogaboom, and Simpson—were stalwarts of the defense in the first few days of the battle. Since Commander Bridget was often at his command post near the Mariveles airstrip, the three Marines provided the key leadership along the front line. The Navy lieutenants and ensigns who commanded platoons took their lead from the young Marine officers. All three Marines were awarded the Navy Cross for their actions at Longoskawayan Point.

A prewar picture of Lieutenant William Hogaboom

Source: Courtesy of Hogaboom's relatives

Despite all their guts and enthusiasm the Naval Battalion did not have the expertise to drive the Japanese back into the sea. Attacking is a more difficult task than defending. The men of the Naval Battalion lacked the weapons and experience to defeat their determined opponents who were using the jungle to great advantage. Additionally, they were fighting with numbers roughly equal to the enemy—not a formula conducive to successful offensive operations. Finally, the defensive firepower of the Japanese was formidable, especially their machine guns.

The arrival of the 2nd Battalion, 57th Infantry (PS) was the decisive turning point in the battle. The Naval Battalion could contain the enemy force, but an experienced infantry unit was needed to finish them off. This the Scouts did in two days of fighting, plus a few days of mop-up.

A few words should be devoted to the Japanese force. The three hundred men who landed at Longoskawayan Point were doomed because they were totally isolated. The Japanese command was not aware of the location of the force that had landed so far south. Indeed, it was not until after the fall of Bataan, when Japanese officers were shown the mass grave of their troops who had fought at Longoskawayan, that the enemy leaders learned the location of this missing unit. Captain Hidaka's diary makes it clear that he quickly determined where his unit had come ashore, but was soon hemmed in by pressure from the Naval Battalion. It is likely that by the last few days of fighting the Japanese were very short of food, water, and ammunition. With no help from other Japanese forces, they fought to the end.

CHAPTER 9

Defeating the First Japanese Offensive

While the battle of Longoskawayan Point was under way fierce fighting was raging on other parts of the Bataan Peninsula. As American and Filipino troops retreated from the Abucay Line the Japanese closely pursued them. The new line stretched across Bataan from Bagac Bay on the west to the little town of Orion on the shore of Manila Bay. The position was sited in the low ground between Bataan's two mountain ranges. As the line was being manned, MacArthur sent a message to General Marshall in Washington declaring: "With its occupation all maneuvering possibilities will cease. I intend to fight it out to complete destruction."[1]

So hasty was the retreat that in some places the new line was not completely sealed and Japanese troops got through the gaps into the rear of the tired Philippine Army divisions that manned the front. In the II Philippine Corps area the Japanese almost got through a hole in the 31st Division's line, but due to quick action by the American general who commanded the division—General Bluemel whom Colonel Howard had interacted with while the 4th Marines was still at Olongapo—reserves were rushed in just in time to seal the breach. Several days of savage fighting followed before the Japanese 65th Brigade was brought to a halt.

After the Americans and Filipinos established their new line across the middle of Bataan the enemy tried to shell the defenses near the shoreline by using small, armed vessels that sailed across the Bay from Manila. These attacks would always take place at night. The II Philippine Corps requested that the Navy try to intercept these attacks because the Philippine Army Q-boats that were under the operational control of the Corps were not able to find the enemy.

On the night of 30–31 January Lieutenant Commander Cheek went on board the gunboat *Luzon* that had the mission to patrol several miles offshore in an attempt to intercept the enemy craft. As the gunboat left South Harbor and headed north two enemy aircraft circled her at low altitude. Strangely, they made no effort to attack; rather they appeared to be searching for something. The planes came so close that *Luzon* opened fire on them three times.[2]

After dark *Luzon* cruised off Bataan's east coast for several hours, but saw no sign of enemy watercraft. While there the crew and passenger did get to observe quite a spectacle, because the gunboat was maneuvering directly opposite the "no man's land" between the Japanese and American lines. Bursting artillery shells, gun flashes, and tracers lit up the sky over the battlefield. To Cheek it appeared to be like the 4th of July, but with the knowledge that men were dying.[3]

BATTLE AT THE POINTS

An even more serious situation had developed in Major General Wainwright's I Philippine Corps on the western half of Bataan. There the retreat to the new line was more difficult because part of the Philippine Army 1st Division had been cut off near Mauban. The Filipino troops had been forced to abandon their heavy equipment and artillery and retreat to the new line via the beach. This prevented an orderly manning of the new battle position. In the confusion, a reinforced battalion of Japanese troops got behind the Filipino-American front and dug in. The so-called Battle of the Pockets lasted from 29 January to 12 February. A considerable number of troops had to be committed before the surviving Japanese retreated through the jungle to their own lines.

Meanwhile, a difficult situation had developed along Bataan's west coast. Recall that on the night of 22–23 January when the three hundred Japanese troops landed on Longoskawayan Point the other six hundred men of the 2nd Battalion, 20th Infantry had come ashore five miles farther north at Quinauan Point. The enemy first encountered poorly trained Army Air Force personnel, now serving as infantry, defending the beaches. The grounded airmen fled without putting up a fight. The Japanese pushed a few hundred yards inland and started to set up defensive positions. Like Captain Hidaka at Longoskawayan Point, the Japanese who landed at Quinauan Point were initially totally lost.

The force at Quinauan Point had the advantage that the Japanese command soon learned their location and took actions to reinforce its troops. On the night of 27 January one company from the 1st Battalion, 20th Infantry traveled by barge to reinforce the men at Quinauan, but instead landed at nearby Anyasan

Point, about a mile north of the now hard-pressed 2nd Battalion. General Wainwright recognized the threat posed by the enemy beachheads behind his front line and committed all the troops he could spare to eliminate the Japanese. He also received reinforcements from the USAFFE reserve; most of the 45th and 57th Infantry Regiments (PS) were committed to the Battle of the Points.

This was a much bloodier battle compared to Longoskawayan Point. During the three weeks of fighting at Quinauan and Anyasan Points the American and Filipino troops suffered about five hundred casualties, despite the fact that tanks were brought in along the jungle trails and there was considerable support from friendly field artillery.

On the night of 1–2 February the Japanese made yet another landing attempt. This time it was the rest of the 1st Battalion, 20th Infantry that would land to reinforce the troops in the Anyasan-Quinauan Points areas. It was hoped that with these additional troops and extra supplies that the Japanese force could take the offensive and move inland to cut the west coast road.

Unfortunately for the Japanese their move to reinforce the toehold on the western Bataan shoreline would be met with fierce resistance. A copy of the order for the landing had been found on the body of a dead Japanese officer on 28 January. The Americans and Filipinos were going to be ready. The troops in the area were alerted to expect the arrival of the enemy landing force, more tanks were moved into the area, and the four serviceable P-40 fighters at the Cabcaben airstrip were armed with 30-pound fragmentation bombs and placed on alert. The Navy also dispatched PT-32 into the area to wait for the arrival of the enemy landing force.

The PT boat, accompanied by the armed yacht *Maryanne*, left Sisiman Cove at 1845 on 1 February and headed through the minefield channel. As they approached the area of Quinauan and Anyasan Points the crew of the PT boat could see flashes of gunfire coming from the area near the Points. This firing was from the Army troops who had spotted the approaching enemy landing barges.

Lieutenant E. G. De Long, the Squadron 3 XO, and Lieutenant (junior grade) V. E. Schumacher, the skipper of the 32 Boat, spotted an enemy ship shortly after 2100, dead ahead at a range of about five thousand yards. Going to Battle Stations, the PT boat started to accelerate to its best speed of 22 knots—only two of the boat's three engines were in operation. The moon was full and visibility excellent. *Maryanne* steered clear of the impending action, continuing her patrol to the north.

As the 32 Boat started to close the range, the enemy vessel was seen to turn away to the north and increase speed. Soon it was observed that the ship was pulling away from the PT boat, meaning that she was probably making over

25 knots. Unexpectedly, the enemy ship then turned eastward toward the Bataan shore. Now the range started to close rapidly.

As PT-32 approached, the enemy ship turned a powerful searchlight on the American craft. Within seconds a two-gun salvo landed in the water about five hundred yards in front of the PT boat as she closed the range to set up for a torpedo shot. Two more enemy salvos hit the water, ahead and astern of the PT boat. At a range of about three thousand yards two torpedoes were launched, and the 32 Boat turned away, firing her .50-caliber machine guns at the searchlight as more enemy shells hit the water near the somewhat faster PT, now minus two tons of torpedoes.

As the 32 Boat completed her turn to starboard, a column of water that seemed to include debris rose in the searchlight beam. Taking this to be a torpedo hit, the PT boat maneuvered away as the enemy ship continued to fire at her. It seemed that the Japanese vessel was slowing as the 32 Boat escaped the searchlight beam and reached the safety of darkness. Rendezvousing with *Maryanne*, the 32 Boat made for the entrance to the minefield. As dawn broke, her crew could see Army P-40s diving over western Bataan in the vicinity of Quinauan-Anyasan Points.

The enemy vessel that PT-32 had attacked was the Japanese minelayer *Yaeyama*, which was supporting the landing of the 1st Battalion, 20th Infantry. According to Japanese records the 1,300-ton minelayer, which was armed with 4.7-inch guns, suffered minor damage that night, but certainly not a torpedo hit. The column of water that the PT boat crew saw could have been from a premature explosion of one of their torpedoes or it might have been a shell splash from one of the Army guns ashore that were firing at the Japanese barges.[4]

While the 32 Boat was doing battle with the *Yaeyama* the troops ashore were providing a hot reception to the 1st Battalion. Under fire from 75- and 155-mm artillery, machine guns, and small arms, and under attack by the P-40s, the Japanese force suffered many casualties as it approached the shore. Several of the twelve landing barges were sunk and the survivors were seen to turn away to the north. Instead of returning to Subic Bay, however, the remaining barges landed at Anyasan Point where they met the battalion's company that had landed there three days before. The battle was going to take longer to resolve now that about three hundred more enemy troops had made it ashore.

By 6 February the surviving Japanese at Quinauan Point had been pushed over the edge of the cliffs at the tip of the point and were holding out in caves along the water's edge. Army troops who attempted to go down the cliffs to eliminate the enemy hideouts suffered casualties. So, a call went out for Navy support.

On the morning of 8 February two of *Canopus'* armed launches left Mariveles for Quinauan Point. On board were Lieutenant Commander Goodall, the Old Lady's XO, and the Navy boat crews. Twenty Army Air Force personnel from the 21st Pursuit Squadron followed in two motor whaleboats. Leading the Army troops was Captain William Dyess, the commander of the 21st. Dyess was in Goodall's launch. The Mickey Mouse battleships were armed as they had been off Longoskawayan Point, with machine guns and 37-mm cannons. Heading north at their best speed, the little flotilla's mission was to engage the Japanese hiding in the caves near the waterline. Captain Dyess' men were prepared to go ashore if need be. Three Marines from Battery A at Mariveles had volunteered to go along to serve as machine-gunners.[5]

The boats arrived off Quinauan Point after dawn and started to engage enemy troops in caves at the base of the cliffs. American and Filipino Army troops had hung white sheets over the edge of the cliffs, directly above the caves. This simple expedient allowed the men on board the launches to spot the Japanese hiding places. Thirty-three enemy troops were killed from gunfire from the two "battleships." Then disaster struck. Four enemy light bombers—probably Japanese Army Ki-30s—flying off the west coast of Bataan spotted the two boats and dove to attack. The four boats headed toward shore and opened fire with their machine guns at the enemy planes. Light 60-kilogram bombs started exploding in the water close to the launches. Gunner's Mate 3rd Class C. H. Kramb was killed as he fired his .50-caliber machine gun at the enemy aircraft.

One of the Mickey Mouse battleships had a large hole blown in its bottom and started to founder. The enemy aircraft came around to strafe with their machine guns. Lieutenant Commander Goodall, who was seriously wounded in both feet, ordered the boats to run for the shore and beach themselves. Two of the four were sunk before they could reach land. Dyess and most of his men swam ashore. By the time the Japanese planes departed three sailors had been killed and fifteen Army and Navy men were wounded, including Goodall. The survivors improvised stretchers for the wounded and carried them inland through the jungle until they reached the west coast road.[6]

A passing Army truck gave the men a ride back to the Old Lady. Goodall was given immediate treatment and then shipped over to the hospital on Corregidor. The other wounded were sent to one of the Army field hospitals on Bataan. The next day men from *Canopus* went to the site where the two boats were beached and stripped them of all useful equipment.[7] The sinking of the launches was an example of what could happen if the Navy's ships or boats operated in daylight outside the anti-aircraft protection of Corregidor.

By 12 February the fighting at Quinauan and Anyasan Points had just about ended. It had been a far longer and costlier battle compared to Longoskawayan Point. Although several hundred Americans and Filipinos had been killed or wounded, two battalions of the Japanese 20th Infantry Regiment had been virtually wiped out.

It was during the fighting at the Points that General Wainwright, the I Philippine Corps commander, requested a naval liaison officer in order to be better aware of the Navy's activities and to expedite naval support. When the request reached Admiral Rockwell he dispatched his flag lieutenant, Malcolm Champlin, to serve with Wainwright. Even after the Japanese landings were defeated Champlin remained with Wainwright; the lieutenant could tell that "Skinny" appreciated the Navy's efforts in the defense of Bataan very much.

On 10 March Wainwright and his immediate staff were driving toward the front lines along Bataan's west coast road. Wainwright wanted to make a check of the troops before heading to Corregidor for a meeting with General MacArthur. Suddenly, Champlin spotted a plane diving out of the sun toward them. He yelled for everyone to get out of the car. The men scattered just in time as a Japanese fighter riddled the car with machine-gun fire. Champlin fired his M-1 rifle at the plane until he was out of ammunition. Wainwright had loaned the rifle to him. Now it became a permanent gift, one that Champlin kept for the rest of his life. He had saved the life of one of the best fighting generals on Bataan.[8]

THE FIRST ARTILLERY BOMBARDMENT FROM CAVITE

The Japanese had occupied the ruined Cavite Navy Yard on 3 January. Within days they started to move westward along the south shore of Manila Bay to establish observation points in order to overlook the fortified islands. By mid-January enemy patrols had occupied the shore several miles west of Ternate. The next step was to bring up artillery to shell the harbor forts.

The first Japanese artillery unit to move into Cavite Province was the Kondo Detachment, named for its commander, Major Toshinori Kondo. Kondo's command was the 2nd Battalion, 8th Field Heavy Artillery Regiment armed with eight 105-mm guns. The Type 92 105-mm weapons could strike targets at a range of up to 20,000 yards. This allowed them to reach Corregidor from firing positions in the vicinity of Ternate. By the morning of 6 February the enemy was ready to start the first artillery bombardment of the harbor defenses.

Most of the Navy's ships were moored in South Harbor between Corregidor and Fort Hughes that morning. Just after 0810 the first Japanese shells began to fall. The 105-mm projectiles sent up shell splashes as the crews were called to Battle Stations and orders given to get under way. An enemy shell hit *Luzon* before she could start moving, but only minor damage was inflicted. Another enemy shell landed less than three hundred yards from the anchored *Mindanao*. Salvos were soon arriving every three to four minutes. The ships of the Inshore Patrol, along with various installations on Corregidor's Tail, were both targeted. As soon as they could the ships started to move around Corregidor's eastern tip to the safer anchorage of the North Channel. Even there it seemed that they would not be completely safe; a few of the Japanese shells sailed all the way over Corregidor and landed in the water between The Rock and Bataan.[9]

The enemy shifted his firing among various targets throughout the morning. Fort Drum, the concrete battleship, was Kondo's primary target. The fort took about one hundred hits that morning but no significant damage was suffered. Drum replied with two 6-inch guns on its south, "port," side and Fort Frank, which also took some hits that day, fired back with its 12-inch mortars. Unfortunately, it was almost impossible to determine where the enemy fire was coming from. Several suspected enemy positions near Ternate and Naic were shelled, but no direct sighting of the enemy was made. Major Kondo had done a good job of concealing his guns in the jungle and on the reverse slope of hills. By 1100 the first bombardment was over.[10]

The first day's action established a pattern that would last for over a month. The Japanese would usually fire during the morning when the sun was low and generally behind them, thus hindering the observation of the Americans on Corregidor and the other islands. By late morning the shooting would normally stop. The Americans could not see the enemy firing locations, having to rely on map surveys to determine where the Japanese might be shooting from. On the other hand, the 35-pound 105-mm shells did relatively little damage.

On the second day of shelling the minesweeper *Quail* was sent to try to spot the hostile firing locations. The ship closed to within three miles of the Cavite shoreline near Ternate in an attempt to find the enemy. With the crew at Battle Stations and guns aimed at the shore, observers on *Quail* tried to spot the Japanese gun positions, but had no luck. On the other hand, the enemy did not fire while the ship was cruising nearby, probably fearing that their muzzle flashes or smoke might be seen.[11]

During the 8th and 9th the Japanese intensified their shelling, this time directing more fire at Corregidor. A number of enemy shells were aimed at the area east of Monkey Point on Corregidor's Tail where Station C had a number of its radio aerials and radio direction finders set up. Apparently the Japanese could see some of the aerials from Cavite, for a fair number of shells were aimed at the area. One morning an enemy shell landed every two minutes around

Station C's equipment on the Tail of the island. Within a few days the area around the direction finders was full of shell craters. Station C personnel had to periodically go into the area to effect repairs on their equipment. The Navy men noticed that on a typical day the Japanese would shell the area from their radio antennas westward to Kindley Field. Some shells also struck the Army's Denver Battery, the 3-inch anti-aircraft unit atop the little ridge just west of Kindley Field.

The area around Malinta Hill and Bottomside also received a number of shells. Several hit the South Dock area, but did little damage. The Army coast defense guns on Forts Hughes, Drum, and Frank fired back as best they could, but it was mostly guesswork based on map estimates of where the enemy artillery *might* be.

On the morning of 9 February the American command decided to conduct an aerial reconnaissance of the area around Cavite. Philippine Army Air Corps captain Jesus Villamor piloted an old PT-13 biplane with a Philippine Army sergeant on board to take photos in an attempt to locate the Japanese gun positions. Escorting Villamor were the five operational P-40s still on Bataan. Villamor crisscrossed the Ternate area several times at about ten thousand feet as his sergeant took over one hundred pictures with the bulky camera.

As the old biplane returned to the airfield on Bataan it was jumped by a Japanese Army Ki-27 Nate fighter; Villamor barely managed to land his damaged aircraft. The precious photos were saved. Meanwhile, a series of dogfights were swirling over Manila Bay as the P-40s engaged six Japanese fighters from the 50th Sentai that had flown over from their base near Manila.[12]

Mindanao was moored in the North Channel where she was safer from the enemy artillery fire coming from Cavite. The crew all came topside to watch the air battle. It was very rare to see American aircraft by that point in the campaign. One P-40 dove low toward the Bay with a Nate on its tail. The crews of the starboard machine guns waited until the Japanese fighter was flying beside the ship at very low altitude, about three hundred yards away, and then opened fire. Thirteen .30-caliber machine guns poured fire at the enemy fighter at virtually point blank range; they fired over 1,500 rounds in less than a minute. The Nate was seen to falter, its wings wagged, and it sped away. The P-40 turned around and took one parting shot at the enemy plane before it managed to escape.[13] Shortly thereafter a Ki-27 was seen making an emergency landing at the Pilar airfield inside Japanese lines along Bataan's east coast. After the plane landed Army 155-mm guns opened fire and destroyed the aircraft on the ground. Possibly this was the fighter that *Mindanao* had damaged with its machine-gun fire.

The American P-40 pilots made no claims for enemy aircraft shot down that day, although it was certain that one U.S. fighter had been lost. So, the pilots

USS Mindanao *before the war in China*
Source: U.S. Naval Institute Photo Archive

were quite surprised to hear a USAFFE press report that evening, claiming that all six Japanese fighters had been shot down. It was another example of the exaggerated reports being generated by MacArthur's headquarters.[14]

The same day as the rare aerial action over Manila Bay *Mindanao* received a regular resupply of rations from Tunnel Queen. It was normal for the ships of the Inshore Patrol to pick up fresh rations every week to ten days. For the roughly 75 men on board on 9 February it was a pretty good allowance: 40 pounds of coffee, 31 pounds of peas, 31 pounds of cherries, 43 pounds of peaches, 39 pounds of sauerkraut, 72 pounds of corned beef, 144 pounds of jam, 84 pounds of beets, 56 pounds of syrup, 75 pounds of pounds of apples, 50 pounds of minced meat, and 630 pounds of fresh beef.[15]

By mid-February that quantity and variety of food would have been almost beyond belief for an 80–100-man Army infantry company on Bataan. Even if the amount of food listed above was expected to last a 75-man ship's crew for a week, it was a far more nutritious and much better balanced ration compared to what the Army was able to serve its troops on Bataan by this time, most of whom were already subsisting on canned salmon and rice, with some carabao meat occasionally added.[16] This record of supply to the gunboat is further evidence of the foresight of the Navy's leadership when they took action in mid-December to move considerable quantities of food to Corregidor and Mariveles.[17]

ENEMY OFFENSIVE COLLAPSES

By the middle of February the Japanese offensive on Bataan was grinding to a halt. Two battalions of the 16th Division's 20th Infantry Regiment had been completely destroyed during the battles along Bataan's west coast. The same regiment's remaining battalion bad been badly battered during the Battle of the Pockets. Along Bataan's east coast the 65th Brigade had been brought to a halt with heavy casualties and forced to go on the defensive. Having started the Bataan campaign with an inadequate force, the Japanese were now almost totally devoid of reserves. By mid-February, of the thirteen battalions of infantry that the 14th Army had committed to Bataan, two had been completely destroyed, an additional battalion was nearly wiped out, and all the remaining units were badly under strength.

By the middle of February a few 150-mm guns had been added to the Japanese artillery detachment in Cavite, but it was not enough to have a serious effect on the Americans. The bombardment from Cavite was a dangerous nuisance as opposed to a significant threat.

The defenders of Bataan had succeeded in driving off the first major enemy offensive. There are no figures on the numbers of casualties that the Army forces on Bataan had suffered by this point after approximately a month of fighting, but it clearly numbered several thousand. It is important to note that Filipino units had done most of the fighting along the main line running from Bagac to Orion. The fighting along Bataan's west coast included a higher percentage of American troops. The Naval Battalion's fight at Longoskawayan Point was one of the battles that helped bring the enemy offensive to a halt.

LEARNING ABOUT MacARTHUR

It was during the initial battles on Bataan that the Navy got a firsthand view of MacArthur's propaganda machine at work. Various commentators have described MacArthur's publicity campaign as decades ahead of its time. That may be so, but there is no denying the fact that MacArthur's dispatches from the Philippines (there were roughly 140 during the campaign) contained numerous lies. While MacArthur could only find the time to visit Bataan once before he left for Australia, he personally scrutinized every press release, indeed, he wrote many of them himself. Below are some examples of the difference between the claims of MacArthur's messages and communiqués and what the Navy really knew to be the truth.

As the retreat from the Abucay Line to the second battle position on Bataan was under way MacArthur released the following communiqué:

> In Luzon our counterattack on the right was a smashing success. Our powerful artillery concentration of 155s was deadly. Our infantry found the enemy completely disorganized in this area; he left hundreds of dead on the field and quantities of supplies and equipment. He is now shifting his center of gravity to the west where his supply lines are secured by his

> Navy. His beach landings on the Subic Bay coast are being cleared up. His pressure on my left forced me to give ground with some loss including guns of the obsolete 2.95 type, but the situation is now stabilized. It was close, but for the present the immediate danger is over.[18]

Two days after the above message was sent, MacArthur sent another dispatch to Marshall that stated the following: "Under cover of darkness I broke contact with the enemy and without the loss of a man or an ounce of material I am now firmly established on my main battle position. The execution of the movement would have done credit to the best troops in the world."[19]

Meanwhile, the 16th Naval District intelligence officer, Lieutenant Commander Cheek, had been visiting American and Philippine Army units on Bataan during the fighting along the Abucay Line. In late January Cheek dispatched, with Admiral Rockwell's approval, an assessment of the situation to the Office of Naval Intelligence (ONI) in Washington. It included this passage regarding the performance of the Philippine Army's 51st Division fighting along the eastern portion of the Abucay Line:

> Learn[ed] from USAFFE reports that the ground I went over on the 14th about one mile in rear of the front line had been taken by the enemy on the 15th following disgraceful retreat by our 51st Division. The Filipino Captain of Co G, 51st Infantry led his company in full flight to the rear upon opening of a light artillery barrage by the enemy. The panic spread to all this regiment, to the 53rd Regiment and even to the reserve (52nd) Regiment a mile in rear of the front. Machine guns, rifles, ammunition and equipment were abandoned—and the former were turned on the disorganized 51st Division by the enemy. This division is one of the poorly trained, all-Filipino-officered new divisions.[20]

During the same trip to Bataan, Cheek met with the U.S. Army colonel who was the senior instructor to the Philippine Army 21st Infantry Regiment. Cheek related that the Army officer was very frank about the performance of his regiment, stating that he started the campaign with 1,700 officers and men, but by the time the unit reached Bataan about 400 remained. Of the 1,300 missing men the colonel was sure that most had deserted, although a few had returned.

As to MacArthur's claim that the retreat from the Abucay position had been "without the loss of a man or an ounce of material," Cheek discovered that in reality the I Philippine Corps alone had abandoned two 155s, eight 75s, thirteen 2.95s, scores of machine guns and thousands of rifles, along with a large amount of motor vehicles, ammunition, and other supplies. He noted that while the Scout units had retreated in good order, some of the Philippine Army divisions had lost 40 percent of their strength, largely through desertions.[21]

Portions of Lieutenant Commander Cheek's assessment was transmitted to the Office of Naval Intelligence (ONI) in Washington in late January. Without naming him, ONI prepared a memo that was sent to the Army's Chief of Military Intelligence Division, also in Washington. Key insights from Cheek's memo were provided to the Army, including the Navy's observations of the poor performance of the Philippine Army. This telling passage was included in the memo that went to the head of Army intelligence: "Many [Army] officers in the frontal area agree with naval views that the stories of the valiant Philippine Army in glorious retreat to the three hundred square miles on Bataan Peninsula and the subsequent defense of the lines there are without foundation in fact."[22]

The Navy intelligence personnel, both from the 16th Naval District and Station C, were also assembling a picture of the Japanese order of battle in the Philippines. They were very surprised to hear the press releases coming from MacArthur's headquarters claiming that 200,000 enemy troops were on Luzon. Based on MacArthur's press releases, this number of Japanese was frequently quoted by the press back in the United States during and after the Bataan campaign.

When Lieutenant Commander Denys Knoll (who took over as District intelligence officer in early March when Cheek departed by submarine) returned to the United States following his evacuation by submarine in early May he was assigned to the Office of the Chief of Naval Operations—Admiral King's personal staff. He prepared a lengthy memorandum covering the period from when he took over from Cheek until his evacuation from Corregidor. His memo described the condescending attitude of MacArthur and his staff toward Navy personnel in the Philippines. In his report Knoll made it quite clear that there was consensus among the Navy intelligence personnel in the Philippines that at no time did the Japanese have more than 60,000 men in the Islands, even following the considerable reinforcements that the enemy received prior to his final offensive in April. Knoll contrasted this to the figures that had been provided to the public—and General Marshall—by MacArthur's staff. It is very likely that Admiral King, who quickly came to detest MacArthur, saw this memo.[23] It should be noted that Knoll highlighted the much improved state of Army–Navy relations in the Philippines once MacArthur departed and General Wainwright took command.

Therefore, as time went by the Navy personnel in the Philippines could see the stark difference between MacArthur's grandiose claims and reality. The lies coming from USAFFE Headquarters were repulsive to those officers who knew the true situation. As word of what was really going in the Philippines gradually filtered out, the Navy's impression of MacArthur became increasingly negative.[24]

CHAPTER 10

The Lull

By mid-February the Japanese offensive had been defeated. Although some members of his staff were still in favor of continuing the attack, General Homma realized that the 14th Army was so badly battered that it might not be able to resist a Filipino-American counter-offensive, much less maintain its own attack. Therefore, he decided to fall back to northern Bataan, tighten the air and sea blockade of the Peninsula and Corregidor, and wait for reinforcements before resuming the drive to eliminate the surprisingly stubborn defenders. It was clear that the need to discontinue the offensive was a direct consequence of the late December decision by Imperial General Headquarters to withdraw the 48th Division and most of Homma's air support.

As it became apparent that the Japanese were withdrawing, morale on Bataan reached an all-time high. The troops knew that they had done well, even if they did not realize that they had outnumbered the Japanese by about three-to-one. The news that Bataan and Corregidor were holding out also electrified the American public. After all, the Japanese were pulling back on Bataan at the same point in time that Singapore was surrendering to the enemy and the fate of the Dutch East Indies was all but sealed.

Now began the middle portion of the campaign, lasting from mid-February to late March. During this period the main American concern was how to get more supplies to the defenders of Bataan and Corregidor before the garrison was literally starved into submission.

THE STATE OF THE BATAAN NAVY

Up to this point in the campaign the Inshore Patrol had lost few ships. Indeed, other than the two PT boats lost in December and January and the Mickey

Mouse battleships sunk in February, the naval force in Manila Bay was essentially intact. The main problem that now confronted Admiral Rockwell was fuel for his ships, and to a lesser extent maintenance and food.

In early February Admiral Hart, now in Java, suggested that several of the gunboats and minesweepers be allowed to head southward from Manila Bay to the Indies where they could be usefully employed. Admiral Rockwell raised the issue with MacArthur and Sutherland, but was turned down. MacArthur stated the Navy ships were performing essential duties such as covering the minefield, patrolling Manila Bay and off the west coast of Bataan, and the areas around the fortified islands. He stated that if the services of the ships were no longer needed, and the opportunity presented itself for an escape, that he would consider allowing selected vessels to try to escape southward. Unfortunately, the decision to allow some of the ships of the Inshore Patrol to try to make their way to the south was never made.[1]

The last time most of the ships had topped off their fuel bunkers had been just before Christmas when Manila was declared an Open City. The Navy had been able to tow a small number of fuel barges to Mariveles in late December. Since then the only new source of fuel had been what could be salvaged from half-sunk vessels around Manila Bay. Occasionally this proved to be a fairly lucrative source. For example, the crew of the Army mine planter *General Harrison* checked out the wreck of the freighter *Don Jose* that was aground just off Hooker Point on the easternmost tip of Corregidor and discovered that some of the ship's fuel tanks were still intact. *Pigeon* assisted in this work, which recovered 160,000 gallons of fuel oil. This was shared among a number of vessels.

Several of the ships were rather bold in their quest for oil, sallying fairly deep into Manila Bay to check out wrecked, half-sunk ships to see if there was any usable fuel on board. That could be a dangerous undertaking because the process of pumping out oil from a wreck took hours. It was too dangerous to continue the work during daylight because Japanese aircraft were sure to attack if the wreck was far from the anti-aircraft defenses of Bataan and Corregidor.[2]

On 15 February *Mindanao* split 20,000 gallons of fuel oil with the *Luzon*. That was the last fuel either ship received during the campaign. By the first week in March it was normal for the gunboats and sweepers to cut their boilers, maintaining just enough pressure to keep lights going and for cooking. The difference in fuel consumption could be considerable. When operating at high speed a gunboat could consume 2,000 to 2,500 gallons of fuel oil in a day. When sitting idle the daily expenditure dropped to 200–400 gallons.[3] Increasingly, the ships' crews were spending time ashore, either in or near Tunnel Queen, dug in near Tunnel Afirm on Corregidor's Tail, or on Fort Hughes. Each day one ship was designated the duty vessel. That ship would maintain sufficient steam to allow it to get under way at short notice.[4]

By the middle of March patrolling by the sweepers and gunboats had basically come to an end. The duty vessel would anchor a few miles east of Corregidor, but would not patrol. With the boilers only occasionally in use it was estimated that most of the ships could continue to operate in this reduced state for five to six months with the fuel that they still had on board. For example, by the end of March *Mindanao* still had approximately 19,000 gallons of fuel oil.[5]

The dry dock *Dewey* proved to be very useful during this period of relative calm. The PT boats of Squadron 3 were lifted into the dock for maintenance, as were the Philippine Army Q-boats. Hulls were scraped and repainted and repairs performed. PT-35 went into *Dewey* as early as 27 January, followed by 41, 34, and 32 Boats, in that order. Unfortunately, the shortage of parts was a major limitation, especially the lack of spare engines. The Old Lady was called on to manufacture parts for the PT boats.[6]

Various attempts were made to boost morale. All hands were desperate for news about how the war was going. Needless to say they were especially interested in any word about a relief expedition heading toward the Philippines. In Tunnel Queen a newsletter was started, the "Navy Evening Gopher." This little rag was published every few days, providing short summaries of the news extracted from the various radio stations that could be heard on Corregidor. This included a number of stations in California. A fortunate few could huddle around short wave radios to hear the broadcasts, but most waited eagerly for the Gopher to reach them. At times these radio broadcasts caused a considerable amount of resentment among the men, especially when some commentator located thousands of miles away dared the enemy to bomb Corregidor. Station KGEI from San Francisco was particularly notorious in this regard.

That the Marines could keep their sense of humor is evidenced by the following piece that showed up in the Gopher. It was titled "The Corregidor Marines' Hymn":

From the holes of Mariveles
To the shores of Cavite
We watch the Nippon bombers
On the land as on the sea.
First to jump for hole and tunnel
And to keep our skivvies clean,
We are proud to claim the title
Of Corregidor Marines.

Our drawers unfurled to every breeze
From dawn to setting sun
We have ducked in every hole and ditch
Where we could quickly run
In the holes of far off hilltops
And in gloomy deep ravines
You will find us always in a hole—
The Corregidor Marines.

Here's holes for you and for our Corps
Which we have dug in dirt
In many a strife we've jumped for life
And damn near lost our shirts
If the Army and the Navy
Ever look out Tunnel Queens
They will find that they are guarded
By Corregidor Marines.[7]

There were other sources of information for the men. Every day the "Voice of Freedom" broadcast from Malinta Tunnel. Philippine Army colonel Carlos Romulo was MacArthur's Filipino public relations officer and also—literally—the Voice of Freedom. The broadcasts were intended to counter the Japanese message to the Filipino people and the troops. Unfortunately, the Voice of Freedom was soon recognized by many of the troops on Bataan and Corregidor as being mostly propaganda and often stirred a considerable amount of resentment, especially among the Americans.[8]

A number of Navy officers who managed to escape from Manila Bay and wrote after action reports for the Navy staff in Washington remarked on the morale of the sailors and Marines in the Manila Bay area. All were highly complementary, stating that the men were surprisingly upbeat, never doubting that help was on the way and that eventually Japan would be beaten. Several of the writers also contrasted what they claimed to be good morale of the naval personnel with many of the Army units, noting that many of the younger Army troops became very demoralized as time went by. As the campaign wore on an increasing number of Army personnel could be found in Malinta Tunnel, apparently doing nothing. It was observed that many of these younger soldiers were suffering from "tunnelitis," which could be described as a lack of willingness to leave the supposed safety of the tunnel once there. This tendency became particularly pronounced following the fall of Bataan.[9]

If there really was a difference in morale between the Army and Navy/Marine Corps personnel it was probably due to the generally greater experience of the latter. On 1 July 1939 the U.S. Army (including the Army Air Corps) numbered only 174,000 active-duty personnel. By December 1941 the Army had grown to 1,686,000 officers and men, roughly a ninefold increase in two and a half years. The Navy and Marines had also expanded, but not nearly so fast. During the same period the Navy had grown from about 125,000 personnel on active duty to some 337,000, about a third of the Army's rate of increase. Similarly, the Marine Corps had grown from 19,400 active-duty personnel in June 1939 to about 66,000 when Pearl Harbor was attacked, a rate of expansion roughly similar to the Navy's.[10]

It was during this period that one of the Navy's "gifts" to the Army went into action. During the evacuation of the Cavite Navy Yard one of the weapons that was salvaged was the spare 1.1-inch four-barreled anti-aircraft gun that had been left by *Houston*. Taken to Corregidor by lighter, the weapon was given to the Army. A scratch crew from the 60th Coast Artillery was assembled, and with the help of some Navy chiefs who were familiar with this type of weapon the painstaking process of disassembling the bulky, water-cooled gun was begun. The plan was to emplace it atop Malinta Hill where it would have an excellent field of fire, particularly of Kindley Field and Corregidor's Tail, as well as South Harbor and North Channel. A spare automobile engine was used for the mount's power supply. The chiefs trained the Army gunners on the use of the weapons once it was assembled atop the hill.

By 11 February the 1.1-inch was in action. Often referred to as a "pom-pom" gun by the crews of the Inshore Patrol, the weapon was ideal for engaging low-flying Japanese aircraft up to about eight thousand feet. This was significantly above the maximum altitude of the .50-caliber machine guns ashore and afloat. Many Navy and Marine veterans of the campaign remembered the streams of tracer rounds that would spew from the 1.1's four barrels as Japanese aircraft tried to swoop in to attack ships anchored in the North Channel.

By this point in the campaign enough had been learned about the Japanese that some insights could be provided to help other American forces preparing to engage the enemy. Colonel Howard prepared a summary of Japanese equipment and tactics. Howard stressed that the enemy made extensive use of infiltration techniques and was particularly good at using camouflage. Enemy equipment was summarized, including Japanese aircraft and ground combat weapons. Howard mentioned that Japanese prisoners had been told by their officers that if captured the Americans would kill them. Most of the prisoners stated that American artillery fire was particularly effective. Howard addressed his report to the Commandant of the Marine Corps; it left Corregidor via submarine.[11] As an aside, by 19 February there were fifty-six Japanese prisoners being held on

Bataan, either at a special ward in Hospital Number 1 or in a stockade. There were no officer prisoners.[12]

STRENGTHENING THE BEACH DEFENSES ON CORREGIDOR AND THE OTHER FORTS

During this period of relative quiet from mid-February to late March some of the Navy and Marine Corps personnel were moved to new locations in the Bay area. The Japanese shelling of the harbor forts increased the concern that the enemy was preparing to the launch amphibious assaults against one or more of the forts from Cavite Province or Manila. Therefore, in mid-February a large portion of the personnel of Commander Bridget's battalion at Mariveles was moved to Corregidor and Fort Hughes to strengthen the beach defenses.

On 16 February Admiral Rockwell directed Commander Bridget to move his Aviation and Headquarters Companies from Mariveles to Fort Hughes. Bridget would be the officer-in-charge of the beach defenses of the fort. The move took place the next day. Nine Navy officers and 336 enlisted men from Mariveles were added to the 4th Marines' rolls. Some of the Navy men, led by Frank Bridget, went to Fort Hughes while the rest joined the force on Corregidor. That same day the Marines of Battery A deployed to The Rock and were absorbed into various companies of the regiment. This left fewer than 100 Marines in the Mariveles area: Battery C that still manned 3-inch anti-aircraft guns.[13]

The next day, 18 February, 26 officers and 705 Filipino enlisted men from the Philippine Army Air Corps were transferred to Corregidor and added to the 4th Marines. A few Marine officers and NCOs were detached from their units and a new company was formed for each of the three battalions. When the Filipinos arrived the Marines were surprised at their poor physical condition—the effect of the Bataan ration—and limited equipment. Most of the newcomers were very young and armed only with rifles. Few had steel helmets, and many only had the uniforms that they wore when they arrived. Interestingly, in the 1st and 2nd Battalions the new companies were not designated as Companies C and G, the two missing units; "Reserve Company" was the title that was used.[14]

Also on the 16th Rockwell ordered that the functions of the Section Base at Mariveles be suspended. Those few personnel who still manned the little base, which by this point had been badly damaged by enemy bombing, were placed under the command of Commander Sackett of *Canopus* who now became the senior Navy officer in the Mariveles area.

During late February the headquarters of the Provisional Tank Group on Bataan recommended that a platoon of light tanks (probably three or four vehicles) be deployed to Corregidor to provide an armored reserve for the 4th

The 3rd Battalion staff on Corregidor. Lieutenant Colonel Adams is on the left, followed by Major Mathiesen, the battalion XO; Captain Golland, the adjutant; Lieutenant Hogshire, USN, the battalion surgeon; Captain Robinton; and Warrant Officer Shimel.
Source: USMC Historical Division, Quantico, Va.

Marines. This was an excellent suggestion; it would have provided tank support for the Marines and other troops manning the beaches. The first Japanese offensive had been defeated and the two American tank battalions on Bataan still had about sixty M-3 light tanks between them (the original strength of the two battalions had been 108 vehicles). The suggestion was, however, turned down, probably because the tanks were considered so vital to the defense of Bataan.[15]

The Marines determined that the enemy might attempt a parachute assault on Corregidor. The two most likely drop zones were the parade ground and the golf course on Topside. Therefore, anti-parachute procedures were developed in concert with the coast artillery batteries that were located around Topside. Although the Japanese did not employ paratroopers against Corregidor, when the Americans retook The Rock in early 1945 an airborne drop was the most important feature of the assault.

By early March Radio Bataan—the Marine radar detachment—was limiting its operations due to the shortage of gasoline for the radar's generators. From this point on the radar would only operate periodically, such as when the few remaining American aircraft were going on a mission. During January and

February the radar had been forced to move on several occasions due to enemy air raids and artillery fire.

OPERATIONS INSIDE THE BAY

By late February the amount of patrolling around the Bay had to be dramatically curtailed due to the fuel shortage. Whereas previously one of the minesweepers or gunboats would patrol on a north–south pattern five to six miles east of Corregidor each night, by the middle of the month this practice had been changed to anchoring one of the ships a few miles east of The Rock to provide an early warning of any enemy craft approaching from the direction of Manila. As dawn approached the duty vessel would proceed back to the North Channel to be under the protection of the anti-aircraft guns of Corregidor and southern Bataan during daylight. South Harbor was rarely used as an anchorage now due to the artillery fire coming from Cavite.

Enemy air attacks took place periodically, but by February the Japanese had a limited amount of aircraft available on Luzon. Nevertheless, they would sometimes go after ships when the opportunity presented itself. On 18 February, for example, *Finch* and *Quail* were sweeping the channel through the minefield to ensure that no mines had become detached when they were attacked by enemy light bombers. No damage was suffered and the enemy aircraft flew off when their ordnance was expended.

For patrols outside the Bay the little converted yachts were frequently used because they were diesel powered and the stocks of diesel fuel were relatively plentiful. So, *Maryanne*, *Fisheries II*, and *Perry* took turns scouting the area off the west coast of Bataan at night to provide early warning of any Japanese amphibious operations against the left flank of Bataan's defenders. Although maintenance was a real problem by this point, the PT boats of MTB Squadron 3 continued to patrol outside the Bay as often as they could.

On the night of 17–18 February PTs 35 and 41 made a reconnaissance into Subic Bay following reports from Army and Navy observers on Corregidor and Bataan that a number of enemy vessels had entered the area. As the 41 Boat approached Grande Island a small vessel of 200–400 tons was spotted and a torpedo fired from a range of about 1,000 yards. It did not explode. Lieutenant Bulkeley, who was aboard the 41, thought that the weapon had passed under the target. The PT boat continued northward into Subic Bay.

Soon a much larger enemy ship was spotted at the Olongapo pier. A second torpedo was launched, and the 41 Boat swung away to the south to exit Subic Bay. As she accelerated, .50-caliber machine-gun fire was directed at a point of land where a Japanese battery was suspected to be. As the PT headed southward a fire could be seen in the area where the torpedo had been aimed. Linking up with the 35 Boat, the two PTs patrolled about fifty miles out to sea west of Corregidor, but nothing was seen. The two boats returned to Manila Bay by dawn.[16] Despite what seemed to be a fire, it does not appear that the American torpedoes hit any enemy vessel.

Japanese artillery fire from Cavite continued throughout the rest of February and into March. As noted previously, when the Japanese started shooting at the ships in South Harbor the vessels of the Inshore Patrol moved into the North Channel on the opposite side of Corregidor. The range was so great from Cavite to Corregidor, much less the North Channel, that the natural dispersion of the enemy shells at those distances made the likelihood of a ship taking a hit mostly a matter of luck. Nevertheless, it was better to take the precaution of staying as far away from the enemy's artillery as possible.

On the morning of 15 February *Oahu* received a much needed 21,000 gallons of fuel from a Navy barge in the North Channel. She then moved to South Harbor and anchored. Suddenly, at 1730 an enemy shell from the guns in Cavite struck the water about four hundred yards from the ship. Battle Stations was ordered, and Lieutenant Commander Smith called down to the engine room from the bridge that he needed steam to get under way—now. The next shell hit about two hundred yards away, followed a couple minutes later by one less than eighty yards off—the Japanese were clearly getting the range. Frantic calls from the bridge urged the engine-room crew to do whatever it took to allow the ship to start moving.

Moments later a shell impacted about forty yards off the ship's side, showering the upper works with fragments. It was then that the ship's engineering officer called to the bridge telling Smith that he could get under way. With the engine telegraph thrown to "full ahead," *Oahu* started to slowly move. The next shell burst on the water twenty yards astern—where the ship had just been. Working up to her top speed of 15.1 knots in less than thirteen minutes, *Oahu* pulled away from the area. Fortunately only three crewmen had been slightly wounded. Lieutenant Commander Smith noted in his log that had it not been for the incredible efforts of the engineers the ship might have been lost.[17]

In the early morning hours of 19 February the enemy artillery on Cavite finally demonstrated how dangerous it could be to the ships. The Army auxiliary mine planter *Neptune* was bringing fuel and other supplies to Fort Frank near the Cavite shoreline, hoping that the night was dark enough to conceal her. Shortly after 0330 hours as the ship was about to start unloading she was hit by a Japanese artillery shell that exploded on her forward deck among the stacked drums of gasoline. The crew jumped overboard as the little ship quickly turned into an inferno.[18]

Quail, *Finch*, and *Tanager* all took turns sweeping the minefield channel. This was to ensure that mines had not come loose and floated into the channel, as well as to confirm that the Japanese did not try to float mines into the area from either inside or outside the Bay or deliver mines by aircraft at night (the enemy never tried to drop mines into the area around Corregidor).

When the ships had some time on their hands—when they were not the duty vessel of the day—they sometimes anchored where they could do some good for the troops ashore. Several times while performing the daily minesweeping duty Lieutenant Commander Morrill of *Quail* had watched Japanese fighters and light bombers attack Cabcaben and Bataan airfields. Both of those airfields ran from west to east with the runways ending very close to Manila Bay. Enemy aircraft would come in from the west and when over Mariveles Mountain they would start their dives, either strafing or dropping bombs and then pulling up close to the water at the end of the runways.

One day in March Morrill moved *Quail* near the Cabcaben airfield and anchored. Some days the Japanese aircraft attacked, most days they did not. *Quail* waited to see what would happen that day. Midmorning arrived and Japanese planes were spotted, getting into position for their run down the mountainside. With the crew at Battle Stations, the men watched the Japanese planes roar down the hillside and drop small bombs on the Army airfield.

USS Quail

Source: U.S. Naval Institute Photo Archive

As the enemy planes pulled out of their dives over Manila Bay nearly a dozen machine guns on the starboard side of *Quail* opened fire. The Japanese planes flew through a mass of .50-caliber tracers. Hits were observed on several of the aircraft as they pulled up. It was nearly the end of the month before the Japanese repeated low-level attacks on Cabcaben Field.[19]

The danger of an enemy attack on Bataan's east coast was taken very seriously. When Manila was abandoned in late December a hasty attempt had been made to scuttle the interisland merchant ships, harbor craft, and small boats that were moored in and around the port. Army engineers and the crews of the Philippine Army Q-boats had this mission, and over thirty vessels were scuttled. Unfortunately, most of the watercraft were disposed of by opening their valves and sea cocks to allow them to flood, as opposed to burning or blowing them up. Since many of the vessels sank upright in shallow water they were relatively easy to salvage. The Japanese lost no time in doing so. As early as the mid-January fighting along the Abucay Line the enemy started using vessels salvaged in Manila to shell the coastal flank of the defenders at night. Fortunately these attacks were very inaccurate, but they raised the specter that at some point the Japanese would attempt a crossing from Manila to land on either Bataan's east coast, on Corregidor, or one of the other harbor forts.

So seriously did the Army take this threat that the 2nd Division of the Philippine Army, composed mostly of men from the Constabulary, was assigned to defend the Manila Bay beaches of Bataan. During March the two Army National Guard tank battalions were positioned near the beaches of eastern Bataan to provide an immediate reserve for the 2nd Division. Interestingly, this is where many of the guns that the Navy had provided to the Army from the stocks at the Cavite Ammunition Depot ended up—as beach defense weapons facing out into Manila Bay.

USAFFE G-2 had a number of Filipino agents working in Manila. These men and women provided information on the strength and activities of the Japanese forces in the city, including the enemy's efforts to salvage and repair ships and boats around the harbor. By early March reports from the agents in the city indicated that the Japanese had put back into service over twenty vessels, including motor yachts, tugs, and interisland steamers. Many of these vessels were being armed with light artillery pieces and machine guns. Additionally, the Japanese had collected an assortment of barges that could be towed across the Bay. Naval intelligence officers, primarily Lieutenant Commander Cheek and Lieutenant Commander Knoll, worked with the Army to assess the enemy's efforts. The conclusion was that by early March the Japanese had sufficient vessels in Manila to transport as many as 12,000 troops. Since Manila was only about thirty miles from Corregidor and Bataan a landing force could easily be moved across that distance under cover of darkness.

Army coast artillery observers high up on Corregidor and Fort Hughes maintained a careful watch on ship movements both outside and inside Manila Bay. By early March they were noting an increasing amount of traffic inside the Bay, mostly fairly close to Manila. Occasionally, they would spot small groups of watercraft in the middle portion of the Bay, at which point the Navy would be alerted to prepare to intercept them.

At 1330 on 25 March observers sighted a group of nine tugs and lighters about ten miles east of Corregidor, moving toward the fortified islands. Inshore Patrol headquarters in Tunnel Queen was informed of the approach of the enemy craft. The *Mindanao* was the duty ship that day. She was ordered by Captain Hoeffel to intercept the approaching vessels.

Being the duty ship the gunboat already had steam up. She left her berth in the North Channel and proceeded eastward. The enemy craft were spotted and *Mindanao* gave chase. As soon as the Japanese saw the approaching gunboat they turned about and headed toward Sangley Point. It now became a race to see if the gunboat could catch the enemy before they reached safety.

When *Mindanao* made her crossing from Hong Kong in early December she had been battered by the typhoons sweeping through the South China Sea. The ship's hull and frames were stressed as she rolled side-to-side up to 49 degrees. Although she made it to Manila, the ship had been strained by the voyage. Now, as she worked up to her best possible speed, vibration got progressively worse. Commander McCracken pressed ahead as fast as possible to get within range. Once the gunboat was close enough to start firing McCracken had to slow down in order to give the gunners a chance to get a good view of the fleeing enemy craft in their gun sights, so bad was the vibration.

At about six thousand yards, the maximum effective range of *Mindanao*'s bow 3-inch gun against a moving target, the order was given to Open Fire. With several of the ship's officers atop the forward deckhouse observing the fall of shot with binoculars, the gunboat fired a total of thirty-five 3-inch shells at the fleeing Japanese boats. It was apparent that some of the enemy craft were hit; one was on fire.[20]

By this point Inshore Patrol Headquarters was insisting that the *Mindanao* return to the safety of the North Channel. The crew was told of the order and immediately protested, wanting to continue the chase. McCracken and his XO, Lieutenant Nash, agreed to press ahead, even though they realized that they were being drawn closer to the enemy's guns on Sangley Point. Most of the other ships of the Inshore Patrol were following the action by listening in on the radio and watching as best they could with binoculars. The crews of the other ships were getting quite a laugh as every few minutes Inshore Patrol headquarters would demand over the voice radio net, "Where are you now, McCracken?"

As the fleeing Japanese boats neared Sangley Point enemy shore guns opened fire on *Mindanao*. Soon the enemy flotilla was rounding Sangley Point, obviously heading for the ruined Cavite Navy Yard. McCracken decided that his crew had had enough fun, and ordered a return to Corregidor. As *Mindanao* made her turn two enemy shells hit the water, one on either side of the ship. Realizing that he had just been straddled, McCracken ordered the helmsman to start zigzagging. The enemy shore guns positioned on Sangley Point continued firing at the gunboat, but scored no hits.[21]

As *Mindanao* turned toward Corregidor three light bombers showed up. The 3-inch guns fired eight rounds in their direction and the ship's twenty-six machine guns put up such an impressive display of tracers that the enemy bombers kept their distance. To put an interesting finishing touch on the day's activities an enemy shell from the guns in Cavite landed about one hundred yards astern of the ship just as she reached the anchorage in North Channel.

RUNNING THE BLOCKADE

With the food situation rapidly becoming desperate USAFFE tried everything it could to bring in more supplies. There were basically three ways to add food to the command's supply: (1) forage around the Bataan Peninsula, both ashore as well as fishing in Manila Bay; (2) bring in food from elsewhere in the Philippines; and (3) bring in more supplies from outside the Philippines. All these methods were tried, with limited success.

The east coast of Bataan had a number of small towns and villages that included rice paddies and fishing ponds. Some of the locals also made their living fishing in the Bay. The Army quartermasters opened three mills to thresh rice waiting to be harvested. Ultimately, daily production reached fifteen tons, a considerable portion of the twenty-five tons of rice required each day by the Bataan garrison, at half rations. Unfortunately, that supply ran out by 12 February.

For a while fishing in the Bay appeared to be a promising source of protein for the troops. At one point in late February the nightly catch was 12,000 pounds of fish. Unfortunately, Japanese attacks on the fishing boats and American and Filipino units on Bataan's east coast accidentally firing at the boats ended this source of supply by early March. Fishing over the side of their vessels did, however, remain a viable option for the Inshore Patrol ships in the Bay. With the ships increasingly immobilized by lack of fuel, crewmen who remained on board could and did use part of their time to catch fish to supplement their rations.

By early March the Bataan Peninsula had been stripped of just about all the food available. There was virtually an unlimited amount of food available in the lush Philippine Islands—the problem was to get it to Bataan. The second option available to the American command was to bring food into the Manila Bay area from sources in the southern islands. The Army had a supply depot at Cebu City in the Visayans, the central islands of the Philippines. By the middle of January the Army quartermasters at Cebu had assembled about twenty-five Filipino-manned interisland ships, most of which had a cargo capacity of three hundred to one thousand tons. Some of these little ships had been in Manila Bay at the start of the war. Indeed, some of them had participated in evacuating Army forces from Manila to Bataan and Corregidor before departing at night for the southern islands.

Philippine president Quezon, in contact with the provincial leadership in the southern islands, directed them to work with the Americans to assemble the ships and food as quickly as possible. For a brief period this method appeared to be promising. Departing from Cebu or Panay under cover of darkness, the small ships would head northward to wait for the right moment to make a dash into Manila Bay at night. They would hide during the day along the southern coast of Luzon or near Mindoro Island and then make the final run at their top speed. These moves were well planned in advance and Army coast artillery and the Inshore Patrol in the Bay were informed when a blockade runner was due to enter the harbor.

Legaspi made the first successful run. She did so under the auspices of Quezon's efforts. Departing Manila Bay on the night of 21–22 January, the ship carried fifty-four Navy officers and eight enlisted men. Led by Captain Dessez who had earlier been in charge of the Mariveles Section Base, the Navy personnel went out to help set up the supply depot at Capiz on the island of Panay and to assist in arranging voyages by the interisland steamers to Manila Bay. About one hundred Philippine Army personnel were also on board. A PT boat escorted *Legaspi* through the minefield channel. Once outside, the ship headed south at her best speed.

Legaspi succeeded in reaching Panay on 24 January. She was quickly loaded with food for the return trip. On the night of 2–3 February she reached Manila Bay and with a PT boat escort the ship passed through the minefield channel and anchored near Corregidor. Unloading started right away. *Legaspi* had brought in several hundred tons of food. The 90,000 personnel on Bataan and the fortified islands consumed about 90 tons per day on half rations. Nevertheless, the success was encouraging. More trips were planned.

By mid-February the Army quartermasters at Cebu and Panay had taken control of the activities of the interisland ships. *Legaspi* made one more round-trip voyage, arriving at Corregidor on 16 February. *Princessa* arrived on the 17th with 700 tons of food. Finally, the *Elcano* entered the Bay on 26 February, bringing 1,100 tons of rations and some 81-mm mortar ammunition. All together, the three ships had brought in about three weeks of food for the garrison.[22]

Elcano's arrival was, however, the end of the blockade runs from the southern Philippines. By late February the Japanese had increased their air and sea patrols. Indeed, once the Japanese focused on the blockade runners, the unarmed and slow interisland ships were quickly shown to be easy picking for the enemy. On 21 February the small (three-hundred-ton cargo capacity) *Cia de Filipinas* was lost off Mindoro. That was the start of a period of disastrous losses. One week later, on 28 February, four ships were lost in the central Philippines. The next day, 1 March, *Legaspi* was discovered off Mindoro attempting to make her third run into Manila Bay. She was forced to run aground while being chased by two Japanese minesweepers. That day the Army called a halt to further efforts to run the blockade.

The Philippine Army Q-boats continued to patrol the area off the east coast of Bataan. The Q-Boats also provided the escort for the Filipino motor vessels *Bohol II* and *Kolambugan* that made several runs outside the minefields to Looc Cove off the west coast of Batangas Province to pick up rice and other food for the garrison. Each of the vessels had a cargo capacity of 400 tons. Over 1,600 tons of rice and other foodstuffs were brought back due to the efforts of brave Filipinos ashore who transported the food to the Cove under cover of darkness. The first run to pick up food was made on 20 January. Several trips were made before the Japanese got wind of the activity and increased the patrols both offshore and on land, thus bringing this method of resupply to an end on 1 March.[23]

From outside the Philippines desperate efforts were made to try to get supply ships to the islands. A number of oceangoing vessels were chartered by Army supply officers in Australia and the Dutch East Indies and loaded with food and other supplies for the run north to the central Philippines. The plan was to transfer the supplies from the larger, oceangoing vessels to the small interisland ships for the final run to Manila Bay.

Only three ships made it to the Philippines. The first was *Coast Farmer*, which arrived in Mindanao from Australia on 20 February carrying 2,500 tons of rations and about 4,000 81-mm mortar rounds. The *Dona Nati* (2,800 tons of food, 1.5 million rounds of .30-caliber ammunition, 100,000 rounds of .50-caliber, 4,000 81-mm mortar shells, and 5,000 rifle grenades) and the *An Hui*

(2,600 tons of food and three crated P-40 fighters) reached Cebu on 10 and 20 March, respectively. Very little of their cargo made it to Bataan and Corregidor; a portion of *Coast Farmer*'s load was on board *Princessa*. All the rest was either lost on board interisland vessels that were sunk or burned in warehouses in Cebu when the Japanese occupied the city in early April. Several other ships dispatched from Australia or the Indies were sunk en route to the Philippines.[24]

THE HEALTH OF THE COMMAND

All these efforts and sacrifice added a few weeks of food to the garrison's stocks. It was nowhere near enough. By the middle of March the situation on Bataan was truly desperate. The so-called half ration was actually far less than that. By late March the men were receiving less than twenty ounces of food a day. That was less than one-third of the normal peacetime ration. By mid-February most American Army personnel had already lost fifteen to twenty pounds, and the worst was still to come.

The weakened state of the troops made them very susceptible to a variety of diseases, including malaria, beriberi (due to the lack of vitamins), and dysentery. By 1 March the supply of quinine, vital to prevent the spread of malaria, had reached a point that preventative doses could no longer be issued. The number of malaria cases immediately skyrocketed. By the end of the month between seven hundred and one thousand new cases a day were being admitted to the various Army hospitals on Bataan. The dreadfully poor decisions of mid-December were now catching up with the Army troops on Bataan, who quite literally were facing starvation.

Although their rations were clearly meager by peacetime standards, the Army troops on the fortified islands were better off. They were getting a smaller portion than they needed, but it was a real half ration and was a much better balanced diet. Whereas the typical Bataan ration by early March consisted of rice and some canned fish, the soldiers on Corregidor and the other forts were getting a relatively nutritious meal, although they were also losing weight. Importantly, Corregidor and the other islands were not infested with malaria-carrying mosquitoes, as was the case on Bataan.

It was not until MacArthur's departure that the Army leadership in Washington learned the actual numbers of men on Bataan and the fortified islands. About three weeks after taking command, in one of his messages to General Marshall urging that food supplies be sent by any means possible, Wainwright stated that there were approximately 90,000 American and Filipino Army personnel on Bataan and the fortified islands. This came as a complete shock to Washington, where the belief was that the garrison was no more than

40,000 men. General Marshall asked that Wainwright confirm the numbers, which he did in a subsequent message. Mr. Stimpson, the secretary of the Army, noted in his diary, "MacArthur kept his figures secret from the very beginning and everyone was astonished when Wainwright revealed the present roster."[25]

The sailors and Marines were also tightening their belts—literally and figuratively—but most of them were certainly better fed than their Army counterparts, particularly the troops on Bataan. Admiral Rockwell and Captain Hoeffel both ordered strict economies of food in order to eke out the supplies as long as possible. Possibly best off of all were the ships' companies. Most of the ships had tried to stock up with food before the evacuation of Manila. So, not only could they draw on the Navy's extensive food stocks in Tunnel Queen, they also had their own food on board. Away from the diseases of Bataan, able to supplement their food by fishing in the Bay, and with on-board medical supplies, the ships were much better off than their Army counterparts and probably better supplied than the Navy and Marine Corps personnel ashore. For example, *Quail*'s senior pharmacist mate had gone ashore to Manila before the city was evacuated and brought back a large quantity of vitamins. These were issued to the crew daily. Amazingly, there were still a few luxury items available. *Canopus* was serving ice cream until sometime in mid-March.

During late February Captain Lloyd Mills, USA, a company commander in the Philippine Scout 57th Infantry, was invited on board *Canopus* along with several other Army officers. The Old Lady was providing a dinner in their honor for their regiment's actions at Longoskawayan Point. Although Mills' company did not fight there, he was all too happy to accept the invitation. What he found stunned him.

A full three-course meal (no half rations that night) was served on white tablecloth in *Canopus*' wardroom. Ice cream was then served for dessert, along with cigars. When they departed that night the Army officers profusely thanked Commander Sackett and the Old Lady's officers for their hospitality. As they headed back to their jungle bivouac Mills thought to himself that he had definitely joined the wrong branch of the military.[26]

It should be stressed that nobody—Army, Navy, or Marine Corps—on Bataan, Corregidor, or the ships in the Bay was enjoying an adequate diet. However, it is clear that the precautions taken by Admiral Hart, Admiral Rockwell, and Colonel Howard were of great assistance to their men during the siege. In mid-March, following General MacArthur's departure, General Wainwright ordered that the Navy's food stocks be pooled with the Army's. When Army quartermasters and Navy Supply Corps officers conducted a joint inventory of the Navy's food stocks in Tunnel Queen and the adjacent supply tunnels the Army officers were taken aback with the amount of food the Navy had available, particularly since the Navy's food supplies were being used to support a relatively small population—fewer than five thousand American and Filipino sailors and the Marines.

MacARTHUR'S DEPARTURE

In early February President Roosevelt and General Marshall were discussing the fate of General MacArthur. By this point it was clear, at least to those in Washington, that the garrison in the Philippines would ultimately be defeated. Therefore, what was to become of America's most famous soldier? On 4 February, Marshall raised the issue with MacArthur, asking for the latter's opinion on evacuation and possible future command positions either in the southern Philippines or in Australia.

Roosevelt finally made the decision on 22 February. MacArthur was told that he was to depart as soon as possible, with Australia as the ultimate destination. Initially it was thought that MacArthur, his family, and immediate staff would be evacuated by submarine to Mindanao, and then flown by Army aircraft to Australia.

Admiral Rockwell was informed of the plan at a 4 March conference with MacArthur and Sutherland. MacArthur offered to take Rockwell and one or two members of his staff with him. Rockwell sent a message to OPNAV in Washington, asking for instructions. The Navy staff in Washington told him to plan to depart with MacArthur.

Various delays by MacArthur pushed the departure date back to mid-March. The submarine *Permit* was designated for the mission and was due to arrive in Manila Bay on the 15th. Starting around 9 March, however, enemy patrol activity around the entrance of Manila Bay started to increase noticeably. This seemed to indicate that the enemy was on to the plan to evacuate the General. It was at that point that the decision was made to evacuate MacArthur's party by PT boat rather than waiting for the submarine. MacArthur would first go to Mindanao, and then by B-17 to Australia.

On the evening of 11 March, MacArthur met with Major General Jonathan Wainwright on Corregidor's North Dock. Wainwright had only learned of MacArthur's departure the day before. He became the senior U.S. Army officer in the Philippines upon MacArthur's departure.

At 1945 PT-41 left Corregidor to meet the 32, 34, and 35 Boats that had loaded their passengers on Bataan that afternoon. A total of twenty-one passengers were aboard the PT boats, including MacArthur, his wife Jean and young son Arthur, the boy's Chinese nurse, and fourteen Army officers (including Sutherland, five other Army generals, and one sergeant). On board the PT-34

PT-41

Source: MacArthur Memorial, Norfolk, Va.

was Admiral Rockwell; Captain Ray, Rockwell's chief of staff, rode on MacArthur's boat. Lieutenant Bulkeley was in command of the PT-41 carrying MacArthur, his family, Major General Sutherland, and Captain Ray.[27]

After an adventurous journey, most of MacArthur's party reached Mindanao by 13 March. More delays followed until adequate air transport could be obtained; MacArthur refused to fly in the old B-17s that were initially sent from Australia; newer, better aircraft had to be sent.

Finally, on 17 March MacArthur and his party reached Australia. The Army officers who escaped with him would stay at his side for the rest of the war. They were to become known in Army circles as "the Bataan Gang"— the great man's true inner circle. Rockwell submitted his report on activities in the Manila Bay area on 1 August 1942.

THE LAST OF THE PT BOATS

The evacuation of MacArthur took MTB Squadron 3 out of the fight in Manila Bay. During the voyage to the southern islands the 32 Boat broke down and had to be abandoned. She was destroyed by the submarine *Permit* in the central Philippines. On 18 March PTs 35 and 41 were sent to the island of Negros to pick up President Quezon and his party to transport them to Mindanao for evacuation by plane. The 34 Boat was under repair at the time.

Now far from the facilities of *Canopus* and *Dewey*, the PT boats, already in poor mechanical shape, deteriorated even faster. A small private shipyard on

Cebu was used to haul the boats out of the water for maintenance, but it was only a matter of time before the end would come.

After dark on 8 April—the night before Bataan surrendered—the 34 and 41 Boats engaged Japanese warships off the southern tip of Cebu island. The two PTs fought a spirited battle against the light cruiser *Kuma*, which put up a vigorous fight with her 5.5-inch guns and automatic weapons. A nearby small Japanese destroyer also got into the fight. Although two lieutenants, Bulkeley and Kelly, thought that they had scored damaging hits, the only hit among the eight torpedoes that were fired was a dud.

Later that night the 34 Boat went aground off Cebu City. Although she freed herself, the boat was attacked by Japanese floatplanes after dawn. She fought as best she could with her machine guns, but was badly hit and had to be run aground. Two of her crew died and the boat was burned and destroyed.

On 12 April, as Japanese troops entered Cebu City following their landing on the island, the 35 Boat was burned on the slipway at the small shipyard. That left only the 41 Boat. On orders from Major General Sharp, the Visayan-Mindanao Force Commander, the PT boat was turned over to the Army at Mindanao. She was to be towed overland to Lake Lanao to serve as a patrol boat to protect the landing areas of American flying boats. With no "fish" left and the boat's engines deteriorating, her days as a torpedo boat were over. In mid-April, as she was being towed overland to the lake, the boat was burned to keep her from falling into enemy hands.

Lieutenant Bulkeley was flown to Australia on 13 April on orders from General MacArthur. He was later awarded the Medal of Honor in a ceremony in President Roosevelt's office. By the end of April Lieutenant Kelly and two of the Squadron's ensigns were also flown to Australia. Their experience with PT boats was considered so valuable that the Navy wanted them saved to serve as instructors.[28]

CAPTAIN HOEFFEL TAKES COMMAND

With Admiral Rockwell's departure Captain Hoeffel became the senior Navy officer in the Manila Bay area. Colonel Howard was still the senior Marine present. At this point in the campaign there were 1,558 Marines and roughly 2,300 American Navy personnel still on Bataan, the ships of the Inshore Patrol, and the fortified islands. Additionally, there were about 500 Filipino naval reservists. The PNAB contractor personnel were still being used to work on tunnels and to keep airfields in operational condition.

After MacArthur and Rockwell's departure General Wainwright moved to Corregidor where he assumed command of the remaining U.S. forces in the Philippines. The senior Army commander on Bataan became Major General

Captain Kenneth Hoeffel. This picture was taken by the Japanese shortly after the surrender of Corregidor.

Source: U.S. Army Military History Institute, Carlisle, Pa.

Edward King, formerly the Luzon Force artillery commander. King was now appointed the commander of the Luzon Force, basically the troops on the Bataan Peninsula. King's headquarters was located near the main road between Hospitals 1 and 2. The Marine detachment that had previously been the guard for the forward USAFFE Headquarters on Bataan now took over the duty as the guards for the Luzon Force command post.

SUBMARINES IN AND OUT OF THE BAY

Although it was very difficult for surface ships to reach Bataan and Corregidor due to the enemy's command of the air and the blockading ships patrolling off the entrance of the Bay, submarines were much more likely to get through. During the course of the siege a number of subs managed to reach the Philippines, bringing in supplies and evacuating key personnel. The main limitation of the submarines was their very small cargo-carrying capacity. Additionally, many in the Navy felt that the main purpose of the submarines should be to attack enemy shipping in the entire Southeast Asian area. In general, the Navy supported using submarines to transport ammunition, but resisted transporting food since it was felt that the amount of food that the subs could bring to the garrison was not worth the effort. When assigned to resupply missions the subs would devote their torpedo rooms to supplies, off-loading most of their bulky torpedoes to make room for cargo.

With *Canopus* still in operation, and with a supply of several dozen torpedoes in Tunnel Queen on Corregidor, submarines could proceed to Manila Bay with as much cargo as possible in their torpedo rooms, unload, and then restock with torpedoes and proceed on with their patrols. If they were required to evacuate personnel the sub might then have to proceed southward to the Indies or Australia.

The first submarine dispatched to the Philippines on a resupply mission was *Seawolf*. When she received her orders to take .50-caliber machine-gun ammunition to Corregidor on 15 January the submarine was at the port of Darwin in Australia. The sub off-loaded her torpedoes onto the submarine tender USS *Holland*, and 675 boxes of machine-gun ammunition and 72 3-inch anti-aircraft shells (unfortunately with the old-type powder train fuzes) were taken on board. Departing Darwin at noon on 16 January, she reached Manila Bay at 0400 on the morning of 27 January. The PT-41, with Captain Hoeffel on board, came out to meet the sub outside the minefield entrance. The submarine followed the PT boat through the minefield channel and submerged in about 130 feet of water to wait out the daylight hours on the bottom. That night she surfaced and off-loaded her cargo. The cargo was welcome; the garrison was very short of .50-caliber ammunition.

Once the ammunition was off-loaded, sixteen torpedoes were taken on board, along with twenty-five passengers—Major Wilkerson, the British liaison officer, twelve Army officers (most of whom were dive bomber pilots who had never received their A-24s), and a similar number of Navy officers and men. Most of the Navy personnel were from PatWing 10; some of the naval aviators had recently fought at the battle of Longoskawayan Point. The submarine departed before dawn on the 29th, reaching the Dutch naval base at Surabaya, Java, on 7 February.[29]

During the first major bombing raids on the fortified islands in late December and early January it had become clear that there was an acute need for more mechanical fuzed 3-inch anti-aircraft ammunition. MacArthur sent a message to the War Department asking that a way be found to expedite the delivery of more of the ammunition that could reach enemy aircraft attacking above 24,000 feet. The Army had the ammunition in its stocks in Hawaii, but how to get it to the Philippines?

On 12 January the submarine USS *Trout* from the Pacific Fleet departed Pearl Harbor with 3,517 mechanically fuzed 3-inch shells on board. The 70 tons of ammunition took up so much room that some of the sub's equipment had to be left behind. She was going to conduct a cross-Pacific voyage directly to the Philippines. Refueling at Midway Island, *Trout* cleared the northern tip of the island of Luzon and arrived at the entrance to Manila Bay on 3 February. After the sun went down, the sub surfaced and was met outside the minefield by PT-41 with Lieutenant Bulkeley aboard. Escorted through the minefield channel, the submarine tied up alongside Corregidor's South Dock. Unloading started right away.[30]

Once the ammunition had been off-loaded, ten torpedoes were put on board. The sub was also topped off with diesel fuel to prepare her for a patrol. However, it was discovered that the boat was still too light; more ballast was needed. The sub's commander, Lieutenant Commander Frank Fenno, requested an additional twenty-five tons of ballast, suggesting sandbags. Admiral Rockwell turned that request down, since sandbags were in very short supply on Corregidor. The admiral had something much more interesting in mind.

When Manila was evacuated the Philippine Commonwealth's gold reserves had been transported across the Bay and stored in the vaults located in Government Ravine on the southeast corner of Middleside. No one wanted the gold to fall into the hands of the Japanese, so the decision was made to use *Trout* as the means to get the precious metal out of the islands. Under cover of darkness, 583 gold bars, some the property of the Philippine government, others owned by mining companies, were loaded on board the submarine. In addition to the 2 tons of gold, an additional 18 tons of silver coins were added to the sub's cargo. Finally, a number of boxes and bags of mail were sent out with the sub. After spending the day submerged on the bottom of Manila Bay, *Trout* departed in the early morning hours of 4 February. She arrived in Pearl Harbor on 3 March, having sunk a small Japanese freighter during the return voyage.[31] Needless to say, her crew was not allowed to keep souvenirs from the most interesting cargo ever carried by a U.S. Navy submarine.

The next sub to reach Manila Bay was *Seadragon*. She arrived on the day that *Trout* departed. *Seadragon* had been damaged during the bombing of the Cavite Navy Yard in December. Now fully operational, she had come in from patrol to get torpedoes and supplies and to evacuate personnel. She was given twenty-three torpedoes and various other equipment, but by far her most important cargo was seventeen men from Station C. Led by Lieutenant Fabian, this was the first contingent of Station C to be evacuated. They took with them various key items of equipment and code books. Several of the Station's Japanese linguists were among the group that was headed for Brisbane, Australia, to begin the process of moving the unit out of the Philippines. A few other Navy personnel and an Army major were among the twenty-one passengers that were on board the sub when she departed on 5 February.[32]

The submarine *Sargo* reached the Philippines on 14 February. She brought in forty tons of .30-caliber ammunition (about one million rounds) from Java to Mindanao. This was a very welcome addition to the supply of the Visayan-Mindanao Force since that command was desperately short of ammunition, having only about one hundred rounds per soldier. When the submarine departed, she took twenty-four Army Air Force ground crew personnel to rejoin their B-17s operating from Java and Australia.

On the night of 19–20 February the submarine *Swordfish* was diverted from her patrol to Manila Bay. Her very important mission was to evacuate the Philippine president, Manuel Quezon, his family, and several members of his staff to the southern Philippines. The submarine reached Panay on the 22nd. The very ill Quezon would remain in the Philippines for several more weeks before being flown out of the islands from Mindanao.

Swordfish was ordered to return to Corregidor, which she reached in the early morning hours of 24 February. This time the yacht *Maryanne*, carrying the U.S. High Commissioner to the Philippines, Mr. Francis B. Sayre, his family and staff, and other evacuees, met the sub. A total of twenty-four passengers were on board when the submarine departed for the south.

Next in was *Permit*. Originally intended to evacuate General MacArthur, that mission was overtaken by events when the General decided to depart by PT boat on the night of 11 March, as we have already seen. *Permit* did, however, make a scheduled rendezvous with PT-32 in the central Philippines on 13 March. It was at that time her skipper, Lieutenant Commander W. G. Chapple, was informed of the change in plans. It was fortunate for the crew of the 32 Boat that they linked up with the submarine, since their PT boat was unserviceable and could not continue on to Mindanao where the other three boats of Squadron 3 had taken MacArthur and his party. The PT boat was destroyed using *Permit*'s deck gun and its crew transferred to the submarine. At that point, the sub was ordered to continue to Corregidor.

On the morning of 16 March the submarine departed from The Rock, heading south. She had on board fifteen officers and twenty-five enlisted men, including Captain Morsell, the 16th Naval District supply officer; Lieutenant Commander Grandfield, the District operations officer; Lieutenant Commander Cheek, the District intelligence officer; and Lieutenant (junior grade) Champlin, Admiral Rockwell's aide. In addition, there were eleven officers and twenty-five men from Station C, the second contingent to be evacuated. When the sub's own crew was added there were 111 men on board. The badly overcrowded submarine eventually arrived at Freemantle, Australia.[33]

When Lieutenant Commander Cheek departed on *Permit* the duties of District intelligence officer were taken over by Lieutenant Commander Denys Knoll. Knoll had started the war as the weather officer of the 16th Naval District. A very energetic officer, he had been assigned to work closely with Cheek as the assistant intelligence officer.

Even before Cheek departed the two intelligence officers had tried to convince the Army to use submarines for supply runs from the central Philippines to Manila Bay. The relatively short distance from Cebu City to Corregidor, about 450 miles by sea, could be traveled by a submarine in three nights of running on the surface. Experience had shown that a submarine could be unloaded at Corregidor in one night. If the sub unloaded all its torpedoes except for the weapons in its tubes it could carry about 45–50 tons of food. This was about a half day's supply for the garrison. In order to increase the carrying potential of the subs the Navy officers suggested to their Army counterparts that a message be sent to the Navy Department specifically requesting that two of the service's large minelaying submarines, USS *Argonaut* and *Narwhal*, be sent to the Philippines to be used in a transport role. At about 3,000 tons' surface displacement, those two submarines were much larger than the typical fleet boats then making the runs to the Islands. Most of the Asiatic and Pacific Fleet submarines were about 1,400–1,500 tons, for example. The two large minelaying subs would probably be able to carry double the cargo of the smaller boats.[34]

Prior to MacArthur's departure these suggestions fell on deaf ears. Indeed, MacArthur's staff was generally indifferent to the Navy and at times hostile. Relations between the two services were cool at best. According to the XO of the 4th Marines, Admiral Rockwell did not have direct access to MacArthur; he had to go through General Sutherland first. This was noted with considerable resentment among the Navy officers in Tunnel Queen.[35]

That changed when General Wainwright took command. To the Navy personnel on Corregidor Wainwright was a breath of fresh air. He stated that he was impressed by the Navy's efforts to assist in the defense of Bataan and Corregidor, and wanted to use the Navy and Marine Corps' assets to the fullest. Wainwright arrived on Corregidor to assume command with firsthand knowledge of the increasingly weak state of the troops on Bataan. MacArthur's only visit to Bataan had been on 10 January, two months before he departed for Australia. During those two months the physical state of the troops had deteriorated alarmingly. Wainwright was desperate to try anything to get more food to the garrison.

During his meetings with Captain Hoeffel and the 16th Naval District staff the subject of using the submarines as interisland ferries came up. Already the OPNAV staff in Washington was trying to free submarines to help move food to Bataan. On 29 March, for example, Admiral King, now the Chief of Naval Operations, sent a message to the Commander, U.S. Naval Forces Southwest Pacific (the U.S. Navy command that took the place of the Asiatic Fleet after the fall of Java in early March) directing that submarines be used to help ferry food to Bataan, saying that the Army was reporting "drastic food shortage."[36]

Convinced that submarines could help, on 30 March Wainwright sent a message to General Marshall in Washington, via the better quality Navy radio on Corregidor, describing the desperate food situation on Bataan. He specifically requested *Narwhal* and *Argonaut* be dispatched to ferry food from the southern Philippines to Corregidor. Unfortunately, Bataan fell before action could be taken.[37]

All the efforts of the submarines added less than one day of food to the Bataan garrison's stocks. The 3,700 rounds of 3-inch ammunition for Corregidor was of greater importance, and the evacuation of key personnel, especially from Station C, was critical. It was clear, however, that submarines of the World War II era were simply not capable of sustaining a large garrison far from the nearest supply base. Perhaps if the suggestion to move the two large minelaying subs had been acted on earlier a bit of a difference could have been made, but even then those two subs could only have moved about 200 tons of food per week given the roundtrip transit and unloading time from Manila Bay to Cebu. Even at half rations, the garrison of Bataan alone needed roughly 80 tons of food each day to sustain about 80,000 men.

STATION C CONTINUES IN ACTION

Even as Station C was being gradually relocated to Australia, the remaining personnel continued to do outstanding work in the effort to break into the Imperial Navy's codes. The British effort was badly disrupted in mid-February when Singapore fell and the intercept station had to evacuate to Ceylon. By this time Station C was leading the Allied assault against the JN-25b code. In February and March the staff at Tunnel Afirm was producing a flood of intercepted Japanese messages, some of which could now be at least partly read. Of almost equal value to actual decoded messages was the traffic analysis that Station C was producing.

By the first week in March Station C had started to detect Japanese intentions to conduct a major new offensive operation, although details were still sketchy. One of Station C's most important insights was that the Japanese were using the designation "AF" to represent Midway Island in the mid-Pacific. This information was passed to both Washington and Commander Joe Rochefort at Station H in Hawaii. This was the very first piece of the intelligence puzzle that eventually led to the great victory at Midway three months later.

THE ONGOING ARTILLERY BOMBARDMENT

The Japanese artillery in Cavite had been conducting a rather ineffective shelling of the fortified islands since 6 February. A few casualties had been inflicted and a limited amount of damage was done, but the overall effect had been negligible. One battalion of 105-mm guns firing at extreme range had little chance of inflicting much damage on the concrete gun emplacements and tunnels of the Harbor Defenses. On the other hand, American counter battery fire against the enemy had been very ineffective. It had proved almost impossible to spot the enemy guns that fired from behind the Cavite hills.

In mid-March, however, the enemy was prepared to conduct a much heavier attack on the islands in the Bay. One of the reinforcements that had arrived following the defeat of the first Japanese offensive was the 1st Heavy Artillery Regiment armed with a total of ten 240-mm howitzers. Although they were World War I–era weapons, the big Japanese guns could fire a 400-pound shell up to 11,000 yards. They were difficult to move and transporting their ammunition was also a major effort, but by 15 March the heavy howitzers were ready to fire from hidden positions in Cavite.

At 0730 on the 15th the Japanese 240s opened fire on Forts Frank and Drum. The concrete battleship's protection again served it well; there was little damage and no one was killed. Fort Frank, however, took a terrific pounding. The island's 3-inch anti-aircraft battery was wrecked and two of its four 155-mm guns were destroyed. Seven of its eight 12-inch mortars were damaged. The following day about five hundred of the big shells hit Fort Frank, doing more damage. On the 21st a shell penetrated the roof of one of the fort's concrete tunnels and burst among a group of troops waiting for vaccinations. Twenty-eight were killed and forty-six wounded, some of whom died within a few days. The American command was becoming increasingly concerned that the Japanese were "softening up" Fort Frank for a possible landing under cover of darkness. Beach defenses on both of the southernmost forts were increased.

Every time the Americans spotted a group of Filipino bancas lined up near the beach they fired at them, wanting to prevent the Japanese from using the little dugouts as landing craft. The American coast artillery batteries fired every day toward Cavite, but as before they had little luck in pinpointing the locations of the enemy guns. In any case, the Japanese did not attempt a landing on either Fort Frank or Drum. By the end of March the Japanese artillery fire was returning to the normal February level—mostly 105-mm fire. This was due to the enemy pulling his big guns out to move them to Bataan in preparation for the final offensive to overwhelm the sick and starving defenders.

THE SECOND BOMBING OF CORREGIDOR

As the end of March approached the Japanese started to step up their aerial activities in preparation for the final offensive on Bataan. Major air and ground reinforcements had arrived. Before they shifted their effort to Bataan, the Japanese Army and Navy air elements were going to have another go at the fortified islands.

The bombing attacks from 24 March to 2 April were the first major enemy air action against Corregidor since the end of the first week in January. Starting at just before 0930 on 24 March Japanese Army Ki-21 Sally medium bombers struck The Rock. Attacking in nine-plane squadrons, the Japanese bombers dropped 550- and 1,100-pound bombs on Corregidor. This was a significant difference compared to the December–January air attacks when mostly light 132-pound bombs had been used. The Japanese also conducted far more night attacks compared to their earlier bombardment. Of the sixty-four air raid alerts during that ten-day period, thirty of the raids were small numbers of enemy aircraft coming in at night.

Another difference was that the Japanese aircraft operated from much higher altitudes. Bombing conducted from well above 25,000 feet showed that the enemy had learned from bitter experience that Corregidor and the other forts in Manila Bay were one of the most heavily defended areas in all of southeast Asia. Often only two Army anti-aircraft batteries could reach the high-flying enemy; these were the batteries armed with the mechanical fuzes that permitted a maximum altitude of just over 30,000 feet.

Over several days of bombing the enemy peppered Corregidor with several hundred bombs. Damage was relatively slight; none of The Rock's major weapons were put out of action. By this time the number of tunnels, bomb shelters, and foxholes was extensive, so the island's garrison had many more places to take cover compared to the December air raids. However, casualties were suffered during the March air raids. For example, on 25 March fifteen Marines were wounded and a Filipino naval reservist assigned as a mess attendant in the 4th Marines was killed.[38]

Due to the very high attack altitudes many of the Japanese bombs missed the island and landed in the water. This gave the ships in the North Channel some anxious moments. On the 30th, toward the end of the second major

Japanese bombing operation, two twin-engine bombers were seen approaching Corregidor at the unusually low altitude of about 22,000 feet. Several 3-inch batteries were alerted but told to hold their fire. Finally, when the enemy planes were within range, four of Corregidor's batteries opened up simultaneously in a spectacular display watched by most of the sailors on the ships anchored in the North Channel and the Marines on the Tail. Both Japanese aircraft erupted in flames and fell toward the Bay.

One of the enemy aircraft lost a wing as it fell. The wing spun around and around with the engine still running as the wreckage descended. It soon became apparent that the wing was going to fall very close to the anchored gunboat *Oahu*. The wing with its still-attached engine splashed less than one hundred yards from the ship. That evening *Mindanao* sent several minced meat pies ashore to congratulate the Army gunners of Battery Denver, the same unit that had watched the gunboat continue firing during a deluge of bombs in December. All that *Mindanao* asked was that the metal tray that the pies were sent on be returned. The next day the Army returned the cooking tray with a thank you note, addressed to the crew of the U.S. "battleship" *Mindanao*.[39]

CHAPTER 11

The Fall of Bataan

By late March it was very clear that the enemy would soon start his long-awaited final offensive to crush resistance on Bataan. The Japanese had been pouring reinforcements into the Philippines since mid-February when their attack bogged down. The force that they assembled by the first week in April was far more formidable compared to the one that had started the Bataan campaign three months before.

The largest new unit that had arrived for the final offensive was the 4th Division, transferred from Shanghai where it had been in Imperial General Headquarters reserve. By early March the entire division had arrived on Luzon. General Homma was not particularly impressed with this unit because it was considerably understrength. Whereas a full-strength, three-regiment Japanese division was authorized roughly 20,000 men the 4th Division had only some 11,076 personnel.[1] Although undermanned, the Japanese 4th Division was slightly stronger than the U.S. Army's Philippine Division had been at the start of the war.

From Indochina came a brigade-sized force from the 21st Infantry Division, the Nagano Detachment. This 3,900-man formation, built around an infantry regiment, was on temporary loan to the 14th Army and was to return to its parent division after the fall of Bataan.

For the battered 16th Division and 65th Brigade about seven thousand replacement personnel arrived. This was enough to bring the 65th Brigade up to roughly full strength, but the 16th Division was still considerably undermanned at the time of the final offensive. There is no mystery why the 14th Army assigned the 16th Division the role of a secondary feint attack on the western side of Bataan.

In addition to the new infantry units, a considerable amount of artillery arrived. The 14th Army artillery order of battle will be reviewed in detail later. There were also major air reinforcements in the form of the Imperial Navy's Takao Kokutai equipped with twenty-four G4M Betty bombers and a squadron of Zero fighters. The Japanese Army contributed two Army bomber regiments with sixty Ki-21 Sallys, redeployed from Burma where they had been fighting the famous Flying Tigers. The air formations started to arrive by early March. These were the units that had bombed Corregidor and the ships in Manila Bay during the last week of March. In addition to the Japanese Army and Navy medium bombers, there were about fifty Ki-30 and Ki-51 light bombers available. The number of fighters was modest, but given the fact that the Americans were down to half a dozen P-40s and P-35s on Bataan and in Mindanao the Japanese felt confident that they would face no meaningful opposition in the air. In preparation for the final offensive the Japanese Army air units in the Philippines were placed under a new headquarters, the 10th Hikotai, while the Imperial Navy's air units were under the 22nd Air Flotilla.[2]

By 1 April the Japanese strength on Luzon had reached its peak, a total of 85,200 Imperial Army and Navy personnel. Of that total 67,100 ground troops were deployed on Bataan; 6,800 of the Army personnel on Luzon were from the Air Force.[3]

The 14th Army's plan was to make the main attack along the Manila Bay side of the Peninsula against the II Philippine Corps. The terrain on the east coast was better, with less jungle. Not wanting to take any chances, the 14th Army decided to initiate the attack with a massive, five-hour air and artillery bombardment to smash the Filipino-American main line of resistance. Assuming the preparatory bombardment went well, the Japanese expected to affect a breakthrough and then advance down the east coast of Bataan toward Cabcaben and Mariveles. The 14th Army staff assumed the final battle of Bataan to take about a month, after which preparations to overwhelm Corregidor would begin. Included in the Japanese plan were preparations to shell the American defenses along the east coast of Bataan by using barges and motorboats that had been salvaged in Manila harbor and armed with 75- and 37-mm guns. The Japanese had used some vessels of this type as early as the Abucay fighting in mid-January; by late March they had a larger number available.

By 2 April all was in readiness. The Japanese 4th Division, the 65th Brigade, and the Nagano Detachment were in place opposite II Philippine Corps, supported by about 150 guns, howitzers, and heavy mortars. The Army and Navy air units at Manila and other bases on Luzon were ready to make a major effort in support of the attack. The offensive would start the next day, 3 April, Good Friday.

THE STATE OF THE DEFENSE

On 2 April there were about 78,100 American and Filipino Army personnel on Bataan,[4] of whom roughly 65,000 were Filipinos. The Navy and Marine Corps personnel still on the Peninsula (about 1,000 Americans and several hundred Filipino naval reservists) were not included in that total. Although theoretically an impressive force in terms of numbers, the defenders were gravely weakened by this point. As related in the previous chapter, the Army had been forced to cut the troops' rations down to the point that by the end of March the typical soldier on Bataan was receiving between 1,000–1,500 calories per day, far below what the men needed. The two main medical facilities, Hospitals 1 and 2, were swamped with patients. Malaria, dysentery, beriberi, and other tropical diseases had swept through the ranks of the weakened, starving troops. The sailors and Marines in the Bataan–Corregidor area were also suffering, but less so compared to their Army counterparts.

During March the Americans and Filipinos had done what they could to strengthen their defenses. Because supplies of barbed wire and other engineering items were very limited, considerable improvisation was necessary. This included covering portions of the front line with sharpened bamboo stakes in lieu of barbed wire. The Navy provided thirty-five depth charges that were converted into large land mines and emplaced along the I Philippine Corps front. Anti-tank obstacles in the form of logs put vertically in the ground were emplaced in areas where enemy tanks could operate. Foxholes, trenches, and weapons emplacements were dug and camouflage improved. Indeed, the jungle of Bataan was of great benefit in providing concealment from Japanese aerial observation, but the jungle was also an ideal breeding ground for the tropical diseases that were ravaging the command, particularly malaria.

In terms of ammunition there were still about 5.5 million .30-caliber rounds, some 50,000 rounds of 75-mm ammunition, and roughly 4,300 155-mm shells on Bataan as of 1 April.[5] The limited number of 155-mm shells was particularly troubling since the 155s had been some of the most effective weapons. When the final Japanese offensive started there were thirty-two 155s on Bataan, divided equally between I and II Philippine Corps. About fifty tanks still remained in the two tank battalions, although they were suffering from a shortage of spare parts. The anti-aircraft defenses still had about forty 3-inch guns, including four Marine Corps weapons and the four guns of *Canopus* that had been mounted ashore near Mariveles. The Army's Bataan Field Flying Detachment was down to two P-40s by the time the Japanese attacked.

It was clear to General Wainwright on Corregidor and General King on Bataan that the extremely weak state of the troops was going to make it very difficult to resist a major enemy attack that was now clearly about to occur. Wainwright desperately continued to press for food shipments, but by the end of March it was obvious that the Japanese blockade was so tight that only submarines, seaplanes, and very small craft could get into Manila Bay under cover of darkness.

THE JAPANESE ATTACK

There was disagreement within the Japanese command as to the exact timing of the final attack. A compromise resulted in 1000 being selected for the start of the preparatory bombardment by aircraft and artillery. The bombardment was to last a full five hours before the tanks and infantry advanced. A special allocation of ammunition had been sent from Japan to ensure that the 14th Army's artillery units would be able to fire for maximum effect against the defenders. The main attack would be made against the Philippine Army 21st and 41st Divisions in II Philippine Corps, directly in front of the high ground at Mount Samat, a key piece of terrain that dominated eastern Bataan.

When the Japanese bombardment began at 1000 on 3 April, roughly 150 guns and heavy mortars opened fire as light and medium bombers roared in to attack the defenders. The Japanese concentrated their barrage against a two-and-a-half-mile-wide sector manned by elements of the two Philippine Army divisions. The shelling continued for five hours and was clearly heard by the residents of Manila, over thirty miles away. The effects were devastating. Senior American Army officers and NCOs who had served in World War I stated that the intensity of the Japanese bombardment was comparable to the heavy shelling of that earlier conflict. On the first day of the attack the Japanese artillery fired over 14,000 shells from 75-mm to 240-mm.[6] By the time the bombardment ended the front had already broken. Most of the demoralized, sick, half-starved Filipino troops in the sector selected for the breakthrough had fled by the time the Japanese infantry arrived; many had died during the five-hour bombardment.

By the morning of 5 April the situation was dire. The enemy poured through the breach in the II Philippine Corps' line. After bitter resistance by some Philippine Army units, Mt. Samat was overrun that day by the 61st Infantry Regiment, giving the Japanese an ideal vantage point to look down on the defenders. An effort was made to hold the Japanese along the little San Vicente

River to the southeast of Mt. Samat and plans were made to launch a counter-attack. The much-weakened all-American 31st Infantry, the Scout 45th and 57th Infantry Regiments, plus the remaining tanks were moved up to lead the attack, but it was hopeless. The defenders were too weak and the enemy too strong.

While the ground fighting was going on, armed motorboats and barges had been shelling the east coast of Bataan at night. The II Philippine Corps staff received reports on the nights of 3 and 4 April that Japanese motorboats were firing toward the shore. Most of the enemy shooting was very inaccurate, but it raised fears that the Japanese were going to conduct an amphibious assault against the east coast of Bataan to complement the ground attack that was smashing through the front line. At 0300 on the morning of 6 April the Corps G-2 report noted: "Considerable artillery firing was observed some distance out in Manila Bay."[7] The Navy's China gunboats were in action against the Japanese.

NIGHT BATTLE IN MANILA BAY

The Americans had good intelligence on the number of small craft that the enemy had available in Manila. It was known that the Japanese had sufficient vessels for a landing of more than a regiment of troops on Bataan's east coast. After several consecutive nights of enemy watercraft firing from out in the Bay there was concern that the enemy was getting ready to make a landing behind the Filipino-American lines. That threat had to be taken seriously. Therefore, on the evening of 5 April the gunboats *Mindanao* and *Oahu* were ordered to raise steam and patrol about 18,000 yards off the east coast of Bataan in order to intercept any Japanese watercraft operating in the area. Given the limited amount of fuel the little ships still had this was certainly considered an important mission.

The water off much of Bataan's east coast was very shallow, ideal conditions for the China gunboats that drew about six to seven feet. The two ships departed from the North Channel as darkness fell and headed north to their patrol area. They planned to run a north–south search pattern.

Mindanao was in the lead with *Oahu* a few hundred yards astern as the two gunboats cruised north about nine to ten miles off the coast. From this vantage point they could see the flashes of gunfire ashore on Bataan as the fighting raged. At about 0200 lookouts on *Mindanao* spotted what appeared to be thirteen to fourteen enemy boats in formation, headed toward Bataan's east coast. They were about nine miles offshore and had apparently not seen the Americans. When initially spotted the enemy boats were astern of the gunboats. They were from the gunboat unit of the 21st Independent Engineer Regiment based in Manila.[8]

Mindanao and *Oahu* turned toward the southwest in order to parallel the enemy formation, keeping them just within sight. At 0300 the two gunboats turned to close in on the enemy and opened fire. At that point the enemy vessels were to port, a few hundred yards away to the southeast. The Japanese promptly returned fire. McCracken estimated from the size of the shell splashes around the gunboats that the enemy was firing 3-inch weapons. That was a good guess, since the 75-mm field pieces on board some of the Japanese boats were almost exactly the equivalent of a 3-inch gun. The Japanese also fired machine guns at the gunboats. *Mindanao* and *Oahu* were firing with everything they had—3-inch and .30-caliber machine guns. *Mindanao* alone mounted twenty-six machine guns, half on either beam of the ship. The enemy formation stared to turn back to the east, at which point the two gunboats swung around to starboard to follow them. McCracken was determined that they not be allowed to escape back to Manila.

The gunboats paralleled the enemy formation, which was now to starboard, heading east. During the exchange of gunfire enemy machine-gun rounds struck *Mindanao* beneath the bridge, hitting a pyrotechnics locker. Almost immediately a fire started and the bridge was filled with smoke. McCracken went outside to the flying bridge, but the smoke was so dense that he still could not see. He directed the helmsman to set a course due north to open the range. While that was going on Yeoman 3rd Class Donald Purling, who was manning a .30-caliber machine gun on the port side just aft of the bridge saw the smoke pouring from the pyro locker. Just as he recalled that there was 3-inch ready ammunition stored close to the pyro, Purling heard an order shouted down from the bridge to throw the burning pyrotechnics overboard. Not seeing anyone else nearby, he crawled over to the fire, grabbed the pyro box, and heaved it over the side.

As *Mindanao* turned north she started firing 3-inch star shells to illuminate the enemy, hoping that Army shore batteries and *Oahu* would be able to better see the Japanese. When the fire was put out, McCracken assessed the situation. It appeared that the enemy formation had heaved to. It was also apparent that the Army shore batteries had not spotted the enemy, or at least they were not shooting at them. McCracken decided to re-engage to try to force the enemy formation closer to Bataan, noting that the Japanese had been sufficiently delayed that they would not be able to make landfall (assuming that a landing was their intention) before daylight. This delay would give the Army forces ashore a good chance to spot and engage them.

With *Oahu* still astern, *Mindanao* swung back to the south and opened fire again. The Japanese machine guns were firing wildly in all directions as the gunboats closed the range. More star shells were fired, which apparently helped

Oahu's gunners more than it did *Mindanao*'s own men. One boat was seen to go up in flames as the enemy formation turned toward the northwest, probably intending to reach that part of the Bataan coast under Japanese control.

Remembering his orders to be back under the protection of Corregidor's anti-aircraft guns by dawn, McCracken set course toward the fortified islands, continuing to fire at the enemy as he withdrew. The two gunboats pulled out of range as dawn approached. As they headed south the gunboat crews could see shell splashes from Army shore defense guns erupt near the enemy boats. By the time the little ships approached Corregidor the sun was up. *Oahu* was attacked by enemy "dive bombers" (probably Japanese Army Ki-51 light bombers), but was not hit. Proud of their night's work, McCracken and Smith reported the results of the action to Captain Hoeffel.[9]

II Philippine Corps' G-2 report noted that shortly after dawn eleven Japanese boats were observed heading north toward Pampanga Bay. Two other vessels, apparently American, were also seen heading south at the same time. As the enemy boats sailed north they fired a few rounds toward the shore without noticeable effect.[10]

This little action is an excellent example of the Navy's role of protecting the Army's seaward flanks on the Bataan Peninsula. It is not known whether this particular Japanese boat formation intended to make a landing on Bataan's east coast, but that was a constant fear of the American command, and the reason why the Army devoted the entire 2nd Philippine Army Division to the defense of the Manila Bay side of the Peninsula. Assuming McCracken's initial count of thirteen or fourteen enemy craft was correct, and again assuming the II Philippine Corps report of eleven vessels spotted at dawn was also accurate, it can be inferred that the two gunboats sank two or three enemy craft. Unfortunately, the situation on Bataan was too far gone by this point. Although *Mindanao* and *Oahu* accomplished their mission, the end of resistance on Bataan was now only three days away.

THE END ON BATAAN

The fighting on 6 April decided the battle. Both sides launched simultaneous attacks that met southeast of Mt. Samat. The battered Philippine Army units broke under Japanese pressure and fled to the south. Although some gains were made by the Scouts of the 45th Infantry attacking into the enemy's flank from the west, by that evening the Japanese had routed most of the opposition to their front and started to advance toward the southern tip of Bataan. By the morning of 7 April the situation was on the verge of collapse. The Scout units and the Americans of the 31st Infantry (all units had been reduced to remnants a few hundred strong by this point), plus the remaining tanks, tried to slow the enemy advance, but it was clear to Major General King, the Luzon Force commander, that the Japanese could not be stopped.

Southern Bataan was heavily bombed on the 8th. Commander Sackett counted roughly twenty air attacks on Mariveles, Cabcaben, Sisiman Cove, and ships in the Bay that day. Fortunately for *Canopus*, she remained untouched. Possibly her months-long ruse of pretending to be an abandoned hulk was still working. At noon on the 8th Sackett was in Queen Tunnel on Corregidor trying to get more information on the situation, and hoping that "Mamasan" might, just might, be allowed to make a run for the southern Philippines should Bataan fall. Captain Hoeffel told Sackett that the Army had informed him that the situation on Bataan was deteriorating fast. Hoeffel instructed Sackett to be ready to execute plans to destroy Navy equipment—and ships—in the Mariveles area. At the time they met in the early afternoon Hoeffel warned Sackett that the Army's plan was to prohibit any personnel from evacuating to Corregidor due to the already crowded situation on the island and the overall shortage of supplies there.

As the situation on Bataan deteriorated the Navy staff on Corregidor was closely monitoring the course of the fighting. Lieutenant Commander Knoll met frequently with his Army counterparts, at times spending most of the day with Colonel Stewart Wood, USA, Wainwright's G-2. By the evening of 6 April it was clear that Bataan would soon fall. Knoll kept Captain Hoeffel and Colonel Howard informed of the progress of the fighting. This was difficult due to the increasingly disorganized and chaotic situation. Southern Bataan was under constant air attack, making movement of troops and vehicles difficult. The area around the southern tip of the Peninsula was becoming jammed with men whose units had disintegrated under the Japanese onslaught. Meanwhile, there were still about 150 Marines and roughly 700–800 Navy personnel in southern Bataan. The Navy leadership on Corregidor was determined that they not be caught when the Peninsula fell to the onrushing Japanese.

By staying in close contact with the Army's operations and intelligence sections on Corregidor, as well as periodically calling King's headquarters on Bataan, Knoll determined that the Luzon Force was on the verge of collapse by 8 April. That afternoon he met with Captain Hoeffel and described what he knew about what was happening on Bataan. Hoeffel realized that the situation was extremely serious. Shortly thereafter Hoeffel asked to meet with General Wainwright to discuss the fate of the Navy and Marine Corps men still on Bataan. Present at the meeting in Malinta Tunnel were Wainwright, Brigadier General Louis C. Beebe, Captain Hoeffel, Colonel Wood, Lieutenant Colonel

Pugh, and Lieutenant Commander Knoll. Hoeffel urged Wainwright to allow all Navy and Marine Corps personnel remaining on Bataan to be evacuated to Corregidor so they could be added to the 4th Marines on the beaches. Hoeffel said that the naval personnel were still in cohesive groups that were under command and could bring with them as much food, fuel, and ammunition as possible. After considerable discussion Wainwright stated that he was prepared to allow up to 12,000 personnel from Bataan to transfer from Corregidor. He was hopeful that major elements of the Philippine Division, in particular the 45th Infantry Regiment (PS), could be brought to The Rock to supplement the beach defenses. Wainwright agreed that all naval personnel should be evacuated to the fortified islands. Once the decision was made those present departed in order to expedite preparations. The sailors and Marines on Bataan had their ticket to escape—if they could do so in time.[11]

As if the earth itself understood Bataan's agony, the southern part of the Peninsula started to shake from a severe earthquake around 2130. This added to the nightmarish scene. Even ships in the Bay could feel the effect of the earth tremors. The roads were clogged with exhausted, frightened men who had run from the approaching Japanese. The end was clearly at hand.

At 2145 Commander Sackett received a call from Captain Hoeffel directing him to put the destruction plans into effect. Unfortunately, the Old Lady was not permitted to try to break out to the south. Given the tightness of the blockade of the entrance to the Bay by this point in the siege it would probably have been a futile attempt resulting in the loss of the ship and many of its crew. *Canopus'* men began readying their ship for its final, short, voyage. Thankfully, Hoeffel's call had included word that Navy personnel would be evacuated to Corregidor, reversing the decision that Sacket had been informed of earlier in the day.

At 2230 formal word arrived at Tunnel Queen from General Wainwright, directing that all naval equipment and facilities on Bataan that could not be evacuated to Corregidor be destroyed and for all naval personnel on Bataan to depart before dawn on 9 April. The Navy had already planned to demolish its stocks on Bataan that could not be moved to The Rock, and to scuttle those ships that could not escape. By the time Wainwright's message arrived Hoeffel had already directed the remaining Navy elements on Bataan to start the demolition of materials and to evacuate all personnel to Corregidor. The situation on the southern tip of the Peninsula was already a nightmare as the remaining sailors and Marines prepared to depart.

Commander Hastings and Lieutenant Weschler had already placed demolition charges—six Army 155-mm artillery shells—in the old *Dewey* dry dock, expecting that this day would eventually come. The sailors assigned to *Dewey* blew the charges and the old servant of the Asiatic Fleet sank in the western portion of Mariveles Harbor where she had been berthed throughout the siege.

The hulk of the minesweeper *Bittern*, which had been wrecked during the bombing of the Cavite Navy Yard four months before, was towed out into the harbor and scuttled. The tug *Napa* was also sunk. The most bitter pill was, without question, *Canopus*. The Old Lady had served both the Army and Navy well during the three month Bataan campaign. At 2200 Commander Sackett directed that the ship be readied for scuttling.

Lighters were brought alongside and the little remaining fuel oil was pumped out for use by other ships. On board the tender's men were removing key equipment. Other items such as large fixed machine tools were wrecked just in case the Japanese might be able to raise the ship after she went down. At 0410 the ship backed out into the middle of Mariveles Harbor under her own power with a skeleton crew. A few hundred yards from her months-long berth the anchor was let go and her sea cocks were opened. Word was passed to abandon ship and the scuttling crew went over the side into three motor launches. Commander Sackett was the last man to leave the ship. *Canopus* went down in fourteen fathoms of water at about 0830.[12]

The Marines of Battery A disabled their four 3-inch anti-aircraft guns that were positioned near the Mariveles airfield. Lighters and motorboats evacuated the gun crews, about sixty-five officers and men, along with their small arms and machine guns to The Rock. By midnight the channel between Bataan and Corregidor was alive with vessels—barges, motor launches, and other small craft—evacuating personnel and supplies. Some were authorized to make the transfer, others were not. Technically, the Filipino naval reservists were not authorized to evacuate to The Rock, but their American Navy comrades brought them along. During the siege the Filipino reservists manned many of the Navy's motorboats that operated between Corregidor and southern Bataan. Now during Bataan's last night of resistance these Filipinos continued to man their small craft, some of them making several runs between the Peninsula and Corregidor. Another group that came over without authorization were about forty-five American civilian personnel from the Pacific Naval Air Bases organization. As the night progressed the situation became more and more chaotic.

Starting at 2100 on the night of the 8th the Army began blowing up its remaining supplies in southern Bataan. There was no time, nor the ability, to warn the mass of personnel flocking into the extreme southern tip of the Peninsula that the ammunition dumps were about to be blown up. At 0200 on the 9th the Army engineers detonated large ammunition dumps located in caves near Hospital Number 1 and General King's headquarters. Throughout southern Bataan, on Corregidor, and on board the small craft in the channel, sailors, Marines, and soldiers watched in awe as the huge dumps of TNT and ammunition were blown. Several remarked that the spectacle far exceeded any 4th of July celebration they had ever seen. The force of the explosions knocked down personnel at Hospital Number 1 and at Luzon Force Headquarters; General King's flimsy headquarters building was blown over by the blast.[13]

Down at Mariveles Harbor the Navy personnel were loading boats with rifles, machine guns, ammunition, food, and fuel. The men themselves were limited to the clothes they were wearing—there was no room in the boats for anything else. The supply tunnels around Mariveles that had served the Navy well were dynamited shut once most of the valuable supplies had been removed.

Just as dawn was approaching three of the last boats to depart Mariveles Harbor pulled away loaded with crewmen from *Canopus*. Suddenly, as the boats were proceeding through the harbor, the caves that had been dynamited closed exploded with a huge roar. It was later guessed that fuel stored inside the caves must have leaked and somehow detonated, which in turn set off the remaining ammunition in the tunnels. The fact that the caves were sealed by the earlier explosions served to magnify the force of the blast. The three boats were only a few hundred yards offshore when the explosion occurred. Giant boulders showered down on them. The boat that Commander Sackett was in had its stern sheared off and sank, but with no casualties. One of the other boats, however, was hit directly by a huge boulder; four Navy men were killed and the boat sank. Nine men were injured. The third boat stopped to pick up the survivors of the two sunken craft and then continued on to Corregidor.[14]

As Bataan was collapsing the Army commanders ordered that the nurses in Hospitals 1 and 2 be evacuated to Corregidor. This was an act motivated in part by knowledge of the barbarous behavior of the Japanese Army during the infamous 1937 Rape of Nanking. The Army leaders wanted to get the nurses to safety on Corregidor, temporary as that may be. Late on the afternoon of the 8th the nurses were ordered to get to Mariveles for evacuation. Many protested leaving their patients, but the orders stood. The nurses at Hospital Number 1 had a relatively easy time getting to Mariveles. Those at Hospital Number 2, however, had a much more difficult journey even though they started from only a few miles farther to the east. By the time the nurses from Number 2 left the hospital the main road was nearly completely jammed with vehicles and retreating soldiers. It took hours to cover just a few miles. The explosion of the big ammunition dumps in the early morning hours of 9 April delayed them even more. Finally, the last group of four nurses made it to Mariveles well after dawn where they were picked up by a passing Navy launch and taken to The Rock. All the American and Filipino nurses were evacuated, total of over ninety women. The Navy's only nurse on Bataan, Ann Bernititus, was among those who escaped. Two Navy doctors, one dentist, and a handful of corpsmen remained behind at the Army hospitals and were taken prisoner by the Japanese.

While the nurses were making their way to Corregidor another critically important evacuation was taking place. On 3 April, the day the Japanese offensive started, the submarine *Seadragon* nosed into Cebu Harbor in the central Philippines. Unloading ten torpedoes and most of the boat's 3-inch deck gun ammunition, Lieutenant Commander Ferrall's sub took aboard 34 tons of food, mostly rice and flour loaded in 100-pound sacks. *Seadragon* arrived off Manila Bay on the evening of 8 April as Bataan was collapsing. The sub surfaced outside the minefield to the west of Corregidor and waited.[15] This was her second trip back to Manila Bay. Again, she was being used to evacuate code breakers.

At about 2100 on the evening of the 8th Ensign Ralph E. Cook was in his bunk at Tunnel Afirm when the phone rang. It was Captain Hoeffel, who wanted to speak to the officer in charge, Lieutenant Lietwiler, right away. Hoeffel told Lietwiler to assemble his men immediately and get to Corregidor's North Dock for evacuation. No baggage was allowed—the men had to depart with only what they were wearing and what little they could stuff into their pockets. Lietwiler, Lieutenant Taylor, and Cook quickly discussed the status of the disassembled and boxed IBM equipment that they had expected to take with them. Lietwiler stated that Captain Hoeffel told him that they would be meeting a sub at sea. That would prevent loading the equipment because the sub's hatches were too small for the boxes to fit without being further disassembled; they would have to be left behind. The key thing now was to get the men out. A total of four officers, three chiefs, and fourteen other enlisted men were all that was left of Station C on Corregidor.[16]

Before departing Lietwiler informed Captain Hoeffel that there were several boxes of materials (the disassembled IBM machines, some code books, and Japanese dictionaries) still in Tunnel Afirm that they did not have time to destroy before heading to the dock. In the days after their departure Hoeffel had the remaining Station C equipment and materials destroyed and sent a message to the Chief of Naval Operations confirming that this had been done. Lieutenant Commander Knoll was in charge of the destruction of the remaining code-breaking materials.

The men proceeded to North Dock where there was a gig waiting to transport them to the rendezvous point where the sub was supposed to be waiting, a location in the outer part of Mariveles Harbor. An Army officer was put on board with them, Colonel George S. Clarke who had commanded the 57th Infantry Regiment (PS) during the initial fighting along the Abucay Line in January.[17] As the men loaded into the small boat they saw the darkness periodically broken with brilliant flashes and loud booms from high up on Topside. This was Batteries Smith and Hearn, Corregidor's two long-range 12-inch guns, firing interdiction missions against Bataan's east coast road. Each of the big guns fired about thirty-five rounds that night in a vain attempt to slow down the enemy's advance along the coast road. As the boat pulled away from North Dock flashes from Bataan could be seen as the battle raged and the Army and Navy blew up ammunition and supply dumps.

The small boat arrived at the designated point, but *Seadragon* was nowhere to be found. The coxswain started to motor about the harbor searching for the missing submarine. Suddenly, a row of tracers ripped ahead of the boat forcing it to heave to. The firing had come from a minesweeper on patrol in North Channel. When the gig inquired as to the whereabouts of *Seadragon* word was passed that the submarine was waiting farther out, near the entrance to the minefield where it was safer. The gig got under way again and shortly thereafter *Pigeon* was spotted alongside the sub. As soon as the small boat tied up to *Pigeon* the Station C personnel went across the rescue vessel over to the submarine. With everyone on edge, and the personnel transfer behind schedule, only about seven tons of the sub's thirty-four tons of food was transferred to *Pigeon* before the unloading of supplies was ended. A message from Captain Hoeffel hastened the departure: "Get the hell out of here." Lieutenant Commander Ferrall was glad to get out of the area. While sitting on the surface the sub had been rocked by the effects of the earthquake that shook Bataan that night. The awesome display of fireworks on Bataan was a clear indication that the Peninsula was on the verge of falling. Navigating his way through the minefield passage, Ferrall took *Seadragon* out into the South China Sea.[18]

With *Seadragon*'s departure the last of the OP-20-G men from Station C left the Philippines. It was critical that those men not fall into Japanese hands. Years later it was revealed by then–Radioman 1st Class Duane Whitlock of Station C that he was part of a discussion in March involving Station C's officers and chiefs where it was agreed that should Corregidor fall before the last of Station C's personnel could be evacuated that they would shoot their own men, and themselves, rather than allow the Japanese to take them prisoner. By 26 April the last of the code breakers had arrived in Fremantle, Australia, where they joined the first two groups who had been evacuated in February and March. Station C was no more. Now this same group of men was operating under the new title of Station Belconin. From there they would continue their outstanding work against the enemy's code system.[19]

At Cabcaben Field the last plane to depart Bataan was being readied. Mechanics were struggling to make last-minute repairs while the pilot, Army lieutenant Roland Barnick, anxiously awaited the arrival of Filipino colonel Carlos Romulo, the "Voice of Freedom" whom MacArthur had personally directed be evacuated from Bataan—the Japanese had put a price on Romulo's head.

When the plane took off from Cabcaben Field at nearly 0120 on the morning of the 9th with six men on board, it was dangerously overloaded. Struggling to rise above seventy feet, Barnick ordered his passengers to throw out everything that was not bolted down. Gradually the old plane gained altitude and headed south. The last plane to escape from Bataan was a repaired Navy J2F "Duck" float plane, one of the aircraft sunk by strafing Zeros in Mariveles Harbor back in early January. Army aviation mechanics and pilots had managed to refloat and repair the plane.[20] Now it headed south toward Panay, leaving Bataan behind in the darkness.

Major General King, acting on his own authority, sent representatives to meet the Japanese early on the morning of the 9th. Recognizing that his disorganized, defeated, starving men could no longer oppose the enemy's advance down Bataan's east coast, King wanted to surrender in order to prevent needless bloodshed. It was a courageous decision. As the situation on Bataan had fallen apart, MacArthur's headquarters in Australia sent messages to General Wainwright ordering him to launch a counteroffensive against the Japanese using the I Philippine Corps on the western flank of Bataan. This was delusional nonsense, as Wainwright, King, and Major General Albert Jones, the I Philippine Corps commander, all knew. The physically weak and sick troops of I Corps were barely able to move their equipment with them as they fell back toward southern Bataan to avoid having their right flank exposed due to the enemy breakthrough on the eastern portion of the Peninsula. From Australia MacArthur also insisted that there be no surrender on Bataan. The tone and substance of MacArthur's messages to both Wainwright and Army chief of staff General Marshall in Washington are quite amazing, clearly showing that MacArthur was totally out of touch with the state of the command in the Philippines. Wainwright was surprised to learn that King had decided to surrender, but was in no position to reverse the decision. By mid-morning on the 9th King had met with the enemy and agreed to surrender the Luzon Force.[21]

RESCUING THE LAST ESCAPEES FROM BATAAN

During the night the commanders of the three minesweepers that were anchored in the North Channel received orders to start working on a new passage through the minefield. With the fall of Bataan imminent the North Channel would no longer be usable by submarines or small surface blockade runners that might still be able to reach Manila Bay. A new passage through the mines was needed on the south side of Corregidor. This was a major undertaking, requiring considerable planning.

On the morning of the 9th a meeting was held on board *Quail*, anchored in North Channel between Bataan and Corregidor. Lieutenant Commander Morrill was the senior officer present, having two years' experience in mine craft. With him were two lieutenants, Thurlow W. Davison, the skipper of *Finch*, and Egbert A. Roth of *Tanager*. Morrill and the other two minesweeper captains began planning how they would approach their new, important, mission. While they were pouring over charts, Morrill's mind was partly on a fuel barge that *Quail* had positioned and then deliberately sunk in Sisiman Cove early in the Bataan campaign; the fuel was a final reserve for a hoped-for breakout to the south. Morrill realized that with the fall of Bataan the precious fuel was probably unrecoverable. He now focused on the task at hand—the new passage through the minefield.[22]

While the minesweeper captains met, other Navy ships were standing close to southern Bataan, trying to assist men onshore who were pleading for help. The three China gunboats, *Mindanao*, *Luzon*, and *Oahu* were all there, along with *Pigeon*, picking up Army refugees. The tug *Keswick* was also standing off Bataan's south coast, trying to lend a hand to the men who were trying to swim to the ships, were coming out in bancas, or were frantically waving shirts or flags from shore, trying to get the attention of the Navy ships.

Three exhausted Army officers rowing a banca reached *Mindanao*. They pointed to where about thirty of their men were still ashore and pleaded that the ship send a boat to get the soldiers. Commander McCracken asked for volunteers. Five crewmen went in one of *Mindanao*'s small boats to pick up the Army troops. When they reached the shore the sailors had to assist some of the weakest soldiers into the boat. The gunboat sailors were shocked to see how emaciated they were. The Army troops were from the all-American 31st Infantry Regiment. As the boat was loaded snipers started to fire at them but the sailors managed to get all the Army personnel on board and headed back out to their ship. Meanwhile, the other gunboats continued to pick up Army refugees.

About an hour after *Mindanao* picked up the Army troops the ships in North Channel suddenly came under fire from Japanese field artillery that had arrived in the area of the southern tip of Bataan. These were almost certainly 70- and 75-mm field pieces accompanying the lead Japanese infantry units sweeping into the area. Seeing the American ships close to shore, the Japanese opened fire.

It was about 1530 and the three minesweeper skippers were finalizing their plans for the new path through the minefield. They had selected a location just to the south of Corregidor where they would be able to use a marker on Hooker Point as a reference point for their work. While the meeting was under way the duty personnel on the bridge periodically informed the three captains of the deteriorating situation on Bataan. Suddenly, *Quail*'s General Alarm sounded. Morrill bolted for the bridge while Roth and Davison ran for their small boats waiting alongside to take them back to their own ships.

When Morrill reached the bridge he quickly sized up the situation. He could see the three gunboats close to the Bataan shore. They were already under fire from Japanese artillery, and were starting to maneuver and shoot back at the enemy. The Army tug *Henry Keswick*, which by this time had a Navy commanding officer and a partly Navy crew, had been hit and was on fire. *Quail* was sitting in the North Channel with steam barely up—the normal procedure to conserve fuel. Morrill ordered his engineers to do whatever it took to give him full power as fast as possible so he could get the ship under way. As *Quail* started to move, Morrill could see *Keswick*'s crew huddled forward as their ship burned while the Japanese continued to fire at her.

Morrill spotted *Mindanao* approaching the stricken tug, gathering speed as she went. When in position between *Keswick* and the Japanese artillery the gunboat let fly with everything she had, 3-inch and .30-caliber, silencing the enemy guns, if not destroying them. *Mindanao* then hauled off to the east, firing at the shore as she went.

Quail now started to get into the fight. While the gunboats engaged the enemy along Bataan's southern shore, Morrill maneuvered *Quail* farther up the coast toward Cabcaben. Spotting a Japanese gun position near the water, the minesweeper zigzagged to close the range. When less than a mile offshore *Quail* opened fire with both her 3-inch weapons. On the second salvo the shells burst squarely among the Japanese guns—wheels and parts of gun carriages flew into the air.[23]

When the Japanese started firing at the ships the patrol yacht *Maryanne* was anchored in the North Channel, her crew watching the gunboats and other craft picking up survivors from Bataan. Chief C. H. Sosvielle and the yacht's skipper, Ensign Fred Newell, were standing together on the deck, somewhat startled that the Japanese had managed to get artillery emplaced so quickly on the southern shore of Bataan. Suddenly, an enemy shell passed *between* them. Both men hit the deck. Once they realized what had happened, including their amazing luck, they broke out laughing. As soon as the seventy-five fathoms of anchor chain was brought in, *Maryanne* got under way and started to maneuver toward the east at her best speed of nine knots.[24]

Pigeon was also working the area between the gunboats and Cabcaben. She was making good use of the 3-inch guns she had pulled off *Sealion* and *Bittern* back in December at the Navy Yard. Blasting away at the enemy that could be seen ashore, she added her fire to the Navy's bombardment. While the gun duel was taking place, *Mindanao* slowed down enough to take on board another thirty Army soldiers who had been picked up by small craft.

The Army mine planter *General Harrison* was also in the North Channel when the Japanese artillery opened fire. Initially the ship's commanding officer, Captain Edgard Rosenstock, USA, tried to dash eastward to get around Hooker Point and into the relative safety of South Harbor. Seeing *Keswick* and some of the smaller craft hit by enemy fire, he reversed course and took his shallow draft ship westward, over the top of the minefield. The mine planter took shelter directly south of Corregidor's westernmost tip. Later the little ship joined the rest of the vessels in South Harbor.[25]

The ships, with the exception of the unfortunate *Keswick*, were getting the best of the Japanese guns ashore. This should not be surprising. The guns firing at the ships were Japanese Army field pieces. Those weapons were not designed to engage moving targets, nor were their crews trained to do so. Once the gunboats, sweepers, and other ships got under way, they had the advantage over the Japanese guns. The minesweepers, gunboats, and *Pigeon* mounted a total of fourteen 3-inch guns, roughly the equivalent of an American or Japanese light artillery battalion.

Quail was getting ready to engage more enemy guns she had spotted farther inland west of Cabcaben when she and the other ships were ordered by Corregidor to stop firing at targets ashore. Army observers on The Rock had spotted long lines of prisoners starting to move northward along the east coast road—the infamous "Bataan Death March" was under way. Not wanting the ships' shooting to endanger the prisoners, Corregidor ordered a cease-fire. General Wainwright had also directed the Army coast artillery on Corregidor to hold its fire for three days to give the enemy a chance to evacuate the tens of thousands of prisoners from southern Bataan.

It was just as well that the ships were told to stop shooting at targets ashore, for by late afternoon they started to come under air attack. With the fighting on Bataan over, the Japanese Army and Navy aircraft were free to engage other targets. On the afternoon of 9 April the most important targets were the Navy ships operating in North Channel. In groups of three the enemy aircraft started to appear. To the Navy men on board the minesweepers and gunboats in North

Channel, the single-engined, fixed-landing-gear attack aircraft appeared to be dive bombers and they did indeed attack in diving mode. In actuality they were Japanese Army Ki-30 and Ki-51 light bombers. As the enemy aircraft started to attack the ships moved deeper into Manila Bay to gain maneuvering room.

During the lull of February and March the ships of the Inshore Patrol had worked out tactics to thwart air attack. They formed groups of three, by type, and started to maneuver in triangle formation at their top speed. The triangle formation was intended to provide mutual protection. Dive bombers tended to come in from astern, where the attack angle was best and most ship's defensive firepower was weak. The defensive triangle would often allow two ships in the triangle to bring their guns to bear on aircraft trying to attack the third vessel. This was the tactic employed on the afternoon of 9 April.

The three gunboats formed up in a defensive triangle, as did the three sweepers. The submarine rescue vessel *Pigeon*, *Maryanne*, and other small vessels maneuvered to try to get mutual support from one of the three-ship groups. As the Japanese aircraft began their attack runs they were confronted with 3-inch fire, followed by dense machine-gun barrages. By this point in the campaign most, if not all, of the gunboats and sweepers mounted twenty or more .30- and .50-caliber machine guns. With all those machine guns firing tracer rounds it must have been quite a spectacle. Maneuvering at their best speeds (13–15 knots), the little ships twisted around Manila Bay, firing as they went.

The air action went on the rest of the afternoon. This was a new experience for the ships in Manila Bay since in previous months a ship would come under air attack by a few planes, but once the attack was over the ship was generally safe for the rest of the day. This time waves of Japanese aircraft appeared. Despite several ships suffering near-misses, not one was hit by an enemy bomb. The Japanese Army light bombers had not been trained to engage moving ships, a fact that was much to the advantage of the Navy vessels maneuvering in the Bay. It is not known if any Japanese aircraft were shot down in the engagement, but the enemy was certainly thwarted in his intent to sink the Bataan Navy that afternoon. But a price had been paid—in fuel. All the ships were short of fuel on the morning of 9 April. Following an afternoon of high-speed maneuvering most were very low by the time the last Japanese plane roared off just before sunset. At that point orders were received from Inshore Patrol headquarters in Tunnel Queen for all ships to return to South Harbor and anchor. Ship captains were ordered ashore for further instructions.[26]

When the little ships moved into South Harbor it was starting to get dark. It had been a very, very long day. When they moored, one of the final tasks of the day was to put ashore the Army refugees that they had taken on board that morning. In the case of *Mindanao* the sixty soldiers she had on board were given the best meal that most of them had had in weeks, and their tattered rags were replaced by the crew's dress white uniforms. The Army troops who had been rescued from Bataan and had participated in a naval action were grateful to be alive. The Navy personnel noted the terrible physical condition of the half-starved Army troops. Wishing them luck, *Mindanao* sent the Army men ashore to Corregidor.

Only the large tug *Keswick* had been lost that day. Hit by Japanese artillery fire soon after the enemy guns took up position in the afternoon, the tug was beached just off Corregidor's Cavalry Point. Her skipper, Lieutenant (junior grade) Trose E. Donaldson, had won the Navy Cross during the bombing of the Cavite Navy Yard. Donaldson remained on board as long as possible, ensuring his crew was ferried off the stricken tug. The last man off the ship, he was in a rowboat heading the hundred or so yards to Corregidor when he was struck in the shoulder by a Japanese artillery shell and killed instantly.[27]

A number of other ships had suffered damage by fragments from near-misses of bombs or artillery shells. *Oahu*'s stack had been riddled by a shell passing through it, for example. Many crew members were amazed that they had survived the day.

Although the ships had put in a great performance, the sailing days of the Bataan Navy were about over. With the enemy now emplaced on southern Bataan, his artillery was much closer than the guns that had been firing from Cavite since early February, and there were going to be far more guns on Bataan than there ever were on the Cavite side of the Bay. The ships were now exposed to crossfire from both sides of the Bay. With little fuel left, it was recognized that it would only be a matter of time before most, if not all, of the ships would be lost to enemy artillery and air attack. Therefore, Captain Hoeffel made the decision to move the crews ashore. The ships' captains were given those orders following their arrival in South Harbor. The move ashore needed to be made that night, since Japanese aircraft and artillery attacks would certainly resume at first light on the 10th.

The crews of the three gunboats went to Fort Hughes where they would man Army heavy coast artillery positions. The Army had never had sufficient personnel to man most of the heavy guns at Fort Hughes. Now it would be the sailors' turn. The crews went ashore that night, taking with them weapons and equipment. In the coming days they would continue to send men out to their ships under cover of darkness in order to retrieve equipment and supplies. The crew of *Luzon* manned the single 14-inch gun of Battery Gillespie high on Fort Hughes' westernmost tip. *Oahu*'s crew took over two

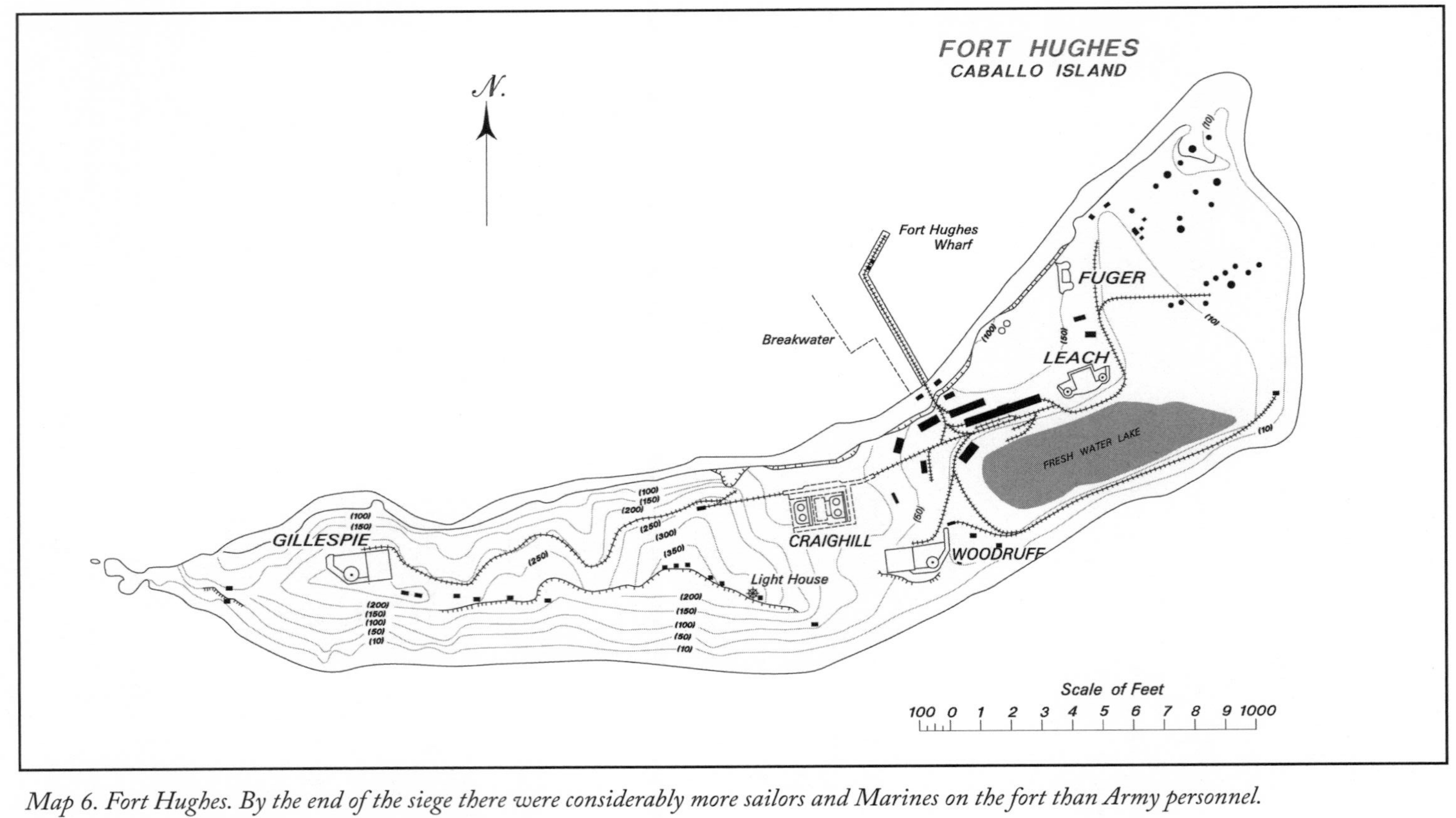

Map 6. Fort Hughes. By the end of the siege there were considerably more sailors and Marines on the fort than Army personnel.

Map prepared for the author by Martyn Keen, based on U.S. Army blueprints

155-mm guns on the low eastern portion of the Fort. Most important of all, *Mindanao*'s crew took over the critical Battery Craighill with its four 12-inch mortars. *Finch*'s crew also moved ashore to Fort Hughes. These moves brought the number of Navy and Marine Corps personnel on Fort Hughes to roughly 530 men, compared to some 270 Army troops.

Some of the men from *Quail* and *Tanager* went to the Navy tunnels on Corregidor, others to Fort Hughes. It was recognized, however, that some of those men would have to return to their ships to cut the new channel through the minefields now that Bataan had fallen. A few men were left on board the sweepers to get ready for that task while most of the crews moved ashore.

Several hundred Navy personnel and the crews of the Marine anti-aircraft guns on Bataan had arrived on Corregidor. Most of the Marines were added to Colonel Howard's Regimental Reserve. The sailors were mostly the crew of *Canopus*. These men were moved to the same area where the Regimental Reserve was located—Government Ravine on the southeast portion of Corregidor's Topside. They would soon be formed into a new 4th Battalion, for the 4th Marines.

On 12 April Captain Hoeffel sent a message to the Chief of Naval Operations reporting that all naval equipment that could not be evacuated to Corregidor had been destroyed and that *Canopus*, *Bittern*, *Napa*, and *Dewey* had all been scuttled. In addition to the men who had withdrawn to Corregidor, Hoeffel reported that 80,000 gallons of fuel oil, 130 tons of diesel, over a million rounds of .30-caliber ammunition, and 45 tons of food had been saved.[28]

Almost all of the Navy and Marine Corps personnel on Bataan had managed to escape to Corregidor, but an unfortunate few had not been able to get away. Seventy-seven Marines were trapped on Bataan the morning of the surrender. The two main groups were "Radio Bataan"—the Marine radar unit that had operated on the Peninsula since early January—and the guard detachment for the Luzon Force Headquarters along the main road between Hospitals 1 and 2. First Lieutenant Mann and First Lieutenant Dobervich and the forty-one enlisted Marines of the guard detachment recognized that Bataan was in trouble shortly after the start of the 3 April offensive. However, the two lieutenants were apparently not kept informed of the details of the worsening situation by the headquarters staff, although they could clearly sense the mounting crisis as the actions of the senior Army officers became more strained.

On the night of 8–9 April they felt the earthquake that shook southern Bataan and they later heard explosions from the Mariveles area as ammunition was blown up. At 0200 the Marines were thrown about as the big nearby Army ammunition dumps exploded; the Luzon Force Headquarters building was knocked down. Still, no word was received as to what they were to do. Finally, in midmorning the Army officers in the headquarters told them that Bataan was surrendering. Some of the Marines broke out the remaining rations and started to eat their largest meal in weeks, others threw their small arms into the jungle, waiting for the arrival of the Japanese.

The second largest group of Marines to surrender was Radio Bataan, the workhorse radar outfit. On 8 April when things were collapsing along Bataan's east coast, orders were received to get the Marines and the radar to Mariveles for evacuation to Corregidor. It was too late; by that point chaos reigned along the roads and trails of eastern Bataan. Lieutenant Schade and Warrant Officer Brainard got the detachment within a few miles of Mariveles, but the massive traffic jams prevented them from getting any farther. After sunrise on the morning of 9 April, when it became apparent that there would be no more ships evacuating men from Bataan, Schade and Brainard ordered the radar equipment destroyed. Later that day the men of the radar detachment were captured by the Japanese.[29] The handful of Navy medical personnel at the Army hospitals were also taken prisoner.

Along with these few Marines and sailors somewhere between 70,000–75,000 American Army, Philippine Scouts, Philippine Army, and Philippine Constabulary troops went into captivity. The exact number of prisoners taken on Bataan will never be known. The Japanese certainly did not keep records of the number of prisoners they took on Bataan; they only started to keep track of the prisoners once they reached prison camps. According to one source, when Corregidor fell the Japanese captured U.S. Army medical records and interviewed American doctors who stated that during the Bataan campaign 365 Americans and 1,938 Filipinos had died from the second week of January until the first week of April. It is likely that those figures do not include all the losses during the final chaotic week on Bataan when many Filipino units were shattered in the first two days of fighting, with the remnants of those units then retreating toward the southern part of the Peninsula.[30] Keeping an accurate count of casualties in those conditions would have been virtually impossible.

As far as the number of American and Filipino prisoners who were taken on Bataan the key, and unknown, variable is the number of troops killed during the final Japanese offensive from 3–9 April. The Japanese suffered about 250 killed in action during the final week of fighting. Filipino-American deaths were certainly much higher, especially in the period 3–6 April when the troops were most exposed to very heavy Japanese artillery fire in the Mt. Samat area. Without question, the vast majority of the defenders killed in the final week of fighting were Filipinos. With the exception of several thousand whom the Japanese permitted to remain in the hospitals on Bataan for a few more days or weeks, the prisoners started the Death March toward prisoner of war camps in central Luzon. No one will ever know how many Americans and Filipinos died along the way. Unofficial estimates range from about 5,000 to as many as 10,000. Of that, as many as 650 were Americans.[31]

Wainwright had hoped to disengage the Philippine Scout 45th Infantry Regiment from the I Philippine Corps for transport to Corregidor to reinforce the 4th Marines on the beaches. Due to the chaotic, clogged roads on Bataan the Scouts could not reach Mariveles in time and went into captivity with the rest of the Luzon Force. A total of about 2,100 personnel had managed to reach Corregidor, of whom about half were sailors and Marines. The stage was now set for the final major act of the Philippine Campaign—the siege of Corregidor.

CHAPTER 12

State of the Beach Defenses

By the time Bataan fell the 4th Marines had been working on improving Corregidor's beach defenses for over three months. To be more accurate, the Marines had really been creating Corregidor's beach defenses because relatively little had been done in the years before the war.

From the time the Army started fortifying Corregidor in the first decade of the twentieth century the emphasis had been on heavy seacoast artillery. The Army had never permanently assigned an infantry unit to Corregidor to defend the beaches. Although the Coast Artillery regiments had a secondary mission of serving as infantry to repel an enemy landing, little emphasis was placed on that role.

A few prewar beach defenses did exist on The Rock. Most of these had been built in the period from before World War I to the early 1920s; however, a few were constructed as recently as 1941. In James Ravine, long recognized as a possible landing site, there was a T-shaped tunnel for troop shelter. This tunnel could, in extreme circumstances, accommodate the better part of an infantry company, some 150 men. It was a well-constructed, concrete-lined tunnel roughly 200 feet long built into the west side of the ravine, with its entrance facing east. It was well hidden from observers on Bataan. In addition to the tunnel, a small concrete infantry trench was just behind the waterline at the entrance to James Ravine. Five hundred yards to the east another concrete infantry tunnel was located behind Battery Point. It was very similar to the James Ravine tunnel and offered good protection from enemy fire from Bataan or aerial bombs.

A small number of concrete positions for 75-mm beach defense guns had been constructed. One was at Battery Point, another near the waterline below Battery Ramsay, while a third was at Infantry Point on the north shore in the

1st Battalion's area. Just to the east of the Middleside Barracks there were prepared pits for four World War I–type Stokes mortars. From this location the mortars could range the beaches of Topside or Bottomside, and as far as Malinta Hill.

Roughly 150 yards east of Malinta Hill were concrete infantry trenches running roughly north to south protecting the east entrance to the tunnel complex. These trenches were envisioned as the last line of defense before the tunnel from an enemy approaching from the Tail of the island. Finally, several concrete machine-gun positions were scattered around the island.[1]

That was about the extent of prewar efforts to defend against an enemy landing force. When the 4th Marines took over the responsibility of beach defenses Colonel Howard directed the battalion commanders to start construction of field fortifications to make the island's beaches as well protected as possible. Since there were few engineers on Corregidor, most of the work had to be conducted by the Marines and the various personnel who were attached to the regiment.

The field works built by the Marines consisted of barbed wire entanglements, trenches and individual foxholes for personnel, emplacements for machine guns and the World War I–type 37-mm guns, and various types of obstacles including tank traps. The 4th Marines and many of the other units on Corregidor dug a large number of small tunnels for protection of their personnel. These improvised tunnels were not as safe as the permanent prewar concrete-lined tunnels or the concrete covered magazines of the seacoast batteries, especially when not properly constructed. Nevertheless, the tunnel digging effort from January through early April certainly saved many lives as the enemy bombardment grew in intensity.

The Marines were able to use local materials such as wood from the many damaged and destroyed buildings around the island. Due to the lack of replacement equipment the men were careful how they used their shovels, picks, and other digging implements; a broken shovel could not easily be replaced. There was also a general shortage of sandbags on Corregidor. This led to an extensive use of wood planks and empty metal powder cans from the anti-aircraft and seacoast guns to hold back the earth along the walls of trenches and other emplacements. A useful source of building material was the stacks of spare wooden ties from the island's now-inoperative trolley system. These were used to line some of the extemporized tunnels and for emplacements for machine guns and 37-mm weapons.

The Fort Mills engineering department was able to build a few small concrete structures after the start of the war. These were mostly emplacements for 75-mm beach defense guns. Overhead concrete cover was provided for these weapons whenever possible. Concrete was also used to help create an anti-tank obstacle in the low ground of Bottomside. Steel rails from the trolley system were set vertically in concrete (a technique very similar to the type of anti-tank obstacles used in the French Maginot Line) to block the inland movement of any Japanese vehicles that might debark at Bottomside. At various points around the island, wooden shoots were rigged so that Air Force 30-pound fragmentation bombs could be slid down over the cliffs to explode on the beaches below. The Marines tested these devices in March; the Regimental Record of Events mentions that the results were excellent.[2]

Recognizing that the Bottomside area represented a potential landing site, a chain of logs was constructed several hundred yards off the north and south shore to obstruct the approach of landing craft. Bottomside was also studded with locally constructed land mines. By the time Bataan fell most of the buildings of the San Jose barrio at Bottomside had been burned down during a series of controlled fires intended to create open fields of fire in the low ground. In addition to the concrete-mounted trolley rails, an anti-tank ditch also covered the southern beach at Bottomside, so concerned were the defenders of the effect of an enemy landing in that area.

By the time Bataan fell the beach defenses were extensive but most were field fortifications made of earth and wood. Experience in World War I had clearly showed that, given sufficient time, artillery could make a shambles of earthen field fortifications unless they were very deeply dug. And while trenches and foxholes could, and did, help minimize casualties, the overall effect of a prolonged artillery bombardment would be to smash gun emplacements, destroy wire telephone lines unless they were very deeply buried, tear apart barbed wire and other obstacles, and disrupt the overall cohesiveness of the defense. This was the reality that the 4th Marines faced as the enemy bombardment got under way in the week after Bataan fell.

By early April the regiment was occupying essentially the same positions that had been designated for the battalions in early January. The 2nd Battalion defended the west end of the island. Lieutenant Colonel Anderson correctly placed his greatest emphasis on James Ravine, the most vulnerable point in the battalion's sector. The middle portion of the island, including the low ground of Bottomside, was guarded by the largest element, the 3rd Battalion. Should the enemy succeed in getting ashore at Bottomside he could immediately threaten Malinta Tunnel, as well as be able to turn westward and advance toward Middleside and Topside.

The long Tail of the island from Malinta Hill eastward to Hooker Point was clearly the most exposed area. Not only was the Tail vulnerable to landing craft

Lieutenant Colonel Adams and one of his Marines on Corregidor

Source: USMC Historical Division, Quantico, Va.

approaching from Bataan, it could also be threatened by enemy craft coming directly across the Bay from Manila. Some of the beaches on the Tail were hardly conducive to landings; sheer cliffs would trap an opponent on the narrow beaches, exposing them to fire from above. In other areas, however, it would be much easier for an attacker to strike inland once ashore, although there was high ground directly behind the shoreline along almost all parts of the Tail of the island.

Since the Tail was the actual Japanese landing site the defenses of the 1st Battalion merit more detailed examination, to the extent that the remaining records and accounts allow. The Army leadership on Corregidor and Colonel Howard recognized that the long Tail was vulnerable. Although the roughly 1,056 officers and men assigned to its defense as of 1 May 1942 appear formidable, the 1st Battalion had some 5,000 yards of beach to defend along the Tail's north shore alone. In total, the battalion had to cover almost 10,000 yards of beaches along the north and south shore of the Tail.

A Company under Major Harry Lang manned the critical beaches along the north shore of the Tail. On 1 May, A Company had three Marine officers and 103 enlisted. No record survives of how many non-Marines were present, but it was probably around 200 men from the Army, Navy, Philippine Scouts, and Philippine Army Air Corps.[3] Additionally, there were men from D Company manning machine guns and 37-mm guns scattered about A Company's area. Therefore, as of 1 May, as the worst of the pre-invasion bombardment was starting, there were probably between 350–400 men manning some 5,000 yards of beach defense positions along the north shore of Corregidor's Tail.

A Company's 1st Platoon under 1st Lieutenant William F. Harris, USMC, was positioned from Infantry to Cavalry Points. The 2nd Platoon, which would absorb the brunt of the enemy landing in the North Point area, was under Gunnery Sergeant John Mercurio, while from east of North Point to the end of the Tail was 3rd Platoon under 1st Sergeant Nobel W. Well, USMC.[4] Also located in the extreme eastern end of the tail was 1st Lieutenant Ray G. Lawrence, USA, of the 92nd Coast Artillery. The night the Japanese came ashore Well was on a mission to the west of the landing site, so Lawrence, whose main mission was artillery coordination, assumed command of the defense on the extreme east end of the island.

Precise information is available regarding the strength of the forces in the 3rd Platoon area. A total of eighty-two men from the Marine Corps, Army, and Philippine Scouts manned the defenses, including the beach defense artillery. Weapons included two 75-mm guns (manned by Scouts) and two Marine 37s, two .50-caliber and two .30-caliber machine guns, eight BARs, rifles for every man, plus a large number of hand grenades.[5] Several of the Marines had Thompson sub-machine guns. The 3rd Platoon also had some of the improvised chutes with which to drop 30-pound fragmentation bombs over the cliffs. Importantly, Lawrence had been personally ordered by Major General Moore not to allow his 75-mm weapons to fire against Bataan; Moore directed Lawrence to keep the guns concealed until a Japanese landing.

B Company was deployed to defend the south shore of the Tail. Given the fact that any enemy landing craft would have to sail around Corregidor's Hooker Point and past Fort Hughes to land on the southern shore of the Tail, it may seem that placing one of the 1st Battalion's two rifle companies there was unnecessary. Nevertheless, the southern shore had to be defended to some extent. On 1 May there were two Marine officers and eighty-three enlisted men in the company, plus an unknown number of men from the other services.

D Company was the battalion heavy weapons unit. Captain Noel O. Castle, a noted marksman in the prewar Corps, commanded the company. Castle's company was the largest in the battalion, with four officers, one warrant officer, and 116 enlisted men from the Marine Corps. As with the other companies, an unknown number of non-Marines were part of the unit. Precise figures are not available, but Castle's company had, in early May, approximately sixteen .50-caliber heavy machine guns, eight 37-mm guns (four M-1916 weapons it had brought from China and four weapons it had received from the Army), and several dozen .30-caliber machine guns of various types (the battalion had roughly forty weapons of this type in mid-January, but more were later acquired from the Army and Navy). Additionally, there were two Stokes mortars with several hundred rounds of high explosive ammunition.[6] By the time Bataan fell the battalion's mortars were deployed in folds in the ground near Malinta Hill. The 37-mm weapons and machine guns had been allocated to the A and B Company areas.

Lieutenant Colonel Beecher had a small Reserve Company under 1st Lieutenant Robert F. Jenkins, USMC. Jenkins' unit, which included most of the Philippine Army Air Corps personnel who had been assigned to the battalion, was deployed on the slopes of Malinta Hill, a very exposed position. Digging in as best they could, Jenkins' men were not very useful as a reserve, since the Malinta Hill area was so critical that a force had to be maintained to protect the east and west entrances.[7] Along the north shore from the east entrance of Malinta Tunnel to Infantry Point was a rifle platoon formed from 1st Battalion's Headquarters Company; from that point eastward A Company took over.

Also in the 1st Battalion's area were six beach defense searchlights (mostly Army 18-inch models), two 3-pounder naval guns manned by sailors, and ten Model 1917 British-type 75-mm guns manned by Philippine Scouts (the two 75-mm guns with lst Lieutenant Lawrence's 3rd Platoon, A Company were counted among these weapons).

Finally, although not directly under the control of the 1st Battalion, there were a variety of other organizations positioned in the Tail of the island. These Army units had the potential to significantly influence the battle should the Japanese get ashore. Denver Battery, 60th Coast Artillery, had four 3-inch semimobile anti-aircraft guns in sandbagged positions on a key ridge just to the west of Kindley Field. On the westernmost point of this small but vitally important ridge were two concrete water tanks that were well-known landmarks on the Tail.

In the immediate vicinity of Kindley Field were two platoons of the 60th Coast Artillery's Mobile Battery. Each platoon had four .50-caliber machine guns. Mobile's 3rd Platoon had one two-gun section positioned near the southwest corner of the airfield, while another two-gun section was on the south side of the field, roughly halfway down the field's length. The 2nd Platoon was positioned on the east side of Denver Battery's ridge, overlooking the airfield, and with a good view of the area of A Company's 2nd and 3rd Platoons. These two Army heavy machine-gun platoons were, essentially, a backstop behind the Marines and other troops along the north and south beaches of the Tail.

There were roughly 120 men of A Company, 803rd Engineers (Aviation). This company had arrived on Corregidor in January to widen and lengthen

Kindley Field in anticipation of the aerial reinforcements that never arrived. The bulk of the 803rd Battalion had surrendered on Bataan. With the Tail of the island under increasing shellfire as April progressed, it was all that the engineers could do to fill in craters so that an occasional aircraft from the southern islands could sneak into Corregidor at night.

All these Army units on the Tail had been badly battered by the time of the Japanese landing. The worst hit was Denver Battery. In its exposed position atop the ridge the battery could be easily seen by Japanese observers on Bataan. Of critical significance was the death on 24 April of Denver Battery's strong and popular 1st Sergeant, Dewey Brady. Brady was killed atop one of the two water towers that dominated the ridge where the battery was located. It had been Brady's norm to position himself atop one of the towers while the battery was engaging enemy aircraft, since from there he had an excellent view of all four 3-inch gun pits and could easily control the unit. His death from artillery fire devastated the morale of the Denver Battery and without question had a major impact on the unit's actions on the night the Japanese landed.[8]

Similarly, the machine-gun platoons of Battery Mobile had only sandbagged positions and foxholes for protection; they were very exposed to enemy artillery fire. This had a bad effect on the morale of the young Army troops, to the point that it probably had a major influence on their willingness to stand and fight when the Japanese landed.

The 1st Battalion had constructed defenses similar to elsewhere on the island. Most men were in individual foxholes, although a few trenches had been dug. Heavy weapons such as machine guns and the 37- and 75-mm artillery pieces had earthen gun pits, most with overhead cover. As the Japanese barrage increased in intensity and many weapons were damaged by shell fragments, permission was granted to move the heavy weapons from the parapets of the emplacements and keep them stored at the bottom of the entrenchments, with orders to be ready to move the guns immediately back to their firing positions in the event of an enemy landing. Tank traps had been dug in several locations. Along part of the shore between Cavalry and Infantry Points a 20-foot-wide and 15-foot-deep trench had been dug a few yards back from the high-water point. Most of the trap was concealed by the trees that had been deliberately left in place to provide natural camouflage. About seventy-five improvised land mines were emplaced directly behind the tank trap.[9]

RESERVES

Colonel Howard had established his Regimental Reserve in mid-February. Initially the reserve was formed by using most of the men from the Headquarters and Service Companies. Major King, formerly the senior officer of Marine Barracks Olongapo, was the initial commander of the reserve. Extra weapons were provided to both companies, allowing each of them to form a machine-gun platoon with four Lewis machine guns. These were easier weapons to carry compared to the heavy water-cooled .30-caliber Browning machine guns that equipped most of the machine-gun platoons in the regiment. When Major King was transferred to Fort Hughes to become XO of the beach defenses on 17 February the command of the Regimental Reserve went to Major Max W. Schaeffer.

At the time Bataan fell the Regimental Reserve had been reorganized into Company O (Captain Robert Chambers) and Company P (1st Lieutenant Hogaboom of Longoskawayan Point fame). By 1 May these two companies had a total strength of 32 officers and 276 men, of whom 20 officers and 143 enlisted men were Marines. Since this total included Colonel Howard and his immediate staff as well as key communications personnel essential for command and control of beach defense operations, not all of the 308 men of Companies O and P would be available to commit against an enemy landing. Since January, these companies had been located in Government Ravine on the southeast side of Topside.

With the fall of Bataan several hundred Navy men became available for use as either artillerymen or infantry. For example, the remainder of the crew of *Canopus* was available for assignment. Many of these men, over two hundred, were sent to Government Ravine on Corregidor's southeast shore, one of the best-protected places on the island because it was sheltered from most enemy observers on Bataan.[10] Here other Navy men from Mariveles and some men from the small craft who had been reassigned ashore joined the *Canopus* sailors.

On the evening of 9 April the sailors were officially formed into 4th Battalion, 4th Marines. In the long history of the Marine Corps this unit stands out as one of the most unusual, an example of how desperate times lead to desperate measures. The battalion was formed with Companies Q, R, S, and T, plus a very small staff. Of the 28 officers and 275 enlisted men in the unit the only Marine officer was the battalion commander, Major Francis H. "Joe" Williams. Five Marine NCOs, 9 Army officers, and 2 Army sergeants were the only other non-Navy personnel in the unit; fully 286 of the personnel were from the Navy, including 16 of the officers. According to another source, the battalion had 316 Navy enlisted men, which would have given the battalion a total strength of 333 personnel.[11]

This unusual organization was formed on the day after Bataan fell. The personnel were assembled in Government Ravine and organized into companies. Apart from the personal gear of each man, there was virtually no unit equipment. Initially, few even had rifles. The battalion quartermaster found boxes of bolt-action rifles, still packed in shipping cosmoline grease, stored in Malinta Tunnel. These were sent to the 4th Battalion, along with boxes of .30-caliber ammunition and several hundred hand grenades. No machine guns or submachine guns were provided, although a few men had BARs. Several hundred hand grenades from the 4th Marine's stocks were issued to the battalion. Nevertheless, the battalion—a key element in the island's reserve—was very weak in weapons. There were no battalion mortars nor 37-mm close support guns. The 4th Battalion was, in the words of one observer, "500 sailors with 500 rifles, nothing more."[12] Indeed, the 4th Battalion did not even have 500 sailors.

Once the men were assembled in Government Ravine, already home to Companies O and P of the Regimental Reserve, training began, such as it was. A large number of the Navy enlisted men were senior petty officers and chiefs from *Canopus*. This fact caused a number of Marines to note that the 4th Battalion was probably the highest paid infantry battalion in the history of the Marine Corps. Of those, at least some had had landing force experience from service in China. Overall, the level of knowledge of infantry tactics among the sailors was quite low, although probably better than the Naval Battalion on Bataan due to the higher general experience level of the Navy men in the 4th Battalion. On the other hand, the Navy enlisted men were, on average, considerably older than a typical young infantryman, a fact that probably offset the generally higher level of experience of the men. In fact, a number of the chiefs had been retired before the start of the war and recalled to active duty when hostilities started.

The officers and chiefs of *Canopus* assigned the men to the platoons and squads, since they knew their men well. The first task was to provide protection for the men. Although they were mostly concealed from Bataan, Japanese observers on the Cavite side of the Bay could see the area where the 4th Battalion was concentrated, and artillery fire during daylight hours was a constant threat. Once foxholes had been dug, and a semblance of organization established, training began. Apart from individual rifles, there was little equipment available for the sailors. Attempts to obtain steel helmets, canteens, first-aid pouches, and other basic equipment were futile.[13] Two of the companies were commanded by Army officers—Captain Paul Moore (Q Company) and Captain Dalness (R Company)—and two by Navy lieutenants—S Company by Lieutenant Edward Little of the 16th Naval District staff and T Company by Lieutenant Butch Otter, from *Canopus*.

Conducting training was very difficult given the need to keep the men under cover during most of the daylight hours. Marine and Army NCOs intermingled with the men, demonstrating the use of their rifles. Some of the sailors had not fired a rifle since basic training, which in some cases was as long as twenty years earlier. Because there was no rifle range, marksmanship training was performed by firing at debris floating in Manila Bay. The veterans of fighting on Bataan conducted lectures on Japanese tactics, and basic fire and maneuver techniques were rehearsed as best they could be under the circumstances. Rudimentary squad- and platoon-level tactics were practiced as the days went by. 1st Lieutenant Otis Saalman, USA, formerly of the 57th Infantry (PS), was assigned to the battalion on 12 April. He was one of the very few personnel in the unit who had experience in ground combat against the Japanese. Along with the five Marine NCOs, Saalman conducted training lectures and sought supplies for the sailors now turned infantrymen.

By all accounts the morale of the 4th Battalion was far higher than one might have expected given the situation the men faced. As Captain Harold E. Dalness, the R Company commander, noted: "The chips were down, and there was no horseplay."[14] Amid the shelling and challenges in training and equipping the men, efforts were made to care for them. Some men who were experts in explosives blasted out a hole in the side of the hill to position the battalion's mess; a welcome improvement because twice Japanese shelling had destroyed the mess, including valuable rations. Most of the daylight hours were spent resting and improving the men's foxholes. The two daily meals were served at 0400 and 2000, both periods of darkness. Even though the ration was sparse by peacetime standards, to the survivors of Bataan it was a virtual feast. In fact, several of the Bataan survivors in the 4th Battalion gained a few pounds back during the four weeks prior to the Japanese landing on The Rock. It was noticed fairly quickly that while enemy artillery fire could be intense during the daylight hours, it was far less heavy at night. The 4th Battalion did its best to get ready for combat, despite the increasingly difficult conditions.

BEACH DEFENSE ARTILLERY

The final major element in the defense of Corregidor was the beach defense artillery. These were a collection of various weapons, mostly Army, some Navy. While the heavy coast artillery weapons' role was to engage Japanese artillery on Bataan and Cavite, the beach defense guns were intended to provide close-in defense against approaching enemy landing craft.

The beach defense weapons were under the overall command of Colonel Delbert Ausmus, USA, a Coast Artillery officer. Before the 4th Marines arrived in December, Colonel Ausmus had been in charge of the island's beach defenses. Scouts of the 91st and 92nd Coast Artillery Regiments manned most of the beach defense guns, although some of the weapons had Navy or Philippine Army crews. Ausmus divided his available weapons into three sectors that corresponded to the battalion areas of the 4th Marines. There were a total of four 75-mm and two 3-inch weapons in the West Sector; one 155, eight 75s, and one Navy 3-inch weapon in the Middle Sector; and ten 75-mm guns in the East Sector.[15]

The totals above do not include the twenty 37-mm weapons (manned by Marines of the battalion weapons companies) and three Navy-manned 3-pounder guns. The weapons of the beach defense artillery were intermingled with the Marines and other troops manning the beach positions. Some had concrete protection while others were in earth and sandbag positions. Japanese artillery or bombing knocked out or damaged most of the beach defense weapons, including the guns on Malinta Hill and at North Point that were in critical locations to oppose a landing on the north side of the Tail. Importantly, however, the Japanese missed the two 75s on Hooker Point.[16]

TABLE 12.1
Personnel Assigned to Corregidor Beach Defenses, 1 May 1942

	4th Mar HQ Company	Regtl Service Company	1st Bn	2nd Bn	3rd Bn	4th Bn	Total
Marines	14 / 79	6 / 64	16 / 344	14 / 307	17 / 429	1 / 4	68 / 1,227
Navy Medical	3 / 7	0 / 1	3 / 13	5 / 18	3 / 19	2 / 6	16 / 64
Navy	1 / 16	0 / 1	1 / 78	4 / 118	1 / 146	16 / 262	23 / 621
Filipino Navy Res	0 / 21	0 / 0	0 / 30	0 / 27	0 / 41	0 / 0	0 / 119
U.S. Army	1 / 0	1 / 0	26 / 286	19 / 98	27 / 146	9 / 2	83 / 532
Philippine Scouts	0 / 0	0 / 0	0 / 33	0 / 13	0 / 18	0 / 0	0 / 64
Phil Army Air Corps	6 / 83	0 / 0	7 / 217	7 / 199	7 / 194	0 / 0	27 / 693
Phil Army OSP	0 / 4	0 / 0	0 / 0	0 / 29	0 / 11	0 / 0	0 / 44
Philippine Constab	0 / 0	0 / 0	1 / 1	0 / 12	0 / 5	0 / 0	1 / 18
Total	25 / 210	7 / 66	54 / 1,002	49 / 821	55 / 1,009	28 / 274	218 / 3,382

The table is based on data from the 4th Marines' Record of Events as of 1 May 1942 showing the manpower assigned to beach defense duties. The Marines listed in this table are those serving on Corregidor. Officers are listed to the left of the slash in each cell, enlisted on the right. Marine totals include men listed as being in the hospital. Besides the 1,295 Marines in headquarters or beach defense positions, 39 Marine officers and men not included in the table were assigned to the 60th Coast Artillery.

In addition to the 1,334 Marines serving on Corregidor, there were 3 officers and 83 men on Fort Hughes and 14 men on the concrete battleship, Fort Drum. An additional 103 Marines were counted as prisoners of war. Of these, 22 men were listed as having been captured in the vicinity of Manila (most of whom were patients at the Naval Hospital when the city was occupied in January), 4 were in Shanghai, and 77 had been taken prisoner on Bataan.[17] All the known or suspected prisoners were still being carried on the regiment's rolls.

It can be seen that by this point in the campaign the majority of the 4th Marine Regiment were men from the other military services, including many hundreds of Filipinos; certainly a situation unique in the history of the Marine Corps. Less than half the men were Marines. Many of the Army personnel were escapees from Bataan and in terrible physical condition. The sailors were for the most part poorly trained for ground combat, as were the Philippine Army Air Corps personnel. Nevertheless, the Marines took these men under their wing and did as much as they could to arm and train them as the enemy bombardment steadily worsened.

CHAPTER 13

The Artillery Duel

With the fall of Bataan the Japanese started to redeploy their artillery into the southern part of the Peninsula in order to be within range of Corregidor and Fort Hughes. Since there was only one road running along Bataan's east coast it took the Japanese several days to move the bulk of their guns, howitzers, and ammunition to the southern portion of the Peninsula in order to bombard Corregidor. Some light artillery companies (the Japanese did not use the term "battery" for artillery units), mostly 75-mm weapons, had accompanied the Japanese infantry as it advanced southward on 8–9 April. These were the weapons that the Navy's ships had engaged the day Bataan fell.

Bataan's fall meant that the days of the fortified islands at the entrance of the Bay were clearly numbered. It was now a question of how long the garrison could hold out, how many casualties could they inflict on the Japanese, and how many men would be lost in the attempt to prolong the defense. Much depended on how well the American artillery on the fortified islands performed against the Japanese guns that were being repositioned into southern Bataan. If the Americans lost the artillery duel with their Japanese counterparts, the men defending the beaches would be at the mercy of the enemy's massed weapons.

JAPANESE ARTILLERY

The Japanese had at their disposal a powerful artillery force with which to reduce the American defenses. Indeed, given the small size of the target this concentration of Japanese weapons meant that the garrison of the fortified islands would be subjected to the most intense artillery bombardment that American troops experienced in World War II. Lieutenant General Kishio Kitajima, the commander of the 1st Artillery Headquarters, had planned the bombardment that devastated the Filipino-American defense line on Bataan on 3 April. Now he was responsible for planning and executing the bombardment to prepare the way for an invasion of Corregidor and the other forts.

Kitajima had at his disposal a variety of artillery units, some of which had been on Luzon since December, while others had arrived for the final offensive on Bataan. By mid-April the Japanese had approximately 120 guns and howitzers in southern Bataan and Cavite with which to bombard the fortified islands. There was a delay in the arrival of many of the Japanese weapons into southern Bataan due to the poor and congested roads. It was not until mid-April that the 240-mm weapons were in position, although most of the 150-mm pieces were in action a few days after the fall of Bataan. Appendix C provides a detailed list of the artillery available to the 14th Army for the siege of the fortified islands. Adapted from a diagram in the Japanese official history, Map 7 shows the locations of most of the Japanese artillery units in Bataan and Cavite.

In addition, the 14th Army had three Independent Mortar Battalions. These units had participated in the 3 April artillery bombardment on Bataan, but none of these mortars could reach Corregidor from the Peninsula. The Japanese intended to transport some of the mortars to Corregidor once an initial lodgment had been gained on the Tail of the island and use them to support subsequent operations on the island.

Assisting Kitajima's staff was the 675-man 5th Artillery Intelligence Regiment and the 1st Observation Balloon Company. The intelligence regiment was equipped with sound and flash locating equipment to pinpoint American artillery positions. The balloon company deployed two World War I–type tethered observation balloons to the area north of Cabcaben on Bataan's east coast, out of range of most of the American guns on Corregidor.

Due to supply and transport limitations the Japanese had to conserve ammunition during most of April. General Kitajima allocated ammunition as follows: 30 percent during the preparatory phase (basically until the end of April); 30 percent in the pre-assault firing from 1–5 May; 30 percent in support of the actual landing and for support of the troops once they started to advance inland from the beaches; and 10 percent held in reserve. For the Army-level artillery alone (guns from 105- to 240-mm) the Japanese determined that they would need 80,800 rounds. When the 75- and 105-mm guns in the 4th and 16th Divisions are added, the total probably rose above 100,000 shells. It is not known precisely how many artillery shells the Japanese actually fired at Corregidor during the 27-day siege of the fortified islands; it was certainly in the many tens of thousands.[1]

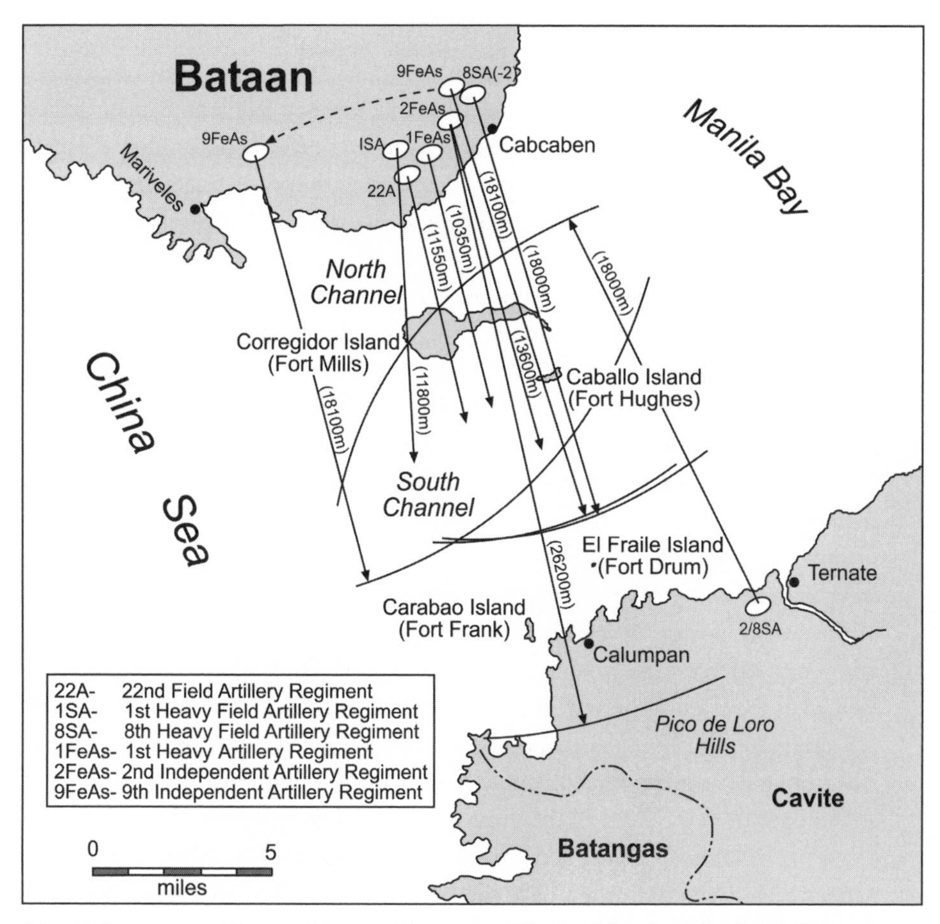

Map 7. Japanese artillery positions on Bataan and Cavite. Note how the fortified islands were in a cross fire once Bataan fell.

This map was adapted from an image in the Japanese official history of the Philippine Campaign.

Kitajima planned to first concentrate on the U.S. artillery batteries, anti-aircraft positions, and command posts, as well as the American ships located in the Bay. Destroying the American anti-aircraft positions would create a much more permissive environment for the Japanese air units that were now readying themselves for the final offensive against Corregidor. Eliminating the American coastal guns and ships would also greatly increase the survivability of the Japanese landing barges when they moved under cover of darkness from Olongapo to inside Manila Bay and, especially, during the actual amphibious assault. Once the artillery duel had been largely won, the Japanese intended to change the focus of the bombardment to the American beach defenses. How well prepared were the Americans to counter this artillery onslaught?

THE ARTILLERY OF THE FORTIFIED ISLANDS

Corregidor and the other forts in the Harbor Defenses had largely been armed and equipped in the years before World War I. The Washington Naval Treaty of 1922 had prohibited any increase or modernization of U.S. defenses west of Hawaii. Therefore, most of the American coast defense weapons were of the World War I era.

All or part of several regiments of Army Coast Artillery manned the seacoast weapons on Corregidor and the other three fortified islands. The nine-battery, 1,300-man, all-American 59th Coast Artillery Regiment commanded by Colonel Bunker manned most of the heavy fixed weapons of 12-inch or larger caliber. The Philippine Scout 91st and 92nd Coast Artillery Regiments had a total of thirteen firing batteries (one battery of the 92nd had surrendered on Bataan) and a combined total of roughly 1,300 personnel. The Scouts primarily manned 155-mm and 6-inch weapons, but on Fort Frank Scouts provided the crews for the heavy seacoast weapons. The Scout regiments also provided most of the gun crews for the beach defense artillery. Finally, there were the 1st and 2nd Coast Artillery Regiments of the Philippine Army. These units had been formed at the start of the war by using Philippine Army Coast Artillery trainees at Corregidor and Fort Wint and had a total of eight firing batteries.[2]

Although these regiments totaled twenty-eight batteries, there were not enough personnel to man all the heavy weapons in the garrison. That is why the crews of *Mindanao*, *Luzon*, and *Oahu* were assigned to Fort Hughes to man a battery each. Even with the use of the Navy personnel not all the gun batteries were manned as the artillery duel began.

There were several different types of weapons at the disposal of the Harbor Defenses: fixed seacoast guns, fixed coast defense mortars, mobile artillery, and turret guns.[3] The fixed seacoast guns were 14-, 12-, 10-, 6-, and 3-inch weapons. The majority of the guns were mounted on disappearing carriages. This pre–World War I design allowed the gun to elevate over a concrete and earth parapet and upon firing the force of recoil would swing the gun back into loading position behind the parapet—hence the term "disappearing." When first introduced in the 1890s these were very capable, appropriate weapons. Although the nature of the disappearing mount limited most of this class of weapon to a 15-degree elevation, that was comparable to the ships of the pre–World War I period. The six 12-inch disappearing guns in Batteries Cheney, Wheeler, and Crockett on Corregidor could range some 17,300 yards firing a 1,070-pound armor piercing shell. The 10-inch guns of Battery Grubbs had a range of 15,000 yards firing a 617-pound shell. The 10- and 12-inch disappearing guns had a maximum rate of fire of about two rounds per minute. The 14-inch weapons of Forts Frank

Battery Gillespie on Fort Hughes. This single 14-inch disappearing gun, shown in the recoil position, was manned by the crew of USS Luzon. *Photo was taken by the Japanese after the surrender. Corregidor is in the background.*

Source: National Archives and Records Administration

and Hughes were of somewhat more modern design; their mounts provided a 20-degree elevation, thus giving a maximum range of 22,800 yards when firing a 1,660-pound armor piercing shell. The rate of fire of the 14-inch weapons was approximately one round per minute. Following the fall of Bataan the crew of the gunboat *Luzon* took over Battery Gillespie on Fort Hughes, a westward-facing 14-inch gun. Although they were very appropriate coast defense weapons early in the twentieth century, the disappearing guns were hardly the ideal weapons for the siege of Corregidor.[4]

The first problem with the disappearing weapons was that their limited elevation meant that they would have difficulty reaching enemy weapons positioned in defilade behind hills. They were very similar to most ship-mounted naval guns—high velocity, flat trajectory weapons. Second, their open, fixed emplacements were totally exposed to air attack and plunging howitzer fire. Finally, there were limited quantities of high explosive (HE) shells that were best suited for attack of enemy artillery positions and troop concentrations. In keeping with the seaward defense focus of the Harbor Defenses, most of the ammunition was armor piercing (AP) intended to penetrate Japanese warships. In fact, there was no high explosive ammunition at all for the 14-inch guns, and only a few hundred rounds of 12-inch high explosive shells. The difference was significant. Not only would AP shells bury themselves twenty to thirty feet into the ground before exploding, they carried a much smaller high explosive filler.[5]

Realizing that there was a shortage of high explosive ammunition for the heavy guns and mortars, on 27 February Fort Mills' ordnance personnel started modifying the fuzes of 12- and 14-inch ammunition. The modification allowed the projectiles to burst faster upon striking the ground, rather than digging deep into the earth before exploding. It was an appropriate move, but the armor piercing shells still contained much smaller high explosive bursting charges compared to HE shells.[6]

There were a few barbette mounts in the Harbor Defenses. The two most important weapons were the 12-inch Batteries Smith and Hearn on Corregidor. These were the two longest-range weapons in the entire garrison, capable of elevating to 35 degrees. This allowed them to fire a 712-pound high explosive shell to 30,000 yards. Unfortunately, both weapons were on flat, totally open circular concrete pads.

The second type of heavy weapon was the seacoast mortar. Starting in the late nineteenth century the U.S. Army Coast Artillery had become the world's leading user of this class of weapon. The concept was to mount four to sixteen mortars in a battery and fire them simultaneously at a high angle of elevation so their heavy shells would plunge steeply down onto the thinly armored decks of warships. The Manila Bay Harbor Defenses mounted a total of twenty-four of these 12-inch weapons. The mortars were disposed as follows:

- Eight Model 1908 weapons were in the two pits of Battery Koehler on Fort Frank.
- Four Model 1912 pieces were in Battery Craighill's two pits on Fort Hughes (manned by *Mindanao*'s crew now onshore).
- Eight were in Battery Geary on Corregidor (the unit that had fired in support of the Naval Battalion in its battle at Longoskawayan Point).
- Four Model 1890 weapons in the single gun pit of Battery Way on Corregidor (one of Way's weapons was unserviceable).

Therefore, the Harbor Defenses had twenty-four 12-inch mortars, of which fifteen could reach Bataan. All the weapons except Craighill had a maximum range of 14,600 yards when firing a 700-pound shell.[7] The longer barreled mortars of Battery Craighill could range up to 19,000 yards.[8]

The mortars were potentially the most important counter battery weapons in the garrison. Battery Craighill on Fort Hughes and Batteries Geary and Way on

Corregidor had sufficient range to reach all the Japanese artillery positions on southern Bataan. Additionally, their steeply plunging shells could reach behind any hill where Japanese artillery might be concealed. As was the case with the disappearing gun positions, the mortar batteries had the disadvantage of being fixed locations and they had a limited supply of high explosive shells.

The mobile guns consisted of 155-mm M-1918 weapons removed from their fixed concrete mounts. The 155s were powerful weapons. Based on a highly successful French World War I design, they were capable of firing a 95-pound shell up to 20,100 yards; a well-trained crew could fire five to six rounds per minute for short periods of time. Some of Corregidor's nineteen 155-mm weapons remained in their fixed positions for the duration of the siege; some were destroyed in those locations. One battery was particularly fortunate. Battery Monja located near the waterline at Wheeler Point had one gun mounted in a concrete casemate and its second gun positioned in a cut between the sides of a hill. This provided Monja's crew far more protection than the other 155 units. In addition to the nineteen 155s on The Rock, Fort Frank had four of these weapons and Fort Hughes had two (manned by the crew of the gunboat *Oahu* after the fall of Bataan), for a total of twenty-five guns.

By mid-April Major General Moore had concluded that these fixed emplacements were simply too vulnerable and a number of the 155s were removed and towed around the island as single-gun "roving batteries." The suggestion to place some of the 155s in a mobile mode had come from Colonel Braly, Moore's operations officer. In some cases the executive officers of batteries would take command of a roving gun along with a crew of ten to fifteen Scout gunners. Usually moving the gun by artillery tractor during the night, the crews would emplace their weapon, bring up ammunition, dig foxholes for protection, and prepare to fire. At any given time, starting about 18 April, there were three or four single-gun roving batteries moving around Corregidor.

Finally, there were the turret guns of Fort Drum, the "concrete battleship." Built from 1908–19, Fort Drum was unique. Not only was the construction of the concrete fort an engineering marvel, it mounted the only turreted weapons used anywhere in the world by the U.S. Army Coast Artillery before the start of World War II. Throughout the pre–World War II period the Coast Artillery had favored disappearing guns, open mortar pits, open barbette mounts, and Panama mounts due to the fact that they were considerably cheaper than turrets. Drum had two turrets each mounting two Model 1909 14-inch guns.[9] In keeping with the era in which they were designed, the elevation was limited to 15 degrees. This resulted in a range of 19,200 yards when firing a 1,660-pound shell. Later in the siege, when Fort Drum's ventilation system had been knocked out, the temperature inside the fort gradually increased to over 100 degrees. The increased powder temperature allowed Drum's weapons to range well over 20,000 yards, thus putting most of the Japanese weapons in southern Bataan within range. Drum's turrets were the most effective installation in the Harbor Defenses because the Japanese could never knock them out with either artillery fire or air attack.[10]

The last available pre-war ammunition record from the Harbor Defenses is dated 31 December 1938. Although there would have been some changes (small amounts of ammunition expended in practice firing in 1939–41), these figures provide a good indication of the amount of ammunition available to the Harbor Defenses at the start of the siege.

TABLE 13.1 Ammunition Available
14-inch armor piercing (AP) = 1,465; providing 183 rounds for each 14-inch gun
12-inch gun AP = 1,736; or 217 rounds per 12-inch gun (8 weapons)
12-inch gun high explosive (HE) = 300; equating to 37 rounds per weapon
12-inch mortar AP = 9,500; 395 each for 24 mortars (23 serviceable)
12-mortar HE = 682; or 28 per mortar
10-inch AP = 1,528; 382 each for 4 guns (2 at Fort Wint)
155-mm HE = 28,996; 1,160 rounds per gun (25 155s)

The data in the table clearly shows that far more armor piercing ammunition was available for the heavy guns and mortars compared to high explosive rounds. It also shows that the 12-inch mortars, in particular, had a considerable amount of ammunition available. Assuming the ammunition was equally divided between the twenty-four mortars in the four mortar batteries, this means that Fort Hughes and Corregidor had between them approximately six thousand mortar shells for potential use against Bataan, albeit most armor piercing.[11]

Mindanao's crew manning the important Battery Craighill was well supplied with ammunition. A 13 March 1942, memo shows that there were 1,249 700-pound and 354 1,046-pound projectiles on Fort Hughes.[12] It is not known how many of Craighill's 700-pound shells were of the high explosive (HE) type that was much better suited for land targets. The figure of almost exactly 400 rounds per mortar corresponds very closely to the average of 423 rounds (AP and HE) based on the 1938 ammunition totals listed in the table. The sailors were, however, short powder charges, only 950 of those being available.

Although the fixed nature of the American coast artillery emplacements meant that the Japanese would, of course, learn their precise locations, there were some compensating features. For example, the concrete emplacements provided considerable protection for the crews, as well as for nearby personnel who might be able to run to the gun position for shelter when a bombardment was striking in their vicinity. In some cases the concrete roofs and walls of the gun emplacements were as much as twelve feet thick.[13] This certainly saved many lives of the gun crews during the siege, since the gunners working in the pits were only a few feet away from shelter when enemy shells started to fall nearby.

In addition, the fixed gun emplacements had, at least at the start of the siege, a good communications network. Buried telephone lines connected the gun emplacements to General Moore's Harbor Defenses headquarters and Colonel Bunker's Seaward Defense command bunker, C-1 Station, on the cliffs above Searchlight Point. Scattered through the islands were a large number of accurately surveyed observation posts that included telephone communications and range and direction finding telescopes to search for and plot targets. The good communications between gun positions, observation posts, and the Coast Artillery battalion headquarters that were located around the islands, and C-1 Station facilitated the coordination of massed fires against the Japanese.

These were the tools the U.S. garrison had at its disposal to contest the Japanese artillery on Bataan. The gun crews who manned the weapons were certainly brave and tried to carry out their assigned tasks as well as they could. But what of the senior-level management and command of the artillery battle?

Colonel Paul Bunker, USA, was sixty-two years old when the war started. He was a career Army Coast Artillery officer who had served in the 59th Coast Artillery Regiment three times. He had, however, no combat experience during World War I. Bunker kept a detailed diary during the 1941–42 campaign that is an invaluable source for historians. Of great significance were his ideas concerning fire direction and control.[14]

Bunker put a great premium on using as little ammunition as possible to engage targets and was very interested in the mathematics of fire direction. He developed the "Bunker System," which placed great importance on the range finding sections quickly and accurately locating the target (in prewar training, a moving ship), the battery plotting sections doing their fire direction computations as rapidly as possible, and the guns assigned to the target having their weapons and ammunition in the best possible state of repair and training so they could quickly place fire on the assigned locations provided to them by the plotting sections.

Although he was clearly proud of "his" system, there are plenty of indications that there was far less confidence among the officers of the 59th. Some even described the Bunker System as "a standing joke."[15] Others noted that while Bunker's techniques that placed great importance on accurate target location and minimal ammunition expenditure were appropriate for use against precise, point targets such as ships, Bunker's methods were far less appropriate, if not dysfunctional, when trying to engage hidden enemy artillery ashore whose precise locations were almost always unknown.

Perhaps the most stinging criticism of Bunker's management of the artillery duel with the Japanese on Bataan came from Colonel Valentine P. Foster, the Fort Hughes commander under whom the Navy's gunboat crews had been placed when they moved ashore following the fall of Bataan. Foster, in addition to being the Fort Hughes commander, was the executive officer of the 59th Coast Artillery, Bunker's second in command. In an early 1960s' interview with James and William Belote, Foster (who was a veteran of artillery duels in France in World War I) described a number of glaring errors on Bunker's part. These included Bunker's lack of appreciation of camouflage, the fact that on several occasions Bunker continued to order batteries to fire while Japanese observation planes were nearby, and Bunker's strange notion that artillery duels were like a boxing match; the battery under fire should be the one to return fire. On the last point Foster was particularly incredulous.[16]

A number of serious errors were made in the manning and employment of the American coast artillery. Despite the fact that the 12-inch mortar batteries were the most appropriate counterbattery weapons, fewer than half of these vital weapons were actually manned when Bataan fell. Battery Geary was crewed by the understrength Battery H, 59th Coast Artillery. Captain Thomas W. Davis III, the battery commander, had only enough men to operate four of the eight weapons at one time. Even more striking, Battery Way was not given a crew until after Bataan fell. Battery E, 60th Coast Artillery, was assigned to refurbish Way's four Model 1890 weapons, but did not have them ready to fire until 28 April, three weeks after Bataan fell. Finally, Battery Craighill, the most modern of the three mortar units that could range Bataan, was given to the Navy personnel of *Mindanao*. The sailors who manned Battery Craighill certainly gave it their best, as will be related later, but given the critical role of that battery it is amazing that such an important installation would be given to a

Navy crew who had absolutely no experience on such weapons and had to learn while literally under fire. Other weapons capable of firing on Bataan also were unmanned. Batteries Grubbs (two 10-inch weapons) and Battery Morrison (two 6-inch guns) on Corregidor's north shore were both unmanned until Battery C, 91st Coast Artillery, escaped from Bataan and was assigned to man them.

Critically, there was virtually no effort made to mass the fires of the American artillery. Immediately after the fall of Bataan the communications between the batteries in the fortified islands, their spotting positions, and their controlling locations such as C-1 Station were good. It was not until late in the siege that communications with the gun positions became difficult as the buried phone lines were cut from constant artillery fire and bombing. The good initial intra-regimental communications provided the means to mass multiple gun batteries on a suspected Japanese gun position. Unlike precise targets such as ships that could be clearly seen, most of the Japanese artillery was well concealed in jungle or behind hills or both. American spotters on Corregidor at times could get a clear view of Japanese artillery, but that was the exception, not the norm. In most cases the Americans had to rely on map reconnaissance to determine likely Japanese firing positions as well as occasionally spotting faint traces of smoke or gun flashes in the jungle. Certainly these were not pinpoint locations of enemy guns. What was needed in these circumstances was to saturate a radius of several hundred yards in all directions from the suspected enemy gun position. In order to do this, several batteries of U.S. guns and/or mortars should have been concentrated on the suspected target for a brisk few minutes of firing. This technique would have had the added benefit of minimizing the exposure time of the gunners in each U.S. battery, rather than giving a single battery the mission and thus forcing its gunners to remain exposed shooting their weapons for a much longer period in order to get the required number of rounds into the target area. Instead, Colonel Bunker's preferred technique was to assign a target to a single firing unit, and limit the amount of rounds that would be fired. It was normal for U.S. fire missions to be conducted by only one unit (a single roving gun, or a single fixed battery) with roughly ten to twenty rounds being fired at the target, often fewer.

A CLASSIC ARTILLERY DUEL

The first three days of the Japanese bombardment saw a gradual buildup of the enemy artillery force in southern Bataan. First the 75- and 105-mm companies went into action, followed by the larger, more cumbersome 150-mm pieces, and finally the big 240s. General Wainwright did not allow Corregidor to return fire until 12 April in order to give the Japanese a chance to remove most of the prisoners from the area. Knowing that many Filipinos and Americans probably remained in Hospitals 1 and 2, all batteries were provided maps that clearly showed their locations and instructed that when adjusting onto a target near the hospitals to begin the shooting well away from the target and gradually adjust the fire closer.

The first significant artillery duel took place on 12 April, the first day free from Wainwright's firing restriction. Japanese shelling began early that morning and grew in intensity. Battery Kysor (two 155s) fired on and sank a Japanese harbor boat off the southeast coast of Bataan, but was promptly taken under fire by the enemy. Next, Battery Geary opened fire on a Japanese gun position that had been spotted and then on a group of Japanese tanks that were parked in the open, but was itself then heavily fired on, and later bombed. In addition to heavy Japanese artillery fire, nine separate bombing attacks were made that day by small groups of Japanese planes. At this early stage of the siege the enemy aircraft had to remain at a respectful altitude; the harbor forts' anti-aircraft weapons were still in action.

It was during the exchange of fire on 12 April that the sailors at Battery Craighill got into action. *Mindanao*'s crew had taken over the four Model 1912 mortars located along the ridge near the center of Fort Hughes. Running directly beside the battery was the main tunnel of the fort, which covered a distance of some 350 feet. The gunboat sailors were trained and assisted by Sergeant Joe West, USA, of the 59th Coast Artillery. Of course, the Navy men had no prior experience on fixed heavy artillery, although it is possible that some of them might have served on big-gun Navy battleships earlier in their careers. Under the tutelage of West, the sailors learned how to load and fire the big mortars. *Mindanao*'s crew also performed the firing data computations from inside the battery's plotting room.

The sound and concussion of a mortar firing inside the confined spaces of the pit was deafening. In their first day of action, the sailors at Craighill fired twenty-six big 12-inch mortar shells at targets on Bataan.[17] After this first day under the guidance of the Army Coast Artillery sergeant, the sailors were on their own.

In the first few days of the duel with the Japanese artillery on Bataan the American gunners were able to dish out a fair amount of punishment. At 0700 on the morning of the 14th a coordinated bombardment of targets on Bataan began. Fort Drum's two turrets fired a total of fifty-two rounds, and two of Corregidor's 12-inch gun batteries together fired sixty shells; Battery Geary added fifty-six of its big 12-inch mortar rounds. *Mindanao*'s crew at Battery Craighill contributed sixty-seven shells to the effort. Additionally, various 155-mm batteries fired several hundred rounds.[18]

On 15 April Craighill fired eighty-eight rounds at various targets, mostly suspected Japanese gun positions. Firing took place from 0700 to 2030 that evening. The Japanese retaliated with shelling of their own; an enemy shell fragment hit one sailor, barely missing his jugular vein. As the days went by, the enemy's artillery fire became more intense and accurate and bombing raids on Fort Hughes increased. The sailors continued to fire back; they shot twenty rounds at various targets on the 17th.[19]

On the night of 18 April Craighill received 100 powder charges from Corregidor. This makes sense given the 13 March ammunition data mentioned earlier, because that report showed Craighill with some 1,600 shells but only 951 powder charges. All the while the Navy men were attempting to put their own mark on the Army fort. By the 19th a Navy galley was in operation inside Battery Craighill's concrete emplacement. Cooking gear, a refrigerator, and ventilation fans were brought ashore from *Mindanao* under cover of darkness and set up inside the concrete tunnels. Dust and flies were everywhere. When the big mortars fired they stirred up huge clouds of dust, as did the near-misses by Japanese artillery shells bursting just outside the gun pits. Occasionally an enemy shell would explode inside one of the pits, sending fragments whirling around the concrete walls.

The Fort Hughes commander, Colonel Foster, provided some of Craighill's targets. Foster's command post occupied part of Craighill's concrete emplacement. Targets located by observers on Corregidor would be phoned into Bunker's C-1 Station, which would then assign an appropriate firing battery on Corregidor, Fort Hughes, or Fort Drum to conduct the fire mission. In other cases Craighill's targets were self-generated. Starting on 22 April Lieutenant Nash would climb up to the top of the island, as he recalled "177 steps, straight up," to a concrete observation post near the Caballo Island lighthouse. From this vantage point Nash, some of his Navy chiefs, and an Army Coast Artillery enlisted man, Private John Son, would search for targets across the Bay on Bataan.[20]

By the second half of April it had become clear to *Mindanao*'s crew that the Japanese had their battery zeroed in, with guns laid and loaded on the target, ready to shoot as soon as they saw any firing from the mortar pits. On 23 April Craighill managed to get off only four rounds. As soon as the sailors fired, Japanese shells were on their way, forcing the men to scurry into the concrete magazine tunnels as soon as they fired a round.

24 April brought severe shelling. Realizing that Battery Craighill was one of their most deadly opponents, the Japanese dedicated a 240-mm howitzer on Bataan to fire at the two mortar pits. For two and a half hours a 240 shell landed roughly every two and a half minutes. Each of the pits took a direct hit

from the big 400-pound shells. One mortar in Pit B was knocked out for the rest of the campaign. The shell that entered Pit A did not explode properly. Instead, the base plug of the round came off when it landed and the shell roared around the inside of the pit like a rocket until its explosive filler was exhausted. Fortunately for the increasingly exhausted and hungry *Mindanao* crew, the next day was much quieter, with the Japanese firing a few rounds at the battery, and the sailors returning a few of their own.

By this time on Corregidor things were becoming very bad. Even before the 240-mm howitzers went into action on 18 April a number of Corregidor's north shore batteries had been knocked out. One factor in the Americans' and Filipinos' favor was the high rate of duds in the Japanese ammunition, especially the 240-mm rounds. General Wainwright visited Battery Geary, which was very heavily shelled by the enemy, and was astonished by how many unexploded projectiles he saw in the immediate vicinity.

On 15 April Battery Kysor in 1st Battalion's area was heavily shelled; one of its two 155s was flipped over by a direct hit that killed five men and wounded fifteen. Also on that day the Philippine Army crew of A Battery, 1st Coast Artillery, manning the four-gun 3-inch Battery James suffered a terrible disaster. The Filipinos had dug a tunnel into the hillside behind the gun position, using if for shelter when shelling or bombing became particularly severe. That day Japanese artillery fire caused a landslide above the tunnel, trapping forty-two men inside; all suffocated before rescuers—most of them Marines from the nearby beach defense positions—could dig through to them.[21]

By 18 April, Battery Grubbs (two 10-inch), Morrison (two 6-inch), Rock Point (two 155s), Kysor (two 155s—one weapon destroyed, the other removed for use as a roving gun), and James (four 3-inch) had all been knocked out. Those batteries were the most visible to Japanese observers on Bataan and thus the easiest targets. Other, better-protected, batteries were also suffering badly by the third week in April.[22]

There were only two American gun positions in the fortified islands that were virtually immune to enemy bombing and shelling. As mentioned earlier, the two-gun 155-mm Battery Monja had one of its weapons mounted in the only concrete casemate on Corregidor, and the other piece was located in a steep cut between two hillsides. Monja's main limitation was that from its location it could only bear on the middle of Mariveles Harbor and westward. The other, far more formidable, American position that the Japanese could not silence was the concrete battleship—Fort Drum.

Drum's naval-style gun turrets had 18-inch-thick armored fronts, 16-inch sides, 13-inch rears, and 6-inch tops. The top deck of the fort (its roof) was on average 20-feet-thick reinforced concrete, while the fort's walls were 20–36 feet of reinforced concrete. Nothing the Japanese had could seriously harm the tiny, but mighty, fortress. Drum was frequently firing at targets on Bataan, as long as they were in range. There is no question that the four 14-inch guns of the concrete battleship were the most effective American counter-battery asset in the Harbor Defenses. The fort's only handicaps were the range limitation due to the 1914-era 15-degree maximum elevation of the guns, and the lack of 14-inch high explosive shells. Although an exact ammunition count for Drum is not available, blueprints indicate that the fort's magazines held at least 440 rounds for the four 14-inch guns.[23]

American and Filipino counter-battery fire did inflict some damage and casualties on the 14th Army's artillery. According to the Japanese official history 403 Japanese were wounded and 41 killed by American fire from 14 April until 4 May.[24] The vast majority of the enemy casualties were men assigned to the artillery units that were shelling the fortified islands, thus proving that at least occasionally the defenders' fire was effective. It is not known precisely how many Japanese artillery pieces the American counter fire destroyed.[25]

As the end of April approached the Americans had already lost the artillery duel with the Japanese. Although this may have been inevitable, the fact remains that the considerable artillery assets that were available to the American command had not been well employed. Too many valuable gun batteries had started the duel unmanned or understrength, thus giving the Japanese an even greater advantage. Critically, virtually no effort had been made to mass the fires of several batteries against known or suspected Japanese gun locations. Despite still having thousands of shells in the magazines of the gun batteries, the volume of the American reply was falling off badly as the end of April approached. And the most intense period of the bombardment had yet to begin. The men manning the beaches were about to feel its deadly effect.

CHAPTER 14

The Final Bombardment

By the last week in April the Japanese were ready to begin their final, very intense, artillery bombardment to break the defenses prior to landing on Corregidor. Most of the shelling from 9 to 28 April had been counter-battery fire against American seacoast and anti-aircraft positions, plus attempts to sink the Navy's ships remaining in South Harbor. The shelling of the Army's fixed coast artillery batteries had been fairly successful; many of the American gun positions had already been silenced as the end of April approached. Less successful had been the attempts to knock out the last of small ships in the Bay.

THE LAST FLIGHT INTO MANILA BAY

On the night of 29 April *Quail* and *Tanager* put out lighted buoys and swept an area to allow two PBY flying boats to land in the Bay. Two PBYs of PatWing 10 departed from Australia on the afternoon of 28 April. The aircraft landed at Lake Lanao on the island of Mindanao, not far from the Army's Del Monte airfield. They had on board a total of 750 3-inch mechanical anti-aircraft fuzes plus several hundred pounds of medical supplies and radio parts. Landing on Mindanao in the early morning hours of the 29th, the two flying boats proceeded northward toward Manila Bay that afternoon, arriving after dark.

After landing in the water south of Fort Hughes their cargo was removed and fifty-four passengers, including nineteen Army nurses, went on board, dangerously overloading both planes. Among the Navy passengers was Commander Frank Bridget, former commander of the Naval Battalion and PatWing 10's senior surviving officer still in the Philippines. The PBY crews had hoped to also take Ensign Trudell, but he was still in the hospital in Malinta Tunnel and unable to be moved due to the head wound he had suffered in the January battle at Longoskawayan Point. Three other Navy officers also went on board the two planes—Lieutenant T. K. Bowers, Commander E. W. Hastings, and Commander C. H. Williams.

The planes took off and headed south, all on board thinking that they had made their escape. Unfortunately, one of the aircraft struck a rock on Lake Lanao and had to be evacuated. Not knowing whether the aircraft could be repaired, the passengers headed for the Army airfield at Del Monte, hoping to be taken out by one of the B-17s or other cargo planes that still occasionally shuttled in and out of the crude base. The PBY was repaired and managed to reach Australia. Its original passengers, however, did not. Unable to get another plane out of the Philippines, they were taken prisoner on Mindanao. Commander Frank Bridget and ten Army nurses were among those the Japanese captured.[1]

THE LAST DAYS OF THE INSHORE PATROL

Most of the Navy's surviving ships had been moved to South Harbor between Corregidor and Fort Hughes following the fall of Bataan. We have already seen that during the night of 9–10 April most of ships' companies had gone ashore. As April ended the Navy's ships were still afloat, although the lack of fuel had reduced their activities to a minimum.

Realizing that the remaining American ships could pose a severe threat to an amphibious landing, as shown by the havoc that *Mindanao* and *Oahu* had created with the Japanese flotilla off the east coast of Bataan on the night of 5–6 April, the enemy devoted artillery to sink the remaining ships. As the Japanese readied more armed launches and improvised gunboats in Manila, they assessed the remaining American naval strength in Manila Bay as: "2 submarines, 3 gunboats, 2 clippers, and 5 or 6 armed merchant ships. The armed forces of Japan will attack and sink these ships."[2]

The Japanese found hitting the Inshore Patrol's ships very difficult; at times they still moved, if only swinging around on their anchor lines as the tide changed. Indeed, small ships were not normal targets for Japanese army artillery units. The typical distance from the Japanese artillery positions in southern Bataan to the middle of South Harbor was 8,000–10,000 yards. At those ranges the natural dispersion of the shells, plus the effect of firing at a small target, combined to reduce the effectiveness of the enemy's firing. Time was, however, on the side of the Japanese. Eventually, the luck of the little ships began to run out.

One day in mid-April *Luzon*'s crew, now manning the 14-inch gun of Battery Gillespie on the western tip of Fort Hughes, watched their ship take two hits, both in the admiral's cabin. That evening Captain Hoeffel went on board the ship and saw the damage done to his uniforms and other personal items. According to the sailors who went with him, the senior Navy officer in the Manila Bay area vigorously commented on the ancestry of the enemy gunners.

Toward the end of April Captain Hoeffel issued orders to prepare the ships that were still afloat for destruction. *Luzon*'s crew placed 5½-pound cans of TNT in the engine room as well as in the fore and after magazines. Additionally, the *Luzon* crew manhandled an old 3-inch .23-caliber anti-aircraft gun up sixty concrete steps on Fort Hughes—stairs set at a 45-degree angle—and positioned the gun so it would bear on their ship. The crew calculated that four 3-inch rounds placed along the hull would sink the ship even if the TNT charges failed to explode.[3]

Despite the increasingly heavy enemy fire, the gunboats were still used at night, portions of the crews going out to their ships in small boats to make use of machinery or to bring ashore supplies or equipment. Since the gunboat crews were concentrated at Fort Hughes, their efforts focused on trying to improve the situation there. For example, the water supply at Fort Hughes was inadequate. Therefore, sailors went back out to their ships at night to run the evaporating plants and bring fresh water ashore before dawn made ship-to-shore movement much more dangerous.

Mindanao and *Oahu* were also accumulating hits during this period. As early as 10 April *Mindanao* took a hit and started to go down by the stern. That night her skipper, Commander McCracken, went out to the ship along with Commander Hastings from the Inshore Patrol headquarters to inspect damage. The ship's engine room and one boiler room were flooded. On the following days *Mindanao* took additional hits from artillery and bombs, but seemed to want to stay afloat. *Oahu*, too, was hit by enemy artillery fire but also refused to sink. On orders from Captain Hoeffel all ships were prepared for destruction but also were instructed to try to maintain the ability to get under way on short notice in case they were needed for one final sortie. As damage accumulated on the vessels this became increasingly difficult. But while the gunboats were more and more idle, the minesweepers still had a very important mission.

With the North Channel directly under the nose of the Japanese on Bataan it was no longer considered usable by small ships or submarines trying to get into and out of Manila Bay under cover of darkness. Since the only passage through the Navy's contact minefield was North Channel something had to be done to clear a new passage to allow whatever final runs might be made to and from the beleaguered forts. Indeed, the orders to open a new passage through the minefield had gone out the day Bataan fell; it was the planning session aboard *Quail* to decide how to open the new channel that had been broken up by the Japanese artillery on the afternoon of 9 April.

Like the gunboats, the minesweepers had moved much of their crews ashore, but in their case the mission of cutting a passage through the minefield meant that more men had to stay on board the sweepers, supplemented by shipmates who would return from Fort Hughes after the sun went down. The technique that Lieutenant Commander John Morrill of *Quail*, Lieutenant Commander Adolph Roth of *Tanager*, and Lieutenant T. W. Davison of *Finch* developed involved using a combination of the minesweepers themselves and the ships' motor launches. The new passage was to be just southwest of Corregidor, wide enough to permit a submarine or small interisland steamer to enter and exit. The sweepers had to gradually cut their way into the field, approaching on a course parallel to the mines, using lines deployed out to the sides of the ship to sweep. The sweeping lines had very sharp cutting knives to sever the cables holding the floating mines onto the harbor bottom. When the knives cut a mine cable, it would come to the surface, where gunfire could blow it up or it could be towed safely away by one of the sweeper's small boats.

Initially, in the first few days after Bataan fell, *Quail* moved over to the area to sweep in daylight as well as night. The Japanese observed this and opened fire on the ship. On 11 April the little vessel took three hits from Japanese shells. The first projectile passed directly through the ship without exploding. Another shell, which Morrill estimated to be from a 6-inch gun (probably a 150-mm gun or howitzer), devastated the ship's bridge. That shell did not explode, rather it struck near the two 3-inch guns forward of the bridge. The armored shields that protected the guns trapped the dud round, which spun around into the bridge, wrecking it. However, since the ship could still be conned from the lower control station she was still functional. After that *Quail* only operated at night. She was carefully moored before dawn at roughly the same spot and did not move during the day. The Japanese probably thought the ship was out of action, since far less fire was directed her way.[4]

Operating only at night also had the effect of saving precious fuel. The goal was to cut a path 400-feet wide into the field, which was seven rows of mines deep. Working every night, *Quail* completed a 400-foot gap by 2 May and was preparing to expand the clearing to 600 feet.

Gradually the little ships succumbed to Japanese artillery and air attack. On 11 April, the same day *Quail* took her first hit, *Finch* was moored along the north shore of Fort Hughes. Lieutenant Davison's intent was to get shelter from the enemy shelling from the Cavite side of the Bay. Unfortunately, the ship was there when a Japanese bombing attack hit Fort Hughes that afternoon. Several Japanese bombs spilled over the top of the island; three landed very close to the sweeper. The blast and fragments from these bombs punctured the ship's hull and she started to settle by the stern. By nightfall she was listing to port, with her stern resting on the bottom. Lieutenant Davison ordered that all the remaining food and ammunition be removed. *Finch* was then officially abandoned, lying derelict alongside the island. Only one crewman had been injured in the bombing, and he was ashore when the attack took place.[5]

On the evening of 1 May Commander McCracken was directed by Captain Hoeffel to report to Tunnel Queen; he was to assume duties of certain officers who were to be evacuated by the next submarine. Lieutenant Nash was to take command of *Mindanao*. Interestingly, Nash's written orders to assume command specifically recognized that he was taking over a sinking ship. Early the next morning McCracken took a boat from Fort Hughes to Corregidor. He had not been in the Navy tunnel long when he was told that *Mindanao* had finally succumbed. The little China gunboat had gone down at roughly 0730. From high atop Fort Hughes some of the crew watched their ship sink close to the south shore of Corregidor. The gunboat's bow and part of the forward superstructure remained above water, very close to Monkey Point.

Oahu managed to hang on until the morning of 6 May, the day Corregidor surrendered. By then she was moored close to the south side of the Tail of The Rock in an attempt to get as much shelter as possible from the enemy artillery on Bataan. It was not good enough. The little gunboat foundered just off Corregidor's Tail due to flooding from several hits and near-misses. Like *Mindanao*, part of her superstructure remained above water.

At 1500 on 4 May *Tanager* was hit several times by Japanese shells and set afire. No attempt was made to get on board to fight the fires. An hour later her ammunition started to explode. Her stern was seen to go under by 1800 and as the sun went down the ship's bow took the final plunge into Manila Bay. That same day an aerial bomb hit the submarine rescue ship *Pigeon* on its starboard quarter. The explosion did massive damage and within eight minutes the ship sank. Fortunately, the ship's crew was ashore so there were no casualties. This left only *Quail*, *Luzon*, *Oahu*, and the little tug *Ranger* still afloat. A few of the Army's watercraft were still available, and there were also a few smaller craft, such as the armed yacht *Maryanne*, which had somehow managed to avoid serious harm.

Map 8 is based on input generously given to the author in 1986 by retired rear admiral John H. Morrill, former commanding officer of *Quail*. Morrill plotted the sinking or final derelict positions of nearly every Navy ship that had survived the fall of Bataan, including his own ship, which was the last to sink.

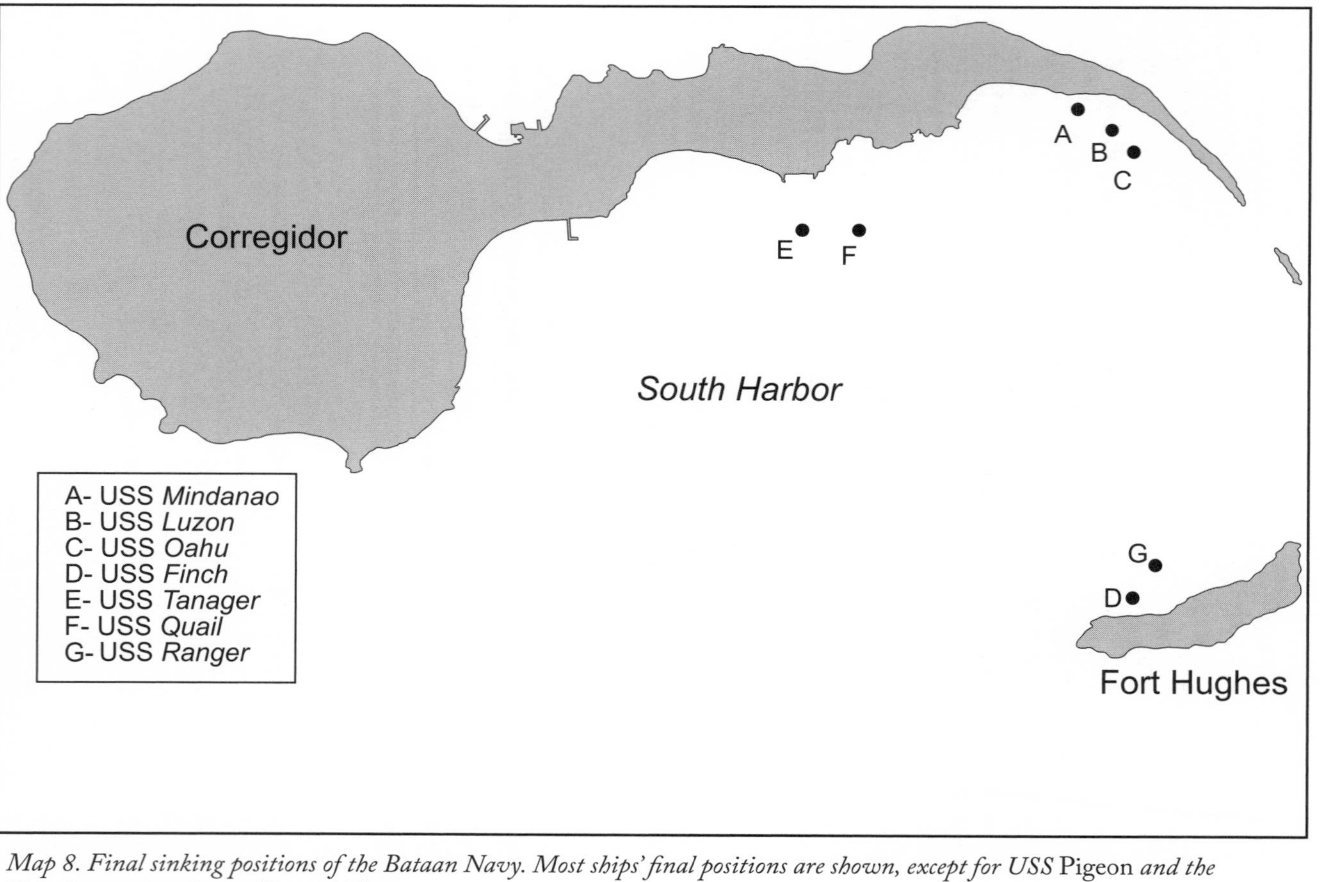

Map 8. Final sinking positions of the Bataan Navy. Most ships' final positions are shown, except for USS Pigeon *and the U.S. Army mine planter* General Harrison.

THE EMPEROR'S BIRTHDAY

General Homma and General Kitajima had planned a special event for 29 April—Emperor Hirohito's birthday. The American command on Corregidor was well aware that the Emperor's birthday would probably bring very intense shelling, and the word was passed to the subordinate commands around the island to prepare for a rough day. At 1830 on the evening of 28 April Sergeant Thomas Hicks of the Regimental Headquarters made the following entry in the 4th Marines Record of Events stating: "Msg to all units: Warning to all bns. Tomorrow is a special Japanese holiday, the birthday of His Imperial Majesty. The enemy may celebrate by unusual aerial and artillery bombardment."[6] The predictions proved to be all too true.

By this point General Kitajima had all his artillery available, including control of the artillery regiments of the 4th and 16th Divisions. His staff divided Corregidor and Fort Hughes into areas of concentration for each Japanese artillery unit. Ammunition limitations earlier in April had caused the Japanese to restrict their firing somewhat, although the suffering Americans and Filipinos would have been amazed to hear that. Importantly, prior to the end of April the Japanese devoted relatively little firing to the possible landing beaches, focusing instead on knocking out the American coastal guns that could threaten their own artillery.

Shelling began at 0745 on Wednesday morning, the Emperor's birthday. In addition to intensely pounding the Army artillery positions on Corregidor and Fort Hughes, the Japanese also concentrated on some of the beach defense positions. The Marine positions at Battery Point east of James Ravine were very heavily shelled. The camouflage was stripped away and the defenses themselves flattened. The Marines had to pull back into nearby tunnels and supplementary positions.

Much of the Japanese shelling was concentrated on Malinta Hill, where damage to above-ground assets was serious. The Navy 1.1-inch anti-aircraft gun atop the hill, which had performed such good service since it was installed in February, was destroyed. Its Army crew had taken shelter in a nearby searchlight tunnel, but a Japanese shell entered the tunnel by plunging steeply down its ventilation shaft. The gasoline supply for the searchlight's generator added to the effect of the explosion; the entire Army crew was killed. The three beach defense 75-mm guns located on Malinta Hill were also knocked out that day. Inside the Malinta Tunnel lights flickered and concussion sent up huge clouds of dust as dozens of 240-mm and smaller shells exploded atop the hill.

The enemy also paid special attention to some of the remaining coast batteries, especially Battery Geary. The sailors and Marines of the Regimental Reserve sheltering in Government Ravine just to the southeast of Geary huddled in their foxholes and dugouts as the area atop the high ground just to the west of their positions was mercilessly pounded by 240-mm howitzers. The Japanese had allocated eight of their ten 240s against this target, resulting in a very heavy concentration of fire against the American mortar battery. Either accidentally or by design, many Japanese shells "spilled over" into Government Ravine to the east of Geary. The company commanders of the Regimental Reserve and 4th Battalion had to keep their men under cover all day due to the severity of the shelling. Battery Geary's commander, Captain Davis, USA, also had to keep his men under cover in the concrete magazines. From his command post a few hundred feet away Davis could actually watch the Japanese shells pass overhead and slam into the battery gun pits and the walls of the concrete magazines. The remaining 12-inch mortars of Pit A were knocked out. Ominously, Davis watched huge chunks of concrete blasted from the walls of the magazines, which although up to twelve feet thick were of unreinforced concrete.

The Japanese heavily shelled both entrances of Malinta Tunnel during the morning. The Bottomside area west of the tunnel was also pounded, raising suspicions that it could be the site of a landing attempt. Before 1000, the 2nd Battalion's Reserve Company sheltering in Middleside Barracks was hit with heavy shelling, forcing the Marines into foxholes dug into the bottom floor of the reinforced concrete building. Thirty minutes later the Japanese began a heavy bombardment of James Ravine. The intense shelling continued all day, sweeping from one point of the island to another.

Japanese aircraft were also out in force to celebrate the Emperor's birthday. The 4th Marines' journal records air strikes at 0730 and 0748 by groups of three and six dive bombers, followed by high level bombers and then nine more of the latter at 0935. All together, the Japanese made 81 sorties against the fortified islands that day, dropping 106 tons of bombs. According to American accounts two enemy aircraft were shot down.

Despite the damage that they had sustained, the 3-inch anti-aircraft batteries were still able to challenge the enemy's air effort. *Mindanao*'s crew at Battery Craighill fired as often as they could, despite a 240-mm howitzer and smaller weapons being dedicated in an attempt to suppress their shooting. Several of the 155-mm roving batteries engaged observed or suspected targets on Bataan, and Fort Drum's four 14-inch guns fired whenever there was a target within range, including interdiction fire along Bataan's east coast road. Colonel Bunker noted in his diary that by 0930 the concrete battleship had fired twenty 14-inch shells at various targets on Bataan. This was also the first day of firing for four-gun Battery Way. This valuable battery should have been fully manned before the fall of Bataan. Instead, the Emperor's birthday—three weeks into the siege—was the first time that the mortars got into action. Bunker noted that Battery Way fired twenty-one rounds that day. Battery Geary fired ten shells before noon.

By that night, The Rock was draped in a shroud of smoke and dust. The exhausted men made efforts to repair damaged defenses and get their evening meal. Casualties had been relatively light, considering the intensity of the enemy bombardment, but worse was about to come.

THE PRE-LANDING BOMBARDMENT

Bad as the shelling on the Emperor's birthday had been, it was merely a prelude to the most intense period of bombardment of the entire campaign. The last phase of the bombardment was to be a heavy shelling of the American beach defenses in preparation for the amphibious landing.

On 30 April the Japanese concentrated their firing on Battery Way, scoring some one hundred hits on the emplacement, although none of the four 12-inch mortars were knocked out. During the day Fort Hughes was bombed three times, and Corregidor six. The Americans continued to fire back as best they could. Well-protected Battery Monja sank a Japanese tug in Mariveles Harbor and then shot at a truck convoy; two of the one-gun roving 155-mm batteries fired on Cabcaben airfield and the surrounding area.

The final bombardment began on 1 May. Although some of the Japanese weapons had been damaged or destroyed by American counter-battery fire during April, there were probably 110 or more guns and howitzers available for the final bombardment of the beach defenses. The Americans quickly noticed that Japanese firing was concentrated on the north shore of the Tail, Bottomside, and in the area around James Ravine. Colonel Howard directed the battalion commanders to keep their men under cover to the maximum extent possible. Several air raids took place during the day, adding to the destruction wrought by the artillery firing from Bataan. So intense was the firing that movement during daylight was very difficult. Nevertheless, unit leaders continued to check positions and the condition of the men. The sailors of the 4th Battalion huddled in foxholes along the southeast coast of Topside came under fire from enemy weapons in Cavite.

By this point so much damage had been inflicted on Corregidor's anti-aircraft batteries that Japanese planes could descend to lower altitudes. Dive bombers struck Forts Drum and Hughes during the morning, as well as targets on Corregidor's Tail. As was normal, most of the bombs aimed at the concrete battleship landed in the water, although one machine gun on the fort was destroyed in the attack.

On 2 May the bombardment intensified, if that were possible. Shelling started at 0730 in the morning and steadily grew in intensity. Bombers were over The Rock by 0800, hitting Malinta Hill and the area around Kindley Field. More air raids followed. The Americans managed to throw up some anti-aircraft fire during a few of the raids, but it could not turn back the Japanese attacks.

By midafternoon the intensity of the Japanese firing had reached an unprecedented level. The Topside area was under a very heavy bombardment, as were the beach positions. Just before 1630 a huge explosion rocked the entire island. A Japanese 240-mm shell had finally penetrated the center magazine of Battery Geary, exploding some 1,600 60-pound powder charges. Thirteen-ton 12-inch mortars were sent flying up to 150 yards—one landing on the Post golf course. Those soldiers at nearby Battery Crockett, less than 200 yards away, who were not under cover were sent sprawling around their positions, knocked down by the massive concussion. A nearby Army 3-inch anti-aircraft battery suffered thirty-five casualties, including one man killed, from the mass of concrete and steel debris that showered their position.

The Marines and sailors of the Regimental Reserve and the 4th Battalion, a few hundred yards to the east of Battery Geary, were sheltering in their foxholes when the huge explosion occurred above them. Debris and unexploded 12-inch shells pelted down on their positions. Some of the foxholes caved in, temporarily trapping the occupants. One of the first responders to the disaster was the 4th Battalion commander, Major Williams, who led a detail of Marines and sailors up the slope to the wrecked Army battery. Incredibly, only six of Geary's gun crew were killed in the blast due to the foresight of their commander, Captain Davis, who had ordered most of the men to take shelter in the most intact of the three magazines. Nevertheless, many men were trapped inside the partly collapsed structure.[7]

Fortunately, Japanese fire temporarily stopped, no doubt due to the spectacular sight of the massive explosion on Corregidor. This allowed the rescue work at Battery Geary to start in relative peace. Within half an hour, however, enemy fire recommenced. Several key communications lines were broken due to the shelling and bombing.

The Americans again tried to fight back as best they could. Fort Drum fired thirty 14-inch shells at three different targets on Bataan, apparently with good effect. Battery Way, now Corregidor's only mortar unit, took several targets under fire, but came in for a ferocious shelling. Two of Way's three operational mortars were put permanently out of action from Japanese shells falling into the gun pit and striking the weapons. That left only one of the valuable 12-inch mortars on The Rock. *Mindanao*-manned Battery Craighill thus became even more important.

Throughout the night Marines, sailors, and Army troops worked to tunnel through to the trapped gun crews at devastated Battery Geary. At 0100 a hole was cut through a magazine wall to four trapped men, allowing food and water to be passed to them. Eventually all were freed, although one died later in the Malinta Tunnel hospital. Incredibly, only six of Geary's gunners had been injured in addition to the six who died in the huge blast. Additionally, five Marines had been killed and nine wounded during the day's fierce bombing and shelling.

That evening Lieutenant Colonel Beecher, the 1st Battalion commander, spoke with Colonel Howard about the state of the beach defenses along the Tail. Beecher had personally conducted an inspection of the positions and discovered the intense Japanese shelling was tearing the obstacles and barbed wire to pieces. Already the telephone lines were damaged to the point that communication was possible only by runner. The laboriously dug tank traps were caving in or being torn up to the point that they presented little obstacle to any tracked vehicles that managed to get ashore. Because he had to keep the men under cover all during the daylight hours during the intense shelling, repairing the obstacles was only possible at night, and the battalion was out of replacement barbed wire. Beecher told the regimental commander that it was very doubtful whether his unit could withstand an enemy landing in force. When Colonel Howard passed that word on to General Wainwright, the latter stated that he would never surrender. Beecher's reply to Colonel Howard was that he was not thinking about surrender, but was obligated to inform his superiors of the increasingly battered state of his unit and the all-important beach obstacles.[8]

Sunday, 3 May began with a Japanese plane flying low over Corregidor at 0645. Machine guns on The Rock drove the enemy aircraft off, but failed to shoot it down. At 0800 the Japanese artillery opened fire on targets on Topside and the beaches. By 0830 the intensity of the shelling had increased significantly. Once again, the Marines and other troops in their foxholes had to hunker down, trying to protect themselves and their weapons.

A brief calm lasted until air raid number 283 sounded at 1125. Bombs fell on the Kindley Field area. There was no answering anti-aircraft fire from Corregidor. By this point the 3-inch batteries were out of action. This was the raid that finished off the Army mine planter *Harrison*. The little ship was struck by two bombs that completely wrecked the entire starboard superstructure and set her afire. The ship's Master, Army Warrant Officer James Murray, and three other men were killed. *Harrison* finally sank the following day.[9]

Another air raid followed an hour later, hitting targets on Topside. While the air raid was under way, 1st Lieutenant Wright's roving battery, now back in action with a new gun, opened fire on enemy trucks parked north of Cabcaben. More air raids followed. As dusk approached, the enemy shelling started to increase in intensity, which was not normal. At 1900 spotters on Corregidor could see considerable truck activity near Cabcaben; clearly an indication that the Japanese were in the final stages of preparation for a landing.

That night the last submarine to reach Manila Bay surfaced to the west of the new gap in the minefield. USS *Spearfish*, commanded by Lieutenant Commander Jim Dempsey, had the mission of evacuating key personnel. Waiting to meet *Spearfish* was Lieutenant Commander Morrill who had led the effort to cut the new passage through the mines. Morrill brought a total of twenty-five passengers for the sub to evacuate. These included fourteen nurses and six Army colonels: C. L. Irwin (Wainwright's operations officer), T. W. Doyle (the commander of the 45th Infantry Regiment of Philippine Scouts on Bataan), Jenks (the USFIP finance officer who brought with him lists of all personnel still alive as of 1 May), M. A. Hill (the inspector general), Ramsey (the command veterinary officer), and Savage (the command's air officer). Five Navy officers, including Commander Earl Sackett, former skipper of *Canopus*, and Lieutenant Commander Denys W. Knoll, the 16th Naval District intelligence officer, were also sent out on the submarine. In addition to the lists of those still alive and recent promotions went other key records, including the precious 4th Marines Regimental Record of Events and the Regimental R-2 (intelligence) log. The last entry of the 4th Marines Record of Events, so dutifully maintained in handwritten form by Sergeant Thomas R. Hicks of the Regimental headquarters, was dated 2 May. That entry recorded the names of the Marine casualties that the regiment had suffered that day. Along with the Regimental journal went the 1 May muster rolls that showed, by company, name-by-name, how the 4th Marines were organized. Various Army and Navy records also were on *Spearfish*, including lists of all personnel still alive as of 1 May. With the departure of the submarine the last evacuation of personnel and records from the Manila Bay area had been accomplished. In the confusion, two stowaways also managed to make it out on the sub.[10]

The 4th of May saw Japanese shelling reach a new level of intensity. The first air raid struck the island at 0730, and within the next half hour Corregidor was under very heavy artillery bombardment. Although there were short pauses in the Japanese shelling, the firing remained steady all day. Five more air raids struck the island by 1800, but it was the artillery fire that caused most of the damage.

Ominously, it was noted by the American command that most of the enemy's firing was against the beach defenses along the north shore of the island.

Again, the Army coast artillerymen tried their best to fire back. As was the norm by this point in the siege, it was the turrets of Fort Drum and the roving 155-mm batteries that provided most of the American counter-battery fire. Various Japanese targets were spotted in the area from Mariveles to Cabcaben. Drum was able to range some of these targets, while the 155s took on those positions that were beyond the concrete battleship's reach. Japanese guns from both Bataan and Cavite engaged Drum, but had no more luck than before in their attempt to silence the concrete fortress. Despite the best efforts of the Army gunners, with so few remaining weapons they could not significantly reduce the amount of enemy fire being directed toward the beaches.

The Marines and other troops manning the beach defenses took a fearsome pounding. It was on this day that A Company's commander, Major Harry Lang, was killed. Lang was inspecting his unit's positions despite the urging of many of his men to stay under cover. Lang visited Private Jack Warner, USMC, whose foxhole was near the cliffs along the western part of Cavalry Point. Warner's position was close to the wreck of the tugboat *Keswick* that had drifted almost ashore after it was hit by Japanese fire the morning that Bataan surrendered. On several nights Warner and other Marines swam out to the tug looking for food and anything else of value. Major Lang stayed to talk for a few minutes at Warner's foxhole, urging him and those in nearby positions to stay calm and remain under cover. Lang then set off to the east as the bombardment continued to grow in intensity to check on more of his men. That was the last time Warner saw Lang alive.[11]

Early that evening Lang reached an earth and sandbag bunker south of North Point to confer with an Army captain who was attached to A Company. The two had just entered the position when it took a direct hit from a Japanese shell. Both were killed instantly. As word spread throughout A Company that Lang was dead it was a shock to the unit. The major had been highly respected by the men. He was the highest ranking Marine killed in action during the Philippine Campaign. After word reached Lieutenant Colonel Beecher that Lang had been killed, Captain Lewis H. Pickup from the battalion staff was assigned to take over the company.

Earlier that day Beecher had to replace the B Company commander, Captain Brown, when it was discovered that he was suffering from shell shock after being buried twice in foxholes from enemy shellfire. Beecher ordered 1st Lieutenant Alan S. Manning from D Company to take over B Company along the south shore of the Tail. Manning had himself already been wounded twice during the shelling. In addition to the loss of Lang, Brown, and the Army captain killed with Lang, three Army officers assigned to the Reserve Company were wounded as was one of B Company's platoon commanders and a lieutenant in D Company.[12]

By midafternoon the entire island seemed to be shrouded in smoke and dust as the Japanese barrage raged across the north shore of The Rock. It was clear to him that the Japanese were getting ready for their assault on Corregidor.

THE FINAL DAY—5 MAY

On this, the morning before the Japanese invasion of Corregidor, there were few in the Filipino-American garrison of the fortified islands of Manila Bay who could not have realized that the Japanese would soon be on their way. During the night a concerted effort had been made to repair telephone lines from General Moore's H Station (Harbor Defenses headquarters in Malinta Tunnel) to Colonel Bunkers' C-1 Station and other outposts around the island. These lines started to break again when the daily shelling and bombing started before 0800. By 0835 the first of several air attacks had struck the island.

As the morning progressed the volume of Japanese fire increased dramatically, with most of it focused on the beach defenses along the north shore. Fort Drum opened fire at 1000 against targets on Bataan, followed by Craighill at 1055. More air raids followed in the later part of the morning, which Corregidor's few surviving anti-aircraft weapons attempted to repel. Although they could not turn back the Japanese bombers it was a brave effort since the anti-aircraft units themselves were also under artillery fire.

At 1230 the Americans opened fire with virtually everything they had left against targets on Bataan. From Corregidor itself the one remaining 12-inch mortar of Battery Way, one 12-inch gun each from Batteries Wheeler and Cheney, the well-protected 155s of Battery Monja, as well as roving batteries Wright, Rose, and Gulick all fired against Bataan. From Fort Frank 14-inch Battery Crofton fired at extreme range at targets near Mariveles, and, of course, Fort Drum contributed to the counter-barrage. Several Japanese batteries were knocked out or temporarily silenced, but the overwhelming enemy shelling continued throughout the day, focused mostly on the beach defenses. At 1800 the defenders attempted a repeat performance against targets on Bataan and Corregidor, but with little effect since by 1830 it was noted that the Tail, Bottomside, and James Ravine were being pounded terrifically by enemy artillery fire. As darkness approached, the volume of Japanese shelling continued to increase, a good clue that a landing attempt would be made that night.[13]

At 2100 Colonel Howard placed the beach defenses on full alert, warning his commanders that the Army's anti-aircraft sound detectors were picking up the noises of engines along Bataan's east coast, almost certainly from large numbers of landing craft. With telephone communications now in such poor shape, the alert had to go out via runner in many cases, which was very dangerous for those young men who performed the duties.

Down on the Tail, Lieutenant Commander McCoy, the 16th Naval District assistant communications officer, was keeping his men inside Tunnel Afirm, under cover from the shelling. With the last of Station C personnel gone, there was more room for others inside the tunnel. In midafternoon a call came in from the Navy headquarters in Tunnel Queen, demanding that McCoy get up there at once. Thinking the order somewhat mad, McCoy nevertheless set off to cover the roughly two miles of ground to Navy headquarters. Dashing from shell hole to shell hole, sprinting from cover to cover as Japanese shells lashed the Tail with unprecedented fury, it took McCoy several hours to make the journey.

When he arrived, somewhat amazed that he was still alive, McCoy was confronted by Captain Hoeffel who had one of McCoy's junior officers in custody. The young Navy officer had been apprehended by Army military police as he was supposedly stocking a small boat with supplies, apparently in preparation for an escape attempt. The Army handed him over to the Navy command and now Hoeffel wanted to know what McCoy intended to do about it. McCoy defended the young officer, telling the Navy's senior officer on Corregidor that the young man was probably only taking prudent precautions for the inevitable, with no intent to desert. This satisfied Hoeffel, who released the officer to McCoy's control.

Upon resolution of the incident McCoy stepped out of Tunnel Queen, climbed a few feet up Malinta Hill and looked eastward toward the Tail of the island and his station on Monkey Point. The sun was going down and the entire Tail was under an incredible artillery bombardment. Realizing that there was no way he would be able to return to his tunnel through that shelling, McCoy concluded that the Japanese would land that night, and he would probably be taken prisoner without his personal effects, which were in Tunnel Afirm. He returned to Tunnel Queen to see what he could do.[14]

CHAPTER 15

The Battle for Corregidor

The Japanese unit assigned the mission of taking Corregidor was the 4th Division. This understrength formation had arrived from China in time to take a leading role in the offensive that overwhelmed the defenders of Bataan. During the final week of fighting on the Peninsula the division had lost 150 men killed in action, modest casualties for a unit of just over 11,000. As the Japanese artillery and aircraft pounded the fortified islands, the 4th Division made preparations for the assault on Corregidor.

The Japanese planned to land a reinforced infantry regiment from the 4th Division on the Tail during the first night of the operation. That unit's mission was to eliminate resistance on the eastern portion of Corregidor, including taking Malinta Hill. One day was allocated to complete those important preliminary operations.

The following night another reinforced regiment would come ashore at James Ravine on the north shore. Meanwhile, the first regiment would attack across Bottomside and drive toward the high ground of Middleside and Topside. If all went well, the operation would be over in two to three days. The assault infantry would be reinforced with engineers, light artillery, and tanks.

During the first week of May the assault elements of the 4th Division assembled along the southeast coast of Bataan, well north of Cabcaben. By this time the Japanese had become very respectful of the 14-inch guns of Fort Drum; therefore they kept the troop assembly areas far enough to the north that they would be beyond the concrete battleship's range.

The Japanese artillery on Bataan would fire in close support of the landings and aircraft would attack American positions during daylight hours. General Homma hoped that the very heavy shelling of the landing beaches, particularly during the period of 1–5 May, would destroy most of the obstacles and kill or drive off the majority of the defenders. There were fifty-two landing barges of various sizes available for the operation. To provide some close support fire for the assault several of the launches that had been seized in Manila and armed with light cannons and machine guns were to accompany the landing forces. These were some of the same watercraft that the enemy had used to shell the east coast of Bataan.

The first landing was scheduled for the night of 5–6 May. H-hour was set for about 2300 when it was still very dark. The moon would rise prior to 2330, giving the attacking troops fairly good visibility soon after they came ashore. The unit scheduled to make the initial landing on the Tail was the 61st Infantry Regiment of the 4th Division, under the command of Colonel Gempachi Sato. The 61st was the unit that had taken Mt. Samat during the final offensive on Bataan in early April. On 1 April the regiment had a strength of 2,180 officers and men. It had suffered modest casualties during the week of fighting on Bataan.[1]

5 May marked a special event in the Japanese calendar—Boys' Day—when young men were supposed to show their pride, strength, and honor. The officers reminded the men of the 61st Infantry of this fact as they made final preparations for the assault. Colonel Sato's reinforced regiment consisted of:

- 61st Infantry Regiment
- One company of the 7th Tank Regiment
- 3rd Battalion, 51st Mountain Artillery Regiment, less one company
- One company of the 2nd Independent Mortar Battalion (two 150-mm mortars)
- One company of the 3rd Trench Mortar Battalion
- 4th Engineer Regiment (less two companies)
- Divisional Wireless Squad
- Half of the Divisional medical unit
- Half of the 1st Field Hospital
- Water and Disease Prevention Section (half-strength)[2]

The plan was for the 1st Battalion and its attached elements, some 790 men riding nineteen landing barges, to come ashore between Infantry and Cavalry Points. Simultaneously, the 785 personnel of the reinforced 2nd Battalion in ten barges were to land slightly to the east toward North Point. Colonel Sato was with his 1st Battalion. The 3rd Battalion was the regimental reserve. It was scheduled to come ashore at 0230. Ten tanks were included in third wave. The assault on Corregidor was to be the combat debut of the brand-new Type 97 Chi-Ha medium tank. Interestingly, one of the vehicles earmarked for the landing on The Rock was an American M-3 light tank that had been captured on Bataan.

The 61st Regiment departed from Lamao on Bataan's east coast shortly before 2200 on the evening of the 5th. As the Japanese barge formation headed south toward Corregidor it was caught in an unexpectedly strong current and carried to the east. The 1st Battalion actually arrived between Cavalry and North Points, several hundred yards east of its planned landing point. The 2nd Battalion had to delay its approach due to its sister unit cutting in front of its intended path. The 2nd Battalion was forced to move even farther to the east, into the area between North and Hooker Points.[3]

THE FIGHT AT THE BEACHES

During the late afternoon of 5 May the Japanese bombardment continued to worsen. After the sun set the shelling intensified further. This was unusual, since on most nights the enemy's firing definitely slackened after dark. There had already been intelligence from Filipino sources that the enemy would try to land on Corregidor on the night of 5–6 May. All units were alerted that the enemy would probably attack that night, although the consensus was that the assault would probably come shortly before dawn on the 6th. Therefore, a decision was made to allow most of the beach defense troops to sleep, as best they could in the face of the shelling, until a couple of hours before dawn. Major Schaeffer, the commander of Companies O and P, and Major Williams, the 4th Battalion commander, were both told to be prepared to move their troops to the vicinity of a landing, which would probably come sometime that night.[4]

At 2100 Colonel Howard was informed that the sound detectors of the 60th Coast Artillery were picking up the noise of many engines along Bataan's east coast. Howard passed the word to the battalion commanders and the Regimental Reserve that an enemy landing attempt was imminent. By this time the telephone lines had largely been torn to pieces by Japanese artillery fire so many of the units had to be alerted by runner. It was very clear that Japanese artillery was concentrating on the north shore beaches, especially around James Ravine (no doubt as a diversion) and the Tail.

Not all the ships of the Inshore Patrol were sunk or sinking—a few still survived. The little patrol yacht *Maryanne* had somehow managed to escape the attention of the Japanese, no doubt due to her small size. The little vessel's crew spent the daylight hours ashore in Tunnel Queen. At night, however, they still conducted patrols to the east and northeast of Corregidor in order to try to detect and provide early warning of any approaching landing force.

On the night of the 5th *Maryanne* was again on patrol to the northeast of Corregidor. Around 2200 the crew spotted a searchlight on The Rock and what seemed to be tracer fire. Next they saw what appeared to be landing barges heading for Corregidor. Reporting this to Tunnel Queen, the ship was instructed: "Do not repeat not interfere. Return to harbor." This was an unfortunate error. Even though the little patrol yacht was armed only with a single 37-mm gun and half a dozen machine guns, she might have been able to seriously disrupt the Japanese landing flotilla as it proceeded toward Corregidor.[5]

THE JAPANESE COME ASHORE

The Marines and other troops huddling in their foxholes were amazed at the intensity of the barrage that swept through their areas. It was the heaviest bombardment of the campaign. Shortly before 2300 the enemy shelling reached its height. The last few salvos included phosphorous shells that sent aloft white up-streamers as the shells burst. Then the firing suddenly stopped. The barrage moved considerably to the west toward Malinta Hill and beyond. As the men along the north shore peered out from their foxholes and weapons pits they spotted enemy barges within fifty to one hundred yards of the shore. Within moments a torrent of fire started to hit the approaching Japanese.

A searchlight on the slopes of Malinta Hill illuminated the approaching enemy boats, giving the men on shore a very clear look. Japanese artillery on Bataan immediately sent a deluge of shells at the light, which was knocked out within three or four minutes. By that point the landing area was being lit up by waves of tracer rounds. Some of the Japanese barges burst into flames, which provided more light.

Near Cavalry Point Private Jack Warner spotted a couple of barges approaching. This was the extreme western portion of the 1st Battalion. He and the rest of his squad fired at the enemy with rifles, BARs, and machine guns. Some of the men threw grenades as the enemy got close to the beach. Warner was sure that none reached the shore alive.[6]

Not far to the east of Warner's position a group of about twenty Army soldiers from A Company, 803rd Engineers were located on the cliffs directly above the landing beaches. As the enemy barges approached the soldiers poured rifle and machine-gun fire at them, killing many enemy troops in the boats.

On the other end of the Japanese line part of the 1st Battalion drifted into the area east of Kindley Field. It was here that 1st Lieutenant Lawrence's men were waiting. Despite the very heavy artillery fire that had hit their positions

Japanese Army Ki-21 Sally bombers flying over Corregidor's Tail after the surrender. This picture shows the area of the heavy fighting on 5–6 May. Fort Hughes is in the background. The beached tug Keswick *can be seen just off Corregidor's Cavalry Point.*

Source: USMC Historical Division, Quantico, Va.

just before the landing barges appeared there were no casualties, so well dug in were the men. When he heard boat motors close to shore Lawrence ordered his one beach defense searchlight to be turned on. Bathed in its light were enemy landing craft about a hundred yards away. Within two or three minutes the light was shot out by small arms fire, but it had revealed the enemy to the men on the 20–30-foot-tall cliffs that overlooked the beach. The two Philippine Scout–manned 75-mm guns that had remained hidden during the bombardment now went into action, firing at Japanese landing barges at a range of less than a hundred yards. Machine guns and 37-mm light cannons ripped up the approaching landing craft. A few of the enemy reached the beach, but were killed by grenades and 30-pound fragmentation bombs thrown over the cliffs. The machine guns and 37-mm weapons had overhead cover made from logs and earth. This served to protect their crews from enemy grenades that were hurled from the beach below. It was a slaughter. The 1st Battalion's easternmost element had been wiped out.

It was in the center portion of the landing area that the Japanese achieved their foothold on the island. Gunnery Sergeant John Mercurio's 2nd Platoon was manning the beaches along North Point. There probably were no more than about fifty men in the area where the bulk of the 1st Battalion, including Colonel Sato, came ashore. Part of the area was steep cliffs, but there were some portions of the beach around North Point where the ground sloped down to the waterline. It was along those paths that the Japanese got ashore and started to head inland.

It was savage fighting, some of it hand-to-hand. The Marines and the American and Filipino soldiers fought the enemy at close range with every weapon they had. Staff Sergeant William Dudley, USMC, of D Company lifted the trails of his 37-mm gun so it could bear down over the edge of the cliffs at barges close to shore. Large numbers of grenades were hurled at the enemy. The fighting was so close that some men were firing pistols. Bayonet fights took place. Private Clarence Graham, USA, was in a foxhole between two dead Marines. He fired all his rifle and pistol ammunition and threw all his grenades, but the enemy kept coming.

Through sheer determination and force of numbers the Japanese made it ashore in the 2nd Platoon's area. The platoon's survivors started to fall back inland from North Point. Some headed westward toward the Denver Battery ridge, others went back across Kindley Field toward Monkey Point. Prior to

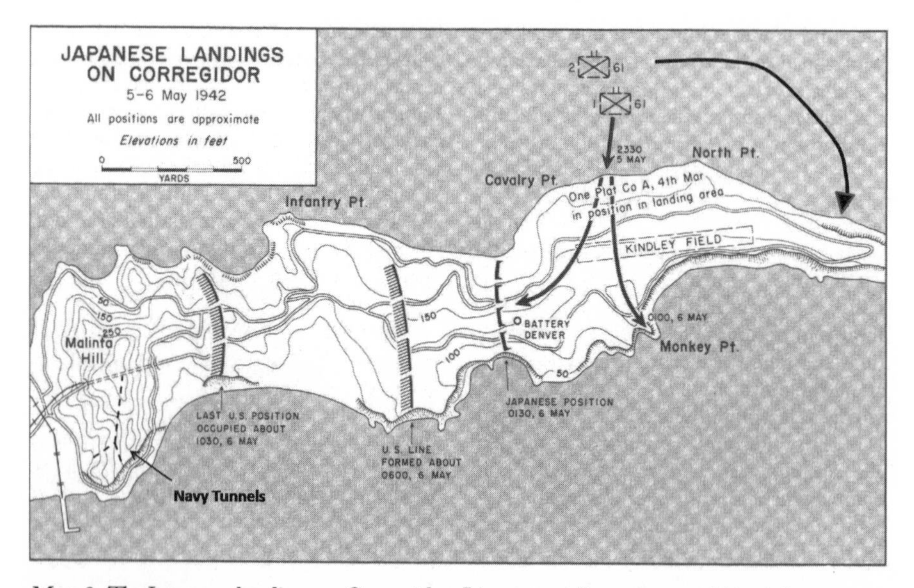

Map 9. The Japanese landing on Corregidor. Lieutenant Lawrence and his eighty-two men who inflicted very heavy casualties on the Japanese were located on the eastern end of the Tail, off the right side of this map.

Adapted from U.S. Army official history

2330 the enemy had established a beachhead in the immediate vicinity of North Point and had started to push inland.

Critically, the machine-gun crews on the eastern end of the Denver Battery ridge pulled out to the west after briefly resisting the enemy. This allowed Colonel Sato's infantrymen to gain access to the eastern end of the highest ground on Corregidor's Tail. On Japanese planning maps the Denver Battery ridge was marked as objective "Chrysanthemum."

Shortly before midnight the first Japanese reached the Denver Battery positions, having bypassed the battery's tunnel where several Marines had created a barricade with railroad ties at the entrance and held the Japanese off from there. The enemy troops cut around the Marines and headed up the hill toward the 3-inch gun positions.

When the Japanese approaching from the east reached the gun pits of Denver Battery some of the Army troops stood their ground and fought them. Most of the battery's personnel had, however, already pulled out, heading toward Malinta Tunnel. Several accounts mention how the battery's morale had been shattered by the loss of 1st Sergeant Brady on 24 April. By the time the Japanese landed much of the fight had gone out of the demoralized Army troops. The fighting in the battery positions was all too brief. As the survivors fled down the ridge and headed west, the Japanese took control of the sandbagged 3-inch gun pits and other emplacements such as the trenches that the Denver Battery personnel had dug. Some of them moved a few dozen yards west to take over the area around the two water towers on the western portion of the ridge. The Japanese now controlled the high ground in the center of the Tail. It was a decisive achievement.

THE SECOND WAVE ARRIVES

Colonel Sato's 1st Battalion had suffered significant casualties when it came ashore. It was, however, the 2nd Battalion that was truly decimated as it approached the island. Confusion offshore had delayed the 2nd Battalion and the tides had forced it farther to the east. Around 2345 most of the unit was approaching the eastern end of the Tail.

Lieutenant Lawrence's 80-odd men were cleaning away the empty shell cases from their gun pits when they spotted enemy barges. By this time the moon had risen and the stars were brilliant, allowing the men to see much farther. The enemy was first spotted about five hundred yards offshore. Again, the 37- and 75-mm guns went into action, followed by the machine guns and small arms. Most of the enemy barges were sunk or shot up well before they reached the beach. A few enemy troops did come ashore below the cliffs of this, the narrowest part of Corregidor. Lawrence's men hurled hundreds of grenades down on them and slid 30-pound fragmentation bombs down wooden shoots to explode among the rocks. There was nowhere for the enemy to hide. Several of the Marines had Thompson sub-machine guns—an ideal weapon for short range fighting. Before the night was over the Marines had expended all of their .45-caliber rounds at the enemy at the base of the cliffs. None of the Japanese who landed in front of Lawrence's position survived.

The forty-five-minute delay between the enemy's first and second waves also gave the surviving coast artillery batteries an opportunity to engage the enemy. *Mindanao*'s sailors at Battery Craighill on Fort Hughes opened fire on preplanned coordinates in the water off Corregidor's north shore. Battery Way on Corregidor also started shooting at the area off North Point with its one remaining 12-inch mortar. According to Japanese sources several 12-inch shells fell ashore into the area around North Point that they were occupying. The 3-inch anti-aircraft battery on Fort Hughes started firing over Corregidor's Tail, setting the fuzes on its shells so they would burst in the air off North Point. The twenty soldiers of the 803rd Engineers isolated on a cliff near Cavalry Point had to take cover as the 3-inch shells burst in the air near their positions.

A few hundred yards south of Corregidor's Tail lay the minesweeper *Quail*. Despite the damage she had suffered from Japanese artillery fire the ship was still serviceable. On board that morning were her skipper, Lieutenant Commander Morrill, and a number of his crew. They had watched the fireworks coming from the Tail and were standing by for orders. Morrill radioed Tunnel Queen and requested permission to take the ship into the North Channel to engage the enemy landing craft. Although he only had part of his crew on board, there were sufficient men to man the engines, the two 3-inch guns, and several machine guns. Morrill was convinced that he could disrupt the enemy landing by wading in among the enemy barges that he was sure were plying between Cabcaben and The Rock. Unfortunately, permission was denied. Morrill and his crew stayed on board, waiting for orders.[7]

There is no precise data on the number of casualties suffered by the 2nd Battalion of the 61st Infantry Regiment. According to one Japanese account the second wave suffered about 70 percent losses. What is clear is that the battalion suffered very heavy casualties. There were no survivors in Lawrence's area where most of the unit had tried to come ashore. A few of the battalion's barges succeeded in dropping their men off by moving farther to the west and landing at North Point. According to one source, of the ten landing barges carrying the 2nd Battalion, eight were lost on or near the shore and one other was sunk as it pulled away after depositing its men.[8]

CONTAINING THE LANDING

From the perspective of the American leadership the situation was confusing. Clearly the enemy was ashore, but there was no word as to exactly where and in what strength. In the previous months the 4th Marines had prepared several fall-back positions behind the beach defenses in order to contain an enemy landing that managed to penetrate inland. One such position ran from the north to south shores of the island, through the Denver Battery ridge. The plan was that if an enemy assault on the east end of the island managed to get ashore, A Company would fall back to man the north part of this line, while B Company would take the southern portion, and the critical center across the ridge would be held by the Army personnel of Denver Battery. The new line, facing east, would hold until reinforcements arrived to counterattack. The current situation seemed to call for the implementation of this contingency plan, so Captain Pickup, USMC, the A Company commander, directed Marine gunner (a Marine artillery warrant officer rank, not to be confused with gunnery sergeant) Harold Ferrell of D Company to go to Denver Battery to contact the Army battery commander.

Taking Pickup's runner, Corporal Orland Morris, with him Ferrell headed east up the road into the Denver Battery position. As he and Morris entered the battery area in the darkness they heard Japanese voices. The corporal quietly crawled forward to observe what was happening. He soon returned with the news that there were enemy troops all over the Denver Battery area. Ferrell headed back to report to Captain Pickup that the enemy now controlled the high ground in the center of the Tail. When he could not find the captain, he assembled a number of D Company Marines and other stragglers and led them forward to the area just west of the Denver Battery ridge, below the two water tanks. Ferrell was putting the men into a quick defensive position to prevent the enemy from advancing westward when the 1st Battalion adjutant, Captain Golland L. Clark, arrived. Ferrell explained the situation. Realizing the seriousness of the situation, Clark sent a runner to report to Lieutenant Colonel Beecher and Colonel Howard that the enemy was ashore and in possession of the Denver Battery ridge. By this time it was probably about 0030 on the morning of the 6th.[9]

The leadership of the 1st Battalion was getting a fragmentary picture of what was happening. Lieutenant Colonel Beecher, who was in Malinta Tunnel, knew the enemy had come ashore around North Point but had few details of what was going on. What he did know was that there was a pressing need to get reinforcements to the Tail, and fast. His own Reserve Company was manning the slopes of Malinta Hill. Due to the possibility of more enemy landings near such a critical location Beecher could not spare many men from that source. A couple dozen men from the 1st Battalion Headquarters and D

Company were rounded up and rushed toward the center of the Tail. At this point Beecher still did not know that the vital Denver Battery ridge had fallen to the enemy. Realizing he needed more troops, the 1st Battalion commander requested the release of the Regimental Reserve to his control. With Colonel Howard also in Malinta Tunnel, permission was quickly obtained. Indeed, the leading elements of the Regimental Reserve were already in Malinta Tunnel, as we will soon see.

Sometime within the next hour Gunner Ferrell linked up with his CO, Captain Noel Castle, and informed him of the situation. After offering to lead the Regimental Reserve from Malinta Tunnel toward the enemy, the commander of D Company assembled a number of his Marines, some men from the 1st Battalion Headquarters Company, plus some Army stragglers, and led them toward the high ground intent on driving the enemy out of the Denver Battery positions. Realizing the situation was confused, Castle sent a quickly formed fifteen-man squad of cooks and drivers to cover his left flank near the north shore. He then headed toward Denver Battery, telling his men, "Let's go up there and run the bastards off." Despite the urgings of Ferrell against him personally taking the lead, the captain (one of the prewar Marine Corps' best marksmen) said, "I'm going to take these people up there and shoot those people's eyes out." Castle apparently also took unauthorized temporary control of one of the platoons of P Company as it moved forward from Malinta Tunnel.[10]

Sometime around 0230 Castle and his men (probably around fifty to sixty) were advancing uphill near the two water tanks on the western end of the ridge when they ran headlong into a group of Japanese who were moving westward. A very close-range firefight started. As his attack stalled, Castle personally retrieved a .30-caliber machine gun and opened fire on the enemy, forcing them back from the area of the water tanks toward the sandbagged gun pits of Denver Battery. Suddenly, he was hit and fell dead. With the captain down, the men fell back, taking up defensive positions west of the water tanks.

Noel Castle was the highest ranking Marine killed on Corregidor during the Japanese assault on the island. Previous accounts of his death are either incomplete or probably in error regarding the time he was killed. Most sources place Castle's death relatively soon after the Japanese came ashore. A key piece of evidence, however, is Lieutenant Hogaboom's article stating that when the Regimental Reserve moved out of Malinta Tunnel, Captain Castle was one of the officers who guided O and P Companies forward. Accounts of the battle agree that when the Regimental Reserve departed Malinta Tunnel it was about 0200. The second telling piece of evidence in Hogaboom's narrative is the statement by his 3rd Platoon leader that "some captain" had ordered him to take his men uphill to the water tanks where they engaged in combat. There is no account of the battle that suggests any significant counterattack was made on the Denver Battery ridge before Castle's abortive attack, which must have taken place after 0200, probably around 0230. What all this indicates is that the Japanese were in possession of the Denver Battery position for nearly two hours before the first significant attempt was made to dislodge them (assuming that an attack by a reinforced platoon can be considered a "significant" effort).

When the survivors of Castle's attack fell back, Captain Clark ordered Gunner Ferrell to place mortar fire on the Denver Battery ridge. Ferrell quickly headed back to the area southeast of Malinta Hill where the 1st Battalion's Stokes mortars were located. About twenty rounds were fired without benefit of observation. Word soon arrived, however, that the mortars shells were bursting too close to friendly troops west of the ridge. Ferrell ceased fire. In the confusion no one could find the Marine who had the range card that listed mortar firing data for targets throughout the 1st Battalion's area. With no observer available to direct their fire, and unable to actually see the Denver Battery hill from their firing location, using the mortars was deemed too dangerous to nearby friendly troops. A potentially decisive source of fire support had to remain silent.

By roughly 0245 the situation was starting to stabilize. The Japanese were in control of Denver Battery's hill, but had suffered heavy losses. Colonel Sato had probably lost between 700–750 of the nearly 1,600 men of the first two battalions to land. One of his battalion commanders was dead. Groups of Americans remained cut off in the Japanese rear. The twenty soldiers from the 803rd Engineers continued to hold out on the cliff near Cavalry Point. Nine Marines were pinned in the north entrance of the Denver Battery tunnel. Lieutenant Lawrence's men on Hooker Point were virtually unscathed, having defeated both enemy attempts to land in front of their positions. Additionally, men from various units—survivors from A Company's 2nd Platoon, men from A Company's 803rd Engineers, machine-gun crews from Mobile Battery, and Marines from B and D Companies—were congregating near Tunnel Afirm on the south side of Kindley Field. Some of the men who reached the Navy tunnel were without weapons. The sailors gave them what spare arms they had. A few Army and Marine Corps officers started to organize a defensive perimeter with the 150 or so men that were in the vicinity of the tunnel. By the early morning hours there were 37 wounded being treated inside the tunnel, including Jack Warner who had been shot in the leg as he withdrew southward from his original position. One of the wounded men did not live through the night.

RESERVES GO INTO ACTION

In Government Ravine on the southeast corner of Topside the men of Companies O and P under the command of Major Max Schaeffer and Major Williams' 4th Battalion watched the fireworks coming from the Tail. There was no doubt whatsoever that the enemy was landing in the 1st Battalion area. Even before the orders to move arrived from Regimental headquarters the officers and NCOs started to get their men ready to go. Companies O and P assembled in the area near the Philippine government vaults and awaited instructions. Just before midnight Major Schaeffer received the order to move to support the 1st Battalion. With P Company in the lead, fewer than 250 officers and men, most of them Marines, but with a sprinkling of sailors and several dozen Philippine Army Air Corps cadets, moved out toward Malinta Tunnel. The first part of the journey was easy. Following the road along the shore that led from Government Ravine toward Malinta Tunnel, both companies crossed Bottomside via a tank trap (which was essentially a deep trench) that ran close to the south beach. Upon entering Malinta Tunnel the men found the situation chaotic.

Wounded were being brought into the tunnel from the east and taken to the hospital laterals. Masses of men, most of them apparently aimlessly wandering or just sitting against the tunnel walls, slowed movement toward the east entrance. When they reached the eastern end of the tunnel the men were directed to sit and await further orders. Additional ammunition was issued while the officers tried to get some information about what was happening out on the Tail. In previous weeks Major Schaeffer had wisely positioned cases of hand grenades, rifle ammo, and extra drums for Lewis machine guns in various locations around Corregidor, including Malinta Tunnel. This allowed the men to move from their bivouac area without being overly burdened. Now that the men were in Malinta Tunnel, awaiting the order to launch their counterattack, the extra ammunition was issued.

Major Schaeffer met with Lieutenant Colonel Beecher who instructed him to counterattack toward Kindley Field where the enemy was known to have come ashore. Around 0200 Schaeffer ordered the move toward the battle area. P Company under 1st Lieutenant Hogaboom was to lead the way and deploy to the left (north) flank when they approached the enemy. Captain Chambers' O Company would follow and deploy on the right (south) flank. Once the two companies were in position they would launch a counterattack. Captain Clark and Captain Castle offered to help guide the men. A number of Marines and sailors from Tunnel Queen volunteered to join Companies O and P to fight or carry ammunition.

With Captain Clark serving as a guide, the two companies started to move out from Malinta Tunnel just after 0200. Hogaboom's P Company led the way. When he reached Road Junction (RJ) 42, a few hundred yards west of the water tanks, Hogaboom's company took the left fork in the road. He deployed his 2nd Platoon facing east, but suddenly discovered that neither the 1st nor 3rd Platoons were to be seen.

After some delay the 3rd Platoon returned, its leader reporting that while he was following the rest of P Company, "some captain had ordered him to take his platoon up around the water towers. There they had engaged the enemy."[11] The officer in question was almost certainly Captain Castle who was, as we have already seen, killed in the first attempt to retake the Denver Battery position.

A few minutes later Hogaboom's 1st Platoon arrived. Now having most of his men present (probably about 110–120), Hogaboom deployed his company into the sloping ground northwest of the water tanks and prepared to advance. Already his men were fighting with Japanese snipers in the darkness. While he was getting his men into position, Hogaboom encountered Lieutenant Harris, USMC, the commander of the A Company platoon that was still manning beach defense positions along the shore northwest of Denver Battery. After quickly conferring with Harris, Hogaboom ordered his men to advance eastward into the general area north of the Denver Battery hill. After they had advanced a few yards they ran into the main Japanese line running from the hill to the north shore. The attack started to bog down as an intense firefight started. While this was under way Hogaboom became aware that O Company, which was supposed to be on his right, was nowhere to be seen.

Whereas P Company had a relatively easy movement from Malinta Tunnel to the area of the Denver Battery position, O Company had been decimated. Captain Robert Chambers led the company from the tunnel, following Hogaboom's P Company. The 1st Platoon was led by Quartermaster Clerk (a warrant officer rank) F. W. Ferguson, the 2nd by Quartermaster Clerk Herman Snelling, and the 3rd by Quartermaster Sergeant John Haskins. Like Hogaboom's P Company, the total strength of Company O was about 110–120 men, mostly Marines.

When O Company cleared Malinta Tunnel it proceeded eastward. As the men moved along they fired upon some unknown personnel seen moving in the darkness. The all-too-American cursing that came back in reply showed that the Japanese were not yet that close to Malinta Tunnel. Ferguson's platoon had almost reached RJ 42 when suddenly he saw a couple of white flares shoot up from not too far ahead. Suspecting that it was a signal for an enemy barrage, he quickly passed the word to his men to be prepared to take cover. Ferguson made a good call; within moments a devastating artillery concentration descended on the company.

Fortunately for Ferguson's platoon there were a number of large, deep, bomb craters in their immediate vicinity when the Japanese barrage came crashing down. He ended up in a large bomb crater along with Captain Chambers and two other men. The intense shelling lasted a few minutes. When it ended the men started to get up from their cover and sort themselves out. Ferguson discovered that he had lost eight men, either killed or wounded. He got his men back on the road and proceeded toward the Denver Battery hill. When they reached RJ 21, just to the west of the water towers, they came under heavy machine-gun fire from atop the ridge. Ferguson got his men into cover near the base of the hill. He expected to see and hear the rest of the company take up positions to his right, but none were to be found.

While the 1st Platoon had suffered fairly modest casualties, the other two platoons had been cut to ribbons by the enemy artillery fire. Quartermaster Sergeant Haskins' 3rd Platoon arrived a few minutes later. He only had five men in addition to himself when he reached the area near the hill. The rest had been killed or wounded. A few of the missing personnel may have been helping evacuate badly wounded men back to the tunnel. Similarly, Warrant Officer Snelling only had four men with him when he reached the area where Ferguson was positioned. Despite the battering that O Company had taken, the Marines were determined to try to counterattack to retake the Denver Battery positions. Along with the few remaining men of O Company, there were some other Marines from A and D Companies in the area, and a few Philippine Scouts from Batteries E and F, 92nd Coast Artillery (PS). By approximately 0245 there were probably less than 75 men in position just to the west of Denver Battery, with roughly another 100–110 in Hogaboom's P Company slightly to the north.

STALEMATE ALONG THE RIDGE

Once contact had been established between Hogaboom's P Company and Chambers' battered O Company the Marines in the battle area started to attack to try to drive the enemy off the high ground. The Marines quickly noticed that the Japanese had deployed a large number of automatic weapons along the top of the ridge near the water towers. As readers will recall from the discussion in the chapter on Longoskawayan Point, this was due to the fact that each Japanese squad had its own light machine gun, in addition to the tripod-mounted machine guns in the weapons companies. Although the Japanese certainly would have lost a considerable number of weapons when many of their landing barges were sunk, the surviving troops still had plenty of machine guns available. These were now sited on the high ground to drive off any counter-attack, which is exactly what now happened.

Hogaboom's three platoons, reinforced by a few men who were already in the area north of the Denver Battery ridge, started advancing into the draw north of the Denver Battery position. The Japanese had set up machine guns in captured American positions on the east side of the draw. The intense enemy fire drove Hogaboom's men to cover. A firefight started that lasted a couple of hours. Some of the Marines managed to use the cover of downed trees to creep toward the enemy firing positions in order to hurl grenades. Although some of the Japanese positions were knocked out, the enemy appeared to have the ability to replace his losses. The situation north of the ridge bogged down into a standoff.

A couple of hundred yards to the south Ferguson started moving his men forward in short, quick advances up the hill. Each time they would make a bit of progress, but men were lost in every attempt. Two Japanese were discovered hiding in a small shack about halfway up the hill between where the men started their advance and the water towers. The pair killed several Americans until they were discovered and eliminated by a BAR.

Three times Ferguson's men attacked. They managed to get to the area of the water tanks, but were then pinned down by fire from the Japanese in the sand-bagged Denver Battery gun positions a few yards to the east. Casualties reached the point that no more attempts could be made. With no weapons heavier than Lewis machine guns, BARs, and hand grenades, the Marines were at a severe disadvantage compared to the dug-in enemy, who also outnumbered them at the point of contact.

It was at this point that an act of bravery occurred that should always be held in highest regard by the Marine Corps. With the advance held up, Sergeant Major John H. Sweeney of the Regimental Service Company, assisted by his close friend Quartermaster Sergeant John Haskins, managed to crawl to the eastern water tower, and climb to the top. It was still dark. Sweeney had stuffed his pockets and shirt with hand grenades. Once atop the water tank he started to hurl grenades toward the enemy in the sandbagged gun positions. Despite being under intense fire from the Japanese, Sweeney managed to knock out at least one enemy machine-gun position, and probably a second. Haskins brought him more grenades, climbing up the tower while under enemy fire. On his second attempt to bring more grenades Sergeant Haskins was killed at the base of the water tower. Not long afterward, Sweeney was shot and killed atop the tower. Ferguson knew both men well; they had served in China together. He remarked that, "they were very close friends in life and it was most fitting that they should go out together."[12]

As dawn approached the American and Japanese lines atop the ridge were very close, about thirty to forty yards apart. The Americans were sheltering among shattered trees and in depressions in the ground. A hundred or so yards to the rear of the American front line was ground that sloped abruptly down to the west, providing some additional cover. There were also some wrecked barracks buildings in the same area. Meanwhile, the Japanese were still in the gun pits and trenches of Denver Battery. Although the Japanese had the support of their artillery on Bataan, the two front lines were so close that the enemy dared not use his firepower. Instead, the Japanese artillery continued to rake the area between Malinta Hill and the battle area west of Denver Battery.

Realizing that he needed more firepower to dislodge the Japanese from their positions along the ridge, Ferguson sent a request to Captain Chambers that a 37-mm gun be moved up to place direct fire on the enemy. Unfortunately, it was decided that the possibility of more Japanese landings meant that the remaining beach defense guns had to remain in position. It was an understandable, but unfortunate decision. One or two 37-mm guns, positioned a few hundred yards west of the ridge, would have been close enough to pick off individual enemy emplacements.

The standoff continued as dawn approached. When Captain Chambers was wounded Ferguson was told to assume command of the remnants of O Company. Around 0400 Ferguson led six men in an attempt to outflank the enemy by following the road that snaked around the south side of the Denver ridgeline. Unfortunately, they were spotted by a Japanese machine gun that was covering the road and five of the men were cut down, either dead or wounded. Ferguson and an Army private from the 803rd Engineers managed to continue and reached a position approximately directly south of the Denver gun pits. Attempts to scale the steep cliff that ran along the road failed.

Suddenly, and much to Ferguson's surprise, Japanese soldiers started leaving the westernmost sandbagged positions and began to move back to the east along the ridge. Ferguson and his Army partner started firing uphill at them with their rifles. The enemy was so close that they could hardly miss; Ferguson thought that he and the private dropped twenty or more of them. As they were firing, the Marine was hit in the face by a rifle bullet. With the help of Private Stewart, Ferguson managed to struggle back to the Marine positions. He reported to Major Schaeffer's command post to relate what he had observed. When he arrived at the temporary CP near RJ 21 he found Schaeffer in conversation with Major Williams. The 4th Battalion was arriving.[13]

THE ENEMY'S FINAL WAVE

The final element of the 61st Infantry had originally been scheduled to land on Corregidor around 0230. However, so many landing craft had been lost bringing the first two battalions to the island that the 3rd Battalion's arrival had to be delayed. It was not until about 0400 that the enemy's final echelon started to head toward Corregidor. Only five of the ten tanks earmarked to reinforce the 61st Infantry could be included in the third wave due to the shortage of barges, so heavy had been the losses of landing craft.

The moon was still providing considerable light at 0445 as the final Japanese wave approached North Point. The enemy was spotted more than a mile from shore and all weapons that could be brought to bear on them opened fire. Fort Drum had been firing four-gun salvos into the area around Cabcaben when observers on Corregidor spotted the approaching landing craft and directed the fort shift its fire to the new threat. Lieutenant Colonel Lewis Kirkpatrick, USA, Fort Drum's commander, replied that he could not see the landing barge so far away through the heavy smoke rising from Corregidor. The answer from the Seaward Defense command post was: "Just fire into the smoke anywhere between you and Cabcaben and you can't miss them." Kirkpatrick directed "turret commander's action" and both of the 14-inch gun turrets started firing independently, varying the deflection and elevation on each salvo so as to pepper the North Channel with shellfire.[14]

Other guns also fired on the approaching enemy. Again Batteries Way and Craighill dropped 12-inch mortar shells into the area off North Point. Some of their shells landed close to Americans along the north shore, and the firing had to be stopped. The few surviving 155-mm guns on Topside also opened fire on the enemy barges. The isolated troops of the 803rd Engineers at Cavalry Point opened fire on the landing craft as they approached; Lieutenant Hogaboom was surprised when he saw fire directed toward the approaching landing craft from *behind* the Japanese he was fighting.

Despite the attempt to thwart the enemy's reinforcement effort most of the 880 men of the 3rd Battalion and its attached elements reached Corregidor. Some landing barges were sunk, however, including one that carried two of the five tanks. The Japanese were fortunate to have not drifted to the east where Lieutenant Lawrence's men were still in position near Hooker Point. Lawrence's position was too far to the east to see the approaching Japanese reinforcements who landed on the western side of North Point.

By this time the enemy's barge losses were very serious. After the barges of the third wave returned General Homma was told that only twenty-one landing craft remained. As dawn broke Lieutenant Lawrence and his men on

Hooker Point started to count wrecked Japanese barges within their field of view. Lawrence could see twenty-two half-sunk barges from his position, each with dead or dying enemy soldiers on board. Four other landing craft were completely full of dead Japanese soldiers. In the surrounding waters many enemy bodies floated, each in an orange life vest.[15]

THE LAST COUNTERATTACK—4TH BATTALION, 4TH MARINES

Around midnight Army major general Moore directed Colonel Bunker to move the coast artillerymen from Batteries B, C, D, and H of the 59th Coast Artillery (a total of about four hundred officers and men) into Malinta Tunnel in order to be prepared to fight as infantry. As Battery C was crossing Bottomside it was caught in a Japanese artillery barrage that killed several of the Army troops.

At about 0130, an hour and a half after Companies O and P had departed, Major Williams received word to move the 4th Battalion into the tunnel and await further orders. The distance from Government Ravine to the tunnel was less than a mile, but Japanese artillery fire resulted in the move taking about an hour. When the battalion reached the western side of Bottomside the area was under intense artillery bombardment; the sailors had to back off about three hundred yards to the west in order to avoid the shellfire. Once the barrage stopped the battalion continued its move it Malinta Tunnel. By the time the 4th Battalion arrived in the tunnel Major Schaeffer's two companies were already in combat.

For the next two hours the 4th Battalion waited in the increasingly awful conditions of Malinta Tunnel. The roughly three hundred men were concentrated near the east entrance. They saw the constant stream of wounded men (around three hundred according to one account) entering the tunnel from the fighting, and periodically suffered from the concussion of enemy artillery shells bursting just outside the east entrance. The heat and dust in the tunnel were nearly unbearable, but all the men could do was wait for the word to advance. Major Williams and the battalion's leadership attempted to get some information about what was happening at the Denver Battery ridge.[16]

Shortly before 0430 Colonel Howard decided to commit his last reserve. He instructed Major Williams to advance eastward, link up with the forces already in contact, and counterattack to drive the enemy off the island. Compared to when Major Schaeffer's companies moved out around 0200 the situation on the eastern portion of the island was now better understood. Colonel Howard and Lieutenant Colonel Beecher knew that the Japanese were in possession of most of the Denver Battery ridge, but were almost certainly unaware that Lieutenant Lawrence's group still held the eastern tip of the island, or that the area around Tunnel Afirm was still in American hands.

Concern for the men in close contact with the enemy resulted in the denial of some requests for fire. Lieutenant Colonel Kirkpatrick, Fort Drum's aggressive commander, called Corregidor suggesting that the troops be pulled back so that he could "sink" the Tail of the island with a hail of 14-inch shells. This recommendation was denied, to the great good fortune of the men cut off on the eastern portion of the Tail.

At 0430 the 4th Battalion moved out from Malinta Tunnel while the Japanese third wave was under fire from Corregidor and the other forts. The order of march was Companies Q, R, S, and T. Major Williams' orders were that when the battalion reached a point about two hundred yards from the firing line that Companies Q and R would deploy to the left (north), while Company T took up position in front of the Denver Battery ridge. Company S would be initially held in reserve behind Company T.

Shortly after the first elements cleared the tunnel they came under long-range machine-gun fire that had little effect. The battalion had proceeded about five hundred yards from the tunnel when it came under artillery fire from Bataan. This barrage caused the battalion to scatter for cover and caused a few casualties, but apparently nothing like the decimation of O Company some two hours earlier. It took about ten minutes for the officers and NCOs to get the men organized and moving again after the barrage ended. 1st Lieutenant Saalman, USA, veteran infantryman from Bataan, was very impressed with the discipline and professionalism of the sailors as they advanced toward the enemy, stating that an experienced observer would have been hard-pressed to tell the difference between them and well-trained infantry, with the exception of their uniforms, of course.

About two hundred yards from the line of contact the companies started to form into lines of skirmishers. Williams ordered Captain Paul Moore, USA, the Q Company commander, to link up with the Marines from Company P who were on the left flank near the north shore and take control of the fighting there. Moore led the men to the north and soon found Lieutenant Hogaboom who was directing the firefight north of the Denver Battery ridge.

To Moore's immediate right, Army captain Dalness led R Company into the firing line on the northwest side of the Denver ridge. A quick check by Dalness showed that he was missing twenty men from his company, probably about a quarter of his unit's strength. Some had been wounded or killed by the artillery fire during the approach march, others had probably become lost and were with other companies; Dalness could never be sure.[17]

Soon after arriving in the area the sailors of Q and R Companies started to come under sniper fire from Japanese soldiers who had gotten past Hogaboom's men. These may have been a small patrol of the enemy that suddenly found themselves cut off behind the Americans when the 4th Battalion arrived. Dalness dispatched a small group of sailors under a Navy chief to hunt the enemy down. About an hour later they returned, the chief stating that they had found and killed three of the enemy, but had lost one man in return.

When R and T Companies entered the line near the water tanks they found very few men manning the area. This was indicative of how heavy the casualties had been during the O Company attacks up the hill. Lieutenant Otter, formerly the gunnery officer of *Canopus*, put his men in position while they were under fire from the Japanese in the Denver Battery gun pits and trenches. Seeing that there were few men to the right of T Company, Lieutenant Little, USN, brought S Company into the line on the right flank of the battalion. By about 0530 most of the men were in position.

As the 4th Battalion moved into position Major Williams linked up with the wounded Major Schaeffer at the latter's command post near RJ 21. Schaeffer agreed that Williams should take over the control of the battle and assume command of the survivors of O and P Companies plus the remnants of other units that were manning the line. With the arrival of the 4th Battalion there were probably about five hundred Americans and Philippine Scouts manning the line that stretched from the north shore just west of Cavalry Point to the south shore of the island around Ordnance Point. This is only an estimate, since there was never a detailed count made of the personnel in contact. Recall that while the 4th Battalion was waiting near the eastern sally port of Malinta Tunnel a large number of wounded personnel were brought in. These men would have been mostly from the 1st Battalion and Companies O and P, plus some Army soldiers. It is likely that by the time the 4th Battalion arrived, Lieutenant Hogaboom's P Company was still relatively intact, with probably eighty to ninety men left. Company O, however, had been reduced to a tiny fraction of its initial strength after being caught in an enemy barrage and two hours of fighting near the water tanks, including the three separate attacks organized by Quartermaster Ferguson. Additionally, there were a few men from Companies A and D, plus some Philippine Scouts and stragglers from the 803rd Engineers and even a handful of Denver Battery still in the line when the 4th Battalion arrived. It was not much considering that the Japanese probably had 1,500–1,600 men on The Rock by this time.*

---

*Some accounts of the battle have claimed that the enemy may have had only five hundred men left on Corregidor by this time. This is far too low a figure. As we will see, according to Japanese sources fewer than one thousand casualties were suffered during the fight on Corregidor on 5–6 May.

The company commanders of the 4th Battalion spent from 0530 to about 0600 getting their men in position, while under fire from the Japanese on the high ground. It is not absolutely clear where the front line was at this point, but apparently the Americans held the ground around the westernmost of the two water tanks, atop the Denver Battery ridge. Hogaboom's men and Q Company were still engaged in a firefight with the Japanese who held the eastern end of the draw on the north side of the ridge. The thinly manned southern part of the American line ended around Ordnance Point; apparently there were few Japanese in that area.

Just before the sun came up Major Williams moved along the firing line and told the company commanders that the 4th Battalion would attack at dawn. He specified 0615 as the jump off time. In the few minutes available to them the company commanders got their men ready. Since the company command posts were virtually in the front line it was relatively easy to contact the platoon leaders and let them know to get their men ready. The sailors of the 4th Battalion, most of them without steel helmets and with no weapon heavier than a BAR and hand grenades, fixed bayonets and prepared to attack.

Promptly at 0615 the sailors of the 4th Battalion, together with Marine and Army survivors of Companies A, B, D, O, and P, launched their assault. Lieutenant Charles Brooks, USN, the 4th Battalion S-2, had once wondered what it would be like to conduct a bayonet charge—now he was in one. Together with the rest of the men, most of them sailors, he was yelling and rushing uphill toward the Japanese. Suddenly he was hit in the leg and was carried down the slope. An Army officer saved his life by applying a tourniquet to his leg as he was carried back to Malinta Tunnel. Once in the hospital laterals his leg was amputated.[18]

On the north side of the line Companies P, Q, and R made good progress and drove the Japanese back about two hundred yards. Directly in front of the Denver positions, however, the attack bogged down in the face of intense Japanese machine-gun fire. Soon after the attack started Japanese flares could be seen, and shortly thereafter enemy artillery fire started to fall in the area of the attack. The men pressed on.

S and T Companies suffered heavily from the automatic weapons fire and were forced to go to ground after advancing fewer than one hundred yards along the top of the Denver ridge. Major Williams noticed that Q and R Companies were pulling out ahead of the sailors struggling atop the ridge and ordered the two northern companies to halt their advance and try to maintain contact with the center of the line.

During their push forward Q Company discovered two Japanese landing barges, still loaded with many enemy soldiers, hung up on the rocks east of Infantry Point. A small group of sailors were sent to eliminate them. Since the landing craft were too far offshore to be reached with grenades, rifle fire had to be used. It took half an hour and several thousands rounds of poorly aimed, clearly novice firing to finish the Japanese off. According to Lieutenant Hogaboom Private First Class McKechine, USMC (who had been the lookout atop Mt. Pucot on Bataan when the Japanese landed at Longoskawayan Point in January) helped the sailors by firing his Lewis machine gun into the barges.

Atop the Denver ridge an intense close-range firefight was under way. S and T Companies suffered many casualties. Lieutenant Butch Otter and a volunteer party of five sailors crawled forward toward the enemy positions in the Denver gun pits. The rest of T Company provided covering fire with their rifles. When they reached a point about twenty-five to thirty yards from the enemy the men rose up and hurled their grenades. One of Otter's burst squarely in the enemy machine-gun pit that had inflicted so many casualties on T Company, killing or wounding the Japanese crew. So many enemy troops were close at hand, however, that the gun was immediately manned again. Otter and four of his men, including Ensign W. R. Lloyd who had served on the Inshore Patrol staff, were killed by enemy fire. Butch Otter was the senior Navy officer killed during the final battle for Corregidor.

Many of the sailors of S and T Companies observed this incident. Otter had been a very popular officer on *Canopus* and his death came as a shock. It also inspired the men, who renewed their attack. A wall of enemy machine-gun fire soon brought it to a halt, however. A grenade fight then developed, with the sailors pitching large numbers of grenades at the Japanese, so close were the front lines.

This was the point, with the sun up, that the Americans would have benefited tremendously from tank support—if they had had it. Recall that back in February the Provisional Tank Group Headquarters on Bataan had suggested sending a platoon of tanks to The Rock. The request had been turned down. Now the sailors, Marines, and soldiers in a furious, close-range battle with the Japanese were in desperate need of armor support.

Major Williams was right in the front line, mostly in the center where the situation was most difficult. He was trying to find a way to break through the enemy line. Sensing that the situation along the left (north) flank was most promising, he directed 1st Lieutnant Saalman, USA, to proceed there to assist Captain Moore and 1st Lieutenant Hogaboom. Saalman led a move that infiltrated near a Japanese machine-gun position on the north slope of the Denver ridge. The men succeeded in getting within hand grenade range of the enemy position without being detected. When they were close enough one of the men with Saalman threw a grenade that dropped into the enemy gun pit. A Japanese soldier was seen picking up the grenade and was getting ready to throw it back at the Americans when it exploded in his hand.

The advance on the north side of the ridge continued, slowly gaining ground. Around 0830 Saalman and some of his men spotted enemy tanks down on the beach east of Cavalry Point. One tank was still in a landing barge; two others had already been unloaded. Word was immediately sent to Major Williams that enemy armor was coming ashore.

The Japanese tanks were the three surviving vehicles from the five that were part of the third wave that came ashore around 0500. Two of the vehicles were brand-new Japanese Type 97 Chi-Ha medium tanks armed with 47-mm guns. The third tank was the American M-3 that had been captured on Bataan. Major Matsuoka of the 7th Tank Regiment commanded the small detachment. When the tanks came ashore in the predawn hours they immediately found themselves trapped on the beach, with sheer cliffs to their front. There were a few exits from the beach through the cliffs, but even there the terrain was steep enough that it was hard to get the tanks up the slopes. Apparently it was the American-made M-3 that managed to get off the beach first; it then helped pull the other vehicles up the slopes. The arrival of Japanese tanks was an ominous development; it helped decide the battle.

THE CONTINUING FIREFIGHT

By about 0900 the situation had bogged down again. The Americans had managed to advance two hundred yards or so in the area north of the Denver ridge, but the attack in the center near the water towers had ground to a halt with heavy losses. Now a firefight started—again—as the two sides blazed away at each other at ranges of fifty to one hundred yards. It was now daylight and the Americans were starting to feel the effects of the little Japanese "knee mortars" (platoon-level grenade launchers) that dropped small grenades into the area they held.

The 1st Battalion tried again to support the advance with 3-inch Stokes mortars, firing another twenty or so rounds at the Denver ridge. Once again the firing was so inaccurate that it endangered friendly troops near the enemy. Gunner Ferrell had to cease firing. This meant that the Americans were still fighting a dug-in enemy with only small arms and hand grenades. Casualties mounted and it appeared that the enemy could not be dislodged. Around 0900 a battery of Army coast artillerymen (probably about one hundred men) under Captain Herman Hauck arrived. Major Williams dispatched them to the left flank to reinforce Companies Q and R where the counterattack had made the best progress.[19] The number of wounded was steadily increasing and the 4th Battalion had precious few medical resources—only one Navy corpsman per company, plus two Navy doctors and two more corpsmen at the battalion level. Evacuating wounded men was very difficult, since the area between Malinta Tunnel and Denver Battery was under Japanese artillery fire. Realizing that he needed more men and heavy weapons, Major Williams sent word to Lieutenant Colonel Beecher and Colonel Howard that he had to have reinforcements. Unfortunately, by this point there were few reserves left except for those Army Coast Artillery batteries that had not yet deployed as infantry. The situation was becoming increasingly grim, but the men did not know that the Japanese were also gravely concerned.

By midmorning Colonel Sato could take pride in the fact that his men firmly held the key high ground on the Tail and had stopped several American counterattacks. However, his situation was far from good. The 61st Infantry and its attached elements had probably suffered around 30–35 percent casualties by this point. More seriously, the Japanese were now desperately short of ammunition. Each Japanese infantryman who landed had come ashore with 120 rounds for his rifle, plus two hand grenades. The light machine guns had 720 rounds per weapon, and the grenade launchers (the knee mortars) had 39 rounds each. Additionally ammunition had been placed in the landing barges of the first two waves, but much had been lost as barges were sunk or frightened boat crews dumped the precious crates into shallow water. The consumption of ammunition had been very heavy during the morning battle. With so few barges left there could be no attempt to bring more supplies to the island, especially now that the sun was up and any approaching landing barge would be seen—and fired upon—long before it reached The Rock. The 61st Infantry was rapidly approaching a crisis point in ammunition, but the Americans did not know it.[20]

At some point after 0900 the Japanese started to emplace light artillery (either 70- or 75-mm guns) atop the Denver ridge. The Americans opened fire on them in an attempt to eliminate the gun crews before the weapons could be put into operation. What was needed, of course, was an intense mortar or artillery bombardment to sweep the top of the Denver ridgeline. Although most of the American coast defense weapons had been knocked out by this point, there were still weapons available on Corregidor, Fort Hughes, and Fort Drum that could be brought to bear on the Denver ridge. No observers had been designated to control the firing, and the communications system was in disarray. The unmanned Battery Ramsay with three 6-inch disappearing guns was on the southeast corner of Topside with a direct view toward the Denver Battery position. One of its guns had been badly torn up by a direct hit from an enemy shell, but the other two had suffered only minor damage. Had Battery Ramsay been manned and had someone controlled its firing, the Japanese atop the Denver ridge could have been pummeled with rapid direct fire by 90-pound high explosive shells.

Around 0900 Lieutenant Little received a chest wound and was evacuated. Major Williams directed 1st Lieutenant Saalman to take over command of S Company; casualties were mounting steadily.

CLIMAX OF THE BATTLE

By roughly 0900 all three Japanese tanks were atop the cliffs around North Point. There is some confusion about exactly when and where the enemy armor went into action, but it appears that the first tank entered the fight around 1000 along the north shore road where Companies P, Q, and R were fighting.

Private First Class Silas Barnes, USMC, opened fire on the lead tank with his machine gun, but with no effect; the rounds bounced off its armor. The tank started firing at American troops in the area north of the ridge. Initially there was some panic among the men and they started to fall back in disorder. Major Williams and the senior NCOs intervened to calm the men and get them back into the firing line. He sent word back to Malinta Tunnel that enemy tanks were in action and requested anti-tank weapons. When the word arrived in the tunnel that Japanese armor was in action it had a profound effect on the American leadership, particularly General Wainwright.

The troops held on for another half an hour. Shortly before 1030 a decision was made to fall back to the concrete infantry trench east of Malinta Tunnel. It is not clear who made the decision to fall back, Colonel Howard or Major Williams. There is no doubt that the introduction of Japanese tanks was a decisive element in the decision, whether the tanks were having much physical effect on the battle or not. Word was passed to the company commanders and the men started to pull back. The withdrawal soon turned into a rout.

When the men started to retreat their movement was immediately spotted by the Japanese on the high ground. Machine-gun fire from the ridge swept the area as the Americans started to retreat. Worse was soon to come. As the sailors and Marines withdrew the enemy called for the artillery on Bataan to bombard the area between the Denver ridge and Malinta Hill. Within minutes the eight hundred to nine hundred yards that the men had to travel was being raked by artillery fire. It rapidly became an every-man-for-himself dash for safety. Captain Dalness recalled that the air was filled with fragments, dirt, and debris from the intense barrage that swept through the area. Casualties were heavy.

Some men did not get the initial word to retreat and got a late start. 1st Lieutenant Saalman was in one such group. He tried to protect his men by having them run behind the enemy barrage, diving into shell holes or bomb craters when the fire got too close. Although no details are available, there is no doubt that some badly wounded men had to be left behind near the front line when the retreat started. These men were almost certainly bayoneted by the Japanese troops when they pursued the retreating Americans.

Around the time the retreat started one group of Americans, mostly coast artillerymen, started an advance along the south shore of the island; apparently they did not get the word to withdraw. It also appears that there were few Japanese troops in the area south of the Denver ridge. These Americans and Filipinos, probably around fifty men, were able to advance through the area near the 3-inch coast defense Battery Maxwell Keyes, sweeping around the south flank of the enemy on the ridge. They continued to slowly advance until around noon by which time they were within sight of Kindley Field; they probably also made contact with the perimeter formed around Tunnel Afirm. When the men came within sight of the little airfield one of the Japanese tanks was still there, possibly suffering mechanical trouble after having been towed up the slope from the beach. Unfortunately, this advance was too little and too late to have any effect on the outcome.

THE END OF THE BATTLE

By the time the remnants of the units that had been fighting near Denver ridge reached the concrete trench east of Malinta Tunnel there were probably only about 150 men left. Some had been killed by Japanese artillery fire as they tried to flee westward. Others had run toward Monkey Point and joined the perimeter on the little hill near the Tunnel Afirm. When the survivors, many of them wounded, reached the mangled trench east of Malinta Tunnel they joined some men manning the position. The few troops already in position included two 37-mm guns from D Company, some .50-caliber machine guns from the 60th Coast Artillery's Mobile Battery that had evacuated the area around Kindley Field in the early morning hours, and a handful of men who had been rounded up in Tunnel Queen by Colonel Howard and Lieutenant Colonel Beecher.

Some groups were still holding on, cut off in small clusters behind the Japanese lines. The largest group behind the Japanese lines was at Tunnel Afirm. Next was 1st Lieutenant Lawrence's group on the extreme end of the Tail. The Army engineers at Cavalry Point were also holding out. Finally, there was the group of coast artillerymen advancing along the south shore of the island. All together, there were about three hundred men behind Japanese lines.

When the survivors of the units that had fought on the Tail fell back into the concrete trench the enemy was not far behind them. Seeing the Americans retreating in broad daylight, Colonel Sato first called in artillery fire from Bataan, then ordered his troops to follow the Americans. One or two of the Japanese tanks accompanied this move. According to a Japanese account a group of about fifty Americans was cut off before they could retreat to the trench near Malinta Tunnel. Fired on by Japanese troops, the group was next attacked by a Japanese plane. As the Japanese closed in from two sides the Americans, described as mostly Marines, threw down their weapons and surrendered.[21]

Major Williams, Captain Dalness, and Lieutenant Hogaboom all survived the retreat to the trenches. They immediately started to organize a defense with the men who had succeeded in retreating, along with the men who were already there. Lieutenant Harris, whose platoon had been manning the beaches northeast of Malinta Hill, brought his men into the trench to reinforce the defenses. It was still pitifully few men to stand between the advancing Japanese and Malinta Tunnel. Still in reserve inside Malinta Tunnel were over 250 Army coast artillerymen—the crews of three heavy coastal gun batteries. Those batteries had not been committed to the battle at the Denver ridge.

The men manning the final line of defense outside Malinta Tunnel asked for reinforcements, but none were sent. Instead, shortly after they got into the trench word was received that they were going to surrender at noon. It was heartbreaking news for the exhausted, hungry men.

CHAPTER 16

Surrender

Lieutenant General Wainwright was in Malinta Tunnel when the Japanese landed on Corregidor an hour before midnight on 5 May. Like the other American leaders on the island he had incomplete, fragmentary information about what was happening. By around midnight it was clear that the Japanese had come ashore in force on the eastern portion of the Tail, but details were lacking. How many Japanese, were they being held or driven back, what was happening to the men fighting east of Malinta Tunnel?

What was clear was that casualties were heavy and increasing. A steady stream of wounded men was being brought back into the tunnel from the fighting to the east; probably two to three hundred before dawn. Around 0400 on the morning of the 6th, as he was trying to piece together what was happening, Wainwright received a final message from President Roosevelt. As was the norm the message arrived via the Navy's superior radio system. The message from the president complimented Wainwright and his command, but was clearly a sign that Roosevelt knew that the defense would soon collapse.

The decisive piece of information was Colonel Howard's report around 1000 that enemy tanks were ashore and advancing westward toward Malinta Hill. "Skinny" Wainwright, a true soldier's soldier, was now in a dreadful situation. He knew that his men were still resisting the enemy's advance, but how long could they hold? What was the point of continued resistance, particularly if it meant very heavy casualties? The enemy was now only about one thousand yards from Malinta Tunnel where several thousand personnel including civilians, nurses, and roughly one thousand wounded were sheltering from the enemy bombardment. There was a strong possibility that the Japanese would fight their way into the tunnel before a surrender could be arranged. The consequences would be dreadful, with possibly thousands killed.

Ultimately it was the presence of Japanese tanks on the island that convinced Wainwright that he had to surrender: "But it was the terror that is vested in a tank that was the deciding factor. I thought of the havoc that even one of these could wreak if it nosed into the tunnel, where lay our helpless wounded and their brave nurses."[1] At 1015 Wainwright met with Major General Moore, the harbor defense commander, and Brigadier General Beebe, his chief of staff, and said that he was going to surrender the harbor defenses at noon. Wainwright considered it critically important to bring the fighting to an end during daylight when control of the situation would be much easier for the Americans—and the Japanese. Wainwright's intent was to surrender only the four forts in Manila Bay. A radio message was sent to the American commanders in the southern Philippines releasing them from Wainwright's command and directing them to continue resistance.

END OF THE BATTLE

A prearranged code word, "Pontiac," had been designated for this situation. Upon receipt of the code word units were to destroy all weapons above .45-caliber. This would allow the troops to retain their small arms, but would set in motion the process of disabling the important heavy coast artillery weapons so the enemy would not be able to use them. Not all units got the message to surrender, while others did not know what "Pontiac" meant when the word was received.

The exhausted men manning the final line outside Malinta Tunnel were told of the decision to surrender as they were trying to reestablish a defense. Lieutenant Colonel Beecher informed Major Williams of the decision when the latter entered Malinta Tunnel looking for additional men and weapons to put into the line. By then it was about 1130.

The word was also passed to the other, still uncommitted, elements of the 4th Marines, the 2nd and 3rd Battalions on Middleside and Topside. Many of the Marines could not believe it; after all they had not engaged the enemy yet. Some cried, others sat dejectedly around their defensive positions. As the word of the impending surrender circulated among the men some smashed their small arms and machine guns in anger and bitterness, whether they knew the intent of "Pontiac" or not.

In Tunnel Queen Captain Hoeffel received word of the impending surrender shortly before 1100. Word was passed to the Navy officers who then informed their men. Many wept openly. The 1st Battalion Navy surgeon, Lieutenant G. T.

Ferguson, who had been the ship's doctor on the little gunboat *Wake* until just before the start of the war, went outside the tunnel and cried, despite Japanese artillery fire still landing nearby. Others took the news in stride, breaking into food supplies to get a really good meal, the first in months for many.

The senior Navy officer in the Philippines drafted a note to be sent by radio. Captain Hoeffel walked into the radio room in Tunnel Queen and handed the message to the duty operator, telling him not to worry about encoding the transmission: "One hundred and seventy-three officers and twenty three hundred seventeen men of the Navy reaffirm their loyalty and devotion to country, families, and friends."[2]

The 2,490 officers and men mentioned in Kenneth Hoeffel's last message must have included the Filipino naval reservists, but did not account for those killed in the past twenty-four hours of fighting. Unfortunately, dozens of sailors had perished in the final battle for The Rock.

After Captain Hoeffel's message was dispatched the two senior Navy communications officers, Lieutenant Commander F. H. Callahan and Lieutenant Commander Melvyn H. McCoy, drafted a final message from Radio Cavite. It was sent to Hawaii in the clear, without code: "Going off air now. Goodbye and good luck. Callahan and McCoy."[3]

Melvyn McCoy thought to himself that he had been correct the afternoon before when he could not make it back to Tunnel Afirm due to the intense Japanese shelling; here he was in Tunnel Queen about to be taken prisoner.[4] Now he wondered what would come next as they awaited the Japanese. As McCoy pondered his fate, the Navy communications personnel in Tunnel Queen proceeded to smash their radio gear and burn their code books.

Colonel Howard was in Malinta Tunnel preparing to join his men in the trench outside the east entrance when he was told of the decision to surrender. For the senior Marine in the campaign it was devastating news. Sam Howard knew how much his men had sacrificed during the past few months. Although he did not know how many had become casualties during the past few hours of fighting on The Rock, he was certainly aware that losses had been heavy; he had seen the procession of wounded being brought into the tunnel during the early morning hours. When word of the surrender arrived the regimental XO, Colonel Curtis, ordered Captain Robert B. Moore of the Headquarters Company to take the 4th Marines' colors outside the tunnel and burn them. When the captain returned to report the job was accomplished Howard finally broke down. Putting his head in his hands, crying, the colonel said, "My God, and I had to be the first Marine officer ever to surrender a regiment."[5]

GOING TO MEET THE JAPANESE

If getting the word out to the scattered American elements around Corregidor and the other harbor forts was hard, the real challenge was informing the Japanese that General Wainwright had decided to surrender. It was essential that the enemy leadership be told that resistance would cease at noon. Japanese artillery was still pounding Corregidor and the other islands and enemy aircraft were making numerous attacks on the fortified islands. Most importantly, enemy troops were closing in on Malinta Tunnel.

As early as 1030 a radio broadcast by General Beebe over the Voice of Freedom was made, telling the Japanese that the American command intended to surrender at noon. When Beebe finished speaking an interpreter read the message in Japanese. No reply was received and no indication came from the enemy that they had heard, or believed, the transmission. The message was repeated at 1230 with no effect; the bombing and shelling continued. There was clearly a need to meet with the Japanese leadership. The duty of taking the surrender message to the enemy fell to the 4th Marines.

Colonel Howard selected Captain Golland Clark and 1st Lieutenant Alan Manning to go forward to the Japanese under flag of truce. Accompanying them was a Marine bugler and an interpreter. Lieutenant Manning carried a white flag. Leaving Malinta Tunnel about 1300 the group headed out past the shattered concrete trench where some men were still in position facing toward the enemy. As the surrender party moved out Major Williams brought the surviving men into Malinta Tunnel to get shelter from the still-falling artillery fire.

The Japanese were not far away. Clark and Manning had only gone a few hundred yards when they met the leading elements of the 61st Infantry cautiously advancing toward Malinta Hill. The Japanese infantrymen had received instructions for this type of possibility; they did not fire on the approaching Americans. The group was taken to meet with Colonel Mooto Nakayama from the 14th Army staff. Coincidentally, Colonel Nakayama was the same senior Japanese officer who had met with Major General King to accept the surrender of the Luzon Force on Bataan nearly a month earlier. Captain Clark informed him of General Wainwright's desire to surrender. The Japanese colonel radioed 14th Army headquarters on Bataan with the news that he was meeting with an American delegation bearing a surrender message. Shortly thereafter Nakayama said he would arrange a meeting of General Wainwright with General Homma, a meeting that would take place on Bataan. Clark returned to Malinta Tunnel and informed General Wainwright of the Japanese proposal.

An hour or so after Clark's return General Wainwright, accompanied by Major General Moore, Brigadier General Beebe, and their aides, proceeded from Malinta Tunnel to the Denver Battery ridge. Captain Clark acted as guide. As they traveled by car and on foot the Americans saw dead and dying men all around them, evidence of just how bitter the battle had been.

Wainwright met with General Homma on Bataan late that afternoon. Expecting the Japanese to accept his surrender, the American commander was stunned to find that Homma insisted that Wainwright surrender all remaining American and Filipino units throughout the Philippines. It had been Wainwright's intent to only surrender the four harbor forts in Manila Bay. When Homma learned this he refused to accept the surrender. Shelling and bombing continued. A crestfallen and profoundly worried Wainwright had to return to Corregidor. With the implementation of "Pontiac" the troops no longer had significant means to resist.[6]

THE STRANGEST SURRENDER

In what was to be possibly the strangest large-scale military surrender in modern times, the Japanese maintained the façade of conducting a real operation for the next two days. On 7 May they occupied the rest of Corregidor, bombing and shelling as they went, despite the complete lack of resistance. American officers kept their men under cover as enemy troops approached; no resistance was offered as the Japanese slowly occupied the island. A number of men were killed in the next day or two as the Japanese continued to shell and bomb the islands before occupying them. During the next two days the surviving troops from around Corregidor turned themselves in or were rounded up by the Japanese.

By late on the afternoon of 6 May Lieutenant Lawrence and his men had not heard any firing for hours. Lawrence gave his men a chance to vote as to what to do next. The vote was clearly for surrender. Lawrence formed the men up and they moved westward. The Japanese did not spot them until they were about at Kindley Field. There they were taken prisoner. Lawrence was convinced that the enemy had no idea that these eighty men were responsible for the destruction of most of the 2nd Battalion of the 61st Infantry. He was sure the Japanese would have killed them had they known.

General Wainwright had to quickly start the process of convincing the commanders in the southern islands to surrender. Throughout that lengthy process he remained concerned that the Japanese would kill the 12,500 prisoners on Corregidor if the commanders in the south refused to give up.

As the Japanese collected prisoners they used them to bury the dead from the fighting on 5–6 May. Burial parties were under Japanese guard and given very little time to dispose of the dead. Japanese corpses had a portion of the body removed for cremation and transport back to Japan. The rest of the body was burned on the island. When the prisoners encountered an American or Filipino body they had to bury it on the spot. Given the rock-hard ground of Corregidor, this was often a difficult task. A hasty, shallow grave was all that could be provided.

After a couple of days when they were under relatively little supervision by the enemy, the prisoners were herded into the area of the 92nd Coast Artillery garage on the south side of the Tail, very close to where the battle had taken place along the Denver ridge. Living conditions were appalling, with little food or water and no latrine facilities other than the nearby sea. On 23 May most of the men were loaded on a ship. The next day the prisoners were moved across the Bay to Manila where they were paraded through the city streets. From there they were broken up into groups and sent to the various prison camps in the Philippines where they joined the survivors of Bataan.

It was not until General Wainwright convinced the remaining units in the southern islands to surrender that the Japanese finally officially honored the prisoner of war status of the Americans and Filipinos who had surrendered on Corregidor. The change of status took place on 9 June, more than a month after the final battle on The Rock.

THE COST

There have been various estimates of how many American and Filipino troops died in the final battle for Corregidor. Some sources have claimed up to five hundred men were killed. That figure is much too high. In the early 1960s when the Belote brothers were researching *Corregidor: The Saga of a Fortress* they interviewed a number of survivors. Some of those men had fought on the Tail, while others had been in the burial parties that combed through the underbrush and craters on the Tail of the island to find American, Filipino, and Japanese bodies. Although there was not then, nor is there today, an accurate count of the Americans and Filipinos killed on the island, those who fought in the final battle or who helped find the bodies afterwards thought that the number of friendly troops killed on the Tail was between one hundred and three hundred.[7]

During the entire Philippine Campaign the 4th Marines (including the 1st Separate Marine Battalion prior to it becoming 3rd Battalion, 4th Marines) lost eighty-nine men. As of 2 May, just before the Regimental Record of Events was carried out on the submarine *Spearfish*, the number of Marines who had died from all causes was thirty-two (including one accidental death and three listed as suicide). During the very heavy bombardment from 3–5 May several other Marines were killed, most notably Major Lang, the A Company commander. Assuming five to ten Marines died in the last three days of shelling and bombing before the Japanese landed, we can infer that about fifty Marines were killed in the twelve hours of fighting on 5–6 May.[8]

As with all personnel issues in this campaign, the Navy records are not as complete as the Marines'. We do know that a large number of sailors became casualties during the final day of battle on Corregidor. The 4th Battalion, 4th Marines was about 95 percent Navy personnel. Other sailors were scattered among the 1st Battalion and the Regimental Reserve. It is probable that about four hundred sailors fought as infantrymen on the Tail of Corregidor. How many died?

At least seventeen, and possibly as many as twenty, crewmen from *Canopus* died including Lieutenant Otter, the highest ranking Navy officer killed in the final battle for Corregidor.[9] The *Canopus* men were all assigned to the 4th Battalion. Other sailors from various Navy organizations were killed in the fighting, although the exact number will never be known. Ensign Lloyd, who died atop the Denver ridge with Lieutenant Otter, was from the Inshore Patrol headquarters, for example. According to Captain Dalness, USA, the 4th Battalion suffered at least 15 officer casualties, along with about 150 enlisted men, roughly 50 percent of the battalion's total strength. Most of these men became casualties either during the fighting around the water tanks on Denver ridge or during the retreat to the final line outside Malinta Tunnel. Due to the very poor medical capability of the 4th Battalion, and the great difficulty in evacuating wounded men from the area of the Denver ridge to Malinta Tunnel it is likely that an unusually high percentage of the wounded perished. The Japanese apparently made no effort to help wounded Americans or Filipinos that they came across as they pursued the retreating Americans toward Malinta Tunnel; those wounded they encountered were almost certainly killed. A precise count is not possible, but when men who were in the 1st Battalion and Companies O and P are included it seems likely that between fifty and seventy-five sailors were killed during the final battle. Several dozen American and Filipino Army personnel also died.

According to a 1 May 1942 estimate by Wainwright's headquarters there were 12,692 military and 2,036 civilians on the fortified islands. Wainwright's report admits that the 1 May estimate was probably not completely accurate, but it is the best available information on the number of personnel still alive on the first day of May. The Japanese claim to have captured 12,495 military prisoners on Corregidor and the other harbor forts. As we will soon see, a few Americans managed to escape the final surrender. If 25 escapees are deducted from the 1 May total of military personnel, and assuming the Japanese prisoner count is correct, it means that about 170 American and Filipino military personnel perished between 3 and 6 May. The vast majority of those deaths would have occurred during the twelve hours of combat after the Japanese landed.[10] This is further confirmation that roughly 150 defenders were killed in the final battle for The Rock.

What of the Japanese? There has long been speculation in English-language accounts of the campaign concerning enemy casualties during the battle for Corregidor. There are, however, very precise, unit-by-unit, casualty figures in the Japanese official history. According to that source, 385 Japanese were killed and 50 were listed as missing during the fighting on 5–6 May. An additional 419 men were wounded in action, for a total of 854 casualties. Apparently the enemy lost 31 out of 52 landing craft that had started the operation; two of the five tanks that embarked for The Rock were sunk with their landing barges.[11] In addition to the losses of troop-carrying landing craft it appears that several of the small gunboats that supported the landing were also destroyed.

A FEW ESCAPE

Late in the morning of the surrender there was considerable confusion on Fort Hughes. Around 1100 the fortress commander, Colonel Foster, USA, lost telephone and radio contact with Corregidor. Foster allowed his remaining guns to continue firing as he tried to find out what was happening.

The sailors of *Mindanao* continued to fire the old 12-inch mortars of Battery Craighill. Up to the final day of fighting they had not lost a man. Then tragedy struck. Two crewmen were killed by enemy artillery fire that morning. Still, the sailors continued to fire during breaks in the enemy barrage when they could get into the mortar pits. In midmorning a very accurate bombing attack took place. Two of their three remaining mortars suffered damage and had to drop out of action. That left one weapon that continued to fire on the enemy.

When word finally came to surrender it did not include any instructions to destroy weapons or equipment. Colonel Foster ordered classified documents to be destroyed, but did not give permission to "spike" the remaining guns. At noon firing stopped. *Mindanao*'s sailors slumped down in the protected concrete magazines and in the adjacent tunnel that ran down toward the eastern end of the island. From 12 April to 6 May they had fired about five hundred 12-inch rounds from their old mortars. Now everyone was wondering what would happen next.

On the island's high western tip the crew of the gunboat *Luzon* were still manning the seaward-facing 14-inch gun of Battery Gillespie. Because their huge weapon could not bear on either Bataan or Cavite the sailors had been sitting out the last four weeks in their concrete magazines with little to do. At least they were protected from enemy shellfire. Now the word came that the fortified islands were going to surrender. About a mile away, just off Corregidor's Tail, lay their ship. Several of the crew asked their officers if they could open fire on the ship with the 3-inch gun that they had pulled up the hillside for just this purpose. Certainly *Luzon* could not be allowed to fall into enemy hands.

Unfortunately the word from the Army command on Fort Hughes was not to destroy equipment unless permission was received from Corregidor. Not really understanding the purpose of such an order, the sailors sat back to await their fate, with their damaged, but still-floating, ship in full view.

That morning Lieutenant Commander Morrill and most of his men were aboard *Quail* a few hundred yards south of Malinta Hill, watching the fireworks on Corregidor. Morrill was very frustrated, having not been permitted to take the ship into the North Channel to engage the enemy landing barges. At roughly 0430 he was directed to move his crew ashore to Fort Hughes. When they arrived via one of the sweeper's motor launches, Morrill reported to Colonel Foster who put some of the crew to work performing odd jobs, while others manned beach defense positions on the eastern end of the island. A few of the crew were on Corregidor in the Navy tunnels.

At 1100 Morrill was thinking that it was time to scuttle *Quail*. Formal orders had not been received to do so; however, Captain Hoeffel had informed his commanding officers days before that they were to scuttle the ships if a series of pyrotechnics were fired above Malinta Hill. This was a backup plan in case the Navy command in Tunnel Queen lost radio contact with its ships. Morrill and Lieutenant Commander Brooks, the commanding officer of *Luzon*, asked Colonel Foster if any of his observers had noticed such a display over Corregidor. The reply was that what appeared to be a 4th of July–like display had been seen a few minutes earlier near Malinta Hill. That was good enough for Morrill. Although he could not raise Tunnel Queen by phone, he decided it was time to scuttle his ship. Brooks was apparently convinced that *Luzon* would sink on her own.[12]

Morrill took five men from the crew out to *Quail* to finish the task of sinking the ship so the Japanese could not take her. They found a 36-foot motor whaleboat and used it to dash from the Fort Hughes dock toward Corregidor's Tail where several Navy ships lay sunk or sinking. Using each hulk as cover, they darted from ship to ship until they reached *Quail*. A few men were spotted on the bow of *Mindanao*; that part of the ship was still above water. Some rifle and machine-gun rounds were fired at them from Corregidor, but no one was hit. When they reached *Quail* it only took a few minutes to open valves to let the sea in. The men reboarded their launch and headed toward the little Army tug

Ranger, which was lying anchored a few hundred yards from the north shore of Fort Hughes.

The tug's crew had abandoned their vessel. Fortunately, there was still a considerable amount of food, weapons and ammunition, water, and diesel fuel on board. Morrill noticed that there were also charts and navigating gear. An idea started to germinate in his mind—a plan to escape. By now it was early afternoon and the firing from the forts had stopped, although Japanese artillery and aircraft were still pounding them. Further evidence of the surrender was seen when the Army started to detonate its mines at the entrance of the Bay. Morrill and his crew watched rows of huge geysers erupt from the entrance of North Channel as the Army exploded its electrically controlled mines. While they hid on *Ranger*, the men watched *Quail* slowly sink, the last ship of the Inshore Patrol to go down in Manila Bay.

After dark Morrill and his men left *Ranger* and returned to Fort Hughes. Although the surrender had taken place, the Japanese had not yet occupied the fort. As many of the ship's crew as could be found, were rounded up. Morrill explained his idea to the men; he planned to escape to the south in the motor whaleboat that was now loaded with provisions, guns, and fuel. The danger was obvious—if the Japanese caught them they would almost certainly be killed. Morrill said each man had to decide whether he wanted to chance it; this would be a voluntary voyage. Some of the exhausted men were clearly not in good enough psychological condition to attempt such a hazardous journey. Realizing the great risk, seventeen men decided to give it a try, including *Quail*'s gunnery officer, Warrant Gunner Donald Taylor.

Just after 2200 on the night of 6 May, over ten hours after General Wainwright had surrendered the harbor forts, eighteen officers and men of *Quail* headed out directly over the minefield in their motor launch. They barely managed to avoid Japanese destroyers still patrolling off the entrance to Manila Bay as they slowly proceeded southward. Many harrowing adventures were to follow as they sailed mostly at night, hiding out ashore during the daylight hours. Sailing through Japanese-controlled territory in the Philippines and the Dutch East Indies they stopped to beg, buy, or trade for fuel and food as they went, always hoping the locals would not turn them in to the Japanese.

On 6 June 1942 Lieutenant Commander John Morrill and the other seventeen officers and men of the minesweeper *Quail* reached the port of Darwin on the north coast of Australia. Their journey had taken a month; they had traveled over two thousand miles. At first the Australian authorities refused to believe they were escapees from Corregidor; nobody could have sailed that far through enemy-controlled waters in such a small boat. Morrill and his crew were arrested. It was not until the senior U.S. Army officer in Darwin arrived to quiz the men about "things American" was it determined that these men were, indeed, who they claimed to be.[13]

The men of *Quail* were the largest group of escapees from the final surrender in Manila Bay. It was a magnificent example of leadership, bravery, and seamanship. Their arrival in Darwin coincided with the end of the initial phase of the Pacific War. Two days earlier the U.S. Navy had won a spectacular victory at the Battle of Midway.

CHAPTER 17

Reflections

The campaign in the Philippines effectively ended on 6 May when Corregidor surrendered. It would take General Wainwright several more weeks to arrange for the surrender of the various units of the Visayan-Mindanao Force in the southern islands, but the troops in the south were so poorly armed that they had no chance of resisting the Japanese in conventional combat. In the coming months and years the Americans and Filipinos who did not surrender on Luzon or in the southern islands slowly built up a guerilla force to contest the Japanese occupation as they waited for the U.S. military to return.

The Philippine Campaign of 1941–42 was largely an Army affair. There were about 87,000 U.S. and Philippine Army troops on Bataan and the fortified islands in early January, compared to about 2,400 American Navy personnel and fewer than 1,600 Marines. The sea services played a supporting role to the Army, but it was an important one.

From the Navy's perspective Manila Bay had become untenable for significant operations once the Cavite Navy Yard was destroyed on 10 December 1941. With the enemy clearly in control of the air, the Navy's larger ships had to leave the northern Philippines. What remained behind—the gunboats, minesweepers, *Canopus* and *Pigeon* to enable submarine operations, the PT boats, and other small craft—supported the Army by patrolling the east and west coasts of Bataan and conducting occasional raids against Subic Bay. Submarines were also able to occasionally make use of Manila Bay for quick refueling and rearming under cover of darkness, usually taking evacuees with them when they departed.

The sailors who remained in the Manila Bay area during the siege were called upon to do some very unusual things in addition to operating their ships.

Fighting as infantry, manning coastal defense guns, and providing maintenance support for the Army were not normal fare for the Navy.

For the Marines the campaign was a frustrating experience in many respects. Never before or since has the Corps lost an entire regiment in combat. For the men of the 4th Marines the experience involved spending months being shelled and bombed, enduring decreasing rations, and working hard at their assigned missions only for most of them to never see direct combat against the Japanese. With the exception of some men who fought at Longoskawayan Point, the 2nd and 3rd Battalions of the regiment never engaged in close combat with the enemy. The 1st and 4th Battalions and the Regimental Reserve fought a bitter battle against the enemy on Corregidor's Tail, but the fight only lasted about twelve hours. The final stand of the 4th Marines on The Rock should always be remembered with pride by the Corps even though less than half the regiment's personnel were Marines by the time of the final battle. The men endured the most severe artillery and aerial bombardment ever suffered by U.S. troops in World War II and still stood their ground, inflicting very heavy losses on their attackers in the final day of battle on Corregidor.

WHAT COULD HAVE BEEN DONE DIFFERENTLY

It is important to recognize that the garrison in the Philippines was going to be defeated, regardless of what they did. The Japanese were much stronger than the combined American-British-Dutch-Australian forces that were available in the western Pacific and Southeast Asia at the start of the war. To borrow from the title of William Bartsch's excellent account of the Army pursuit squadrons in the Philippines, the garrison was truly "doomed at the start" even if the men and their leaders did not realize it at first. The only issues were how long were they going to be able to hold out, how much was it going to cost the Japanese to overwhelm the defenders, and how many men would be lost in the process of trying to extend the campaign as long as possible. This situation was precisely what the planners foresaw in the two decades before the war.

Given that reality, could some things have been done differently that would have improved the Navy and Marine Corps contribution during the defense? The answer is without doubt, yes.

First, the Navy's submarines should have performed better. Both Admiral Hart and General MacArthur were counting on the submarines to inflict serious damage on an approaching invasion fleet. The main reasons for the failure to do so was the very poor-quality torpedoes with which the submarines were armed and a lack of aggressiveness on the part of a number of the submarine commanders. Bad torpedoes were not the fault of the Asiatic Fleet. That was the responsibility of the Navy Department during the period between the two world wars; the weapons had not been properly tested. On the other hand, Admiral Hart and Captain Wilkes could have deployed more subs in the immediate vicinity of the likely main landing areas, especially Lingayen Gulf.

The Navy should have moved more fuel oil to Bataan before Manila was declared an Open City in late December. In large part this was the Army's fault for not giving Admiral Hart more advanced warning that WPO-3 was about to be ordered. Thinking that Manila would soon be occupied, the Navy pulled most of its assets out of the capital and Sangley Point by Christmas Day, blowing up or burning most of its remaining fuel supplies during the two days that was available before the Philippine capital was supposed to be declared an Open City. Had more of that fuel oil been moved to Bataan and Corregidor during the period 13–25 December the activities of the ships of the Inshore Patrol would not have been as badly curtailed by early March.

Even with the limited amount of fuel available the ships of the Inshore Patrol could have been employed more aggressively, especially in January and early February during the first battle on Bataan. For example, the gunboats could have made nightly raids along the east coast of Bataan firing at the Japanese onshore. That is exactly what the Japanese were doing with the watercraft that they had salvaged and armed in Manila. Given the short distance from their anchorages to the front lines on eastern Bataan, gunboats (but not the minesweepers; the water off the northeast coast of Bataan was too shallow) could have conducted bombardment missions during the hours of darkness and still been back under the protection of Corregidor's anti-aircraft guns by dawn.

Elements of the 4th Marines could have been used to conduct raids on Cavite Province to harass or eliminate the Japanese artillery that was firing on the fortified islands. Some middle-grade Marine officers suggested such a course of action, but were turned down. The Inshore Patrol had plenty of ships to carry raiding parties of one to two hundred Marines over to Cavite at night. In addition to the ships' guns, raids around Ternate and Naic could have been supported by the Army's coastal artillery on Forts Frank, Drum, and Hughes.

Prior to the fall of Bataan, when it had become clear that the enemy would attack Corregidor from Bataan rather than from either Cavite or outside the Bay, Colonel Howard should have strengthened the defenses on the north shore of the island and created a stronger reserve. As it was, the Regimental Reserve—the force that would decide the battle once the enemy landed somewhere on The Rock—consisted of fewer than two hundred trained Marines in Companies O and P and the roughly three hundred poorly trained sailors of the 4th Battalion. Although movement around Corregidor became increasingly difficult following the fall of Bataan as more and more Japanese artillery got into action, reshuffling troops at night was an option. According to all accounts Japanese artillery fire was far less intense after dark until the last few days when the enemy was conducting his final pre-assault bombardment of the landing beaches on the north shore of the island. Therefore, it would have been possible to take companies from the 2nd and 3rd Battalions—trained Marines—who were manning beach defense positions facing south and westward on Topside and replace them with the sailors of the 4th Battalion. That would have provided more well-trained and better armed Marines for the all-important reserve.

Assuming that the 4th Battalion was to be the final reserve, it needed more heavy weapons to support a counterattack. The battalion went into action with nothing heavier than hand grenades, BARs, and rifles. Clearly it needed some heavier weapons to provide fire support. Several 37-mm guns and mortars should have been withdrawn from other parts of the regiment and provided to the 4th Battalion in a weapons company while the unit was forming in Government Ravine during April. As an absolute minimum a couple of machine-gun platoons should have been created for the battalion.

Finally, the mid-February decision by the Army not to send a tank platoon to Corregidor was a mistake. There were certainly enough tanks still on Bataan to spare three or four vehicles for Corregidor. If the defenders had had even one or two tanks during the counterattacks on the Denver Battery ridge it is quite likely that they would have overwhelmed the Japanese and driven them off the island.

Note that I have not criticized the use of the 4th Marines as beach defense troops on Corregidor. It is true that the 4th Marines could have been employed as a unit on Bataan. That is clearly what Colonel Howard wanted when he spoke with General MacArthur and Major General Sutherland in Manila on Christmas Eve 1941. However, given the perception that the regiment needed more field training after the long years in Shanghai, and the importance of protecting Corregidor from amphibious or airborne assault, the decision to employ the Marines on The Rock was appropriate.

In the final analysis, however, all the possible steps listed above—and more—would still not have saved Bataan or Corregidor. Perhaps if the Japanese had delayed going to war until April, as MacArthur had hoped, the defense might have been much more successful. In December 1941, however, there was no doubt that the Japanese would eventually win. It took the American leadership in Washington until February to finally come to the realization that the garrison was doomed. Perhaps mercifully, most of the soldiers, sailors, and Marines fighting in the Manila Bay area did not reach the same conclusion until sometime later. They existed on hope.

ARMY–NAVY RELATIONS IN THE AFTERMATH OF THE PHILIPPINE CAMPAIGN

From the end of 1935 when he stepped down as chief of staff of the Army to the summer of 1941 when he was recalled to active duty, MacArthur had been the military adviser to the Philippine government. The commanders of the Asiatic Fleet during those years had relatively little need to interact with him. Rather, their formal Army point of contact in the Philippines was always the active-duty major general who commanded the Army's Philippine Department. It was not until late July 1941 when MacArthur was recalled to active duty and placed in command of USAFFE that he started to interact with the sea services on official matters. The experience was not a good one for the U.S. Navy.

MacArthur's treatment of Admiral Hart became increasingly bad during the fall of 1941. Although Thomas Hart was one of the very few people who could say that he had somewhat of a friendship with MacArthur, in the last few weeks before the start of the war the relationship between the two deteriorated dramatically. Hart was becoming wary of MacArthur's judgment and motives, while becoming ever more aware of MacArthur's huge ego that often crossed the line into megalomania. Shortly before the start of the war Hart confided to his wife his feeling about the General whom he had once been able to call a friend: "Douglas is, I think, no longer altogether sane—he may not have been for a long time."[1]

Once war started MacArthur showed his true colors. In the immediate aftermath of the disaster of Clark Field on the first day of war he started to manipulate the news coming out of the Philippines. The General also looked for others to blame for the deteriorating situation in the Philippines. As we have seen, he turned on the Navy. Hart's reputation took such a beating due to MacArthur's claims that the Navy was not supporting him, and had a "defeatist" attitude, that this very honorable, capable, and realistic admiral was recalled to the United States in mid-February.

When Hart got back to Washington he spoke with the senior Navy leadership about his experiences in the Philippines and his dealings with MacArthur. Additionally, Navy officers in the Philippines wrote official reports on what was *really* happening, as opposed to MacArthur's often fictitious press releases and messages to General Marshall in Washington. A number of Navy officers managed to escape from the Manila Bay area before the surrender of Corregidor. Some of them, like Lieutenant Commander Cheek and Lieutenant Commander Knoll, understood the big picture in the Philippines due to the positions that they held as 16th Naval District intelligence officers. They *knew* what had really happened and were not at all hesitant to write and talk about it within Navy circles. Admiral Rockwell also had the opportunity to discuss the events in the Philippines with the Navy leadership. It soon became clear to the Navy's senior leaders what had happened to Thomas Hart at the hands of Douglas MacArthur. Long before the fall of Bataan the Navy leadership knew exactly what they were dealing with in Douglas MacArthur. By the spring of 1942 the Navy clearly understood what this man was all about.

It was in large part due to their experience with MacArthur in the Philippines that the Navy absolutely refused to agree to a unified Pacific Theater Command under the General. At this point in the war Army chief of staff George Marshall was still supporting and defending MacArthur (although as the war progressed, Marshall became increasingly skeptical of MacArthur's judgment). The Navy, however, was wise to him. In particular, the new CNO, Admiral King, would not consider the idea of the Pacific Theater, which the Navy had for decades considered its main area of operations, coming under MacArthur's control. The Navy's bad experiences with MacArthur in the first Philippine Campaign contributed directly to the Pacific being divided into the Southwest Pacific Area under the General, and the Central Pacific commanded by Admiral Chester W. Nimitz, MacArthur's better in every way, except in the area of generating publicity.

In the first few decades after World War II the public perception of MacArthur was quite positive. In the past thirty years, however, the view historians have developed regarding the General has changed profoundly—and not for the better. As one recent study of the war put it: "His erratic performance in the Philippines should have led to his relief and retirement, but, instead, the Medal of Honor and a flood of media attention, encouraged by Roosevelt, diverted attention from America's military disasters. Then, having created a monster, FDR and the Joint Chiefs of Staff had to live with MacArthur and his powerful friends."[2] A recent devastatingly critical biography described MacArthur as a classic case of an extreme narcissistic personality disorder, and a profoundly flawed man.[3]

One of George Marshall's biographers noted that, "the Navy hated MacArthur, really hated him." The United States Navy had every right and reason to hate Douglas MacArthur.[4]

WHAT HAPPENED TO THEM

The data on Navy and Marine casualties during the campaign contains some inconsistencies. As with other personnel data, the information on the Marines is more precise than that available for the Navy. According to official sources, during the first Philippine Campaign the Navy suffered 337 officers and men killed in action or died of wounds, not including casualties among the Filipino naval reservists. There is no accurate record of the number of Navy personnel wounded in action, but it certainly numbered a few hundred. The Marine Corps lost 89 men killed in action or died of wounds during the same period. Officially, 167 Marines were wounded in action, although due to the confused situation of the last few weeks of the siege of Corregidor it is possible that total is low.[5] Of the 426 sailors and Marines who died during the fighting at least 100 were killed during the final twelve hours of resistance on Corregidor.

The nearly three and a half year period of captivity was more deadly than the five months of combat. The best estimate for the 4th Marines is 474 personnel died in captivity out of roughly 1,480 prisoners of war. The Japanese took about 2,050 sailors prisoner on Corregidor and the other harbor forts. Additionally, approximately 250 Navy personnel had been captured in Manila in early January. According to the Navy's postwar official accounting of personnel, about 630 sailors captured in the Philippines died while prisoners of the Japanese. Some of the men were murdered by their captors, others died from neglect (disease and malnutrition), and many perished on board the "Hell Ships" that were inadvertently sunk in 1944 by U.S. submarines and aircraft.[6]

I regret that space permits only a limited recounting of what happened to various Navy and Marine Corps personnel who helped defend the Philippines.

Admiral Hart. Thomas Hart returned to the United States in February 1942 and was placed on the retired list in July of that year. He was asked to serve as a member of the Navy's General Board that influenced ship design and production. Hart was appointed as a U.S. Senator in 1945, filling a vacant seat from his home state of Connecticut; he did not seek reelection. He never made any adverse comments about MacArthur in public. After his departure from the Senate this very honorable man retired from public life to his home in Connecticut. Admiral Thomas C. Hart died in 1971 at the age of ninety-four.

Admiral Rockwell. Francis Rockwell remained on active duty for the rest of World War II. Upon arriving in Australia he commanded the U.S. submarine force based on that country's east coast. He later commanded the Amphibious Force, Pacific Fleet, leading the assault on Attu Island in the Aleutians in 1943. Following the Aleutians Campaign he took command of Fleet Operational Training Command, Atlantic Fleet. Retiring from the Navy as a vice admiral in 1948, he died in 1979.

Colonel Howard. The senior Marine in the Philippines, Samuel Howard survived prison camp. Immediately after release at the end of the war he wrote a narrative of the 4th Marines' experience for the Commandant of the Marine Corps. He retired from the Marines in 1953 having reached the rank of lieutenant general. He died in 1960, having spent thirty-eight years in the Marine Corps.

Captain Hoeffel. Kenneth Hoeffel also survived the war. A generally quiet, reserved man, Hoeffel carried a great burden after the departure of Admiral Rockwell. Although he can be faulted for being rather cautious in the employment of the Inshore Patrol, he cared for his sailors and Marines as best he could. Hoeffel retired from the Navy as a rear admiral in 1953. He died in 1971, age seventy-seven, and is now buried in Arlington National Cemetery not far from President John Kennedy.

Commander McCracken. This China gunboat sailor took *Mindanao* through thick and thin. Alan McCracken was liberated when U.S. forces entered Manila in February 1945 and wrote a memorandum on the actions of *Mindanao* for the Secretary of the Navy. He stayed in the Navy after the war, retiring as a rear admiral. He died in 1989.

Lieutenant Commander Morrill. The skipper of *Quail* and his seventeen men were the largest group to escape from the Philippines. Retiring as a rear admiral, John Morrill died in 1997 at the age of ninety-four.

1st Lieutenant Hogaboom. The son of an Army National Guard brigadier general, this hero of Longoskawayan Point and the fighting on Corregidor managed to write down his experiences while in prison camp. Tragically, Bill Hogaboom was on board *Oryoku Maru* when it was sunk by U.S. aircraft off Olongapo in December 1944. He got free of the sinking ship and managed to reach shore. Too far gone to survive, he died on the beach. Fortunately for the annals of the Marine Corps his account was found after the war and published in *Marine Corps Gazette* magazine in 1946.

All of the ships of the Inshore Patrol were lost. The map prepared by Admiral Morrill for the author is the most authoritative source of the final resting place of most of the ships of the Bataan Navy. Interestingly, the gunboat *Luzon* and minesweeper *Finch* were put back in operation by the Japanese. *Luzon* had not been scuttled by her crew due to the fact that the order to destroy equipment (including ships) did not reach Fort Hughes on the morning of 6 May at the time of the surrender.[7] While *Mindanao* and *Oahu* had both foundered, *Luzon* was still afloat, despite several hits from enemy artillery fire. By August the Japanese had repaired her and put her into commission as the gunboat *Kuratsu.* Still operating in the Philippines, her bow was blown off by a torpedo fired by the U.S. submarine *Narwhal* in March 1944. *Luzon* was finally sunk near Manila in February 1945. *Finch* was lying half-sunk alongside Fort Hughes when the enemy occupied the fortified islands. Like *Luzon*, the Japanese were able to put *Finch* back into commission, renaming her *Patrol Boat Number 103.* She was finally sunk in February 1945 by U.S. carrier planes that caught her at sea between Luzon and Formosa. The enemy also seized the little *Maryanne.* She had been moored off Corregidor's south dock the morning of 6 May and her crew was unable to return to the ship in order to scuttle her after they were informed of the surrender. The little yacht's final fate is unknown. The Japanese raised and put the old dry dock *Dewey* back into action, but it too was destroyed by U.S. forces in 1944. The Philippine Army's Q-111 was also salvaged by the Japanese.

FINALE

The campaign in the Philippines in 1941–42 was the worst battlefield defeat ever suffered by the U.S. military. At the time, however, it was seen by the American public as a gallant attempt to stem the Japanese tide in the first months of the war. One has but to look at a war map of the western Pacific on 1 April 1942 to see that the enemy had overrun Malaya, Singapore, Hong Kong, the Dutch East Indies, Guam, Wake, and most of Burma. Meanwhile, two tiny specks remained deep inside enemy-controlled territory—Bataan and Corregidor. Although MacArthur's communiqués were clearly disingenuous, they did stir the U.S. public. "Remember Bataan, Remember Corregidor" were second only to "Remember Pearl Harbor" as rallying cries during the war.

The roughly 2,400 American sailors, 1,560 Marines, some 650 Filipino Navy Reservists, and the 400–500 contractors of the Pacific Naval Air Bases organization gave a good account of themselves during this campaign, even in defeat. Hopefully this narrative, incomplete or flawed as it might be, has done justice to their story.

APPENDIX A

Asiatic Fleet, 7 December 1941

- **Commander in Chief, Asiatic Fleet** Admiral Thomas C. Hart
  –**Chief of Staff** Rear Admiral William R. Purnell
- **Task Force 5** (Rear Admiral William A. Glassford)
  –USS *Houston*[1]
  –USS *Marblehead*[2]
  –USS *Boise*[3]
- **16th Naval District**
  –District Commandant, Rear Admiral Francis W. Rockwell
  –Chief of Staff, Captain Herbert J. Ray
  –Commanding Officer, Section Base Mariveles, Commander W. H. Harrington
  –Captain of the Cavite Navy Yard, Commander R. G. Deewall
  –Captain of the Olongapo Naval Station, Lieutenant (junior grade) V. C. Prewitt
- **Patrol Wing 10** (Captain F. D. Wagner)
  –Patrol Squadrons (VP) 101 and 102 with a total of twenty-eight PBY-4 flying boats
  –Utility Squadron with five OS2U "Kingfisher" and four J2F "Duck" seaplanes
  –Tenders USS *Langley*, *Childs*, *William B. Preston*, and *Heron*[4]

- **Inshore Patrol** (Commander Kenneth M. Hoeffel)
  - –Gunboats *Ashville* and *Tulsa*
  - –River gunboats USS *Oahu*, *Luzon* (flagship), and *Mindanao*[5]
  - –Converted yachts *Isabel* and *Lanikai*

- **Destroyer Squadron 29** (USS *Paul Jones*)
  - –Destroyer Division 59: USS *Pope*, *Peary*, *Pillsbury*, and *John D. Ford*
  - –Destroyer Division 58: USS *Stewart*, *Bulmer*, *Barker*, and *Parrott*
  - –Destroyer Division 57: USS *Whipple*, *Alden*, *John D. Edwards*, and *Edsall*

- **Submarines, Asiatic Fleet**
  - –A total of twenty-nine submarines in three squadrons (six were old World War I–era "S-boats," the rest more modern fleet submarines)
  - –Tenders included USS *Canopus*, *Holland*, and *Otus*
  - –Rescue vessel USS *Pigeon*

- **Minecraft**
  - –USS *Quail*, *Bittern*, *Tanager*, *Lark*, *Finch*, and *Whippoorwill*

- **Miscellaneous vessels**
  - –Floating dry dock *Dewey*
  - –Naval tugs USS *Napa*, *Genesee*, and *Vega*[6]

U.S. Navy Personnel, 1 December 1941

Shore commands	=	800*
Cruisers	=	2,150
Destroyers	=	1,650
Submarines	=	1,590
Gunboats	=	680
PT boats	=	85
Tenders, oilers	=	3,300
Minesweepers	=	450
Patrol Wing 10	=	420
Total	=	11,125

Note: These totals are an approximation, based on all available sources.

*Includes Asiatic Fleet staff, 16th Naval District staff, Cavite Navy Yard, Olongapo Naval Station, Canacao Hospital, tugs and harbor craft, and radio intercept personnel

APPENDIX C

Japanese Artillery Units Available for Bombardment of Corregidor

- 1st Heavy Artillery Regiment. Armed with eight Type 45 240-mm howitzers. These powerful weapons could hurl a 400-pound shell roughly 11,000 yards. This was the same unit that had inflicted considerable damage on Fort Frank in the second half of March.
- 1st Field Heavy Artillery Regiment. Armed with twenty-four Type 96 150-mm howitzers with a range of 12,970 yards.
- 9th Independent Heavy Artillery Battalion. Armed with eight Type 89 150-mm guns; its weapons could range up to 21,800 yards.
- 8th Field Heavy Artillery Regiment. Armed with sixteen Type 92 105-mm guns capable of ranging to 20,000 yards. Half of the 8th's weapons were located in Cavite near Ternate to provide a crossfire effect against the Harbor Defenses.
- 3rd Independent Mountain Gun Regiment. The regiment was armed with twenty-four Type 41 75-mm mountain guns capable of a range of only 7,000 yards. Before the final offensive on Bataan some of the 3rd Regiment's weapons had been mounted on board small vessels that had been seized in Manila and used to shell the American defenses on the east coast of Bataan under cover of darkness. Following the fall of Bataan the 3rd Regiment mounted more of its guns on board barges and motorboats in order to provide fire support for the landing on Corregidor.
- 3rd Battalion, 51st Mountain Artillery Regiment. This battalion was part of the 21st Division whose main body was still in Indochina. It had supported

the regimental-sized Nagano Force from that division during the final offensive on Bataan. The battalion was armed with twelve Type 41 mountain guns. Like the 3rd Independent Regiment, some of this battalion's weapons were mounted on board barges or motorboats to provide fire support to a landing force.

- 4th Field Gun Regiment. This was the divisional artillery regiment of the 4th Division. Armed with sixteen Type 38 75-mm mountain guns (range of 13,080 yards) in its 1st and 2nd Battalions, and eight Type 91 105-mm howitzers (range of 11,500 yards) in its 3rd Battalion.
- 22nd Field Gun Regiment (less one battalion). This was the artillery unit of the 16th Division, which had fought throughout the Bataan campaign. While the other elements of the 16th Division did not participate in the Corregidor operation, the 22nd Regiment deployed twelve Type 38 75-mm mountain guns and twelve Type 91 105-mm weapons for the pre-invasion bombardment.
- 2nd Independent Heavy Artillery Company. This unusual unit consisted of two Type 96 240-mm howitzers (range of 11,000 yards) and two Type 96 150-mm guns with the exceptional range of 27,450 yards.[1]

Notes

Chapter 1. The Navy and Marine Corps in the Philippines

1. "Admiral Thomas Charles Hart," www.microworks.net/pacific/biographies/thomas_hart.htm
2. "Narrative of Naval Activities in Luzon Area, December 1, 1941 to March 19, 1942," Memorandum from Rear Admiral F. W. Rockwell to commander-in-chief, U.S. Fleet, 1 August 1942, 2–5, Louis Morton Collection, U.S. Army Military History Institute, Carlisle, Pa. (hereafter cited as Rockwell Narrative).
3. "Bechtel Corporation: 1940–1945: Bechtel Goes to War," www.bechtel.com/BAC-Chapter-2.html
4. Terrance McGovern and Mark A. Berhow, *American Defenses of Corregidor and Manila Bay, 1898–1945* (Oxford: Osprey Publishing, 2003), 11.
5. Interview with Vice Admiral Kenneth Wheeler, USN (Ret.), March 1986.
6. Celedonio Ancheta, *The Wainwright Papers*, vol. II (Manila: New Day, 1980), 10.
7. Telephone interview of Rear Admiral John H. Morrill, USN (Ret.), by the author, May 1986.
8. Letter to the author from Mr. Rico Jose, Philippine military historian, October 1987.
9. Although often referred to by writers as "Station Cast," the correct designation for the Philippine intercept station is Station C.
10. *Intercept Station C, from Olongapo through the Evacuation of Corregidor, 1929–1942* (Pensacola, Fla.: U.S. Naval Cryptolog Veterans Association, 2003), 4–13, 102–108.

11. Strength of the 4th Marines was determined from the regiment's muster roll reports for 1 December 1941, which are available on microfiche at the Marine Corps Historical Center, Quantico, Va. (hereafter cited as 4th Marine Muster Rolls).
12. 4th Marines Record of Events, 18 December 1941, obtained from the Marine Corps History Division, Quantico, Va.
13. 1 May and 1 December 1941 Muster Rolls, 1st Separate Marine Battalion, obtained from Marine Corps Historical Center, Quantico, Va.
14. William Hogaboom, "Action Report Bataan," *Marine Corps Gazette*, April 1946 (hereafter cited as Hogaboom).
15. Michael Miller, *From Shanghai to Corregidor: Marines in the Defense of the Philippines* (Washington, D.C.: Marine Corps Historical Center, 1997), 3.
16. 4th Marines Record of Events, 14 January 1942.
17. Ibid., 18 December 1941.
18. Lewis Morton, *The Fall of the Philippines* (Washington, D.C.: Office of the Chief of Military History, 1953), 49.

Chapter 2. The Final Days of Peace

1. Memorandum from CINCAF to Commanding General, USAFFE, Subject: Control of Air Operations over Water, 23 October 1941, MacArthur Archives, Norfolk, Va.
2. Memorandum from USAFFE Commander to CINCAF, Subject: Control of Air Operations over Water, 7 November 1941, MacArthur Archives.
3. Memorandum from Army Chief of Staff to Lieutenant General MacArthur, 5 December 1941, MacArthur Archives.
4. Richard Connaughton, *MacArthur and Defeat in the Philippines* (New York: Overlook Press, 2001), 150; Admiral Thomas C. Hart, "Narrative of Events for the Asiatic Fleet Leading to War, and for 8 December 1941 to 15 February 1942," 23, Louis Morton Collection (hereafter cited as Hart Report).
5. Rockwell Narrative, 2–4.
6. www.historycentral.com/Navy/MISC 2/Whippoorwill.html
7. Kemp Tolley, *Yangtze Patrol: The U.S. Navy in China* (Annapolis, Md.: Naval Institute Press, 1971), 278–280.
8. "Report on the Operation, Employment and Supply of the Old 4th Marines from September, 1941 to the Surrender of Corregidor, May 6, 1942 Made from Memory and Some Notes," Memorandum from Brigadier General Samuel L. Howard, U.S. Marine Corps to

Commandant of the Marine Corps, 26 September 1945, 3–4, Marine Corps Historical Center (hereafter cited as Howard Report).

9. Ibid., 3–4.
10. Ibid., 7–8.
11. Deck Log, USS *Pigeon*, 24 November–4 December 1941, National Archives, College Park, Md.
12. Deck Log, USS *Finch*, 3–4 December 1941, National Archives.
13. Tolley, *Yangtze Patrol*, 279–282.
14. "Activities of USS *Mindanao* from September 6, 1941 to May 2, 1942," Memorandum from Commander Alan McCracken to the Secretary of the Navy, June 1945, 2–5, Naval Historical Center (hereafter cited as *Mindanao* Report).
15. Martin Middlebrook and Patrick Mahoney, *Battleship, The Sinking of the Prince of Wales and Repulse* (New York: Charles Scribner's Sons, 1979), 1–71.
16. Connaughton, *MacArthur and Defeat in the Philippines*, 158.
17. Hart Report, 34–36.
18. W. G. Winslow, *The Fleet the Gods Forgot* (Annapolis, Md.: Naval Institute Press, 1982), 255–256.
19. Kemp Tolley, *Cruise of the Lanikai, to Provoke the Pacific War* (Fredericksburg, Md.: Admiral Nimitz Foundation, 1994), 41–54.
20. James Leutze, *A Different Kind of Victory: A Biography of Admiral Thomas C. Hart* (Annapolis, Md.: Naval Institute Press, 1981), 222–224.

Chapter 3. War Begins

1. A photocopy of Hart's message can be seen in Samuel Eliot Morison's *Rising Sun in the Pacific 1931–April 1942* (Boston: Little, Brown, and Company, 1975).
2. 4th Marines Record of Events, 8 December 1941.
3. Dwight R. Messimer, *In the Hands of Fate, the Story of Patrol Wing Ten, 8 December 1941–11 May 1942* (Annapolis, Md.: Naval Institute Press, 1985), 35–38.
4. "War Diary," 16th Naval District, 8 December 1941, National Archives.
5. Messimer, *In the Hands of Fate*, 40–42.
6. FEAF Report, "Airplanes in the Philippines—Present and Projected," 19 November 1941, MacArthur Archives. This document lists 247 aircraft of all types on hand as of 19 November. On 25 November an additional 24 P-40s arrived by ship.
7. Christopher Shores, Brian Cull, and Yasuho Izawa, *Bloody Shambles*, vol. 1 (London: Grub Street, 1992), 165–166.

8. William Bartsch, *December 8, 1941: MacArthur's Pearl Harbor* (College Station: Texas A&M University Press, 2003), 410–424.
9. Shores, Cull, and Izawa, *Bloody Shambles*, vol. 1, 169–175.
10. Two of the Clark-based B-17s were airborne on a reconnaissance mission; four others were damaged. Only one bomber on the ground was completely missed by the enemy. There were an additional sixteen B-17s at Del Monte Field on Mindanao.
11. Shores, Cull, and Izawa, *Bloody Shambles*, vol. 1, 163–174.
12. Clay Blair, *Silent Victory: The U.S. Submarine War against Japan* (New York: Bantam Books, 1975), 127–130.

Chapter 4. The Bombing of the Cavite Navy Yard

1. William H. Bartsch, *Doomed at the Start: American Pursuit Pilots in the Philippines, 1941–1942* (College Station: Texas A&M University Press, 1992), 121–135.
2. A Kokutai was an Imperial Navy air formation consisting of several squadron-sized units. It was a rough equivalent to a western Air Group.
3. Shores, Cull, and Izawa, *Bloody Shambles,* vol. 1, 177–178.
4. Memorandum from Commander Patrol Squadron 101 to Commander PatWing 10, Subject: "Bombing Attack on Japanese Battleship on 10 December 1941," 31 December 1941, Navy Historical Center, Washington, D.C.
5. "Information Regarding Strength and Composition of Japanese Forces, Philippine Islands, Dec 41–May 42," Prepared by U.S. Army G-2 for Army Historical Division, 15 August 1949, 2, Louis Morton Collection.
6. In March the *Takao Maru* was destroyed by Filipino guerillas before the Japanese could salvage the ship.
7. Bartsch, *Doomed at the Start*, 136–150.
8. Shores, Cyull, and Izawa, *Bloody Shambles,* vol. 1, 176–182; Bartsch, *MacArthur's Pearl Harbor*, 149–153.
9. Deck Log, USS *Mindanao*, 10 December 1941, National Archives.
10. J. Daniel Mullin, *Another Six Hundred* (self-published, 1984), 37–44.
11. Messimer, *In the Hands of Fate*, 52–56.
12. Miller, *From Shanghai to Corregidor*, 7.
13. John Morrill and Pete Martin, *South from Corregidor* (New York: Simon and Schuster, 1943), 197–199.
14. "USS Pigeon," www.mississippi.net/-comcasts/tenders/023/0
15. Morrill and Martin, *South from Corregidor*, 199–201.

16. Jake Hertel, *Otus* crew member, letter to the author, December 1986.
17. Memorandum for Commanding Officer, USS *Otus* from the ship's medical officer, 14 December 1941, Subject: Men wounded in air raid, Louis Morton Collection.
18. Miller, *From Shanghai to Corregidor*, 8.
19. Shores, Cull, and Izawa, *Bloody Shambles*, vol. 1, 182.
20. Deck Log, USS *Oahu*, 10 December 1941, National Archives.
21. Robert J. Bulkley, *At Close Quarters: PT Boats in the United States Navy* (Washington, D.C.: Naval History Division, 1962), 5.
22. Malcolm Champlin, "December, 1941," Naval Institute *Proceedings*, December 1971; Letter from Captain Champlin, USNR (Ret.) to the author, February 1986.
23. In his 1986 letter to the author, Champlin was adamant that the Japanese *decreased* their altitude after the first bombing run over the base. The Japanese formation leaders probably noticed that the bursting anti-aircraft shells were several thousand feet below them on their first run, and felt they could lower their attack altitude on their following passes.
24. The 1st Separate Battalion had a very limited number of the more modern mechanical fuze 3-inch rounds that were capable of reaching above 30,000 feet, but the quantities were so small as to be essentially meaningless.
25. John Toland, *But Not in Shame* (New York: Random House, 1961), 73.
26. Miller, *From Shanghai to Corregidor*, 9.
27. John A. Glusman, *Conduct under Fire* (New York: Viking, 2005), 58–61.
28. Rockwell Narrative, 10 December 1941.
29. The surprisingly low total of 25–30 dead from the 16th Naval District is partly corroborated by a statement by Admiral Hart. In Hart's biography, author James Leutze quotes Hart as saying after the raid that some twenty-five of "his young men" were lost. *A Different Kind of Victory*, 233; "US Navy Personnel in World War II, Served and Casualty Statistics," www.history.navy/library/online/ww2_statistics.htm#active_enl
30. A. V. H. Hartendorp, "Story of the First Bombing of Cavite, the Pan American Airways Station, Olongapo," *The American Chamber of Commerce Journal*, Manila, October 1953.
31. "War Diary," 16th Naval District, 20 February 1942, 9 December 1941, Louis Morton Collection.
32. Memorandum from Commander, Mine Division Nine to Commandant, 16th Naval District, 5 March 1942, Subject: "USS *Bittern*, War Damage Received and Abandoning Of," Naval Historical Center.

33. John Prados, *Combined Fleet Decoded* (New York: Random House, 1995), 215.

Chapter 5. Waiting for the Main Attack

1. Interview by the author of Rear Admiral Morrill and Commander Taylor, 1987.
2. Deck Log, USS *Napa*, 11 December 1941, National Archives.
3. Memorandum, USAFFE, 20 December 1941, no subject line, describing the number and type of Navy guns provided to the Army, National Archives.
4. 16th Naval District War Diary, 16 December 1941.
5. Handwritten notes taken by Rear Admiral Purnell at the 13 December meeting, National Archives.
6. Interview by the author of Vice Admiral Wheeler, USN (Ret.), April 1987.
7. 16th Naval District War Diary, 17 December 1941.
8. Morton, *The Fall of the Philippines*, 138–144.
9. Shores, Cull, and Izawa, *Bloody Shambles*, vol 1, 183–184.
10. Messimer, *In the Hands of Fate*, 59–63; "R-2 Journal," 4th Marines Daily Intelligence Summary, 8 December 1941 to 3 May 1942; 12 December 1941 entry, Marine Corps Historical Center; Shores, Cull, and Izawa, *Bloody Shambles*, vol. 1, 184–185.
11. 4th Marines Record of Events, 13 December 1941.
12. Ibid.
13. Ibid.
14. Deck Log, USS *Mindanao*, 16 December 1941.
15. Bulkley, *At Close Quarters*, 7–8.
16. A. V. H. Hartendorp, "The Sinking of the SS *Corregidor*, December 17, 1941," *The American Chamber of Commerce Journal* (Manila), September 1953.
17. Memorandum from Brigadier General E. P. King, USAFFE Artillery Officer, to USAFFE Chief of Staff, 12 November 1941, MacArthur Archives.
18. P. S. Anderson, *Medical Supply in World War II* (Washington, D.C.: Office of the Surgeon General, 1968), 401.
19. 1st Separate Marine Battalion Muster Roll, 1–31 December 1941.
20. Deck Log, USS *Oahu*, 19 December 1941.
21. Rockwell Narrative, 20–21 December 1941.

22. Message from General MacArthur to General Marshall, 10 December 1941, Louis Morton Collection.
23. Memorandum from Flagship US Asiatic Fleet, 10 December 1941, MacArthur Archives.
24. H. P. Willmott, *Empires in the Balance: Japanese and Allied Pacific Strategies to April, 1942* (Annapolis, Md.: Naval Institute Press, 1982), 185, 189.
25. Radio message from General MacArthur to General Marshall, 13 December 1941, MacArthur Archives.
26. Message from General MacArthur to General Marshall, 14 December 1941, MacArthur Archives.
27. Memorandum from MacArthur to CinCAF, 19 December 1941, MacArthur Archives.
28. Message from OPNAV to CinCAF, 17 December 1941, Louis Morton Collection.
29. Memorandum from CinCAF to Commanding General USAFFE, 20 December 1941, MacArthur Archives.
30. Radio message from OPNAV to CinCAF, 23 December 1941, MacArthur Archives.

Chapter 6. The Retreat to Bataan and Corregidor

1. Morton, *Fall of the Philippines*, 125–126.
2. Ibid., 133–138.
3. Blair, *Silent Victory*, 138–141.
4. Ibid., 145–152.
5. Morton, *Fall of the Philippines*, 162.
6. Memorandum from 16th Naval District Intelligence Officer to the Director of Naval Intelligence, Subject: "War Diary," 20 February 1942, Lieutenant Commander Cheek, Naval Historical Center (hereafter cited as Cheek Memorandum).
7. Howard Report, 9–10.
8. Sutherland Diary, Louis Morton Collection.
9. Ancheta, *The Wainwright Papers*, vol. II, 19.
10. Howard Report, 11–12.
11. Interview with Vice Admiral Wheeler, March 1987.
12. Deck Log, USS *Mindanao*, 25 December 1941.
13. Messimer, *In the Hands of Fate*, 102–104.
14. Message from CNO to CinCAF, 29 December 1941, MacArthur Archives.

15. Message from Admiral CinCAF to OPNAV, 2 January 1942, MacArthur Archives.
16. Morison, *The Rising Sun in the Pacific*, 311–312.
17. Morton, *Fall of the Philippines*, 261.

Chapter 7. Settling in for the Siege

1. Mullin, *Another Six Hundred*, 59–60.
2. 4th Marines Record of Events, 24–25 December 1941.
3. Mullin, *Another Six Hundred*, 62–63.
4. 12 January 1942 USAFFE memorandum on strength of all units in the Bataan Service Command area, MacArthur Archives.
5. Letter to the author from Rico Jose, Manila, October 1987.
6. Bulkley, *At Close Quarters*, 5.
7. Howard Report, 13.
8. James H. Belote and William M. Belote, *Corregidor: Saga of a Fortress* (New York: Harper and Row, 1967), 6–9.
9. Ibid.
10. Ancheta, *The Wainwright Papers*, vol. II, 49–53.
11. Undated postwar narrative of Lieutenant Colonel R. F. Jenkins, Marine Corps Historical Center. During the siege Jenkins was a lieutenant in the 1st Battalion, 4th Marines.
12. E. M. Perry, *The Spirit of Canopus* (self-published, 2007), 76–80.
13. Deck Log, USS *Mindanao*, 29 December 1941.
14. Deck Log, USS *Oahu*, 29 December 1941.
15. Ancheta, *The Wainwright Papers*, vol. II, 69.
16. 4th Marines Record of Events, 4 January 1942.
17. Howard Report, 15.
18. Miller, *From Shanghai to Corregidor*, 16–17.
19. 16th Naval District War Diary, 31 December 1941.
20. Messimer, *In the Hands of Fate*, 178–185.
21. Perry, *Spirit of Canopus*, 84–86.
22. 16th Naval District Memo, "Disposition of Employment of Naval Forces, Manila Bay Area," 14 January 1942, Louis Morton Collection; 4th Marines Record of Events, 13–15 January 1942.
23. 4th Marines Record of Events, 14–15 January 1942.
24. Ancheta, *The Wainwright Papers*, vol. II, 7.

25. Elizabeth Norman, *We Band of Angels: The Untold Story of American Nurses Trapped on Bataan by the Japanese* (New York: Random House, 1999); Naval Historical Center Oral Histories, "U.S. Navy Nurse in the Pacific Theater During World War II," http://history.navy.mil/faqs/faq87–3b.htm
26. Ancheta, *The Wainwright Papers*, vol. IV, 55.
27. Ibid., 54–55.
28. Interview with Rear Admiral Morrill, 1987.
29. "Contract No. 4175," 16th Naval District Memorandum, 16 February 1942, National Archives.
30. Memorandum from Commander Motor Torpedo Boat Squadron Three to Commandant 16th Naval District, Subject: "Report of Attack on Enemy Vessel in Port Binanga, 19 January 1942," 20 January 1942, MacArthur Archives.
31. Cheek Memorandum, 19 January 1942 entry.

Chapter 8. Longoskawayan Point

1. 16th Naval District Headquarters Memorandum for Captain Dessez, 9 January 1942, Louis Morton Collection.
2. Memorandum from Commander Bridget to Commandant of 16th Naval District, 9 February 1942, Louis Morton Collection.
3. Miller, *From Shanghai to Corregidor*, 20.
4. Captain E. L. Sackett, USN, "History of the USS *Canopus*," Office of Naval Records, 1942, 12, Louis Morton Collection (hereafter cited as Sackett Report).
5. Ibid.
6. The 65th Brigade, originally intended as a garrison unit for the conquered Philippines, had three two-battalion regiments with a total of roughly 6,700 officers and men. One of its regiments went to the west coast, and was replaced by the stronger, three-battalion 9th Infantry Regiment from the 16th Division. When the 65th attacked down the east coast of Bataan it was reinforced by the 7th Tank Regiment (some fifty Type 89 medium tanks), two field artillery regiments, and an artillery battalion. The artillery units were armed with forty-eight 150-mm and 105-mm guns and howitzers. Morton, *Fall of the Philippines*, 261–264.
7. 4th Marines Record of Events, 16 January 1942; Colonel John Olson, USA (Ret.), *Anywhere-Anytime: The History of the 57th Infantry (PS)* (self-published, 1991), 85–86; Miller, *From Shanghai to Corregidor*, 17.
8. Morton, *Fall of the Philippines*, 279–285.

9. Ibid., 263.
10. Gordon L. Rottman, *Japanese Army in World War II: Conquest of the Pacific* (Oxford: Osprey, 2005), 28–32, 45–48; George Forty, *Japanese Army Handbook, 1939–1945* (Gloucestershire: Sutton Publishing, 1999), 121.
11. Morton, *Fall of the Philippines*, 126, 345.
12. Donald Young, *The Battle of Bataan* (London: McFarland and Co., 1991), 97–98.
13. Diary of Captain Hidaka, 23 January 1942 entry, MacArthur Archives.
14. Cheek Memorandum, 23 January 1942 entry, Louis Morton Collection.
15. Diary of Captain Hidaka, 23 January 1942 entry.
16. Young, *The Battle of Bataan,* 104.
17. Miller, *From Shanghai to Corregidor,* 21.
18. Letter from E. G. Pollack, former member of PatWing 10, to Rear Admiral Kemp Tolley, April 1971, Kemp Tolley Collection, Nimitz Library, U.S. Naval Academy.
19. Hogaboom, 27–28.
20. Miller, *From Shanghai to Corregidor*, 21.
21. This was an old British design from 1898. The inadequate recoil system meant that the weapon had to be tied to the ground before firing. Its advantage was that the little gun could be disassembled and moved fairly easily through poor terrain.
22. Commander Francis Bridget, USN, "Action of Longoskawayan Point against Japanese Forces," Memorandum to Commandant 16th Naval District, 9 February 1942, Louis Morton Collection (hereafter cited as Bridget Report).
23. Diary of Captain Hidaka, 23 January 1942 entry.
24. Ibid., 24 January 1942 entry.
25. Keith Barlow, ed., *Bunker's War* (Novato, Calif.: Presidio Press, 1996), 43.
26. Diary of Captain Hidaka, final entry dated 25 January 1942.
27. Sackett Report, 14.
28. Hogaboom, 28. There is inconsistency in the sources regarding the number of shells fired by Battery Geary in its first shoot. The official record of the Harbor Defenses and USAFFE shows that nine shells were fired.
29. USAFFE G-2 summary, 2 February 1942, MacArthur Archives.
30. Olson, *Anywhere-Anytime*, 20, 89.
31. The Japanese Army issued swords to officers and some NCOs. Some of the swords carried by officers were ancient family heirlooms.

32. USAFFE G-3 Journal, 28 January 1942, MacArthur Archives.
33. Olson, *Anywhere-Anytime*, 112–113.
34. USAFFE G-3 Daily Report, 28 January 1942, MacArthur Archives.
35. Ibid., 29 January 1942, MacArthur Archives.
36. The description of *Quail*'s action is based on an interview with Rear Admiral John Morrill in 1992 and his 30 January 1942 official report to the Commandant of the 16th Naval District, Subject: "Action at Longoskawayan Point, morning of January 29, 1942," Louis Morton Collection, and Morrill and Martin, *South from Corregidor*, 169–181.
37. I Philippine Corps G-2 Report, 31 January 1942, MacArthur Archives.
38. Ibid., 1 February 1942.
39. Bridget Report.
40. Olson, *Anywhere-Anytime*, 118.
41. Letter from E. G. Pollack, former member of PatWing 10, to Rear Admiral Kemp Tolley, April 1971, Kemp Tolley Collection.

Chapter 9. Defeating the First Japanese Offensive

1. Morton, *Fall of the Philippines*, 295.
2. Cheek Memorandum, 31 January 1942 entry.
3. Ibid.
4. Morton, *Fall of the Philippines*, 318–319; Bulkley, *At Close Quarters*, 14–15; Memorandum from Motor Torpedo Boat Division Nine to Commandant 16th Naval District, 3 February 1942, Subject: Attack of USS PT-32 on Enemy Cruiser During Night of 1 February 1942, MacArthur Archives.
5. 4th Marines Record of Events, 8 February 1942.
6. Letter from Commander Goodall to Mr. George Groce, Army Historical Section, 17 August 1948, Louis Morton Collection.
7. Perry, *The Spirit of Canopus*, 98–99; Walter Karig and Welbourn Kelly, *Battle Report, Pearl Harbor to Coral Sea* (New York: Farrar & Rinehart, 1944), 317–318.
8. Duane Schultz, *Hero of Bataan: The Story of General Jonathan M. Wainwright* (New York: St. Martin's Press, 1981), 195–196; interview of Captain Champlin, USNR (Ret.), by the author, May 1987.
9. Deck Log, USS *Mindanao*, 6 February 1942.
10. Memorandum prepared by headquarters, Harbor Defenses of Manila and Subic Bays, 6 February 1942, MacArthur Archives.
11. Interview of Rear Admiral Morrill, USN (Ret.), by the author, 1987.

12. Bartsch, *Doomed at the Start*, 310–313.
13. Kemp Tolley, ed., *American Gunboats in China* (Monkton, Md.: Yangtze River Patrol Association, 1989), 317.
14. Shores, Cull, and Izawa, *Bloody Shambles*, vol. II, 134–135.
15. Deck Log, USS *Mindanao*, 9 February 1942.
16. Ancheta, *The Wainwright Papers*, vol. IV, pg. 71.
17. Deck Log, USS *Mindanao*, 9 February 1942.
18. Radio message from MacArthur to Washington, 25 January 1942.
19. Radio message from MacArthur to the War Department, 27 January 1942.
20. Cheek Memorandum, 16 January 1942 entry.
21. Ibid., 22 January 1942 entry.
22. Memorandum, Office of Naval Intelligence, Washington, D.C., to Chief of Military Intelligence Division, 29 January 1942, Louis Morton Collection.
23. "Intelligence Report, Sixteenth Naval District during Period March 12 to May 3, 1942," Memorandum from Lieutenant Commander Denys W. Knoll to Vice Chief of Naval Operations (Director of Naval Intelligence), undated, 1, Louis Morton Collection (hereafter cited as Knoll Report).
24. Discussions with Captain Champlin, USNR (Ret.), 1987–88; H.P. Willmott, *The Barrier and the Javelin: Japanese and Allied Pacific Strategies, February to June 1942* (Annapolis, Md.: Naval Institute Press, 1983), 165–166.

Chapter 10. The Lull

1. Rockwell Narrative.
2. "USS Pigeon," wwww.mississippi.net/-comcents/tendertale.com/tenders
3. Examination of the daily Deck Logs of USS *Mindanao* and *Oahu* during January–March 1942. The gunboats had a maximum fuel capacity of about 60,000 gallons.
4. Tolley, *American Gunboats in China*, 317.
5. Deck Log, USS *Mindanao*, 31 March 1942.
6. 16th Naval District War Diary, 27 January 1942.
7. Navy records folder, Louis Morton Collection.
8. Connaughton, *MacArthur and Defeat in the Philippines*, 256.
9. Cheek Memorandum.
10. George Forty, *US Army Handbook 1939–1945* (Phoenix Mill: Alan Sutton Publishing, 1995), 1–9; Frank O. Hough et al., *Pearl Harbor to Guadalcanal: History of the U.S. Marine Corps Operations in World War II*, vol. I (Washington, D.C.: Historical Branch U.S. Marine Corps, n.d.), 47–56;

Navy Personnel in World War, www.history.navy.mil/library/online/ww2_statistics.htm

11. Memorandum from Commanding Officer, 4th Marines, to the Commandant of the Marine Corps, Subject: "Intelligence Summary," 4 February 1942, Marine Corps Historical Center.
12. Memorandum for General MacArthur, Subject: Japanese prisoners, 19 February 1942, MacArthur Archives.
13. 4th Marines Record of Events, 16–18 February 1942.
14. Ibid.
15. Ancheta, *The Wainwright Papers*, vol. II, 160.
16. Memorandum from Commander Motor Torpedo Boat Squadron 3 to Commandant 16th Naval District, Subject: "Night Operations, PT-35 and 41 off Subic Bay, the Night of 17–18 February 1942," MacArthur Archives.
17. Deck Log, USS *Oahu*, 15 February 1942.
18. Ancheta, *The Wainwright Papers*, vol. IV, 27.
19. Interview of Rear Admiral Morrill by the author, 1987.
20. Deck Log, USS *Mindanao*, 25 March 1942.
21. *Mindanao* Report, 4–5.
22. Ibid., 67–69.
23. Ibid., 68.
24. Morton, *Fall of the Philippines*, 392–397.
25. Schultz, *Hero of Bataan*, 227.
26. Interview of Colonel Mills, USA (Ret.) by the author, Philippine Scout reunion, San Antonio, Texas, April 1986.
27. Rockwell Narrative; Morton, *Fall of the Philippines*, 354–360.
28. Bulkley, *At Close Quarters*, 24–26.
29. Robert L. Underbrink, *Destination Corregidor* (Annapolis, Md.: Naval Institute Press, 1971), 43–48.
30. Belote and Belote, *Saga of a Fortress*, 80.
31. Underbrink, *Destination Corregidor*, 51–55, 157–163.
32. Ibid., 162–167.
33. Malcolm Champlin, "Escape from Corregidor," *Shipmate*, March 1972; *Intercept Station C*, 143.
34. Knoll Report, 2–3.
35. USMC Oral History Transcript, Interview with Brigadier General Donald Curtis, USMC (Ret.), USMC headquarters, 1974, 58–59.

36. Message from COMINCH to COMSWPACFORCE, 29 March 1942, Louis Morton Collection.
37. Radio message from Radio Cavite to General Marshall, via Admiral King, 30 March 1942, Louis Morton Collection.
38. 4th Marines Record of Events, 25 March 1942.
39. *Mindanao* Report, 4–6.

Chapter 11. The Fall of Bataan

1. Most Japanese infantry battalions had four rifle companies and a machine-gun company. In the case of the 4th Division (and the 65th Brigade, which had been fighting on Bataan since January) there were only three rifle companies in each battalion. "Information Regarding Strength and Composition of Japanese Forces, Philippine Islands, Dec. 41–May 42," Prepared by U.S. Army G-2 for the Army Historical Division, 15 August 1949, 8, Louis Morton Collection.
2. Shores, Cull, and Izawa, *Bloody Shambles,* vol. II, 136–137.
3. "Information Regarding Strength and Composition of Japanese Forces, Philippine Islands, Dec. 41–May 42," 6.
4. Luzon Force Strength Report, 29 March 1942, MacArthur Archives.
5 John W. Whitman, *Bataan: Our Last Ditch* (New York: Hippocrene Books, 1990), 458.
6. *Offensive Operations in the Philippines: From Lingayen to Corregidor* (Tokyo: Japanese Defense Agency Research Center, 1966), Table entitled "Second Offensive of Bataan, Plan and Use of Artillery," MacArthur Archives.
7. II Philippine Corps G-2 Report, 5–6 April 1942, MacArthur Archives.
8. Japanese Monograph No. 2, *Philippine Operations Record*, 162, Army Historical Center.
9. *Mindanao* Report, 4–6 April 1942.
10. USFIP G-2 Journal, 6 April 1942, MacArthur Archives.
11. Knoll Report, 15.
12. Perry, *The Spirit of Canopus*, 111–114.
13. Morton, *Fall of the Philippines*, 460.
14. Karig and Kelly, *Battle Report*, 321.
15. Blair, *Silent Victory*, 194–195.
16. *Intercept Station C*, 83–87.
17. Colonel Clarke had been relieved of command in January due to inability to cope with the stress of combat; he was being sent out of the Philippines in order to pass on information about Japanese tactics.

18. *Seadragon* had some interesting moments on her way back to Australia. Two days after picking up the Station C personnel she engaged two Japanese destroyers. As was so common at that point in the war, her torpedoes malfunctioned and missed.
19. *Intercept Station C*, 107, 118–129, 177.
20. Bartsch, *Doomed at the Start*, 365–366.
21. Morton, *Fall of the Philippines*, 454–467.
22. Morrill and Martin, *South from Corregidor*, 3–5.
23. Ibid., 6–13.
24. C. H. Sosvielle, "USS *Maryanne*," *Ex-POW Bulletin*, September 1992, 36–40.
25. Arnold A. Bocksel, "The USAMP *General Harrison* in the Harbor Defense of Manila and Subic Bay," *Coast Artillery Journal*, November–December 1946, 54.
26. Morrill and Martin, *South from Corregidor*, 6–19; interview with Rear Admiral Morrill (Ret.), by the author, Bland, Va., 1987.
27. Knoll Report, 19. In some accounts *Mindanao* is credited with rescuing *Keswick*'s crew, supposedly coming alongside to take the men off during the gun battle in North Channel. This did not take place. Neither Lieutenant Commander Knoll's memorandum nor Captain McCracken's report credit *Mindanao* with rescuing *Keswick*'s men. A letter to the author from Captain Nash, then *Mindanao*'s XO, also refutes this claim, although Nash does confirm that the gunboat did engage enemy guns that were firing at *Keswick*.
28. Message from COM 16 to CNO, 12 April 1942, MacArthur Archives.
29. Miller, *From Shanghai to Corregidor*, 12–14, 16–19.
30. Japanese Monograph No. 2, *Philippine Operations Record*, 42.
31. For an excellent discussion of the Death March and the possible number of deaths, see Stanley L. Falk's *Bataan, the March of Death* (New York: PEI Books, 1962).

Chapter 12. State of the Beach Defenses

1. U.S. Army maps of Corregidor, dated 1935 and 1941, National Archives; Ancheta, *The Wainwright Papers*, vol. II, 11–15, 57–64.
2. Letter to the author from Brigadier General Austin C. Shofner, USMC (Ret.), September 1985.
3. Muster Roll of Officers and Enlisted Men of the U.S. Marine Corps, Company A, 1st Battalion, 4th Marines, 1 May 1942, Marine Corps Historical Center, Quantico, Va.

4. 1st Sergeant Well was the platoon leader; however, 1st Lieutenant Lawrence, USA, certainly had the prominent role in the defense of the extreme Tail of the island, and clearly outranked Well. It is likely that the two reached an arrangement regarding responsibilities.
5. Belote and Belote, *Saga of a Fortress*, 146–147.
6. Data on the weapons of 1st Battalion come from several sources. The most important source of information is the 4th Marines Record of Events. The 14 January entry shows the battalion with thirty-nine .30- and two .50-caliber machine guns, four 37-mm guns, and two mortars.
7. Undated postwar memorandum written by Captain Jenkins, Marine Corps Historical Center.
8. "War History of Battery D, 60th Coast Artillery," Captain Paul R. Cornwall, http://corregidor.org/ca/btty_denver/d/htm
9. Letter to the author from General Austin C. Shofner, September 1985.
10. Although the Belotes stated that Government Ravine was "defiladed" from enemy fire, that is not correct. The Japanese howitzers on Bataan could easily have sent plunging shells into Government Ravine—and in fact they did, as the accounts of surviving Marines and Navy personnel attest. What made it somewhat safer was the fact that most locations within the ravine could not be directly seen from Bataan. Therefore, most Japanese shellfire falling there was "unobserved," and therefore less precise.
11. Undated postwar memorandum written by 1st Lieutenant Otis E. Saalman, Marine Corps Historical Center.
12. The figure of "500 sailors" was certainly too high. The figure of 303 officers and men in the battalion is based on the 4th Marines Record of Events.
13. Harold E. Dalness, "The Operations of the 4th Battalion (Provisional) 4th Marine Regiment in the Final Counterattack on the Defense of Corregidor 5–6 May 1942," Advanced Infantry Officers Class No. 2, 1949–50, Fort Benning, Ga., 5–6, U.S. Army Infantry School Library (hereafter cited as Dalness).
14. Ibid., 7.
15. Ancheta, *The Wainwright Papers*, vol. II, 86–88.
16. Ibid., vol. III, 86.
17. 4th Marines Record of Events, 1 May 1942.

Chapter 13. The Artillery Duel

1. Japanese Monograph No. 2, *Philippine Operations Record*, 19, 203–205.
2. Ancheta, *The Wainwright Papers*, vol. II, 54–57.

3. Data on the seacoast armament of Corregidor and the other harbor forts is taken from a variety of sources, most importantly, Belote and Belote, *Saga of a Fortress*, and Ancheta, *The Wainwright Papers*, vol. II.
4. Ian V. Hog, *British and American Artillery of World War 2* (London: Arms and Armor Press, 1978), 203–221.
5. *Table of United States Army Cannon Carriages and Projectiles*, data section for 12-inch guns (Washington, D.C.: U.S. Army Office of the Chief of Ordnance, January 1924), National Archives.
6. Belote and Belote, *Saga of a Fortress*, 91–92.
7. A number of earlier works have mentioned American 12-inch mortars firing a 670-pound high explosive shell. No such projectile existed in the U.S. inventory. The armor piercing shell came in two weights: 1,046 and 700 pounds. The high explosive version was 700 pounds. Data from *Table of U.S. Army Cannon Carriages and Projectiles*.
8. Although some of the official data on the M-1912 mortar indicates a range of 16,000 yards, statements by Colonel Foster, Fort Hughes' commander, clearly indicate that prewar test firings resulted in ranges of just over 19,000 yards.
9. Some accounts have said that Drum's turrets and guns were naval designs. While certainly inspired by the Navy's battleships, both the turrets and guns were specifically designed for the Army.
10. John Gordon, "The Gallant Stand of the U.S. Army's Concrete Battleship," *Army*, March 1986.
11. U.S. Army Report, "Ammunition on Hand in Harbor Defenses, Philippine Department, December 31, 1938," National Archives.
12. Headquarters Fort Hughes memorandum prepared for Colonel Foster, 13 March 1942, Louis Morton Collection.
13. The magazines of Navy-manned Battery Craighill had overhead cover of five feet of reinforced concrete and eleven feet of compacted dirt atop the concrete. This level of protection was somewhat less than the other mortar batteries, and was a cause of some concern to the Harbor Defenses leadership.
14. Belote and Belote, *Saga of a Fortress*, 67–69.
15. Interview of Colonel T. W. Davis III, U.S. Army (Ret.), by James Belote, 9 November 1963. Copy of the interview letter provided to the author by James Belote.
16. Undated (early 1960s) interview of Colonel V. P. Foster, U.S. Army (Ret.), by James Belote, Belote interviews, Army Historical Center.
17. Letter from Captain David Nash, USN (Ret.), to William H. Bartsch, August 1977. Copy of the letter provided to the author by Captain Nash, July 1986.

18. USFIP G-2/3 Report, 14–15 April 1942, MacArthur Archives.
19. Letter to the author from Captain David Nash, USN (Ret.), July 1986.
20. Ibid.
21. Belote and Belote, *Saga of a Fortress*, 114.
22. Ibid., 111–112.
23. The deck plans indicate storage for 440 14-inch projectiles, but more may have been stored in the fort at the time of the siege. www.concrete battleship.org
24. *Offensive Operations in the Philippines: From Lingayen to Corregidor* (Tokyo: Japanese Defense Agency Research Center, 1966), Table entitled "Corregidor Island Attack—War Dead, Injured, Sick Incidence," MacArthur Archives.
25. Belote and Belote, *Saga of a Fortress*, 121.

Chapter 14. The Final Bombardment

1. Messimer, *In the Hands of Fate*, 285–300.
2. "Translation #3, Japanese Documents: Field Diaries # 9, 10," Historical Division, Pacific Section, U.S. Army, undated, Louis Morton Collection.
3. Jim Marclay, "*Luzon*'s Last Days," in Tolley, *American Gunboats in China*, 216–218.
4. Letter from Rear Admiral Morrill to the author, May 1986.
5. Deck Log, USS *Finch*, 11 April 1942, National Archives.
6. 4th Marines Record of Events, 28 April 1942 entry.
7. Ancheta, *The Wainwright Papers*, vol. II, 45–46.
8. Hough et al., *Pearl Harbor to Guadalcanal*, 189.
9. Bocksel, "The USAMP General Harrison."
10. Ancheta, *The Wainwright Papers*, vol. II, 46.
11. Interview of Mr. Jack Warner, former member of A Company, 4th Marines, by the author, 2007.
12. Belote and Belote, *Saga of a Fortress*, 130–131.
13. Ancheta, *The Wainwright Papers*, vol. II, 48.
14. Telephone interview of Captain McCoy, USN (Ret.), by the author, 1987.

Chapter 15. The Battle for Corregidor

1. "Information Regarding Strength and Composition of Japanese Forces, Philippine Islands, Dec. 41–May 42," Louis Morton Collection.
2. Japanese Monograph No. 2, *Philippine Operations Record*, 48.

3. Morton, *Fall of the Philippines*, 554–555.
4. Miller, *From Shanghai to Corregidor*, 28.
5. C. H. Sosvielle, "Corregidor," in Tolley, *American Gunboats in China*, 142.
6. Interview of Mr. Jack Warner, 2007.
7. Interview of Rear Admiral Morrill, USN (Ret.), by the author, 1987.
8. Miller, *From Shanghai to Corregidor*, 31.
9. Memorandum by Gunner H. M. Ferrell, prepared for Marine Corps headquarters, 1946, Marine Corps Historical Center (hereafter cited as Ferrell Memo).
10. Ibid.
11. Hogaboom, 32.
12. Undated postwar narrative of Captain F. W. Ferguson, "From 8 December 1941 to 6 May 1942, While Serving with the Fourth Marines," 17–18, Marine Corps Historical Center.
13. Ibid.
14. Gordon, "The Gallant Stand of the U.S. Army's Concrete Battleship."
15. Letter from Lieutenant Colonel Ray Lawrence to Dr. James Belote, October 1963, Belote interviews, U.S. Army Historical Center.
16. Dalness, 13.
17. Ibid.
18. Belote interview with Rear Admiral Charles B. Brook, USN (Ret.), October 1963, Louis Morton Collection.
19. Ferrell Memo.
20. Miller, *From Shanghai to Corregidor*, 39–40.
21. Kazumaro Uno, *Isle of Delusion* (N.p.: Press Bureau of the Imperial Army General Headquarters in China, 1942), 35.

Chapter 16. Surrender

1. Jonathan Wainwright, *General Wainwright's Story* (Garden City, N.Y.: Doubleday and Company, 1946), 119–120.
2. Tolley, *Yangtze Patrol*, 291–292.
3. Toland, *But Not in Shame*, 374.
4. Interview of Captain McCoy, 1987.
5. Miller, *From Shanghai to Corregidor*, 41.
6. Morton, *Fall of the Philippines*, 564–584.
7. Belote interviews with Corregidor survivors, American Defenders of Bataan and Corregidor convention, May 1964, U.S. Army Historical Center.

8. 4th Marines Record of Events, 2 May 1942.
9. Perry, *The Spirit of Canopus*, 191.
10. Ancheta, *The Wainwright Papers*, vol. II, 102–103.
11. *Offensive Operations in the Philippines: From Lingayen to Corregidor*, Table entitled "Corregidor Island Attack–War Dead, Injured, Sick Incidence."
12. Morrill and Martin, *South from Corregidor*, 49.
13. Interview of Rear Admiral Morrill, 1987.

Chapter 17. Reflections

1. Connaughton, *MacArthur and Defeat in the Philippines*, 148.
2. Williamson Murray and Allan R. Millett, *A War to Be Won: Fighting the Second World War* (Cambridge, Mass.: The Belknap Press of Harvard University Press, 2000), 205.
3. Russell D. Buhite, *Douglas MacArthur: Statecraft and Stagecraft in America's East Asian Policy* (Lanham, Md.: Rowman & Littlefield Publishers, Inc., 2008), 161–171.
4. Leonard Mosley, *Marshall, Hero for Our Times* (New York: Hearst Books, 1982), 485.
5. Miller, *From Shanghai to Corregidor*, 42; Daniel D. Howell, *The Battle for Corregidor, December 1941–6 May 1941, the 4th Marine Regiment Hung Out to Dry* (Manila: Dizon and Company, 2003), 272–278.
6. U.S. Department of Veterans Affairs, Former Prisoners of War, April 2005, 5, www.history.navy.mil/faqs11–1.htm
7. Jim Marclay, "*Luzon*'s Last Days," in *American Gunboats in China*, 216–218; telephone interview of Rear Admiral Morrill by the author, 1987.

Appendix A. Asiatic Fleet, 7 December 1941

1. *Houston* was at the central Philippine port city of Iloilo on Panay Island when war started.
2. *Marblehead*, together with USS *Paul Jones* and the four flush-deckers of Destroyer Division 58 were at the port of Tarakan on the northeast coast of Borneo when war started.
3. *Boise* actually belonged to the U.S. Pacific Fleet.
4. *Langley* had been the Navy's first aircraft carrier in the early 1920s. *Childs* and *Preston* were converted World War I "flush deck" destroyers, while *Heron* was a converted World War I *Owl*-class minesweeper.
5. *Mindanao* was at sea, en route from Hong Kong when war broke out.

6. Multiple sources were used to compile the list of ships and other elements in the Asiatic Fleet, including Morison's *Rising Sun in the Pacific*, 157–160, and the 1 October 1941 Asiatic Fleet officers roster, Kemp Tolley Collection.

Appendix C. Japanese Artillery Units Available for Bombardment of Corregidor

1. Data on range of Japanese artillery taken from Donald B. McLean, *Japanese Artillery, Weapons and Tactics* (Wickenburg: Normount Technical Publications, 1973). The list of Japanese artillery units is from The Corregidor Historical Society web site: http://corregidor.org/J1/bataan_and_corregidor.htm

Selected Bibliography

Books

Ancheta, Celedonio A. *The Wainwright Papers*, vols. I–IV. Manila: New Day Publishers, 1980.

Barlow, Keith, ed. *Bunker's War: The World War II Diary of Colonel Paul D. Bunker*. Novato, Calif.: Presidio Press, 1996.

Bartsch, William H. *December 8, 1941: MacArthur's Pearl Harbor*. College Station: Texas A&M University Press, 2003.

———. *Doomed at the Start: American Pursuit Pilots in the Philippines, 1941–1942*. College Station: Texas A&M University Press, 1992.

Belote, James H., and William M. Belote. *Corregidor: The Saga of a Fortress*. New York: Harper and Row, 1967.

Blair, Clay, Jr. *Silent Victory: The U.S. Submarine War against Japan*. New York: Bantam Books, 1975.

Breuer, William B. *Sea Wolf: A Biography of John D. Bulkeley, USN*. Novato, Calif.: Presidio Press, 1989.

Buhite, Russell D. *Douglas MacArthur: Statecraft and Stagecraft in America's East Asian Policy*. Lanham, Md.: Rowman & Littlefield Publishers, 2008.

Bulkley, Robert J. *At Close Quarters: PT Boats in the United States Navy*. Washington, D.C.: Naval History Division, 1962.

Burton, John. *Fortnight of Infamy: The Collapse of Allied Airpower West of Pearl Harbor*. Annapolis, Md.: Naval Institute Press, 2006.

Condit, Kenneth W., and Edwin T. Turnbladh. *Hold High the Torch: A History of the 4th Marines*. Washington, D.C.: Historical Branch, G-3 Division, Headquarters Marine Corps, 1960.

Connaughton, Richard. *MacArthur and Defeat in the Philippines*. New York: Overlook Press, 2001.

Edmonds, Walter D. *They Fought with What They Had*. Boston: Little, Brown and Company, 1951.

Falk, Stanley. *Bataan, the March of Death*. New York: PEI Books, 1962.

Forty, George. *Japanese Army Handbook, 1939–1945*. Gloucestershire: Sutton Publishing, 1999.

——. *US Army Handbook, 1939–1945*. Gloucestershire: Sutton Publishing, 1995.

Francillion, Rene. *Japanese Aircraft of the Pacific War*. Annapolis, Md.: Naval Institute Press, 1979.

Glusman, John A. *Conduct Under Fire: Four American Doctors and Their Fight for Life as Prisoners of the Japanese, 1941–1945*. New York: Viking, 2005.

Hog, Ian V. *British and American Artillery of World War 2*. London: Arms and Armor Press, 1978.

Hough, Frank O., et al. *Pearl Harbor to Guadalcanal: History of the U.S. Marine Corps Operations in World War II*, vol. I. Washington, D.C.: Historical Branch U.S. Marine Corps, n.d.

Howell, Daniel D. *The Battle for Corregidor, December 1941–6 May 1941, the 4th Marine Regiment Hung Out to Dry*. Manila: Dizon and Company, 2003.

Hoyt, Edwin P. *The Lonely Ships: The Life and Death of the U.S. Asiatic Fleet*. New York: David Kay Company, 1976.

James, D. Clayton. *The Years of MacArthur*, vols. 1 and 2. Boston: Houghton Mifflin Company, 1970.

Jose, Rico T. *The Philippine Army, 1935–1942*. Manila: Ateneo De Manila University, 1992.

Jowett, Philip. *The Japanese Army, 1931–1945*, vols. 1 and 2. London: Osprey Publishing, 2004.

Karig, Walter, and Welbourn Kelly. *Battle Report, Pearl Harbor to Coral Sea*. New York: Farrar & Rinehart, 1944.

King, Otis H. *Alamo of the Pacific*. Fort Worth, Texas: Branch-Smith, 1999.

Leutze, James. *A Different Kind of Victory: A Biography of Admiral Thomas C. Hart*. Annapolis, Md.: Naval Institute Press, 1981.

Mallonee, Richard C. *The Naked Flagpole: Battle for Bataan*. San Rafael, Calif.: Presidio Press, 1980.

McGovern, Terrance, and Mark A. Berhow. *American Defenses of Corregidor and Manila Bay, 1898–1945*. Oxford: Osprey Publishing, 2003.

McLean, Donald B. *Japanese Artillery, Weapons and Tactics*. Wickenburg, Ariz.: Normount Technical Publications, 1973.

Messimer, Dwight R. *In the Hands of Fate: The Story of Patrol Wing Ten, 8 December 1941–11 May 1942*. Annapolis, Md.: Naval Institute Press, 1985.

Metcalf, Clyde H. *A History of the United States Marine Corps*. New York: Putnam and Sons, 1939.

Middlebrook, Martin, and Patrick Mahoney. *Battleship: The Sinking of the Prince of Wales and Repulse*. New York: Charles Scribner's Sons, 1979.

Morison, Samuel Eliot. *The Rising Sun in the Pacific 1931–April 1942*. Boston: Little, Brown, and Company, 1975.

Morrill, John, and Pete Martin. *South from Corregidor*. New York: Simon and Schuster, 1943.

Morton, Louis. *The Fall of the Philippines*. Washington, D.C.: Office of the Chief of Military History, 1953 (official U.S. Army history of the Philippine Campaign).

———. *Strategy and Command, the First Two Years*. Washington, D.C.: Office of the Chief of Military History, 1962 (part of the official U.S. Army history of World War II series).

Mosley, Leonard. *Marshall, Hero for Our Times*. New York: Hearst Books, 1982.

Mullin, J. Daniel. *Another Six Hundred*. Self-published, 1984.

Murray, Williamson, and Allan R. Millett. *A War to Be Won: Fighting the Second World War*. Cambridge, Mass.: Belknap Press of Harvard University Press, 2000.

Norman, Elizabeth, M. *We Band of Angels: The Untold Story of American Nurses Trapped on Bataan by the Japanese*. New York: Random House, 1999.

Offensive Operations in the Philippines: From Lingayen to Corregidor. Tokyo: Japanese Defense Agency Research Center, 1966 (this is the official Japanese history of the Philippine Campaign).

Olson, John E. *Anywhere-Anytime, The History of the 57th Infantry (PS)*. Self-published, 1991.

Perry, E. M. *The Spirit of Canopus*. Self-published, 2007.

Prados, John. *Combined Fleet Decoded*. New York: Random House, 1995.

Rottman, Gordon L. *Japanese Army in World War II: Conquest of the Pacific 1941–42*. London: Osprey Publishing, 2005.

———. *US Marine Corps Pacific Theater of Operations, 1941–43*. London: Osprey Publishing, 2004.

———. *US Patrol Torpedo Boats*. London: Osprey Publishing, 2008.

———. *World War II Japanese Tank Tactics*. London: Osprey Publishing, 2008.

Schultz, Duane. *Hero of Bataan: The Story of General Jonathan M. Wainwright.* New York: St. Martin's Press, 1981.

Shores, Christopher, Brian Cull, and Yasuho Izawa. *Bloody Shambles*, vols. 1 and 2. London: Grubb Street, 1996.

Smith, Michael. *The Emperor's Codes: Breaking Japan's Secret Ciphers.* New York: Arcade Publishers, 2000.

Smith, S. E. *The United States Marine Corps in World War II.* New York: Random House, 1969.

Toland, John. *But Not in Shame: The Six Months after Pearl Harbor.* New York: Random House, 1961.

Tolley, Kemp. *Cruise of the Lanikai, to Provoke the Pacific War.* Fredericksburg, Md.: Admiral Nimitz Foundation, 1994.

——. *Yangtze Patrol: The U.S. Navy in China.* Annapolis, Md.: Naval Institute Press, 1971.

——, ed. *American Gunboats in China.* Monkton, Md.: Yangtze River Patrol Association, 1989.

Underbrink, Robert L. *Destination Corregidor.* Annapolis, Md.: Naval Institute Press, 1971.

Uno, Kazumaro. *Isle of Delusion.* N.p.: Press Bureau of the Imperial Army General Headquarters in China, 1942.

Wainwright, Jonathan. *General Wainwright's Story.* Garden City, N.Y.: Doubleday and Company, 1946.

White, W. L. *They Were Expendable.* New York: Harcourt, Brace, and Company, 1942.

Whitman, John W. *Bataan: Our Last Ditch.* New York: Hippocrene Books, 1990.

Willmott, H. P. *Empires in the Balance: Japanese and Allied Pacific Strategies to April, 1942.* Annapolis, Md.: Naval Institute Press, 1982.

Winslow, W. G. *The Fleets the Gods Forgot: The U.S. Asiatic Fleet in World War II.* Annapolis, Md.: Naval Institute Press, 1982.

Young, Donald J. *The Battle of Bataan.* London: McFarland and Co., 1991.

Zaloga, Steven J. *Japanese Tanks 1939–1945.* London: Osprey Publishing, 2007.

Articles

Baldwin, Hanson W. "The Fourth Marines at Corregidor." *Marine Corps Gazette*, November 1946–February 1947.

Bocksel, Arnold. "The USAMP *General Harrison.*" *Coast Artillery Journal*, November–December 1946.

Braly, William C. "Corregidor: A Tradition." *The Coast Artillery Journal*, July–August 1946.

Champlin, Malcolm M. "December 1941." *Shipmate*, March 1971.

——. "Escape from Corregidor." *Shipmate*, March 1972.

Dalness, Harold, E. "The Operations of the 4th Battalion (Provisional) 4th Marine Regiment in the Final Counterattack in the Defense of Corregidor 5–6 May 1942." Infantry Officer Advanced Officers Class No. 2, 1949–50, U.S. Army Infantry School Library, Fort Benning, Ga.

Gordon, John, IV. "The Gallant Stand of the U.S. Army's Concrete Battleship." *Army*, March 1986.

Hartendorp, A. V. H. "Story of the First Bombing of Cavite, the Pan American Airways Station, Olongapo." *The American Chamber of Commerce Journal* (Manila), October 1953.

Hogaboom, William F. "Action Report: Bataan." *Marine Corps Gazette*, April 1946.

Johnson, Judith. "Laura Cobb, A Kansas Nurse in a Japanese Prisoner of War Camp." *U.S. Navy Medicine*, January–February 2003.

Marclay, Jim. "*Luzon*'s Last Days," in Tolley, ed., *American Gunboats in China*, 1989.

Markland, Herbert F. "A Coast Artilleryman's Experience." *The Coast Artillery Study Group Journal*, February 1996.

Nash, Davis. "Last Days of the USS *Mindanao* (PR-8)." In Tolley, ed., *American Gunboats in China*, 1989.

Prickett, William F. "The Naval Battalion on Bataan." Naval Institute *Proceedings*, November 1960.

Purling, Donald T. "Minda Action." In Tolley, ed., *American Gunboats in China*, 1989.

Sosvielle, C. H. "Corregidor." In Tolley, ed., *American Gunboats in China*, 1989.

——. "USS *Maryanne*." *Ex-POW Bulletin*, September 1992.

Welsh, Shawn. "A Coast Artilleryman's Experiences on Fort Mills." *The Coast Artillery Study Group Journal*, February 1996.

"Yangtze Patrollers, Bilibid POWs." *U.S. Navy Medicine*, January–February 1986.

Pamphlets

Intercept Station C, From Olongapo Through the Evacuation of Corregidor, 1929–1942. Pensacola, Fla.: Special Publication by the U.S. Naval Cryptolog Veterans Association, 2003.

Miller, J. Michael. *From Shanghai to Corregidor: Marines in the Defense of the Philippines*. Washington, D.C.: Marine Corps Historical Center, 1997.

Santelli, James. *A Brief History of the 4th Marines*. Washington, D.C.: Historical Division, Headquarters United States Marine Corps, 1970.

Shaw, Henry I. *Opening Moves, Marines Gear Up For War*. Washington, D.C.: Marine Corps Historical Center, 1991.

Official Documents

"Action of Longoskawayan Point against Japanese Forces." Memorandum from the Battalion Commander to the Commandant 16th Naval District, 9 February 1942. Louis Morton Collection, U.S. Army Military History Institute, Army Heritage and Education Center, Carlisle, Pa.

"Activities of USS *Mindanao* from September 6, 1941 to May 2, 1942." Memorandum from Commander Alan McCracken to the Secretary of the Navy, June 1945. Naval Historical Center, Washington, D.C.

"Ammunition on Hand in Harbor Defenses, Philippine Department, December 31, 1938." U.S. Army Report. National Archives, College Park, Md.

"Bombing Attack on Japanese Battleship on 10 December 1941." Memorandum from Commander Patrol Squadron 101 to Commander PatWing 10, 31 December 1941. Naval Historical Center, Washington, D.C.

"Contract No. 4175." 16th Naval District Memorandum. 16 February 1942. National Archives, College Park, Md.

Deck Log, USS *Finch*. 1941–42 entries. National Archives, College Park, Md.

Deck Log, USS *Mindanao*. 1941–42 entries. National Archives, College Park, Md.

Deck Log, USS *Napa*. 1941–42 entries. National Archives, College Park, Md.

Deck Log, USS *Oahu*. 1941–42 entries. National Archives, College Park, Md.

Deck Log, USS *Pigeon*. 1941–42 entries (reconstructed after the war by her senior surviving officer). National Archives, College Park, Md.

Diary of Captain Hidaka. Captured enemy document. MacArthur Archives, Norfolk, Va.

"Disposition of Employment of Naval Forces, Manila Bay Area." 16th Naval District Memorandum. 14 January 1942. Louis Morton Collection, U.S. Army Military History Institute, Army Heritage and Education Center, Carlisle, Pa.

Ferguson, F. W. "Personal Experiences of Captain F. W. Ferguson, USMC, From 8 December, 1941 to 6 May, 1942, While Serving With the Fourth Marines." Undated memorandum prepared for Headquarters USMC, 1946. Marine Corps Historical Center, Quantico, Va.

Ferrell, H. M. Untitled memorandum prepared for Headquarters USMC, 1946. Marine Corps Historical Center, Quantico, Va.

Goodall, H. W. Letter to Dr. George Groce. U.S. Army Historical Section, 17 August 1948, pertaining to sinking of "Mickey Mouse Battleships" off Bataan on 8 February 1942. Louis Morton Collection, U.S. Army Military History Institute, Army Heritage and Education Center, Carlisle, Pa.

Hart, Admiral Thomas C. "Narrative of Events for the Asiatic Fleet Leading to War, and for 8 December 1941 to 15 February 1942." 1942. Louis Morton Collection, U.S. Army Military History Institute, Army Heritage and Education Center, Carlisle, Pa.

Headquarters Fort Hughes memorandum prepared for Colonel Foster, 13 March 1942. Louis Morton Collection, U.S. Army Military History Institute, Army Heritage and Education Center, Carlisle, Pa.

"Information Regarding Strength and Composition of Japanese Forces, Philippine Islands, Dec 41–May 42." Prepared by U.S. Army G-2 for the Army Historical Division, 15 August 1949. Louis Morton Collection, U.S. Army Military History Institute, Army Heritage and Education Center, Carlisle, Pa.

"Intelligence Report, Sixteenth Naval District during Period March 12 to May 3, 1942." Memorandum from Lieutenant Commander Denys W. Knoll to Vice Chief of Naval Operations (Director of Naval Intelligence), undated. Louis Morton Collection, U.S. Army Military History Institute, Army Heritage and Education Center, Carlisle, Pa.

"Interview of Brigadier General Donald Curtis (Ret.)." USMC Oral History Transcript, History and Museums Division, Headquarters USMC, Washington, D.C., 1974. Marine Corps Historical Center, Quantico, Va.

Japanese Monograph Numbers 1 and 2, *Philippine Operations Record, Phase I, 6 November 1941–30 June 1942.* Office of the Chief of Military History, U.S. Army Military History Institute, Army Heritage and Education Center, Carlisle, Pa.

Jenkins, Robert F. Undated postwar memorandum written by Captain Jenkins. Marine Corps Historical Center, Quantico, Va..

Memorandum from CINCAF to Commanding General, USAFFE, Subject: Control of Air Operations over Water, 23 October 1941. MacArthur Archives, Norfolk, Va.

Memorandum from Commander, Mine Division Nine to Commandant, 16th Naval District, 5 March 1942, Subject: "USS *Bittern*, War Damage Received and Abandoning Of." Naval Historical Center, Washington, D.C.

Memorandum from Commander Bridget to Commandant of 16th Naval District, 9 February 1942. Louis Morton Collection, U.S. Army Military History Institute, Army Heritage and Education Center, Carlisle, Pa.

Memorandum from 16th Naval District to Commanding General, Philippine Department, Subject: "Anti-Aircraft Defense of the Cavite-Sangley Point Area." 16 September 1941. MacArthur Archives, Norfolk, Va.

Muster Rolls, 4th Marine Regiment and 1st Separate Marine Battalion, December 1940 through May 1942. Held in microfiche format at the Marine Corps Historical Center, Quantico, Va.

"Narrative of Naval Activities in Luzon Area, December 1, 1941 to March 19, 1942." Memorandum from Rear Admiral F. W. Rockwell to Commander in Chief, U.S. Fleet, 1 August 1942. Louis Morton Collection, U.S. Army Military History Institute, Army Heritage and Education Center, Carlisle, Pa.

"I and II Philippine Corps G-2 and G-3 Daily Journals." December 1941 to April 1942. MacArthur Archives, Norfolk, Va.

"Philippine Department Plan—Orange" (1940 revision, updated to April 1941). Headquarters, U.S. Army Philippine Department. MacArthur Archives, Norfolk, Va.

"Record of Events." 8 December 1941 to 3 May 1942, prepared daily by Sergeant Thomas R. Hicks, Headquarters Company, 4th Marines (the official regimental record of events for the 4th Marines). Marine Corps Historical Center, Quantico, Va.

"Report on the Operation, Employment and Supply of the Old 4th Marines from September, 1941 to the Surrender of Corregidor, May 6, 1942 Made from Memory and Some Notes." Memorandum from Brigadier General Samuel L. Howard, U.S. Marine Corps to Commandant of the Marine Corps, 26 September 1945. Marine Corps Historical Center, Quantico, Va.

"Roster of Officers and Seniority List, 16th Naval District, 1 November, 1941." Published by 16th Naval District, November 1941. Kemp Tolley Collection, U.S. Naval Academy Library.

"R-2 Journal." 4th Marines Daily Intelligence Summary, 8 December 1941 to 3 May 1942. Marine Corps Historical Center, Quantico, Va.

Saalman, 1st Lieutenant Otis Edward. Undated and untitled memorandum. Marine Corps Historical Center, Quantico, Va.

Sackett, Captain Earl L., USS *Canopus*. "The History of the USS *Canopus* (AS-9)." Undated. Louis Morton Collection, U.S. Army Military History Institute, Army Heritage and Education Center, Carlisle, Pa.

Table of Organization, Type 1935 Regiment, United States Marine Corps. Marine Corps University, Quantico, Va.

Table of United States Army Cannon Carriages and Projectiles, data section for 12-inch guns (Washington, D.C.: U.S. Army Office of the Chief of Ordnance, January 1924). National Archives, College Park, Md.

USAFFE G-2 and G-3 Daily Reports. December 1941 to May 1942. MacArthur Archives, Norfolk, Va.

"War Diary." Memorandum from Lieutenant Commander Marion C. Cheek, 16th Naval District Intelligence Officer to Director of Naval Intelligence, 20 February, 1942. Naval Historical Center, Washington, D.C.

"War Diary." 16th Naval District, 20 February 1942. Louis Morton Collection, U.S. Army Military History Institute, Army Heritage and Education Center, Carlisle, Pa.

Letters and Interviews

Champlin, Malcolm M., USN (Ret.). Captain Champlin was Admiral Rockwell's flag lieutenant and the U.S. Navy liaison officer to Major General Jonathan Wainwright's I Philippine Corps on Bataan in February–March 1942.

McCoy, Melvyn H., USN (Ret.). Captain McCoy was the assistant District Communications Officer of the 16th Naval District.

Mills, Lloyd, U.S. Army (Ret.). As an Army lieutenant, Colonel Mills served in the 57th Infantry Regiment (Philippine Scouts).

Miller, Michael. Miller is a senior historian at the Marine Corps Historical Center at Quantico, Va.

Morrill, John H., USN (Ret.). Rear Admiral Morrill was the CO of the minesweeper USS *Quail* (AM-15).

Nash, David, USN (Ret.). Captain Nash was the XO of USS *Mindanao*, PR-8, one of the three China river gunboats that fought in Manila Bay.

Olson, John E., U.S. Army (Ret.). Colonel Olson was the Regimental Adjutant of the 57th Infantry Regiment (Philippine Scouts) while serving as a first lieutenant in the Philippines.

Purling, Donald T., USN (Ret.). Don Purling was a yeoman on board USS *Mindanao.*

Shofner, Austin C., USMC (Ret.). Brigadier General Shofner was a captain commanding the provisional "reserve company" of 2nd Battalion, 4th Marines during the siege of Corregidor.

Sosvielle, C. H., USN (Ret.). Chief Sosvielle served on board USS *Maryanne*, armed yacht in Manila Bay.

Warner, Jack. Warner was a member of A Company, 4th Marines.

Wheeler, Kenneth R., USN (Ret.). As a lieutenant (junior grade), Vice Admiral Wheeler was one of the 16th Naval District supply officers.

Index

About the Author

John Gordon graduated from The Citadel in 1977. Following a career in the U.S. Army he joined a Washington think tank as a defense analyst. He has written numerous articles and books on military subjects and has been researching the 1941–42 Philippine Campaign for many years. He has a BA in history from The Citadel, an MA in international relations from St. Mary's University in San Antonio, an MBA in business administration from Marymount University, and a PhD in public policy from George Mason University. In addition to his senior defense analyst position, he is an adjunct professor at George Mason and Georgetown Universities, teaching public policy and defense-related courses.

The **Naval Institute Press** is the book-publishing arm of the U.S. Naval Institute, a private, nonprofit, membership society for sea service professionals and others who share an interest in naval and maritime affairs. Established in 1873 at the U.S. Naval Academy in Annapolis, Maryland, where its offices remain today, the Naval Institute has members worldwide.

Members of the Naval Institute support the education programs of the society and receive the influential monthly magazine *Proceedings* or the colorful bimonthly magazine *Naval History* and discounts on fine nautical prints and on ship and aircraft photos. They also have access to the transcripts of the Institute's Oral History Program and get discounted admission to any of the Institute-sponsored seminars offered around the country.

The Naval Institute's book-publishing program, begun in 1898 with basic guides to naval practices, has broadened its scope to include books of more general interest. Now the Naval Institute Press publishes about seventy titles each year, ranging from how-to books on boating and navigation to battle histories, biographies, ship and aircraft guides, and novels. Institute members receive significant discounts on more than eight hundred Press books in print.

Full-time students are eligible for special half-price membership rates. Life memberships are also available.

For a free catalog describing Naval Institute Press books currently available, and for further information about joining the U.S. Naval Institute, please write to:

Member Services
U.S. Naval Institute
291 Wood Road
Annapolis, MD 21402-5034
Telephone: (800) 233-8764
Fax: (410) 571-1703
Web address: www.usni.org